The Silverlake Experiment

LAW IN ACTION
A series edited by
Sheldon Messinger
University of California, Berkeley

THE SILVERLAKE EXPERIMENT

Testing Delinquency Theory and Community Intervention

LaMar T. Empey
and
Steven G. Lubeck

University of Southern California

ALDINE PUBLISHING COMPANY
Chicago

First published 1971 by
Aldine Publishing Company
529 South Wabash Avenue
Chicago, Illinois 60605

Library of Congress Catalog Card Number 70–123591
ISBN 202–30065–X
Printed in the United States of America

Contents

Part IV: Implications and Reformulations

Appendices

Preface

THE HISTORY of society's effort to deal with the juvenile delinquent is not happy. There are many grounds upon which to question the effectiveness of current practices, especially for that group who are more than one-time offenders. But perhaps even more distressing is the lack of sound knowledge by which to define what their problems are and, therefore, by which to build more successful approaches for dealing with them. Our difficulties do not stem merely from a punitive attitude toward lawbreakers or the lack of humanitarian concern. Our basic problem, in the last analysis, is a lack of knowledge.

This lack of knowledge is a function mainly of (*a*) the immaturity—the theoretical and methodological inadequacies—of the sciences that are concerned with the incredibly complex problems of explaining human behavior, and (*b*) the nature of our correctional systems, which inevitably make difficult either the conduct of research or the rational utilization of available knowledge.

Responses to these problems have followed traditional and divergent patterns. Social scientists have been preoccupied with theoretical and methodological issues, while correctional people have had to do whatever seemed most sensible for them to do. In the absence of proven methods for delinquency control, they have relied upon the accumulated products of experience, professional and otherwise, as the basis upon which to proceed. The consequence has not been satisfying to either group, but in practical terms it has been the best available.

Throughout the whole process has always been the hope that, through interdisciplinary collaboration, some better solutions might be found. This hope has been based upon the recognition that if many kinds of knowledge are to be acquired, collaboration between scientists and practitioners will be necessary. In attempting to understand the nature of court and correctional systems, for example, or to experiment with alternative approaches, the necessary investigations could not be conducted unless they were sponsored and supported by both groups. In the interest of accumulating knowledge, some compromise of traditional differences and ideologies was always required.

One of the major difficulties in effecting this compromise has been the lack of effective frameworks within which the divergent interests of the social scientist and the practitioner could be reconciled. We have failed to develop the kinds of experimental models by which theoretical, operational, and research issues could be jointly addressed and jointly studied. This brings us to the Silverlake Experiment.

The Silverlake Experiment was a field experiment that attempted to remedy these problems. However, rather than being devoted exclusively to the study of a delinquency reduction effort, which is so often the practice in studies of this type, it was concerned with two other matters of equal importance: (1) a test of delinquency theory upon which the reduction effort was based, and (2) the development of a field experimental model that might be used to guide future correctional research.

This report attempts to communicate with practitioners and social scientists on the results of the effort. The reasons for this twofold communication are simple. Since both practitioners and scientists were involved in the endeavor, it is equally important for both to be informed about it: the efforts that were made to negotiate a contract of agreement, binding on both parties; the way in which a body of theory was used as the foundation upon which to build a delinquency reduction effort; the kind of intervention strategy that emerged from the theory; the strengths and limitations of the research that was conducted; and, finally, an assessment of findings not only in terms of theory and strategy but in terms of the lessons learned from this kind of endeavor.

Since it was a foregone conclusion that this particular experiment would not constitute a panacea, it was hoped that it would contribute to the search, both for a better understanding of the delinquency problem and for the use of the field experiment as a knowledge-generating device. And it was hoped as well that the report would be of ultimate value to the delinquent boys in whom all of us are ostensibly interested for reasons other than as subjects in an experiment or as sources of employment for a long list of police, judicial, and correctional workers.

Acknowledgments

IT IS IMPOSSIBLE to acknowledge the many contributions that different people and organizations make to a project like this, and the following list is only a fragment of what it might be. We are deeply indebted:

to the board of trustees and the director of Boys Republic, Frank Graves, for their moral, administrative, and financial support;

to the funding agencies that made the research possible: the Rosenberg Foundation, its board, and its executive director, Ruth Chance; the Ford Foundation and Program Associate Robert Chandler; and the National Institute of Mental Health Grant MH 14397–02 for funds to complete the data analysis;

to the staff members at Boys Republic, and especially those at the experimental residence who endured the pains, not only of innovation but of being monitored by research: Anthony J. Manocchio, the residence director, Ray Rodelander and Robert Leach, his two major assistants, and staff members David Elliott and Patrick McNally;

to the young men involved in the experiment who, while they might quarrel with the details of research, were always supportive of its goals;

to several dedicated research assistants, most notably George E. Newland, for four years of data collection and analysis, William Yee for computer assistance, Truman Jolley for data collection, and Gary Bolli and Suzanne Schwellenback for data preparation;

to agencies such as the Juvenile Court of Los Angeles County and Judge William McFaden; the Los Angeles County Probation Department, and executives Harold Muntz, Donald T. Loughery, Jr., and many other understanding and helpful officers and administrators; the Los Angeles City Schools and William R. Ruess and Robert W. Caveney; and the Los

Angeles City Police and Inspector George N. Beck and former Captain
W. L. Richey;

to the Health Sciences Computing Facility at UCLA (sponsored by
NIH Grant FR–3);

to the many residents of the Silverlake area of Los Angeles who not
only tolerated the experiment but came to its assistance when assistance
was needed;

to Sheldon Messinger, Clarence Schrag, Herbert L. Costner, and
Sanford I. Labovitz for their detailed and most helpful reviews of the
manuscript;

and, finally, to one of those faithful and long-suffering secretaries without
whom no book would ever be completed, Elaine Corry.

PART I

Overview

CHAPTER ONE

Construction of an Experimental Model

> Scientists and engineers have had very little impact . . . on the overall operations of the criminal justice system and its principal components: police, courts, and corrections. More than 200,000 scientists and engineers have applied themselves to solving military problems and hundreds of thousands more to innovation in other areas of modern life, but only a handful are working to control the crimes that injure or frighten millions of Americans each year. Yet, the two communities have much more to offer each other: science and technology is a valuable source of knowledge and techniques for combatting crime; the criminal justice system represents a vast area of challenging problems (President's Commission on Law Enforcement and Administrations of Justice, 1967a: 1).

This account of the Silverlake Experiment presents the opportunity to consider in microcosm some of the hopes expressed by the President's Commission on Law Enforcement and Administration of Justice (1967a) for research and experimentation in corrections. This field experiment attempted to unite the scientific functions of theory and research with the correctional functions of administration and intervention. It is devoted to a study of the problems inherent in an innovative attempt to deal more successfully with serious delinquents. And, although the size of the experiment was infinitesimal when compared with the gargantuan size of the entire criminal justice system, its experience illustrates many of the problems that might be anticipated in other attempts to unite scientific and correctional functions.

The experiment joined together in a common enterprise the resources of Boys Republic, a private institution for delinquents, and the Youth Studies Center of the University of Southern California. Prior to the introduction of the experiment, Boys Republic had concentrated its efforts on the operation of an institutional program for delinquents. However, reflecting the contemporary concern for finding alternatives to incarceration, it was interested in developing a community-based operation. Consequently, the director of Boys Republic sought out research personnel from the Youth Studies Center to see if some kind of an experimental program might be initiated.

Rather than leading to precipitous action, however, his approach resulted in a series of negotiations and planning sessions that are instructive because of their implications for a study of this type. Lewin (1968: 441) described the importance of such planning as follows:

> Planned social action usually emerges from a more or less vague "idea." An objective appears in the cloudy form of a dream or wish, which hardly can be called a goal. To become real, to be able to steer action, something has to be developed which might be called a "plan." The transition from an idea to a plan presupposes that: (i) The objective has to be clarified; (ii) The path to the goal and the available means have to be determined; (iii) A strategy of action has to be developed. These three items together make up the "general plan" which is to precede action.

Lewin's comments describe very well the vague conception with which the Silverlake Experiment began and allude to the complex planning which followed. Such planning was a very critical phase of the study because both parties were cautious about the form in which any collaboration should occur. Experimental efforts between correctional and research people in the past have not been notably successful, and, it was hoped that, through careful planning, many of the problems that have become virtually traditional might be avoided. This chapter is devoted, therefore, to a description of the experimental model upon which the Silverlake Experiment was based.

Organizational Problems

The first problem encountered was organizational. Suchman (1967: 147) and Miller (1958: 2–3) have noted that organizations tend to perpetuate themselves in traditional form. In addition to the pursuit of such manifest goals as delinquency reduction, the goals of organizational survival, stability, power, and growth also become highly important. Thus, if the operation of an experimental study were perceived as a threat to those latter objectives, that study might be resisted, either overtly or covertly. A first basic step, therefore, required an explicit understanding of what kind of an innovation it was that the Boys Republic sought and what implications that innovation might hold for the organization as a whole.

Perhaps without realizing it, Boys Republic was seeking changes of considerable magnitude. It was a relatively old institution which, since 1907, had perpetuated a traditional way of dealing with delinquents that had considerable visibility and public appeal. The name of the institution, Boys Republic, is, in itself, very descriptive of this tradition. Guided by the assumption that delinquents are immature, impulsive, and lack adequate controls, Boys Republic had developed an institutional program that stressed citizenship, education, work, and discipline. Consequently, its program components included a boy government system, an accredited high school, vocational training, a farm and dairy, recreational facilities, and individual counseling. In most of its aspects, it conformed to the public notion of what a correctional organization should be.

Yet, in organizational terms, Boys Republic was very similar to what Goffman (1961: 5–6) calls a total institution: (1) all aspects of the program were conducted at the same place and under the same single authority; (2) each phase of the members' daily activities was carried on in the company of several others; (3) all phases of the day's activities were tightly scheduled and regimented; and (4) the various enforced activities were brought together into a single rational plan designed to fulfill the official aims of the institution. Thus, the assumptions and organizational structure upon which Boys Republic was based would be likely to differ considerably from any new community program, especially if that new program were to be theoretically conceived and experimentally designed and evaluated.

Contrast with Community Model

Consider what was implied in the interests of Boys Republic in developing a community program. While it was impossible in the initial negotiations to describe for the director of Boys Republic exactly what form an experimental community program might take, a number of suggestions had been made that indicated it might be vastly different from what Boys Republic, its governing board, and its donors had been used to.

"All of the past phases in the evolution of corrections," noted the President's Crime Commission (1967b: 164),

> accounted for criminal and delinquent behavior primarily on the basis of some form of defect within the individual offender. The idea of being possessed of devils was replaced with the idea of psychological disability. Until recently, reformers have tended to ignore the evidence that crime and delinquency are symptoms of the disorganization of the community as well as of individual personalities, and that community institutions—through extending or denying their resources—have a critical influence in determining the success or failure of an individual offender.

Similarly, Block (1958) has accused both the legal and treatment professions of ethnocentrism, of constructing their intervention programs to conform to the middle-class American image. And Szasz (1963) has raised similar questions regarding mental illness. Both have been sharply critical of the confusion of social, ethical, medical, and legal concepts and of the tendency to locate most problems within the offender.

To be sure, successful readjustment on the offender's part may require some kind of personal reformation, but it may also require a much greater emphasis upon the problems of reconstructing social institutions. Reintegration for an offender may succeed or fail, depending not only upon what he does but, as Becker (1963: 1–15) notes, upon the community's labeling and reacting processes. If the latter are such as to permit the offender to discard the label of criminal and to adopt another identity, the integration process will be aided. But if they tend to hold the offender at arm's length, then any desire on his part for reintegration may be of little consequence. Until the labeling and reacting processes are changed, he will remain by definition an offender, an outsider.

The problem is highlighted by Erikson's (1964: 16) argument that, although we have elaborate rites-of-passage by which we induct the offender into a deviant status, we have no concomitant rites-of-passage back out of that status. There is no elaborate ritual equivalent in impact to the commitment ceremony by which the offender is inducted socially back into a non-deviant status. Reflecting an awareness of this problem, the field of correction has recently shown increasing concern with finding alternatives to older methods. For offenders, on one hand, who would otherwise have been incarcerated, residential centers having no physical restraints, work-furlough programs, daily nonresidential programs, and halfway houses have been created (*cf.* Empey, 1967a). Rather than emphasizing total surveillance and isolation, these alternative programs have taken on a broker's role by attempting to mediate between the perceptions and needs of the offender and the needs and demands of the community.

The main thrust of this reintegrative philosophy is to develop a new institutional form: a *mediatory* institution whose major function would be to reverse the processes of stigmatization and to develop rites-of-passage for the offender back into a non-delinquent status. Its role would be that of a broker, mediating between the needs of the community and the needs of the offender.

In contrast to the traditional assumptions and practices of Boys Republic, then, the implementation of the mediatory philosophy in the community would require radical alterations in its thinking and practice. A mediatory program would be much more concerned with an outward perspective than with an inward one; that is, it would be far more concerned than Boys Republic had been in the past with resolving problems that are precipitated by the offender's interaction with the community. Sometimes its efforts would require changes in the behavior of the offender, but they would also be directed toward changing the behavior of officials and the public. The rules of the whole correctional "game" would be altered. Thus, one issue Boys Republic had to consider was whether it was not only prepared to alter some of its basic thinking about delinquents but also to take on all the problems of a mediatory program: dealing with a resistant public, obtaining the support of courts, police, probation and the schools, locating and training new staff, or running the inevitable risks of having serious offenders free in the community. The type of program Boys Republic had operated in the past had had a kind of public appeal that could not be ignored. Not the least of the director's difficulties, therefore, would be that of obtaining the moral and financial support of his governing board. It was highly possible that they would not be supportive once they considered all the facts.

Use of Theory and Research

A second major problem to be considered was the interest of Boys Republic and the Youth Studies Center in conducting the new program on an experimental basis. Even though society has come a long way from the day in which cruelties and excesses were the primary reactions to crime, the bleak fact is that we know surprisingly little about ways to be more effective. Just as the monstrous punishments of the eighteenth century failed to curtail crime, so during the twentieth century have we likewise failed to do so. The reason, say McCorkle and Korn (1954: 94–95) is that we have equated humanitarianism with effectiveness and failed to recognize that the humane care of offenders is not necessarily the same thing as helping them or preventing new crime.

This state of affairs placed everyone involved in the planning stages of this study on the horns of a dilemma. On one hand, there was no guarantee that the introduction of scientific theory and research methods would result in a correctional outcome for Boys Republic that was any better than that which it had already achieved. In fact, the result conceivably could be worse. Research people were certainly not in possession of a panacea.

On the other hand, if Boys Republic were to invest in a new program *without* conducting any research, it was not likely to learn much. It would simply be repeating the traditional pattern of corrections in general that has been guided more by what Wright (1965: 38–40) calls a *strategy of activity*—more by a kind of intuitive opportunism and goal-oriented guessing—than by a well-defined *strategy of search*. While vast sums have been expended on a series of crime- or delinquency-reduction efforts, similar sums have not been expended on the disciplined study of those efforts.

As a result, there is a growing belief that until improvements are made in the theoretical and research foundations upon which intervention is based, changes in correctional structures and practices, by themselves, will be unlikely to produce dramatic improvements. The delinquency reduction models of the past have not been adequate.

Thus, Boys Republic was confronted with the problem of deciding whether it wished to run the double risk, first, of trying to start a mediatory program and, second, of having it evaluated. On the other side of the coin, however, was the compelling possibility that experimentation might be productive, both for Boys Republic and the field in general. While the use of research would not guarantee improved correctional effectiveness, there was still the hope that an innovation might be stimulating to the organization and also result in useful information. In fact, if these possibilities were not of interest to Boys Republic, there was no need for collaboration with the Youth Studies Center. Boys Republic could even start a community program, if it wished, without having to deal with the problems of relating research to it.

A Contract of Agreement

After considering the issues, the officials of Boys Republic decided in favor of experimentation. However, in order to concretize its interests so that they coincided with those of the Youth Studies Center, it was decided to work out a "contract of agreement" between the two. This contract would not be a formal document in the legal sense, but would constitute a statement of understanding, specifying three things: (1) the kind of organizational model needed to conduct the experiment; (2) the basic objectives for that model; and (3) the methods by which the experiment would be financed and operated. Such a contract would provide the ground rules for the conduct of the experiment, and might help to avoid some of the disastrous consequences that have characterized many attempts at action-research collaboration in the past. If agreement could be achieved, negotiations might then move to the more detailed specification of the structure and context of the experiment.

THE EXPERIMENTAL MODEL

Since, as mentioned above, most efforts at delinquency reduction have been based upon a *strategy of activity*, it was agreed that a model favoring a *strategy of search* should be constructed. If a body of correctional theory were to be tested, the nature of the experimental program, the actions of the staff, and the conduct of research would all have to be organized within a common framework.

After considering the alternatives, the model that seemed most appropriate was a *field experimental model* (FEM). The "field experiment" is a special type of research endeavor that is conducted in naturalistic social settings (French, 1953). The investigator does not rely totally on sampling and statistical operations to assess causal relations, nor does he rely on the often artificial atmosphere of the experimental laboratory. Instead, he attempts to manipulate and ascertain the effects of a number of variables as they operate in a normal social environment.

In this case, the development of a field experimental model (FEM) was extremely complex because of its departure from both research and correctional traditions. Nothing less than a new structural base for the conduct of an innovation was required. An FEM was needed that could provide not only an intervention and research foundation for the study but that would also facilitate collaboration between ordinarily disparate action and research people. Besides objectives for the model, therefore, a detailed specification of the structural elements of the model would also be necessary.

THE OBJECTIVES

Agreement upon objectives is a crucial component of an FEM because administrators, practitioners, and research people often share different sets of interests and priorities. Administrators are usually concerned with the stability and maintenance of their organizations, practitioners with delinquency reduction, and research people with theory and methods. If effective collaboration among these individuals is to be realized, then, differences must be examined and reconciled.

In the present case, the negotiation of a contract to this point had implied that the Silverlake Experiment was to be concerned, first and foremost, with building basic knowledge. Otherwise, why use a strategy of search rather than a strategy of activity? However, experience indicates that the pursuit of such an approach cannot be left to chance. There are too many opportunities for a lack of understanding and communication. Consequently, the basic contract had to be given substance in the form of a basic set of objectives.

After considerable discussion, it was agreed that the objectives of the experiment should be to accomplish the following:
1. to determine the capacity of a particular theory of delinquency to explain delinquent behavior, and, thus, to suggest effective measures for intervention;
2. to learn about the operational and organizational problems of a delinquency reduction effort based upon that theory;

3. to study the problems of the FEM as a knowledge-generating device.

The selection of these objectives did not mean, of course, that those involved in the experiment would be insensitive to the ethical issues involved in work with delinquents, unconcerned with delinquency reduction, or oblivious to the organizational problems of Boys Republic or the Youth Studies Center. But, as explained above, it seemed likely that the chances of the experiment to make a lasting contribution would result more from its ability to document theoretical, research, and operational problems than from a preoccupation with any single one of these issues. That is why these particular objectives were chosen and why they served to structure the conduct of the study in a particular way.

FINANCING AND OPERATION

A vital part of the contract was some agreement on financing and operation. It seemed likely that if both organizations were to be committed to the successful completion of the experiment, both should share the burdens. Thus, it was agreed that Boys Republic would provide support for the action component of the study, while the Youth Studies Center would provide for the research. The latter, of course, would require the preparation and submission of a research application.

It was also tentatively agreed that the experimental program should operate for three years, with an additional year being devoted to the follow-up of subjects. However, since the substance of the FEM still remained to be defined, it was difficult to be precise on such issues at that time. Further work on the details of the FEM had to be specified and are discussed in the next section.

Elements of Experimental Model

Despite prolonged discussions on the need for common objectives and a field model, nothing had been specified in concrete terms regarding the basic theoretical assumptions upon which the experiment would be based, what research and action staffs would be expected to do, or what form the intervention strategy would take. Yet, not inconsequentially, the ultimate success of the FEM would depend upon the extent to which action and research people conceived of themselves as having a common framework for action. A theoretical and organizational blueprint was needed that would relate them together in such a way that their various roles could be seen as functional and complementary, rather than dysfunctional and oppositional.

After considerable thought, it was concluded that the basic elements of the FEM should include the following:

1. A body of *theory* designed to explain why some juveniles become repeat offenders
2. An *intervention strategy* logically related to the delinquency theory and comprised of a set of intervention principles and guidelines
3. A body of *research* designed to reflect both upon the delinquency theory and the intervention strategy
4. An *assessment of the implications* of the research findings for delinquency theory, for correctional intervention, and for future field experimentation

The rationale for selecting each of these elements is described below.

DELINQUENCY THEORY

There were several reasons why some theoretical assumptions about delinquency were necessary. In the first place, if the list of alternatives for responding to delinquency had been narrow, well defined, and supported by empirical evidence, the task of selecting among them would not have been difficult. But this was not the case. The choice of alternatives was broad, ill defined, and lacking adequate supporting evidence. One way out of this maze, therefore, was to exercise considerable rigor in making assumptions explicit and submitting them to test.

It appeared that if the Silverlake Experiment were to proceed on a rational basis, a set of postulates would have to be developed upon which both intervention and research could be based. Furthermore, if these postulates were to be usable, they would have to be defined with considerable precision and clarity. Any test of theory is profoundly difficult at best, but research that attempts to evaluate programs incorporating a host of ill-defined and competing assumptions may be worse.

This attempt to construct theory would represent a radical departure from correctional tradition. Attempts by correctional personnel to construct and use theory, in any formal sense, have been negligible, first, because of a general distrust of theory and, second, because the task of theory construction is profoundly difficult. Theory is generally seen by correctional personnel as totally abstract and divorced from reality; it does not seem to be applicable to everyday problems. Since it is often difficult for even the scientist to translate the symbolic representations utilized by theory—concepts, syntactical terms, propositions—into phenomena that are readily observable in the everyday operation of society, it is even more difficult for the action person to conceive how they could be used in any action program (*cf.* Empey, 1964: 56–57).

Yet these difficulties were not adequate to discredit the overall utility of theory. In the first place, it would have been a mistake to assume that practitioners do not use theory. Although they do not do their theorizing in a very sophisticated way, most of them have explanations for delinquency that are not only theoretical but that tend to become highly rationalized belief systems. These belief systems are intellectual prisms that dictate perception and determine what those who use them will see and on what they will concentrate their efforts. Such prisms, notes Glaser (1956: 433), not only determine what correctional people look for but what they overlook!

In other words, the ill-defined explanations that are used every day do precisely what a formally derived theory does: they define certain variables as important, focus attention upon those variables, and assume that certain outcomes will be the product of their manipulation. The key difference, however, between poorly constructed theory and the kind sought here was (1) in the logic and construction of the explanatory scheme and (2) in the extent to which the scheme was both operational and testable. The social scientists in the experiment, therefore, could make a distinct contribution by developing a formal body of theory that could serve as the basis for defining the delinquency problem to be addressed and for organizing both the action and research components of the experiment.

INTERVENTION STRATEGY

The second element required for the FEM was an intervention strategy. Such a strategy would be comprised of a set of intervention principles and a set of operational guidelines. The principles would be comprised of an abstract set of statements, derived from the delinquency theory, and would indicate how the problems of delinquents should be addressed in the experimental program. Furthermore, such principles would be of use not only to the action component of the experiment but to the research component as well. They would provide the invaluable function of helping to clarify the relation between the two; that is, action would be concerned with implementing basic principles and research with assessing the success and consequences of that implementation. The principles that gave meaning to action would also give meaning to research.

Operational guidelines would be concerned with translating principles into action. Any new intervention strategy required answers to a host of organizational as well as staff-related questions: What is the nature of the organization that is needed to operationalize intervention principles? What shall be the nature of its norms, social structure, and sanctions? What are the consequences for this kind of organization within the network of organizations that already exist?

In terms of staff, what new roles are required? What kinds of training are necessary? What kinds of difficulty might be anticipated? The operational guidelines would be designed to answer such questions.

This attention to the explicit definition of an intervention strategy would hope to overcome the historical inclination to define "treatment" in narrow terms as though it were confined exclusively to the relationships between a practitioner and a client. This is an extremely limited point of view. "Treatment" of any kind is comprised of a host of relationships, organizational as well as interpersonal. Consequently, even though efforts to define the intervention strategy in broad terms could never hope to anticipate all of the problems that would occur, the experimental program could still be no better than the logical guidelines and specifications that went into its preparation.

RESEARCH STRATEGY

The third major component needed for the model was a research strategy. In order to achieve basic objectives, recall that research would have to be concerned with testing delinquency theory, reflecting upon the implementation and adequacy of the intervention strategy, and providing information upon the problems and prospects of the overall FEM.

In order to accomplish this, it seemed that research information of four kinds would be needed: (1) information on program *input*—on the characteristics of the offender population and the theoretical assumptions made about them; (2) information on program *process*—on the nature of the program, whether it was ever implemented according to basic design, and what is contribution to outcome was; (3) information on program *outcome* —on the results produced by the program; and (4) information on the capacity of the FEM to join administrative, action, and research people effectively together in the accomplishment of a complex experimental task. Further, the research effort would require the random selection of experimental and control groups from a common population of offenders—the experimental group to be placed in the mediatory community program, and the control group in the more traditional program of Boys Republic.

The substantive content of these different bodies of research will be described in Chapter V. The important thing to note at this point is that research, like other components of the FEM, would flow logically from the basic objectives set for the study, and the basic theory and principles that gave them substance. Rather than obtaining data from arbitrarily selected points, based upon their unique interests, research people would gather data that would be most relevant for the realization of a broader set of goals.

ASSESSMENT OF IMPLICATIONS

The final element of the experimental model would involve an assessment of the experiment in terms of its implications for basic theory, for the pragmatic aspects of correctional experimentation, and for the future of the field experiment as a methodological device. In terms of basic theory, this assessment would involve a reformulation of the delinquency theory and intervention principles upon which the experiment was based. Although it was conceivable that the findings might confirm the conceptual structure of the study, that eventuality was unlikely. The reasons are twofold.

First, it was likely that weaknesses or inaccuracies in the basic theoretical structure would be revealed by empirical findings. Some basic assumptions and principles would not be confirmed. The tools for testing theory in the social sciences are crude; measurement problems would inevitably be encountered. Thus, attempts should be made at the end of the study to reformulate the theoretical structure in light of measurement problems. A reformulation of this type might help not only to improve the structure and accuracy of the theory, but to present it in such a way that it could be operationalized more effectively for the purposes of research examination by others.

Second, the findings of the study would be assessed in terms of their implications for corrections, *per se:* the relative utility of community *vs.* institutional alternatives, the comparative costs of the two approaches, the implications of the experiment for Boys Republic, and the problems that might be anticipated in attempting community, as well as staff and offender change.

Finally, the assessment of implications would be concerned with what might be called the sociology of the field experiment—the problems of relating action, theory, and research in a common endeavor, the ethical and philosophical issues that were encountered, and the potential of the FEM for future research. If the proper perspective were retained throughout the study, it might contribute substantially to an understanding of a number of crucial problems that have plagued both social scientists and correctional people for a long time.

FEM Operation: A Preview

The writing of the contract, the joint definition of objectives, and the specification of elements for the FEM served as the basic framework for organizing the Silverlake Experiment. However, even after these steps had been taken, much remained to be done. The skeletal structure for the FEM, its theoretical, intervention, and research elements, still required substantive content. Staff members had to be located and trained. Contacts with important community agencies, legal, educational, and otherwise, had to be made and their cooperation solicited. Facilities to house the experiment were also required, as well as the acquisition of research funds. However, rather than going further into these issues at this time, they will be discussed throughout the book in appropriate places. In fact, the book is organized to conform to the general structure of the FEM; that is, the first major section is concerned with the theoretical, strategic, and research structure of the study, the second section with research findings, and the third with implications. Thus, the remainder of this chapter is devoted to providing the reader with a brief preview of the study, since later chapters will provide the information in detail.

EXPERIMENTAL PROGRAM

The Theory

The delinquency theory upon which the experiment was based was derived largely from the sociological literature. In brief, it was assumed that the greater part of delinquent behavior is not a private and secret deviation but one in which others participate, share extensive knowledge, provide techniques, or give sanction. It is behavior that, in a particular social context, attracts peers and gives status to its perpetrators.

Intervention strategy

In deriving *principles* for intervention, the assumptions made about delinquents suggest that seriously delinquent boys simply cannot become non-delinquent unless organizational mechanisms are available by which to do so. One of the most contradictory characteristics of the traditional correctional setting has been its continual demand that offenders behave legitimately and responsibly without ever providing mechanisms and peer support by which to behave in these manners. The development of such mechanisms, therefore, is necessary as a means of establishing a social climate in which boys can better accept the purpose of the change process, identify themselves closely with it, and grant prestige to those who succeed in it. If they could, in fact, become a genuine member of a re-formation group, they might then be more effectively alienated from pro-delinquent, pro-inmate points of view. Furthermore, assuming that the offender can be motivated to learn new skills and to develop new social relationships, the job is still only half done. It is not just old patterns he must discard, but new patterns he must find. His need is for a positive reintegration in pro-social, legitimate relationships and activities as an alternative to his illegitimate relationships of the past.

When the above principles were translated into operational guidelines, the experimental program was organized as follows:

1. A mediatory community program was set up in order to avoid some of the negative aspects of institutional life. Location of the program in the community would permit the delinquent to retain some degree of freedom, place him in a better position to be reintegrated in non-delinquent activities

and institutions, and provide him with some rewards for any changes that occurred.

2. Experimental and control subjects were randomly selected from a common population of offenders in Los Angeles County. Experimentals were assigned to the new community program, controls to the traditional program of Boys Republic. Only repeat offenders, ages 15 through 17, were included. Offense histories ran the usual gamut. The median number of official offenses was four, and three of the most common violations were incorrigibility, auto theft, and breaking and entering. The only exclusions included serious sex offenders, narcotics addicts, and seriously retarded and psychotic boys.

3. No more than twenty boys were assigned to the experimental program at any one time. A larger number, it was hypothesized, would make difficult any attempts to establish a unified and cohesive system.

4. The experimental program deliberately attempted to create a program culture in which a considerable amount of power and decision-making was invested in the offender as well as the staff segment of the system. As mentioned in the change assumptions, an attempt was made to establish a climate in which boys could better accept the purpose of the change process, identify themselves with it, and grant prestige to those who succeeded in it. If they could, in fact, become a genuine member of the reformation group, they might then be more effectively alienated from pro-delinquent, pro-inmate points of view.

5. A daily group meeting was instituted as the formal mechanism through which attempts at collaboration and problem-solving were implemented. The resident population of twenty boys at the experiment was broken into two groups of ten boys, each of which was led by a professional staff member and met for one and one-half hours, five days a week.

Group meetings were patterned after the technique of Guided Group Interaction. In general, this technique implies that behavior that departs from accepted legal and ethical norms should be viewed not so much as some kind of disease but as a way a person has learned of coping with environmental demands. Group treatment, then, becomes a problem in social learning. From the delinquent's point of view, it has three main goals: (1) to question the utility of persistent delinquency; (2) to provide alternative ways for behavior; and (3) to provide recognition for a boy's personal reformation and for his willingness to help reform others.

The role of the adult leader in these daily group meetings was extremely important. He sought to become a functional rather than an authoritarian member of the group. His objective was not that of always imposing his will on the group but of increasing the capacity of the group to analyze its own problems and to resolve its own difficulties. These meetings, then, had the dual purpose of evolving and maintaining a new and different correctional culture and at the same time of providing an environment in which individual social learning could be maximized.

6. Boys in the experimental program attended the local high school and returned to their own homes in the community each weekend. They were also responsible for maintaining the experimental residence and assisting with other work in it.

7. Program staff were selected on the basis of their capacity to implement the intervention strategy. Before they were hired, they were asked to agree to the basic ground rules of the contract between Boys Republic and the Youth Studies Center. It was important that they understand the basic objectives of the study and that their personal approaches to corrections would not inhibit the implementation of the strategy just described.

Consistent with the emphasis upon encouraging decision-making and the use of power among delinquents, the size of the action staff was kept deliberately small. A director was found who was willing to live at the experimental residence. The only staff hired in addition was another full-time group leader, a part-time tutor who worked at night, a part-time work supervisor, and a part-time cook.

BOYS REPUBLIC: THE CONTROL PROGRAM

By way of contrast, consider the assumptions and intervention strategy of the Boys Republic Institution.

The Theory

Boys Republic had assumed traditionally that the problems of delinquents are twofold. First, delinquent boys are immature and impulsive; their difficulties stem from a lack of adequate, internal controls. Second, they lack adequate educational, vocational, and interpersonal skills. As a result, their need is for a highly structured living environment in which both sets of inadequacies may be addressed.

Intervention Strategy

Translated into action, these assumptions led to the development of Boys Republic as a small, self-sufficient community in which school and work were given the strongest emphasis.

1. The physical plant included an accredited, four-year high school facility, program services buildings, an auditorium, a dining hall and kitchen, a chapel, cottages (each of which housed 25 boys), and extensive physical education facilities. It also possessed considerable farm and grazing land, plus an award-winning dairy.

2. Daily activities were full and quite regimented. They began with morning clean-up and breakfast and then were divided into seven periods.

Five of these periods were spent attending academic classes. The other two comprised work activities, some of which were related to the farm, dairy, and kitchen, and others which, as one boy caustically described them, "consist of such highly academic things as raking leaves, digging holes, and cutting grass."

In addition to these seven periods of academic and vocational training, there were two periods designed for recreation, one between 4:00 and 5:00 P.M., and another between 7:30 and 9:00 P.M. Much of this time involved a strong and well-coached athletic program. Boys Republic engaged in athletic activities with other small, local high schools, both acting as a host and journeying to other schools.

3. A male counselor and a housemother were assigned to each of five 25-boy cottages. In addition, there was a small supervisory staff responsible for the custodial operation of all the cottages. The housemothers were affectionately called "Grannies" and some believe that the influence of these housemothers was the most pervasive at Boys Republic. In any event, the presence of these women in the boys' living quarters indicated the attempt by Boys Republic to foster a more normal, homelike atmosphere than is ordinarily found in correctional institutions.

4. Boys Republic had traditionally attempted to legitimate and formalize a role for boys in the operation of a student government. In an accreditation report, this student government was described as follows:

> Organization of the student government at Boys Republic follows the lines of city government, with a councilman from each cottage representing the students of that cottage on the council, and a mayor representing the student body at large. In addition to the council, there is a chief of police, a judge and a district attorney. These officers meet regularly to consider matters of student interest. They are elected each semester and have certain specified responsibilities. They are looked up to as leaders in all phases of student life (Boys Republic High School, Evaluation Report, 1966: 5).

It is difficult to say just what contribution this student government made, either to the operation of Boys Republic or to the rehabilitation of the individuals involved. There is no question but that the supervisory staff has made some use of the boy government as a control device. In terms of Boys Republic's guiding philosophy, however, the purpose of boy government was to teach boys citizenship and to prepare them for meaningful participation in society, not just to excercise control.

In summary, Boys Republic was an open institution in which only moderate attention was paid to custody and considerable attention to other activities. Due to the long-term emphasis upon school and a comprehensive kind of adjustment, the average length of stay for program graduates at Boys Republic was relatively long, an average of 13 months. A few boys stayed as short a time as six months and some stayed as long as two years.

RESEARCH STRATEGY

The research strategy has already been outlined. However, it should be noted that the same general criteria used for selecting program staff were used in selecting research staff. They were expected to conform to the demands of the FEM. In addition to the research director, they included two research assistants and a secretary. Arrangements were made for them to occupy a small building adjacent to the experimental residence.

Great care was taken to structure the research role so that both delinquents and program staff would understand that whatever data were collected from delinquents would be privileged in the sense that it could not be used directly for or against any individuals. Whenever it was discovered, through research, that the experimental program was not being implemented according to design, that information might be used to alter existing practices, but never was it used to punish or reward a given boy or group of boys.

TRAINING AND INTEGRATION OF TOTAL STAFF

In addition to hiring staff on the basis of their abilities to implement the FEM, rather elaborate steps were taken to inform them further about its demands and to insure continuity of operation throughout the life of the experiment. Prior to initiating the experiment, therefore, the same model that has been discussed above was presented to the staff. In addition, the content of the theory and the intervention and research strategies were also presented and discussed in detail, including not only the combined action and research staffs, but the director of Boys Republic and the research director as well. The goal was to help staff members recognize their role in the total scheme of things.

Besides the initial training sessions, this same group of people met weekly to review problems and progress. In contrast to traditional staff meetings, however, emergent problems were analyzed not on an *ad hoc*, case-by-case basis, but on the relation of those problems to the basic design of both intervention and research strategies. Quite often, delinquents also participated in these sessions. Thus, whether a problem involved action or research issues, it was discussed in terms of the total context of the FEM. While it was impossible to deal adequately with all issues, especially to see how they could be adequately resolved in theoretical terms, regular staff meetings proved to be invaluable and provided for an essentially cooperative environment.

RELATION TO EXTERNAL SYSTEMS

Important agencies in the community, of course, could not be ignored, especially the police, courts, the probation department, and the schools. Therefore, prior to initiating the experiment, the FEM was explained to them. Further, arrangements were made throughout the life of the study to present an annual progress report to them. This included a written document they received beforehand and a luncheon and verbal report at the experimental residence. Attendance at these sessions was good and included not only representatives from the agencies mentioned above, but key members of the Boys Republic staff, the funding agencies, and university people.

DURATION OF EXPERIMENT

The experimental program was conducted for a period of three years, followed by an additional year in which follow-up data were gathered on experimental and control subjects. In all, 261 boys participated in the experiment, 140 experimentals and 121 controls. The research findings presented later cover this period of time and include the 261 subjects just mentioned.

Summary

This chapter has described the attempt that was made to design and implement a field experimental model. Of importance is the fact that the model was constructed not merely for the purpose of learning more about the problems of delinquency reduction, but also for the potential utility of such a model for future research. In order to implement the model, it was necessary to establish a contract of understanding between the action and research agencies involved, to specify in great detail the elements of the model, and to seek and train staff who were willing to work with it. We will proceed now to discuss more about its structure, what occurred when it was implemented, and what implications it seems to hold for both corrections and social science.

References

BECKER, HOWARD S. 1963. *Outsiders: Studies in the Sociology of Deviance*. New York: Free Press of Glencoe.

BLOCK, HERBERT A. 1958. Legal, sociological, and psychiatric variations in the interpretation of the criminal act. In Richard W. Nice, Ed., *Crime and Insanity*. New York: Philosophical Library.

Boys Republic High School. 1966. Evaluation Report for Western Association of Schools and Colleges. *Accreditation Program* (March).

EMPEY, LAMAR T. 1964. The application of sociological theory to social action. *Social Problems,* 12 (Summer): 56–67.

1967a. *Alternatives to Incarceration.* Washington, D.C.: U.S. Government Printing Office.

ERIKSON, KAI T. 1964. Notes on the sociology of deviance. In Howard S. Becker, Ed., *The Other Side.* New York: The Free Press.

FRENCH, JOHN R. P., JR. 1953. Experiments in field settings. In Leon Festinger and Daniel Katz, Eds., *Research Methods in the Behavioral Sciences.* New York: Holt, Rinehart and Winston.

GLASER, DANIEL. 1956. Criminality theories and behavioral images. *American Journal of Sociology,* LXI (March): 443–444.

GOFFMAN, ERVING. 1961. *Asylums.* New York: Doubleday.

LEWIN, KURT. 1968. Feedback problems of social diagnosis and action. In Walter Buckley, Ed., *Modern Systems Research for the Behavioral Scientist.* Chicago: Aldine Publishing Company.

MCCORKLE, LLOYD W., and RICHARD KORN. 1954. Resocialization within walls. *Annals of the American Academy of Political Science,* 293 (May): 94–95.

MILLER, WALTER B. 1958. Inter-institutional conflict as a major impediment to delinquency prevention. *Human Organization* 17 (Fall): 20–23.

President's Commission on Law Enforcement and Administration of Justice. 1967a. *Task Force Report: Science and Technology.* Washington, D.C.: U.S. Government Printing Office.

1967b. *The Challenge of Crime in a Free Society.* Washington, D.C.: U.S. Government Printing Office.

RECKLESS, WALTER. 1955. *The Crime Problem,* 2nd ed. New York: Appleton–Century–Crofts.

SUCHMAN, EDWARD A. 1967. *Evaluative Research.* New York: Russell Sage Foundation.

SZASZ, THOMAS S. 1963. *Law Liberty and Psychiatry.* New York: Macmillan.

WRIGHT, JOHN C. 1965. Curiosity and opportunism. *Trans-Action,* II (January–February).

PART II

Theory and Strategy

CHAPTER TWO

Delinquency Theory

There are many links in [a theoretical] argument, and the weakness of any one may shake the plausibility of the whole. A spurious plausibility may sometimes be achieved by leaving certain vital assumptions unspoken and hence less likely to attract critical appraisal. The more explicit we make each link in the argument, the more we facilitate the task of the critic. Inviting criticism in this manner is not a masochistic gesture. None of us enjoys the public mutilation of the theories on which we have long labored and with which we have become identified. However, if there is anything of merit in those theories, it is out of such criticism that there grows the further research and the logical reconstruction of the arguments which are necessary to bring theories into closer correspondence with the reality they are designed to explain. If there are fundamental flaws in the argument, some critic, friendly or otherwise, will eventually bring them to light anyway, and it is vouchsafed to very few to propound an explanation of a complex social phenomenon so logically neat and so empirically well grounded as to remain indefinitely invulnerable to criticism (Cohen, 1955: 109–110).

While Albert Cohen's remarks are applicable to the need for explicitness in the statement of any scientific theory, they are especially applicable to theories having to do with delinquency control. As mentioned in Chapter One, the systematic implementation of a field experimental model (FEM) at Silverlake required a formal body of theory upon which to base both action and research components of the model. If we were to adjudicate more efficiently among the various alternatives open to us, we would have to begin by applying considerable rigor to the development and presentation of our theoretical framework. Both the knowledge-building and operational functions of the study would depend upon it. If such a framework were constructed, it could then be used to guide the implementation of the

25

experimental design, to invite criticism, and to develop research by which its basic postulates could be tested.

Three basic steps were taken in developing the theory: (1) the population for whom it would be applicable was defined; (2) the theory was stated in narrative or descriptive terms; and (3) the theory was then formalized. It was felt that these steps would be the most effective means for making each link in the theoretical argument explicit.

Definition of Population

Since offenders assigned to the experiment could not be drawn from the universe of all delinquents, some delimiting criteria had to be established. The most obvious delimiting characteristic was the fact that the experiment would be concerned only with those juveniles who are *officially* defined as lawbreakers, not with all lawbreakers in general. There is a tremendous difference between the two and an explanation that might be suitable for one need not be suitable for the other.

Delinquent behavior, in *official* terms, is defined by two essential elements: (1) it is behavior that violates the legal norms of society, and (2) it is behavior that evokes official responses by the various elements of the juvenile justice system (Cloward and Ohlin, 1960: 3). Thus, the inclusion of official response as an essential element makes official delinquency a far different thing from unofficial lawbreaking.

Official response, quite aside from the mechanics of arrest, trial, and treatment, serves the social function of labeling and publicizing the deviant. Without it, the adolescent who breaks the law but remains undetected retains his non-delinquent status. With it the adolescent who breaks the law but is detected is assigned a new status: "delinquent." This new status vastly alters his whole network of interactional relationships. He is now assigned a new role in society that itself brings new responses from others and new, reciprocal responses from him. Official processing, therefore, is an important part of the whole sequence of events that ultimately produces official delinquency. Furthermore, if official delinquency is to be understood, the role of official processing must be assessed and included as part of the whole explanatory mosaic. More will be said on this subject later.

A second, and related, general characteristic is the fact that most official delinquents are lower class. Arrest records, probation reports, reformatory data, and demographic studies, over the years, all seem to suggest that the official offender is likely to be a member of the lowest social and economic groups, a child of the slum or a poor neighborhood, a school dropout, and without employment (Burgess, 1952; Cohen, 1955: 37–44; Dirksen, 1948; President's Commission on Law Enforcement and Administration of Justice, 1967b: 60; Shaw and McKay, 1942; Wattenberg and Balistrieri, 1950).

Numerous objections have been raised, of course, regarding this conclusion and the accuracy of the official delinquency records upon which it is based (Barron, 1956: 32; Cressey, 1957: 230–241; Kvaraceus, 1958: 331–332; Porterfield, 1946: *passim*; President's Commission on Law Enforcement and Administration of Justice, 1967b: 266–267; Warner and Lunt, 1941: 427). If studies of undetected delinquency are even partially correct, they indicate that official statistics may greatly distort the epidemiological character of law-violating behavior and lend credence to an inverse relationship between class and actual law violation that is misleading (*cf.* Empey, 1967b, for a summary of these studies). Yet, in one sense, this issue was beside the point in considering the Silverlake population.

The experiment would be concerned only with adjudicated offenders and for that reason both theory and intervention would have to take that fact into account. Theoretical postulates were needed by which two important questions could be answered: (1) Since the majority of official delinquents seem to be lower class, how could their delinquency be explained? (2) What kind of an intervention strategy would be needed to work with this lower class population?

SPECIFIC EXPERIMENTAL CRITERIA

In addition to these general issues, a few specific criteria were also needed. The first criterion had to do with the experiment as an alternative to incarceration. Ordinarily, first-time offenders are not incarcerated. Consequently, most of those assigned to the experiment would probably be repeated offenders. Theory construction would have to take that fact into account.

Second, the Boys Republic population included only boys, ages 16 through 18. This is an age at which the incidence of delinquency is high and during which, after a history of prior trouble, an offender is most likely to be incarcerated. The age variable, like virtually every other variable, had important theoretical implications also. For example, the theoretical model that appears later in this chapter is a sequential model. It suggests that delinquency does not emerge full-blown at time of first offense but is the product of a series of experiences. Thus, by implication, an intervention strategy that might be appropriate for one age level might not be appropriate for another age level. With young children, one might want to concentrate much more heavily upon home and family relationships, while at an older age level, he would want to concentrate upon peer and community factors.

Finally, because Boys Republic ordinarily excluded all boys who were known to be psychotic, seriously retarded, violent sex offenders, or drug addicts, these offenders would also be excluded from the experiment.

In summary, a body of theory was needed to explain the official delinquency of a population of 16- to 18-year-old repeat offenders whose backgrounds were most likely lower class and for whom the experiment would be an alternative to institutionalization. They would be without psychosis, severe mental retardation, addiction to drugs, or a history of violent sex offenses.

Causation Theory

Before presenting the causation theory for this population in formal, axiomatic terms, the second step involved a statement of it in informal, narrative terms. Such a statement was of use in providing action and research people with the substantive content of the formal statement that was to follow. This next section, therefore, is devoted to the narrative task. The four basic postulates of the theory are presented as topic subheadings and the literature that is relevant to each of them is presented under those headings.

I. The lower the social class, the lower the subsequent achievement.
Fundamental to the whole theory construction was the lower class background of most official delinquents. Prevailing theory, accompanied by some evidence, suggests that such membership is the fundamental starting place in the sequence of experiences and events leading to official designation as delinquent. A review of the factors contributing to such a designation suggests an environment of early deprivation, one which retards and disrupts learning processes (Dennis, 1960; Deutsch, 1967: 31; Goldfarb, 1953; Hunt, 1961).

Summaries of research findings by both Deutsch (1967: 31) and Metfessel (1965) suggest that lower-class children suffer disabilities of almost every kind when it comes to effective participation in the school and other middle-class institutions, the gateways to achievement in modern, industrial society. They typically lack language skills, their vocabularies are extremely limited, and they have not had experience with the kinds of words and language that enable them to develop listening abilities and to attend to long, orderly, and focused verbal interaction. As a result, they speak less articulately, with a less varied vocabulary, and with poorer sentence structure than do their higher-class peers. In a day when achievement depends so much upon verbal interaction, communication of abstractions and interpersonal relations, these are distinct liabilities.

Membership in the lower class also has an adverse effect on the interpersonal relationships of the child in the school environment. Lower-class children, typically, are disciplined by physical force. In the school, by contrast, discipline is administered through deprivation of privilege or through attempts at reason and insight-building. Lacking experience with these techniques—which are indeed middle-class manners and folkways—lower-class children find it difficult to understand the causes and consequences of behavior as defined by the school. Consequently, they do not possess the requisite cognitive skills or social strategies for coping with the formal, grade school situation. But how does all this relate to delinquency?

Based largely upon post-hoc analyses, research indicates that such problems may be even more acute for the lower-class child who becomes delinquent than for lower-class children in general. First, although the evidence is not conclusive, it suggests that the incidence of broken homes and family disorganization is greater among delinquents than non-delinquents (Monahan, 1957; Shulman, 1949; Toby, 1957). If this is the case, then the socialization of the delinquent, and his emotional supports, may be even more limited than those just described for lower-class children in general.

Second, some studies have found that delinquents score lower on conventional tests of intelligence, when social class is held constant, than non-delinquents (Reiss and Rhodes, 1961; Short and Strodtbeck, 1965: 237). If true, this places them in a double bind because intelligence has also been found to vary directly with social class: the lower the class, in general, the lower the quotient (Erickson and Empey, 1965: 6–7). This would mean, of course, that official delinquents are at the bottom of the heap, first, because they are lower class, and, second, because they suffer even greater intellectual disabilities than their lower-class peers.

It has been noted, of course, that one cannot attribute greater inherent stupidity to delinquents based on such findings because to do so would be to misinterpret grossly the meaning of intelligence tests. Although such tests may have some utility in measuring innate ability, they are, first and foremost, measures of achievement—measures of the cultural backgrounds and educational experiences of those who take them. As Cohen (1955: 103) put it, intelligence tests measure abilities "that are prized by middle-class people, that are fostered by middle-class socialization, and that are especially important for achievement . . . in middle-class society."

On the other hand, the practical implications of Cohen's remarks are that lower-class children, and especially delinquents, are measurably inferior when it comes to their ability to satisfy middle-class teachers and to compete with middle-class peers—in sum, to achieve, first, in middle-class schools and, later, in middle-class society (*cf.* Erickson and Empey, 1965). The most significant thing about this state of affairs is that this group of young people are failures when it comes to effective participation in the one major institution in society that is charged with bridging the gap between childhood and adulthood, the one institution that is devoted exclusively to the socialization of the young.

The school, in turn, either through its failure to recognize these kinds of deficiencies or through a lack of resources, has been unable to compensate for them (*cf.* Elliott, 1966). In fact, the reverse seems to be true. Rather than becoming a place in which deficiencies diminish, the school becomes a place in which they accumulate. Low expectations are established, failure is anticipated, and, true to the Mertonian self-fulfilling prophecy (Merton, 1957: chap. XII), failure occurs.

The point of this particular part of the theoretical narration, however, is not that cultural deprivation and the lack of achievement in school lead inevitably to delinquent behavior. That is not being suggested. What is being suggested is that these influences may be but one of a series of stages that lead to delinquency. The lack of achievement in school may increase the amenability of the child to other influences which, coming later in his life, can eventually lead to delinquent behavior. What, then, are the other stages in the sequence that generates delinquency? The next section has to do with the possible impact upon the potential delinquent of his failure to achieve in school.

II. Decreased achievement results in increased strain.
From a conventional standpoint, it would be logical to assume that failure on the part of lower-class juveniles to achieve in school and community would be productive of strain for them. But one cannot automatically make that assumption. Their failure to achieve does not mean necessarily that they experience strain, a lowered sense of self-worth, social alienation, or loss of status. The lack of achievement is problematic only if lower-class children have internalized a set of values that defines the lack of achievement as "bad." If they have not, then the lack of achievement in conventional ways may be irrelevant in terms of the values they hold.

Theorists have not been in total agreement on this issue. Miller (1958; Kvaraceus and Miller, 1959), for example, has argued that lower- and middle-class values are not the same. The focal concerns of lower-class people, he says, are with trouble, toughness, smartness, excitement, fate, and autonomy, not with achievement in middle-class institutions and patterns. The behavior of the lower-class child may be seen, therefore, as an attempt to adhere to the standards of value as they are defined within lower-, not middle-class, culture. His failure with respect to middle-class values would not be a source of strain to him.

In contrast, a number of other theorists take an opposing point of view.

They have suggested that there is essential agreement among the classes on major goals and values. According to this view, the democratic and egalitarian character of American culture results in the indoctrination of all social classes with a desire for high social status and economic success, despite the fact that the means for reaching these goals are differentially distributed. By implication, therefore, the lower-class child whose abilities are limited and who lacks conventional access to institutional channels for upward mobility is especially discomfited. He is likely to experience strong feelings of frustration and deprivation because of his inability to achieve (*cf.* Merton, 1957: chaps. IV–V).

Cohen (1955: 121–137) says this problem, above all, is a status problem. The thought is dominant in American society, he says, that one's sense of personal worth is at stake in comparison with all comers. The capacity of the individual to compete is judged by one set of prevailing criteria. Since the lower-class child, either in association with middle-class teachers or peers, is unable to compete successfully, status frustration is the inevitable result.

Cloward and Ohlin (1960: 86) agree with Cohen in general terms:

> The disparity between what lower-class youth are led to want and what is actually available to them is the source of a major problem of adjustment. . . . Faced with limitations on legitimate avenues of access to [conventional] goals, and unable to revise their aspirations downward, they experience intense frustration; the exploration of nonconformist alternatives may be the result.

In summary, these theoretical statements are part of a larger body of theory that suggests that, since the subparts of any complex society are intimately tied up with the whole, it should come as no surprise that the members of different classes share common values. Lower-class children, for example, watch television, listen to the radio, go to the movies, and attend middle-class dominated schools like everyone else. Since they are conditioned by stimuli that reflect the prevailing perspectives and values of American society, they internalize the American tradition of wanting to succeed.

Research evidence has tended to confirm the view that American values are generally shared, especially the view that the American tradition of wanting to get ahead is a powerful motivating force. In fact, experimental studies of levels of aspiration in the social-psychological literature suggest that the lower classes may be even more strongly motivated to achieve than are those on strata above them (Empey, 1956; Gould, 1941). And with specific reference to delinquents, both Kobrin (1951) and Short and Strodtbeck (1965: chap. 3) suggest that delinquents, no less than non-delinquents, are inclined to legitimate official values. The delinquents

Short and Strodtbeck studied did not seem to be alienated from the goals of the larger society and "even the gang ethic," say Short and Strodtbeck (1965: 59, 271), "is not one of 'reaction formation' *against* widely shared conceptions of the 'good' life." Gang, lower-class and middle-class boys, Negro and White "evaluated images representing salient features of the middle-class styles of life equally high."

These findings, which confirmed those of Gold (1963) in Michigan, lend greater support to theorists who argue that lower-class children do internalize basic values than to those, such as Miller (1958), who argue that class differences are exclusive. In fact, Short and Strodtbeck (1965: 74), after considering these issues concluded that Cohen (1955) and Cloward and Ohlin (1960), as well as Miller (1958) had actually understated the meaningfulness of middle-class values to members of delinquent groups. For that reason, we chose to emphasize the sharing of basic values and the strain they produce as basic ingredients of our theory and to discard the Miller formulation. In fact, given the strength of emerging evidence, one wonders whether we are correct in referring to prevailing values as "middle-class" values or whether we should be using some more inclusive term. Traditional values favoring achievement seem to be widely shared.

If this is true, the paradoxical quality of the problems it poses should not escape unnoticed. People are prone, as Cohen (1955: 137) suggests, to assume that those things we define as evil, such as delinquency, have their origins in separate and distinct features of society or in unique pathological qualities of individuals. But this analysis suggests that this assumption is incorrect. Those very values that are at the core of "the American way of life," those values that help to motivate the behavior we esteem most highly, may also help to produce problematic and undesirable behavior.

Having accepted the idea that the way to respect, status, and success lies in pursuing the values of middle-class society, yet finding themselves without the necessary advantages, qualifications, and opportunities for achievement, the chances of lower-class youth for the attainment of fundamental goals are slight. Their desire to succeed and their inclination to evaluate their progress by the same measuring rod as other adolescents, coupled with their personal disabilities and lack of access to institutionalized channels, generate problems of adjustment that are compelling in their need for resolution. Intense strain is likely to result. What alternatives, therefore, are available to resolve this strain?

III. Increased strain results in identification with delinquent peers.
Cohen (1959) suggests the availability of three general alternatives. The first is a conformist alternative with long-range implications in which the individual joins others in adhering to conventional expectations despite

the likelihood that he will have to carry a chronic load of frustration. Acceptance of the conformist alternative means that he will have to play the status game according to middle-class rules, even though it will probably mean a docile acceptance of a low-status position, with all its limitations. He may eventually acquire a limited education, a job, and a family and become a stable member of lower-class society. There is the possibility, of course, that by exerting great effort and by deferring gratifications, he may be able to attend college. If he does, he may then become the exception who is upwardly mobile, and part of the American dream.

The major virtue of this alternative is the official support it receives from others. Conformity to basic values brings moral and symbolic validation. Frustration, therefore, is easier to bear knowing that one will not have to encounter the moral uncertainty and social sanctions that would be the result of deviation.

A second major alternative, as Cohen (1959) suggests, is for the individual to break with conformist reference groups and to join with new reference groups whose norms legitimate a deviant solution to the strain that is experienced. This solution may involve "shopping around" to find already existing deviant reference groups or to join forces with others in creating them. The virtue of this alternative, at least in the short run, is its ability to provide more immediate gratification.

There is nothing new about this resolution of strain, about the notion that boys get into trouble with other boys, or that they join with others in the attempt to resolve their problems. The idea for which it stands, as Cohen (1955: 1) notes, is commonplace in everyday as well as scientific thinking.

In anthropology and social psychology, as well as sociology, it has long been postulated that people who share common problems of adjustment tend to work out new and collective forms of adjustment, not only in lower-class areas but in emerging nations, in political parties, in prisons, mental hospitals, or factories. That is why subcultures, cliques, and power groups evolve. What is surprising, however, is how little attention has been paid to this alternative in explaining lawbreaking or in constructing ameliorative programs and strategies of intervention.

The third and final alternative is for the individual to "resolve" his problems by "going it alone," wandering, consciously or subconsciously, into solitary forms of deviant behavior or by becoming mentally ill. This would appear to be the most improbable and least common alternative, because it is the most costly, personally and socially. Only when group solutions are precluded will the problem-solving become completely personal and thus completely explainable in psychogenic terms. To be sure, it does occur but it is a relatively rare event.

Of these three alternative modes of adjustment, the most commonly chosen, of course, is the conformist alternative. The majority of lower-class adolescents do not become persistent delinquents, at least not officially. The second most common is likely to be the collective, deviant adjustment. In addition to all the theoretical speculation in support of this conclusion, there is also a large body of evidence in support of it.

First, in general terms, as Coleman (1961: 3–4) has pointed out, in separating our children for many years of schooling, we tend to cut them off from the rest of society and to force them inward upon their own age groups. Young people constitute one or more small societies, each of which has many, if not most, of its most important interactions within itself. As a result, there is likely to be conflict between adults, on one hand, and even the most successful of students, on the other, because of the identification of the latter with peers. But what about the unsuccessful student?

The possibilities for conflict and peer identification are even greater here. After failing in school, there is only one direction to go—aside from complete isolation—and that is further into a society of like-minded peers— a society, in this case, made up of failures. Polk (1965: 12–13) says that this involvement is both quantitative and qualitative. Quantitatively, unsuccessful students are almost twice as likely to spend their evenings with friends than are successful youths (64 *vs.* 38 per cent). Qualitatively, they are much more likely to have friends who have dropped out of school (43 *vs.* 16 per cent). Furthermore, failures are far more likely than successful students to give peer-oriented responses and, at the same time, to consider either grades or school activities as being unimportant in providing status for them. School failures, then, seem to be twice-removed from adults and at least once-removed from successful students (*cf.* Erickson and Empey, 1965). However, even though this may be true, it does not explain delinquent behavior. We need answers to additional questions: What evidence is there that differential peer association leads to delinquent behavior? How does the collective attempt to resolve strain among some juveniles lead to a delinquent adjustment? These questions are discussed most appropriately under the next major postulate of our theory.

IV. Identification with delinquent peers results in delinquency.
First, let us consider an important body of evidence. In their pioneering study, Shaw and McKay (1931) reported that, of 5,480 known offenders in the Chicago Juvenile Court in 1928, 82 per cent had committed their delinquent acts with one or more companions. Stealing and offenses against property were especially group-centered, with 9 out of 10 offenses so related (*cf.* Lohman, 1957: 8, for later Chicago figures). Twosomes and threesomes were the most common. An examination of the charts and

diagrams presented by Shaw and McKay, showing the web of interlocking combinations of boys, was strongly suggestive of a transmission process at work of delinquency from boy to boy, or group to boy.

In their study of 500 delinquents and 500 non-delinquents, the Gluecks (1950: 163–164) painted a similar picture. They reported that 98 per cent of the delinquents, but only 7 per cent of the non-delinquents, had companions who were delinquent. Fifty-six per cent of the delinquents, but only 6 per cent of the non-delinquents, were members of gangs. Similar figures could be cited for California (Fenton, 1935: 182), Elmtown (Hollingshead, 1949: 332–411), and elsewhere (Healy and Bronner, 1936: 52–64; Kvaraceus, 1945: 115).

Group-related delinquency, furthermore, does not seem to be solely an American phenomenon. In a summary article, describing a variety of studies going back to 1920, Scott (1956) reports percentages from London, Scotland, and "typical provincial towns" in England ranging between 60 and 80 per cent for delinquents operating in groups. The figures were much the same as those reported in the U.S. studies. Likewise, Geis (1965: 4–16) indicates that delinquency, as a group phenomenon, has been characteristic of juveniles in a variety of different cultures at a variety of different times.

One investigator (Plant, 1948: Part 1, 24) was so impressed by the available evidence that he was led to conclude that "with the possible exception of marriage, no human arrangement is of a more social nature than delinquency." Even though this is probably an overstatement, the relationship between group and delinquent behavior is so pervasive that it seems to require explanation wherever delinquency occurs. However, when the Gluecks (1956: 42–43) encountered this phenomenon (98 per cent of their delinquents had delinquent companions), they rejected peer association as an explanatory variable because they felt that it occurred after, not before, the onset of delinquency. They conjectured, instead, that family dynamics, physique, temperament, emotional attitudes, and psychological set were what caused delinquency and that association with other delinquents, like delinquency itself, was the product of these prior variables (Glueck and Glueck, 1950: 281–283). Companionship would not be an important cause.

Eynon and Reckless (1961), on the other hand, produced findings that seriously questioned the conclusion reached by the Gluecks. Almost three-quarters of the delinquent boys they studied, whether pre-adolescent or adolescent, were with companions when they committed the first delinquent act that brought them to the attention of officials. Their findings strongly suggested that companionship is important in the genetic sequence. Why this striking difference between the two studies? How could it be explained?

The difference was inherent in the measures of "onset" that were used.

The Gluecks used psychiatric interview to establish "onset," while Eynon and Reckless used official detection and arrest. The result was that when psychiatric criteria were used, onset in 90 per cent of the cases was said to have begun before age 10, and usually without companions, while the comparable figure, using official data, was only 19 per cent before age 10. Thus, the two different sets of findings were the product of different research criteria and procedures. Furthermore, Eynon and Reckless protested the use of psychiatric criteria (1) because such criteria include acts that are far different from those that are socially and legally defined as delinquent, and (2) because of the growing body of literature that indicates that psychiatric diagnoses are extremely unreliable. Actually, it is our feeling that neither of these two interpretations is entirely correct. Instead, as Tannenbaum (1938) suggested, delinquent behavior and association in delinquent groups may be interdependent.

Tannenbaum (1938), indeed the whole "Chicago School" (Shaw, 1940a, 1940b; Shaw and McKay, 1942; Thrasher, 1927), postulated a sequential model of causation in which interaction between disassociated youths in the community led first to loosely structured associations among these youth, followed later by the emergence of delinquent groups with strong internal ties. In the absence of adequate direction from the community, the delinquent group developed as a subcultural refuge for disassociated youth.

According to this point of view, associations with delinquent peers both cause and result from delinquent behavior. They are interdependent. At the outset, boys who are unintegrated into the institutional paths of society engage in mischievous and annoying behavior. As the community imposes increasing sanctions upon them, they are forced ever further into delinquent group associations as a refuge. Thus, a self-fulfilling prophecy is set up that tends to evoke and make worse the very behavior that was complained about in the first place. That is why, as Tannenbaum (1938) suggested, the process of labeling a person deviant and then making him self-conscious of that label, may make the problem worse, not better.

What his analysis failed to provide, of course, is the way in which the sanctioning activities of the community may have produced conformist, as well as deviant, behavior. Some boys are undoubtedly deterred by the imposition of negative sanctions; some boys would not become further enmeshed in the process but would withdraw from it. Tannenbaum's failure to explain this phenomenon is a common one. No theory, as yet, is able to pinpoint with precision the factors, both personal and social, that determine which course an individual will follow.

Reckless, Dinitz, and Murray (1956) concluded, on the basis of their research, that the self-concept may serve as an "insulator" against delinquency. Well-"insulated" boys do not internalize delinquent values and are willing to play the game as defined by significant others who are conformists. It seems likely, however, that boys who are well "insulated" are those who are least likely to become enmeshed in the whole defining process in the first place. For that reason, we are still at a loss to explain the gaps left in Tannenbaum's formulation. Even so, there is great inherent value in it because of its emphasis upon the learning of delinquent behavior that takes place in the interactional process among boys, and between boys and the community. It implies the great importance of distinguishing between the disabilities the majority of lower-class boys possess and the factors that eventually produce delinquent behavior among only a minority of them. Social disabilities and delinquency are not necessarily the same thing. Thus, even without pinpointing the precise factors that introduce a boy to the wandering interaction that leads to involvement with delinquent groups, we may still be able to identify the factors that lead to delinquency itself, once involvement occurs.

What is being suggested is that individuals adopting this form of adjustment do not simply experience strain, view alternatives, and make a sudden and solitary choice to become delinquent. This form of adjustment would depend upon the availability of existing delinquent groups or individuals who are experiencing similar problems. In the event such groups or persons were available, the individual's interaction with them initially would be half-concious, groping, and tentative, not intimate, deliberate, and rational (*cf.* Cloward and Ohlin, 1960: chaps. 4–6; Cohen, 1959: 469–473; Parsons, 1951: 249–251). His choices in favor of delinquency would be fraught with dangers as well as satisfactions. They would pose the possibility of alienating as well as attracting significant others, of hindering as well as encouraging important kinds of interaction.

The key thing to remember is that without the eventual moral support and validation of delinquent peers and subculture, such an adjustment, short of mental pathology, would not be possible. Delinquent activities are understandable primarily in terms of the values, norms, and sentiments implicit in delinquent associations because the delinquent's only defense against the moral encroachments of the middle class is his repudiation of these encroachments and the substitution of an inverted moral code that is supported by others. In other words, the moral code of the delinquent subculture is the direct antithesis of the middle class. It functions, as Bordua (1961) suggests, "simultaneously to combat the enemy without and the enemy within, both the hated agents of the middle-class and the gnawing sense of inadequacy and low self-esteem. It does so by erecting a counterculture, an alternative set of status criteria." It is the means by which lower-class boys can achieve the status and attention they have been conditioned to want instead of succumbing to the sense of failure they would experience if they were to use conventional criteria.

Cloward and Ohlin (1960) present some distinctive features on the theme of a drift into delinquency. They do not believe it is initiated by the reaction formation Cohen (1955: 32–33) suggests or by the random play activities implied by Tannenbaum (1938). It is initiated, instead, by alienation. What distinguishes children who do become delinquent from those who do not is their withdrawal of legitimacy from established social norms.

They suggest further that delinquent association may appear in different forms depending upon the opportunity structures existing in various communities. In that community in which there is an integration of different age levels, criminal traditions may be transmitted from adults to juveniles. Youngsters are recruited into a criminally oriented delinquent subculture.

In disorganized or unorganized communities, which cannot provide either legitimate or illegitimate means for achievement, *conflict* subcultures emerge. Since social controls and opportunities in such communities are weak, the young are deprived of both conventional and criminal opportunity. The results are wild untrammeled activities that symbolize protest against the meaninglessness of the social experience.

Finally, a *retreatist* subculture, characterized primarily by the use of narcotics or alcohol, may develop in disorganized communities in lieu of conflict or career-oriented delinquent subcultures. Retreatists, however, are double failures who choose to withdraw from frustration rather than fighting it.

In any event, all three modes of adaptation are symbolic of failure and blocked opportunities, not the repudiation of fundamental, societal goals. In each case, illegitimate activity and subcultural standards develop as alternative means for the satisfactions which all people seek.

Finally, Matza (1964: 63–64) has yet another theory, which emphasizes a subtle but important distinction. He argues that "there is a subculture of delinquency, but it is not a delinquent subculture." Matza's point (1964: 33–68) is that American culture is not a simple puritanism exemplified by the middle class. Instead, it is a complex and pluralistic culture in which, among other subcultural traditions, there is a subculture of delinquency, one with its own particular norms and rationalizations (*cf.* Bell, 1959: 115–136, for an example of Matza's point among adults).

The persons most likely to participate in this subculture, he believes, are "drifters": those lower-class adolescents spoken of here who are most likely to be cut off from institutional ties and conventional activities (Matza, 1964: 27–30). In the absence of such ties, they are far more dependent than most adolescents upon peer relationships. As a result, they are more likely to drift into delinquent activities, especially since most of them live in high delinquency areas. Even so, their delinquent behavior

will be highly situational, more the product of spontaneous group interaction than of highly structured and long-standing relationships.

What Matza implies is that delinquents, like non-delinquents, possess a
repertory of possible behaviors, some conformist, some deviant, that are
applied in different social contexts. In conventional settings, they can, and
usually do, behave conventionally; in delinquent settings they do likewise.
Being "drifters," however, they are highly susceptible to "shared misunderstanding," highly likely to stereotype one another so that, in delinquent situations, they attribute greater commitment to delinquency to
each other than any one of them actually feels. For example, Thrasher
(1963: 300–303) describes three boys who begin to phantasize about robbing
a post office. Subsequent interviews with them revealed that none of them
wanted to commit the actual robbery but the more they talked the more
they became involved, each believing that the others wanted to continue
and each fearing to "chicken out." The result was that they robbed the
post office and ended up in legal custody.

Matza's point of view, like Cohen's, would place the delinquent in a
vulnerable and ambivalent position over his delinquency. His awareness
of conventional values and his lack of ties to a close-knit group would
cause him to experience doubt about the norms he violates and to exhibit
guilt and shame when called to account for his delinquent acts. He would
be totally insulated neither by a shield of ignorance regarding conventional
expectations nor by a wall of peer solidarity with which to ward off the
effects of self-condemnation and social sanctioning. Sykes and Matza
(1957) suggest, however, that the subculture of delinquency provides the
offender with a series of intricate rationalizations by which to "neutralize"
his own delinquent acts, even though he might subscribe, in an abstract
way, to laws in general. These "techniques of neutralization" help to
justify his acts both to himself, psychologically, and to others, socially, in
much the same way as borderline business practices or income tax violations
are justified by their adult perpetrators. "It is by learning these techniques
that the juvenile becomes delinquent, rather than by learning moral
imperatives, values or attitudes standing in direct contradiction to those
of the dominant society" (Sykes and Matza, 1957: 667). In other words,
delinquent subculture is not an all-or-none set of standards which is totally
opposed to conventional standards. Instead, it stands alongside conventional standards to be used selectively as the situation dictates.

Narrative Summary

One could never hope to reconcile all of the subtle differences implicit in
these different points of view. Nevertheless, there are certain major themes

present throughout, and it was these which formed the basic theoretical argument used at Silverlake:

1. Lower-class boys, especially those who become delinquent, are ill-prepared to achieve in the context of middle-class institutions.
2. The lack of achievement in a success-oriented society produces strain, a serious problem of adjustment.
3. For a significant number of those caught in this situation, an almost exclusive association with peers, similarly circumstanced, is the result.
4. This differential association with peers results in the emergence of delinquent subcultures through which boys achieve the status, recognition, and sense of belonging that have not been achieved in a conventional way.

The ultimate validity of this argument, and especially its utility in dealing with delinquents at Silverlake, would depend upon its logical consistency and the empirical evidence that could be garnered in favor of it. In order to move, then, to matters of program development and empirical test, it was felt that the theory should be formally presented.

Formal Construction of Theory

The task of theory construction might have been concluded with this summary, once basic assumptions had been made reasonably explicit. However, some compelling arguments in favor of formal construction have been made.

First, Gibbs (1967: 74) has argued that, although significant theories have been stated informally, as in this case, this mode of construction hardly improves a theory.

> Even if one grants that formal theory construction does not insure empirical validity, it may play a crucial role in attempts to *test* the theory. Equally important, it is difficult to assess the logical consistency of a theory without reducing it to formal statements. Moreover, the use of formal statements does not make it impossible for a theoretician to 'make a case' for plausibility. The theory can be (and should be) presented in a narrative form, followed by a formal restatement. Finally, a better way than formal construction to reveal the pretentiousness of a theory scarcely can be imagined. When a theory is presented in a narrative form, its ostensible significance may evaporate when restated formally.

Furthermore, formality in stating a theory is important, not just in terms of deductive logic, but in terms of falsifiability as well.

> If a theory generates predictions about events or things that cannot be confirmed or refuted by experience, it is not falsifiable. . . . Whatever the interpretation of the results, theories must be testable, which is to say that they must be stated in such a way that they are falsifiable (Gibbs, 1967: 87).

The issue of falsifiability seemed especially important in this case where theory was to provide the basis for an intervention strategy. If such a theory were not falsifiable, then serious doubts about its continued use should be raised. The field of corrections, indeed all fields involving intervention in people's lives, have been plagued by the use of theories that not only have been vaguely articulated, but that are virtually untestable. Consequently, Gibb's emphasis upon formal theory construction seemed particularly applicable to our experimental endeavor.

Second, in terms of the *criteria* for assessing a theory, Schrag (1967: 229) has suggested that,

> The main task of any theory is to construct a calculus of relationships among classes of events such that the derived statements are (1) logically valid, (2) accurate in their claims regarding observable data, and (3) useful in describing, explaining, and controlling the course of events with which they are concerned.

In other words, Schrag is suggesting that the pragmatic adequacy of a theory, as well as its logical and empirical adequacy, is important. Thus, if this criterion were joined with those suggested by Gibbs, the basic concepts and relationships of the theory should be made as explicit as possible. The ultimate utility of our argument would depend upon its direct relevance for the purposes of intervention, as well as for the purposes of explanation.

Formal Theory Construction

Given our needs, it seemed that an axiomatic model for formalizing our narrative statement would be the most useful. This form of theory construction has been employed by a number of investigators to develop theories in a variety of content areas (Catton, 1961; Gibbs and Martin, 1962; Gould and Schrag, 1962; Zetterberg, 1954, 1963, 1965). According to Zetterberg (1954: 18–25), the axiomatic system has the following advantages: (1) the concepts and postulates offer the most parsimonious summary of research findings, (2) the axiomatized theory has the highest plausibility per amount of empirical data, (3) through the use of an axiomatic model, strategic research problems may be located, (4) the source of failure of an hypothesis to meet empirical test may be efficiently discerned, and (5) the axiomatic model permits clear distinction between propositions that are definitions and those which are hypotheses.

Axiomatic theory, in the form in which we would use it, would be comprised of two major types of statements or propositions: *postulates* and *theorems*. Postulates would be the fundamental building blocks of the theory, the basic statements of relationships from which the remainder of the theory would be derived. If we had had invariant laws regarding delinquency from which to begin, these would have been our postulates; they would have provided the most logical starting points in the construction of our axiomatic system. However, since such laws did not, and may never, exist, we had to begin with what seemed to us to be some of the strongest statements regarding delinquency that could be derived from our review of existing theory and fact.

The theorems, on the other hand, would be statements derived according to logical rules from the postulates. They would not have as high a degree of empirical support as the postulates but instead would be the logical consequence of them. Once the postulates and theorems of the axiomatic system were established, it would then be possible to examine their logical coherence as a whole, their correspondence with empirical fact, and their pragmatic implications for purposes of intervention and control.

Once these decisions had been made, a presentation of the theory in formal terms required attention to the definition of the basic concepts in the theory, the nature of the relationships between these concepts, and, finally, the rules that would govern the process of logical deduction. Each of these three areas is examined briefly below.

CONCEPTS

Only five major concepts were used in constructing the theory: "social class," "achievement," "strain," "identification with delinquent peers," and "delinquent behavior."

1. *Social class* is an ordinal concept used to denote groups of individuals who share similar attributes along a socioeconomic continuum. The concept derives its meaning only within the context of a single societal or community network, and the continuum of attributes is defined in terms of the possession of such socially sought goals as prestige, wealth, power or some loosely formulated combination of these components (Gould and Kolb, 1964: 648–650). For example, a nonskilled laborer who makes a very low income would be ranked toward the lower end of the social class continuum. At the upper extreme of the continuum would be ranked powerful and wealthy persons with such prestigious occupations as court judge, bank president and physician.

2. *Achievement* also derives its meaning within a social context. In our theory, it refers to the attainment of goals, *through legitimate means*, that are endorsed and defined as important by society. For adolescents, legitimate achievement is usually defined in terms of successful goal attainment in the family, in school and, to a lesser extent, in work. For example, in general societal terms, a successful adolescent might be expected to exhibit good scholarship, to conform to school rules, and to begin experimentation

with adult roles by demonstrating competence and skill at a job. Even further achievement might be measured in terms of athletic prowess in organized games, the attainment of membership in school clubs and societies, or election to office in church, club, or classroom.

3. *Strain,* as defined in the context of this theory, is comprised of two major components: (1) a disaffection or detachment from existing institutional relationships and activities, and (2) a dynamic state of tension implying a strong need for resolution.

4. *Identification with delinquent peers* refers to the process of internalizing the norms and beliefs of specific delinquent groups, of adopting subcultural standards and points of view. Identification occurs when the individual makes the delinquent group a primary reference group.

5. *Delinquent behavior* refers (1) to the commission of an illegal act by a juvenile that (2) results in the adjudication of that act by the court as officially delinquent. Both ingredients—illegal behavior and subsequent adjudication—must be present before behavior is considered "delinquent."

NATURE OF RELATIONSHIPS

Since statements of relationships dealing with absolute certainty are rare or nonexistent in the social sciences, all of the relationships expressed in the following axiomatic theory will be probabilistic in nature. A probabilistic relationship is one that does not deal in absolute certainties. Instead of assuming that "X *always* results in Y," a probabilistic statement is one assuming that "X is *likely* to result in Y." *Thus, postulates in this theory are meant to be probabilistic in nature, even though actual probabilities are not explicitly stated.* Perhaps a better way of saying this is that the postulates imply correlations, and that we do not expect the correlations to be perfect since factors other than those explicity identified in the theory will also affect the relationships.

Furthermore, all of the relationships expressed in the theory are asymmetric, meaning that the occurrence of a causal factor is followed in time by its effect, rather than occurring simultaneously with it, and that the observed causal sequence is not reversible. For example, the statement "smoking causes cancer" is an expression of an asymmetric relationship. It would be absurd to state that "cancer causes smoking." The utility of stating postulates in asymmetric form lies in the fact that they lead to more powerful deductions in the context of an axiomatic model than statements that are made in symmetric or covariance form without regard to temporal order and irreversibility (Costner and Leik, 1964: 823–825). Thus, when we state that "an increase in X results in a decrease in Y," we are assuming that Y is likely to follow X in time and that Y does not result in an increase in X.

RULES FOR DEDUCTIONS

In any search for a set of logical rules to guide the deduction of theoretical statements, one is confronted by an almost total lack of meaningful alternatives. This situation seems to be due, in part, to the primitive state of conceptual development and measurement in the social sciences, especially in the area of delinquency and corrections. On the one hand, it would have been optimal to use the powerful rules of mathematical logic and calculus to interrelate the concepts, but the lack of interval measurement seemed to preclude the use of this alternative. Our levels of measurement were at best ordinal (*cf.* Stevens, 1960: 141–149).

On the other hand, it might have been possible to use the categorical syllogism as originated by Aristotle. The rules of syllogistic logic are clear and unambiguous, but they also have a characteristic that made them unsuitable for our purposes. The categorical syllogism is used to describe logical relationships among nominal classes, not among relationships based on ordinal measurement. We were interested in studying the correlative relationships among the concepts in our theory (*e.g.*, an increase on *X* results in an increase on *Y*). Thus, the categorical syllogism was not suitable for our purposes either. What we needed was a set of rules that would enable us to construct a theory on the basis of the ordinal measures that we would use.

Two rules have been employed recently by social scientists to perform logical deductions of the type in which we were interested. These rules, called the *sign rule* and the *transitivity rule*, seem to have been developed to handle the unique, logical requirements of axiomatic, sociological theory as we wished to develop it.

1. *The Sign Rule.* Costner and Leik (1964) define this rule very simply: "The sign of the deduced relationship is the algebraic product of the signs of the postulated relationships." In more precise terms, the sign rule deals with certain measures of association and requires that the sign of the relationship expressed in the conclusion of explanandum of an argument must be the algebraic product of the signs of the relationships expressed in the two postulates or explanantes of the same argument. This means that if both postulates of an argument express positive correlations, or if both express negative correlations, the conclusion must be positive. If, on the other hand, the sign of one of the postulates is negative while the other is positive, the conclusion must necessarily be negative. This rule leads to three possible types of deductions, illustrated in formal terms below:

Type 1 (both postulates express positive correlations)
Postulate A: An increase in *X* results in an increase in *Y*. (positive)
Postulate B: An increase in *Y* results in an increase in *Z*. (positive)

Conclusion: An increase in X results in an increase in Z. (positive)

Type 2 (one postulate positive, the other negative)
Postulate A: A decrease in X results in an increase in Y. (negative)
Postulate B: An increase in Y results in an increase in Z. (positive)
Conclusion: A decrease in X results in an increase in Z. (negative)

Type 3 (both postulates express negative correlations)
Postulate A: An increase in X results in a decrease in Y. (negative)
Postulate B: A decrease in Y results in an increase in Z. (negative)
Conclusion: An increase in X results in an increase in Z. (positive)

Notice that in each of these three examples, the sign of the conclusion is the algebraic product of the signs of the postulates. In purely logical terms, this is a simple rule to use. On an *empirical* level, however, validation of the sign rule can become very complex. Actual correlations among sets of variables do not always conform to the three cases illustrated above. Nevertheless, there are specific empirical conditions under which the rule must hold true. A consideration of these conditions, however, will not be made until the theory is evaluated on an empirical level in Chapter Eleven.

2. *The Transitivity Rule.* In basic terms, this rule may be stated as follows: "If A implies B, and B implies C, then A implies C" (Gould and Schrag, 1962: 69; Schrag, 1967: 223). For example, if smoking might result in cancer, and if cancer might result in death, this implies that smoking might result in death. Many types of relationships, however, are not conducive to this type of rule; the statements that John is the father of Bill and Bill is the father of Pete do *not* imply that John is also the father of Pete. This implication would be an absurdity, at least in the present kinship structure of our society. The transitivity rule holds true only for certain types of statements and logical connections.

Furthermore, when postulates are presented in asymmetric form, as they are in this theory, the "middle term" of the explanans must occupy a specific position if the transitivity rule is to hold true. It must be the final term of the first postulate and the initial term of the second postulate. In abstract terms, a causal argument must take the following form in order to meet the requirement of transitivity (Schrag, 1967):

X leads to Y
Y leads to Z
therefore: X leads to Z

Notice that the middle term, Y, appears at the end of the first postulate and at the beinning of the second one. If the argument were stated in any other form, such as:

X leads to Y
Z leads to Y

then no valid conclusions about the causal sequence between X and Z could be reached because the transitivity rule could not be applied.

The Formal Theory

The four basic *postulates* of the theory described in the narrative statement were as follows:

Postulate I: The lower the social class, the lower the subsequent achievement.

Postulate II: Decreased achievement results in increased strain.

Postulate III: Increased strain results in identification with delinquent peers.

Postulate IV: Identification with delinquent peers results in delinquency.

The causal sequency implied by these postulates could be diagrammed as follows:

Lower Social Class ⟶ Decreased Achievement ⟶ Increased Strain ⟶ Increased Identification ⟶ Delinquency

Using the postulates as basic premises, the following first-order theorems were deduced:

Theorem I: The lower the social class, the greater the subsequent strain (deduced from Postulates I and II).

Theorem II: Decreased achievement results in identification with delinquent peers (deduced from Postulates II and III).

Theorem III: Increased strain results in delinquency (deduced from Postulates III and IV).

These three theorems exhaust the implications of the four postulates. Using one postulate and theorem, however, three second-order theorems may also be deduced.

Theorem IV: The lower the social class, the greater the subsequent identification with delinquent peers (Postulate I and Theorem II).

Theorem V: Decreased achievement results in delinquency (Postulate II and Theorem III).

Theorem VI: The lower the social class, the greater the subsequent delinquency (Postulate I and Theorem V).

The above set of four postulates and six theorems exhaust the deductive implications of the theory.

A Concluding Comment

Before proceeding to the guidelines for intervention that were derived from this theory, an important comment on its adequacy is in order. There are potential liabilities as well as strengths in stating the theory in axiomatic form, liabilities that are more apparent today than when we started the experiment several years ago. Possibly the most notable is the likelihood that the formal statement oversimplifies the complex processes involved. For example, the narrative statement emphasized the likelihood that the stigmatizing effects of official labeling—the negative reactions of the community to the delinquent—are likely to isolate him further from conventional institutions and activities. If this is so, then two things are implied which the theory did not take into account: (1) the presence of "stigma" as an important concept and (2) the likelihood that relationships among such concepts as strain, peer identification, and delinquency are interdependent rather than independent.

The increasing conflict of the delinquent with the community, and the stigmatizing effects of official labeling, imply a progressive increase in strain which is likely to increase even more his identification with delinquent peers. Thus, it may be that if the theory is to take adequate account of both "stigma" and the interdependence of important concepts, the theory should be diagrammed as follows:

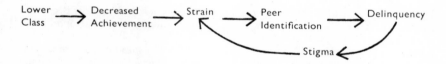

For any explanation of persistent delinquency, therefore, a more complex model than our original one would be needed.

In making this report of findings, we could have revised the formal statement to include this, and perhaps other revisions. However, since both the intervention strategy of the experiment and the data collection were based upon that statement, it seemed best to report the study as it was originally conceived, and to reserve comment on the adequacy of the original statement until it is actually tested in Chapter Six. As will be seen at that time, there are findings which confirm the notion that a more complex model is needed. Furthermore, in Chapter Seven, an attempt will be made to reformulate the theory in a way that will better take into account the problems of theory construction, the empirical findings of the study, and improved methods of measurement.

References

BARRON, MILTON A. 1956. *The Juvenile in Delinquent Society*. New York: Alfred A. Knopf.

BELL, DANIEL. 1959. *The End of Ideology*. Glencoe, Ill.: The Free Press.

BORDUA, DAVID J. 1961. A critique of sociological interpretations of gang delinquency. *Annals of the American Academy of Political and Social Science*, 338 (November): 120–136.

BURGESS, ERNEST W. 1952. The economic factor in juvenile delinquency. *Journal of Criminal Law, Criminology and Police Science*, 43 (May–June): 29–42.

CATTON, WILLIAM R., JR. 1961. The functions and dysfunctions of ethnocentrism: a theory. *Social Problems*, 8 (Winter): 201–211.

CLOWARD, RICHARD A., and LLOYD E. OHLIN. 1960. *Delinquency and Opportunity: A Theory of Delinquent Gangs*. New York: The Free Press.

COHEN, ALBERT K. 1955. *Delinquent Boys: The Culture of the Gang*. New York: The Free Press.
1959. The study of social disorganization and deviant behavior. In Robert Merton, Leonard Broom, and Leonard Cottrell, Eds., *Sociology Today*. New York: Basic Books.

COLEMAN, JAMES. 1961. *The Adolescent Society*. Glencoe, Ill.: The Free Press.

COSTNER, HERBERT L., and ROBERT K. LEIK. 1964. Deduction from axiomatic theory. *American Sociological Review*, 29 (December): 819–835.

CRESSEY, DONALD R. 1957. The state of criminal statistics. *National Probation and Parole Association Journal*, 3: 230–241.

DENNIS, W. 1960. Causes of retardation among institutional children. *Journal of Genetic Psychology*, 19: 47–59.

DEUTSCH, MARTIN, and associates. 1967. *The Disadvantaged Child*. New York: Basic Books.

DIRKSEN, CLETUS. 1948. *Economic Factors in Delinquency*. Milwaukee: Bruce.

ELLIOTT, DELBERT S. 1966. Delinquency, school attendance and dropout. *Social Problems*, 13 (Winter): 307–314.

EMPEY, LAMAR T. 1956. Social class and occupational aspiration: a comparison of absolute and relative measurement. *American Sociological Review*, 21 (December): 703–709.
1967b. Delinquency theory and recent research. *Journal of Research in Crime and Delinquency*, 4 (January): 28–42.

ERICKSON, MAYNARD, and LAMAR T. EMPEY. 1965. *School Experiences and Delinquency* (with Max L. Scott). Washington, D.C.: President's Commission on Juvenile Delinquency and Youth Crime.

EYNON, THOMAS G., and WALTER C. RECKLESS. 1961. Companionship at delinquency onset. *British Journal of Criminology*, 2, 2 (October): 167–170.

FENTON, NORMAN. 1935. *The Delinquent Boy and the Correctional School*. Claremont, Calif.: Claremont Colleges Guidance Center.

GEIS, GILBERT. 1965. *Juvenile Gangs*. Washington, D.C.: President's Committee on Juvenile Delinquency and Youth Crime.

GIBBS, JACK P. 1967. Identification of statements in theory construction. *Sociology and Social Research*, 52, 1 (October): 72–87.

GIBBS, JACK P., and WALTER R. MARTIN. 1962. Urbanization, technology and the division of labor: International patterns. *American Sociological Review*, 27 (October): 667–677.

GLUECK, SHELDON, and ELEANOR T. GLUECK. 1950. *Unravelling Juvenile Delinquency*. Cambridge, Mass.: Harvard University Press.
1956. *Physique and Delinquency*. New York: Harper.

GOLD, MARTIN. 1963. *Status Forces in Delinquent Boys*. Ann Arbor: University of Michigan, Institute for Social Research.

GOLDFARB, W. 1953. The effects of early institutional care on adolescent personality. *Journal of Experimental Education*, 12: 106–129.

GOULD, JULIUS, and WILLIAM L. KOLB. 1964. *A Dictionary of the Social Sciences*. New York: The Free Press.

GOULD, LEROY C., and CLARENCE SCHRAG. 1962. Theory construction and prediction in juvenile delinquency. In *Proceedings of the Social Statistics Section of the American Statistical Association*. Seattle, Wash.: University of Washington Press.

GOULD, R. 1941. Some sociological determinants of goal striving. *Journal of Social Psychology*, 13 (May): 461–473.

HEALY, WILLIAM, and AUGUSTA F. BRONNER. 1936. *New Light on Delinquency and Its Treatment*. New Haven, Conn.: Yale University Press.

HOLLINGSHEAD, A. B. 1949. *Elmtown's Youth*. New York: John Wiley.

HUNT, J. M. 1961. *Intelligence and Experience*. New York: Ronald Press.

KOBRIN, SOLOMON. 1951. The conflict of values in delinquency areas. *American Sociological Review*, 16 (October): 653–661.

KVARACEUS, WILLIAM C. 1945. *Juvenile Delinquency and the School*. New York: World.
1958. *What Research Says to the Teacher: Juvenile Delinquency*. Washington, D.C.: National Education Association.

KVARACEUS, WILLIAM C., and WALTER B. MILLER. 1959. *Delinquent Behavior*. Washington, D.C.: National Education Association.

LOHMAN, JOSEPH D. 1957. *Juvenile Delinquency*. Cook County, Ill.: Office of the Sheriff.

MATZA, DAVID. 1964. *Delinquency and Drift*. New York: John Wiley.

MERTON, ROBERT K. 1957. *Social Theory and Social Structure*. Glencoe, Ill.: The Free Press.

METFESSEL, NEWTON S. 1965. Conclusions from previous research findings which were validated by the research and evaluation of project potential. Los Angeles: University of Southern California, (Mimeo.)

MILLER, WALTER B. 1958. Lower-class culture as a generating milieu of gang delinquency. *Journal of Social Issues*, 14: 5–19.

MONAHAN, THOMAS P. 1957. Family status and the delinquent child: a reappraisal and some new findings. *Social Forces*, 35 (March): 257.

PARSONS, TALCOTT. 1951. *The Social System*. Glencoe, Ill.: The Free Press.

PLANT, JAMES S. 1948. Who is the delinquent? In Nelson B. Henry, Ed., *Juvenile Delinquency and the Schools*, Part I. 47th Yearbook of the National Study for the Study of Education. Chicago: University of Chicago Press.

POLK, KENNETH. 1965. *Those Who Fail*. Eugene, Ore.: Lane County Youth Project. (Mimeo.)

PORTERFIELD, AUSTIN L. 1946. *Youth in Trouble*. Fort Worth, Tex.: Leo Potisham Foundation.

President's Commission on Law Enforcement and the Administration of Justice. 1967b. *The Challenge of Crime in a Free Society*. Washington, D.C.: U.S. Government Printing Office.

RECKLESS, WALTER C., SIMON DINITZ, and ELLEN MURRAY. 1956. The self-concept as an insulator against delinquency. *American Sociological Review,* 21 (December): 744–746.

REISS, ALBERT J., and ALBERT L. RHODES. 1961. The distribution of juvenile delinquency in the social class structure. *American Sociological Review,* 26 (October): 730–732.

SCHRAG, CLARENCE. 1967. Elements of theoretical analysis in sociology. In Llewellyn Gross, Ed., *Sociological Theory: Inquiries and Paradigms.* New York: Harper and Row.

SCOTT, PETER. 1956. Gangs and delinquent groups in London. *British Journal of Delinquency,* VII (July): 4–26.

SHAW, CLIFFORD. 1940a. *The Jack-Roller: A Delinquent Boy's Own Story.* Chicago: University of Chicago Press.
    1940b. *The Natural History of a Delinquent Career.* Chicago: University of Chicago Press.

SHAW, CLIFFORD, and HENRY D. MCKAY. 1931. Social factors in juvenile delinquency. *Report on the Causes of Crime,* Washington, D.C.: U.S. Government Printing Office.
    1942. *Juvenile Delinquency in Urban Areas.* Chicago: University of Chicago Press.

SHORT, JAMES F., JR., and FRED L. STRODTBECK. 1965. *Group Process and Gang Delinquency.* Chicago: University of Chicago Press.

SHULMAN, HARRY M. 1949. The family and juvenile delinquency. *Annals of the American Academy of Political and Social Science,* 261 (January): 21–31.

STEVENS, S. S. 1960. On the theory of scales of measurement. In Arthur Danto and Sidney Morgenbesser, Eds., *Philosophy of Science.* Cleveland: World.

SYKES, GRESHAM M., and DAVID MATZA. 1957. Techniques of neutralization: a theory of delinquency. *American Sociological Review,* 22 (December): 664–670.

TANNENBAUM, FRANK. 1938. *Crime and the Community.* New York: Columbia University Press.

THRASHER, FREDERIC M. 1927. *The Gang.* Chicago: University of Chicago Press.
    1963. *The Gang.* Abrd ed. by James F. Short, Jr. Chicago: University of Chicago Press.

TOBY, JACKSON. 1957. The differential impact of family disorganization. *American Sociological Review,* 22 (October): 505–512.

WARNER, LLOYD, and PAUL S. LUNT. 1941. *The Social Life of a Modern Community.* New Haven, Conn.: Yale University Press.

WATTENBERG, WILLIAM W., and J. J. BALISTRIERI. 1950. Gang membership and juvenile delinquency. *American Sociological Review,* 15 (December): 744–752.

ZETTERBERG, HANS L. 1954. *On Theory and Verification in Sociology.* Stockholm: Almquist and Wiksell.
    1963. *On Theory and Verification in Sociology.* (Rev. ed.) Totowa, N.J.: Bedminster Press.
    1965. *On Theory and Verification in Sociology.* (3rd enl. ed.) Totowa, N.J.: Bedminster Press.

CHAPTER THREE

Intervention Principles

> One rather common view regarding the treatment of offenders is that once an appropriate structure is provided for rehabilitative efforts, including larger budgets, small case loads, wider use of probation, better classification programs, more trained workers in corrections, higher salaries, and the like, dramatic reductions in recidivism will quickly follow. This is a position of unbridled and undue optimism, for there is little empirical basis for such a faith. Improvements in correctional structure could have little effect upon recidivism until improvements are also made in the practice theory of treatment, and even then, dramatic reductions in delinquency and criminality may be unlikely (Gibbons, 1965: 15).

The causation theory sketched in Chapter Two described the process of becoming delinquent as a sequential process. The causal sequence suggests that delinquency is not the product of any single relationship or happening in the life of the child, but is an emergent form of adjustment involving a cumulative series of experiences and relationships. Therefore, the use to which one might want to put that theory for the purposes of intervention would depend upon the age of the population one had in mind and whether one were interested in prevention or rehabilitation. For example, if one were dealing with pre-adolescents, and were concerned primarily with prevention, then one might pay greatest attention to the first two postulates of the theory:

Postulate I: *The lower the social class, the lower the subsequent achievement.*

Postulate II: *Decreased achievement results in increased strain.*

If he could find means by which to increase the achievement of lower-class children, he might avoid some of the problems implied by Postulates III and IV.

51

Postulate III: *Increased strain results in high identification with delinquent peers.*

Postulate IV: *Identification with delinquent peers results in delinquency.*

He would hope by his early intervention to interrupt the delinquency-generating process in which, because of failure, lower-class children reject conventional alternatives and turn to delinquent peers. By integrating these children more effectively with conventional institutions, he might avoid their introduction into the compensatory and delinquent peer systems in which delinquency is learned.

If, on the other hand, one were concerned with the *rehabilitation* of an already-convicted group of older offenders, as was the case in the Silverlake Experiment, a different form of intervention would be implied, one that would concentrate greater attention upon the delinquent group activities described in Postulates III and IV. The theory suggests that it is only in the later stages of the adjustment process, where one associates with delinquent groups, that delinquency is actually learned. The lack of achievement by some children and the strain that is generated thereby do not, by themselves, produce delinquency, even though they are important antecedents to it. The actual learning of delinquent behavior, the learning of its techniques, its rationalizations, and its rewards occur largely in association with others. Without this learning and the moral support and validation of the peer group, delinquency is not likely to occur. Consequently, in the establishment of priorities for the purposes of *rehabilitation*, the theory suggests that one should concentrate initial, if not greatest, attention upon those factors that immediately precede the onset of delinquency.

This argument rests upon the assumption that the closer any developmental stage is in temporal proximity to delinquent behavior, the more pertinent would be its applicability to rehabilitative intervention. While earlier stages might be important for prevention, they would have lesser import for individuals who have already become persistently delinquent and officially identified as such. There are two indirect kinds of support for this conclusion.

In the first place, the axiomatic format that was used in constructing the theory resulted in a listing of etiological stages in decreasing order of their proximity to the occurrence of delinquent behavior. Each of the basic concepts in the theory was related directly to delinquency by the statements of the theory in the following order:[1]

Postulate IV: *Identification with delinquent peers results in delinquency.*

1. For a review of the definitions, the nature of relationships among variables, and the rules for deduction that governed the development of these theoretical statements, see Chapter II.

Theorem III: *Increased strain results in delinquency.*
Theorem V: *Decreased achievement results in delinquency.*
Theorem VI: *The lower the social class, the greater the subsequent delinquency.*

Thus, these statements imply that the first etiological stage to be addressed should be *identification with delinquent peers,* followed by *strain,* then by *decreased achievement* and, finally, by *social class.*

Second, causal inferences based upon correlational analysis might suggest the same conclusion. The causal sequence outlined by the theory is shown in Figure 3.1.

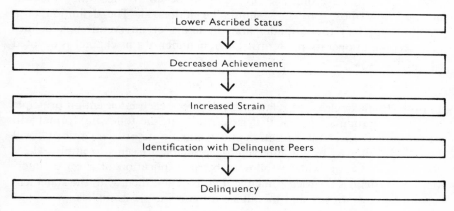

Figure 3.1. The Causal Sequence

For purposes of illustration, let us assume that the absolute values of the correlations between each of the adjacent variables in our chain are 0.70. What, then, would be the separate relationships of each of the causal variables to delinquency? By assuming that the causal model is valid and by utilizing the analytical techniques suggested by Blalock (1964: *passim*) and Simon (1965: chap I), we could expect the following correlation between each variable and delinquency:

$r15$ (ascribed status and delinquency) $= (r12) \times (r23) \times (r34) \times (r45) =$
$$= (0.70)^4 = 0.24$$
$r25$ (achievement and delinquency) $= (r23) \times (r34) \times (r45) = (0.70)^3 = 0.34$
$r35$ (strain and delinquency) $= (r34) \times (r45) = (0.70)^2 = 0.49$
$r45$ (peer identification and delinquency) $= (r45) = (0.70)^1 = 0.70$

Using this particular model, then, it would appear that as we move further down the causal chain, each of the variables has a higher direct relationship to delinquency and thus has a more direct and logical applicability to an intervention model. Although all variables might play an equally important part at some stage in the etiological sequence, their immediate applicability and relevance to the construction of a rehabilitative model is not the same. One would concentrate upon the most immediate antecedent to delinquency as the starting point for rehabilitative intervention.

Whether right or wrong, then, this reasoning was followed in establishing priorities for the Silverlake Experiment. But while these priorities, and the theoretical statements that gave rise to them, were explicit as to what one should pay most attention in setting up a correctional program, they were not explicit as to what the contents of that program should be. While they were useful in indicating the problems to be confronted, they did not indicate how those problems should be addressed. The definition of a solution still had to be made, first, in terms of intervention guidelines and, second, in operational terms. The remainder of this chapter is devoted to the first task.

Intervention Principles

In order to make clear the relationship between each intervention principle and the causation statement that gave rise to it, the following format will be utilized. Each of the causation statements, in its order of priority, will be stated, followed by the intervention principle it seems to imply. These statements, in turn, will be followed by an explication of a set of intervention guidelines for each principle. Let us begin, then, with the statement having highest priority and the intervention principle it implies.

Causation Priority 1: *Identification with delinquent peers results in delinquency.*
Intervention Principle 1: *The delinquent group should be made the target of change.*

This principle suggests that the most effective context in which to change the attitudes and behavior of offenders would be a group setting: (1) because they tend to be cut off from conventional groups and activities, making them far more dependent than their non-delinquent counterparts upon one set of peers and one set of group standards, and (2) because of reference group theory, which seriously questions whether an individual who acquires delinquency from a group can be dealt with individually without regard for the persons or norms of the system with which he identifies. As Cartwright (1951: 388) has suggested, conversion to a new mode of adjustment would probably be most effective if conducted in a group context, if it became a mutual conversion.

To begin with the most general proposition, we may state that the behavior, attitudes, beliefs, and values of the individual are all firmly grounded in the groups to which he belongs. How aggressive or cooperative a person is, how much self-respect and self-confidence he has, how energetic and productive his work is, what he aspires to, what he believes to be true and good, whom he loves or hates, and what beliefs and prejudices he holds—all these characteristics are highly determined by the individual's group memberships. In a real sense, they are properties of groups and of the relationships between people.

Whether they change or resist change will, therefore, be greatly influenced by the nature of these groups. Attempts to change them must be concerned with the dynamics of groups, Cartwright (1951: 388).

Similarly, Lewin (1947: 35) notes that:

Experience in leadership training, in changing of food habits, work production, criminality, alcoholism, prejudices, all seem to indicate that it is usually easier to change individuals formed into a group than to change any one of them separately. As long as group values are unchanged, the individual will resist changes more strongly the farther he is to depart from group standards. If the group standard itself is changed, the resistance which is due to the relationship between individual and group standards is eliminated.

The first intervention principle suggested that techniques were required for dealing not just with the individual but with his group, not just with his unique characteristics but with those characteristics he shares with others. His delinquent values, beliefs, and rationalizations must be replaced with new values, beliefs, and rationalizations, and with means by which he can then realize conventional satisfactions. Group techniques might become the means by which a new set of rules could be defined for the individual and different kinds of behavioral expectations established and rewarded. Once his peers could accept the legitimacy of new rules and new behavior, he would be more inclined to go along.

GROUP AS TARGET OF CHANGE: EMERGENT GUIDELINES

Cressey (1955) has enunciated four guidelines relative to the task of making the delinquent group the target of change. The first (p. 118) suggests that "if [delinquents] are to be changed, they must be assimilated into groups which emphasize values conducive to law-abiding behavior and, concurrently, alienated from groups emphasizing values conducive to [delinquency]." Since convicted delinquents may experience considerable difficulty in securing effective contacts with non-delinquent groups, special groups for the reformation process must be created. This is especially true for persistent offenders such as those assigned to the Silverlake Experiment. Although it would have been desirable if intensive and frequent contacts could have been established with non-delinquent groups at the very beginning of the experiment, it seemed unlikely that such contacts were

possible. Community groups are not ordinarily willing to assume responsibility for the kinds of intensive and painful group experiences of the
kind implied here. That day may come eventually, but it is not now a likely
possibility.

Second, Cressey (1955: 119) suggests that "when the entire group is the
target of change . . . strong pressure for change can be achieved by convincing the members of the need for change, thus making the group itself
the source of pressure for change." This guideline suggests first that, if one
is to make constructive use of group pressures, then the group must become
the *medium* as well as the target of change. Since change can be either
supported or blocked by group pressures, then only by using the group as
a *medium* for change can support be effectively generated.

This guideline also suggests that unless pressures favoring change are
generated within the delinquent group, the usual exhortations by correctional workers, their vocational classes, or counseling may do little to
change the group's subcultural standards. What will happen, instead, is
that individuals will exhibit two behavioral repertoires, an official repertoire
for the correctional worker and a delinquent repertoire for their peers.
Since the objective is to have offenders discard the latter, effective use of
the group as a *medium* for change would seem to be imperative.

Cressey's third guideline (1955: 118) suggests that "the more relevant
the common purpose of the group to the reformation of [delinquents], the
greater will be its influence on the [delinquent] members' attitudes and
values." The allusion here is to the need for organizing a group whose
specific purpose is the changing of delinquent behavior, norms and
rationalizations. For a delinquent, membership in a group designed merely
to satisfy his personal needs or his recreational or educational interests is
not enough. The total network of delinquent relationships and the problems and rewards it promises must somehow be addressed.

The final guideline has both a personal and a group connotation. As
Cressey (1955: 119) puts it, "The most effective mechanism for exerting
group pressure on members will be found in groups so organized that
[delinquents] are induced to join with [non-delinquents] for the purpose of
changing other [delinquents]." In personal terms, the principle implies
that the offender who is willing to play a reformation role by attempting
to change other offenders may be changed himself, perhaps more successfully than those he is trying to change. In order to help the other person,
he must necessarily change his own perspective and adopt some of the
values and prosocial views of the non-delinquent. Cressey (1955: 119) calls
this "retroflexive reformation." If a delinquent is serious in his attempts
to reform others, he must accept the common purpose of the reformation
process, identify himself closely with others engaged in it, and grant prestige

to those who succeed in it. In so doing, he becomes a genuine member of the reformation group and in the process may be alienated form his previous pro-delinquent groups.

The basic objective in applying these guidelines would be to provide means by which the young person could be stopped from conceiving of himself as delinquent and, stimulated by his own efforts and those of his peers, encouraged to conceive of himself as non-delinquent. His delinquent set of attitudes, rationalizations, and goals could be replaced by a non-delinquent set that defines his illegal activities as undesirable, shameful, and disruptive of his search for personal success and satisfactions. This kind of change could be accomplished more effectively if offenders became active members of groups whose sanctioning systems oppose delinquent activity and reward conventional behavior.

Granting the importance, then, of making the delinquent group the target of change, other important problems must be addressed if the group effort is to be successful. The theory of causation presented in Chapter Two suggests that delinquent groups and delinquent behavior are a direct consequence of strains generated in society at large. By the same token, inmate resistances to change are often the direct product of the strains generated in correctional organizations themselves. Consequently, any effort to make the group the target of change is unlikely to succeed without some attention to these other matters, without some attention to the social and correctional strains that make the change-resistant delinquent group meaningful to delinquents. The need for attention to strain, then, leads us directly to the next causation statement and the intervention principle it implies.

Causation Priority 2: *Increased strain results in delinquency.*
Intervention Principle 2: *Strain among delinquents should be reduced.*

Two major problems must be addressed in any attempt to implement this principle. The first has to do with the precise nature of the societal strain delinquents experience and the second with the capacity of any correctional organization to deal with that strain. Since, with regard to the first problem, it was hypothesized that most delinquents seek a resolution of this strain by becoming members of delinquent groups, certain questions must be asked about the adequacy of this adjustment. The radical separation of delinquent groups from conventional successes and satisfactions leads to the presumption that these groups must be successful in supplying alternative satisfactions for their members. But is that the case? How rewarding is group membership?

GROUPS AND GRATIFICATIONS

As a matter of fact, conflicting themes run through the literature regarding this issue. The degree to which delinquents derive gratifications from their groups is not clear. The first theme, exemplified most clearly by Thrasher (1927) and the Chicago school, emphasizes the idea that delinquent groups are characterized by internal cohesion: *esprit de corps,* solidarity, cooperative action, shared tradition, and a strong group awareness. The key to this theme is its emphasis upon the culture-generating qualities and attractiveness of the peer group.

The second theme, as Bordua (1962: 245–246) notes, is inherent in much contemporary theory (Cloward and Ohlin, 1960; Cohen, 1955; Miller, 1958). "Gang boys are driven," he notes, "not attracted. Their lives are characterized by desperation rather than fun," by frustration, negativistic retaliation, alienation, and radical separation from conventional institutions and activities. This theme is much less romantic in its emphasis than the first, and implies, not internal attraction, but external pressure as the source of group cohesion.

Some recent evidence has been supplied in support of this point of view. Short and Strodtbeck (1965: 231) depreciate nostalgic references to "that old gang of mine" and question the image of the delinquent group as carefree and cohesive. They believe that such an interpretation may derive more from the projections of middle-class observers than from the realities that dominate street life (*cf.* Short and Strodtbeck, 1965: Chaps. 10 and 12).

They found that, compared with others, delinquent boys were not only characterized by a long list of "social disabilities," such as unsuccessful school adjustment, limited social and technical skills, a low capacity for self-assertion and lower intelligence scores, but that these characteristics diminished their capacity to derive marked satisfactions from their group associations. Group members tended to hold each other in low esteem and their interactions with each other were characterized by an omnipresent tone of aggression. Low personal skills and insecurities seemed to make for low group skills and collective insecurities as well.

This account is complemented by Matza's (1964: 53–55) use of the term "sounding" to refer to the incessant plumbing and testing through insult by delinquent boys of one another's status and commitment to delinquency. Likewise, Miller (1958: 519) speaks of the "focal concerns" of the lower-class gang culture as toughness, smartness, and excitement. Whatever the terms, it appears that delinquent boys are under constant pressure to protect status and assert masculinity.

While this pressure to project a particular image may not be qualitatively different from any of the highly stylized kinds of interaction found in a host of other status-conscious groups, the point is that such interaction is not characteristic, at least hypothetically, of *primary* groups. *Primary* groups, ideally, are supposed to involve the total person and to provide warmth and support for the individual as well as whatever tensions and insecurities may be involved. With the constant "sounding" that goes on in delinquent groups, it is questionable as to whether lower-class gangs are that kind of group.

Klein and Crawford (1967: 63) present additional arguments to indicate that the internal sources of lower-class group cohesion may be weak. It is their feeling that, were it not for the external pressures of police and other officials, the threats of rival groups, or the lack of acceptance by parents and employers, many delinquent groups would have nothing to unify them. By themselves, such groups do not develop the kinds of group goals and instrumentally oriented activities which are indicative of much organization.

The overall picture painted by the evidence of recent years, then, suggests that gang members, like inmates in a prison, may be held together not by feelings of loyalty and solidarity, but by forces much less attractive. It is not that social structure is lacking, but rather that it is defensive and highly stylized, not especially supportive and gratifying.

As if these problems were not enough, the fact that delinquents often display elaborate mechanisms of repression and defense by which to "neutralize" (*cf*. Sykes and Matza, 1957: 664–70) the conventional norms they violate is some evidence that conventional values may continue to press for recognition, perhaps to have some attraction for them. The need to neutralize conventional values implies the possible existence of ambivalence among delinquents. A delinquent adjustment may not be without its psychological price. As Cohen (1955: 132) puts it:

> Moral norms [i.e. basic American values], once effectively internalized, are not lightly thrust aside or extinguished. If a new [delinquent] moral is evolved which offers a more satisfactory solution to one's life problems, the older ones usually continue to press for recognition, but if this recognition is granted, the apple cart is upset.

Delinquent associations may provide the offender with some social status and acceptance, but a considerable build-up of conflict may also be implied. To the degree that the delinquent identifies with legitimate values and groups, his delinquent solution will be imperfect and adulterated. His adjustment will be a tenuous one. Membership in a delinquent group will not be entirely successful in resolving the strains he feels but may, in fact, add to them.

This argument suggests, then, that the delinquent is not subject to just one kind of strain, but rather to several: the strain that is instrumental in causing him to become delinquent in the first place—*i.e.*, the lack of achievement in a success-oriented society; the strain that is inherent in the fact that the delinquent group, even though it is a kind of last resort, is a marginal refuge at best; and, finally, the strain inherent in his internalization of conflicting norms. He is ambivalent.

The possibility suggests that he may be in the market for a solution. Ambivalent feelings might have considerable utility if they could be unveiled in such a way that an individual could see that his doubts and fears about delinquency are not unique but are shared by other delinquents as well. The existence of mixed feelings could constitute a fulcrum upon which other alternatives might be considered, alternatives that would help to diminish the overall strain delinquents feel. How capable, then, are correctional programs of reducing strain? The answer to that question could be the key to correctional success.

CAPACITY OF CORRECTIONS TO REDUCE STRAIN

Unfortunately, evidence indicates that most correctional systems are not designed to capitalize upon delinquent ambivalence nor are they in a position to provide conventional alternatives for which peer support could be gained. In the case of serious offenders of the type with which we are concerned here, the usual correctional alternative is incarceration. Let us consider, therefore, the problems associated with incarceration.

Under conditions of incarceration, it is not only difficult for correctional people to provide alternatives to the delinquent's alliance with his delinquent group, but the deprivation of liberty only seems to confirm prior, negative perceptions of authority and to heighten resistances to change. The reasons are not difficult to discover.

On one hand, the deprivation of liberty, even among such non-delinquents as prisoners-of-war or mental patients inevitably seems to produce an informal inmate system resistant to rather than supportive of change (Clemmer, 1940; Cressey, 1961; Goffman, 1961; Schrag, 1954; Sykes, 1958; Sykes and Messinger, 1960). In his study of Nazi concentration camps, for example, Abel (1951: 153) noted that

> One of the more interesting observations is the fact that in every one of the more than two hundred large concentration camps, identical patterns of reaction developed among inmates in spite of the virtual absence of contact between them as well as the heterogeneity of their populations.

Captivity, quite aside from one's delinquent or non-delinquent history, seems to generate an inmate code whose function is resistance to formal authority and the maintenance of self-dignity for inmates.

On the other hand, several investigators have noted that inmate organization is by no means completely successful in mitigating the devastating effects of social rejection and captivity. Institutional life is also characterized by a high degree of personal isolation and fear (Clemmer, 1940; Glaser,

1964; Morris and Morris, 1963). There is a great deal of inmate predation upon inmate, forced homosexuality, and exploitation.

To complicate this matter further, there is a lack of unity among officials as well. The notion of a monolithic official structure is a myth (Schrag, 1961). Officials usually possess different ideologies and are fragmented into competing subsystems by virtue of their different roles. The most notable fracture exists between treatment and custody people. But even within these groups, there are competing vested interests; clinical personnel, diagnosticians, and counselors are often at odds with educational and vocational specialists. They simply do not agree with respect to basic goals and methods. The official organization may be as fragmented internally as the inmate organization.

Perhaps the most devastating aspect of this anomalous state of affairs is the tremendous set of conflicts that it poses, even for the prosocial inmate. Overall, a place of confinement is a caste system. Inmates and authorities are divided into discrete groups, and even though the ostensible role of the organization is to have offenders adopt the same goals, expectations, and patterns of behavior as staff members, conditions of caste make it difficult, if not impossible, for them to do so. And, if this were not enough, life within each caste is characterized by a jungle-like existence involving competing subgroups, exploitation, and fear. It is little wonder, then, that places of confinement have been singularly unsuccessful in providing inmates with the kinds of direction and support they need to become something else. If one accepts the theory that an individual's self-concept and behavior are not separable from the social relationships in which he lives, one could expect little but personal chaos and confusion.

The total institution, notes Goffman (1961), "is a social hybrid, part residential community, part formal organization" that attempts both to punish and, at the same time, to reform the offender. It is a striking example of the problems posed by conflicting punitive and reform ideologies. It is so full of logical contradictions that, while it effectively suppresses the offender, it can do little to change him.

OTHER IMPEDIMENTS TO "TREATMENT"

Correctional people, of course, have not been totally unaware of these problems. The reform revolution in corrections, with its emphasis upon individualized treatment, has generally been considered to be an antidote to the caste-like character of correctional organizations and the punishment philosophy out of which they grew. The recent study of places of confinement for delinquents by Street, Vinter, and Perrow (1966) documented the existence of correctional organizations whose approach to control ranged all the way from tight to loose. Correctional goals and practices varied considerably, from ideologies of custody to ideologies of treatment. But, paradoxically, one must be cautious about the extent to which the adoption of a treatment ideology in a total institution can successfully do away with the problems just mentioned.

The reason lies in the tendency for the treatment philosophy, like the punishment, to locate virtually all of the difficulty within the offender. The problems of change have not really been conceived in structural terms. As a consequence, the treatment philosophy has never seriously challenged the social functions of punishment and indicated the extent to which caste-like, correctional organizations may seriously hamper efforts to prepare offenders for return to an open, democratic society. Its main function, instead, has been to add a cloak of sophistication and professionalism to the correctional scene. But whether the offender's behavior is defined as "wicked" and in need of punishment or "pathological" and in need of treatment, the result is much the same. Removing the offender for purposes of "treatment" has the same social function as removing him for purposes of punishment: it validates the diagnosis of undesirability and excuses basic institutions—family, school, and work—from responsibility. It raises the question as to whether the offender's problem is correctable, suggesting that it may be a permanent malignancy rather than a temporary disability (Empey, 1968a: 9–10).

In organizational terms, moreover, the caste-like character of many treatment programs is revealed by the fact that treatment personnel, even if highly trained, have a symbiotic relationship with clients that is subtle and paradoxical. The status of the professional, his "helping" role, his very place in the whole scheme of things heavily depends upon the client remaining in a subordinate relationship to him. The paradox is, therefore, that, although the professional role ostensibly exists to help the client, it is, in fact, one which relies upon a superordinate-subordinate relationship. As a result, it is difficult for the client to change unless his relationship to those above him changes also. The old problem of the caste system remains. Organizational arrangements are not available through which to encourage the client to stop conceiving of himself as "delinquent," "inmate," or "patient," and to conceive of himself, instead, as "non-delinquent," "employee," or "student."

In fact, nothing is quite so revealing of the problem as this very discussion itself and the language it uses. In the absence of adequate role designations by which to describe some new continuum of positions an individual might fill in moving from a delinquent to a non-delinquent status, roles are dichotomized: "offender–non-offender," "delinquent–non-delinquent," "deviant-conformist." In describing the relationship of the offender to staff members in a correctional organization, the same kinds of dichotomies occur: "patient-therapist," "client-caseworker," or "guard-inmate."

In our present ways of thinking, these are mutually exclusive categories, designating permanent positions filled by either offenders or staff members. Little or no effort has been devoted to ways by which an offender might be moved, step by step, into new roles—roles that connote change in some desired direction, roles that carry with them new expectations and rewards for conventional behavior, roles that decrease the stigma associated with an offender or inmate status and decrease the social distance between staff and inmate groups.

It was for these reasons that it seemed imperative at Silverlake to derive a set of intervention principles that might address more successfully the problems of strain delinquents bring with them to the correctional setting and the strains correctional organizations, themselves, seem to have created.

REDUCTION OF STRAIN: EMERGENT GUIDELINES

Actually, there are some suggestions in the literature as to how these problems might be dealt with in a combined way. First, with regard to the strain, the ambivalence, hypothesized to exist among delinquents because of the adulterated and tenuous character of their delinquent adjustment, Empey and Rabow (1961: 683) have suggested a first guideline; namely, that the protection and rewards provided by any change program for *candor* should exceed those provided either by delinquents for adherence to a delinquent code or by officials for rigid conformity and "good behavior." If it is assumed that a change in basic loyalties, attitudes, and values is desirable, then delinquents should be as free to express delinquent points of view as staff members are to express non-delinquent values. To deny delinquents this opportunity is to deny, by implication, a candid examination of the non-delinquent side of the coin; namely, the points of view, the rationalizations, and the exploits that characterize *non*-delinquent behavior.

If ambivalence among delinquents is to serve any purpose, if they are to weigh the alternatives open to them, they must have the opportunity to consider those alternatives in as open and objective a way as possible. Without candor, it is difficult for the delinquent individual to become aware of the extent to which other delinquents share conventional as well as delinquent aspirations; without candor, it is virtually impossible to have them examine the ultimate utility of each; and without candor, offenders are encouraged to adopt the two repertoires of behavior that have so long characterized correctional settings: the official repertoire exhibited by offenders for the benefit of staff and the delinquent repertoire exhibited for the benefit of peers. The maintenance of these two repertoires signifies not only the underground character of the delinquent repertoire, but the dualism of most correctional organizations and their inability to come to grips with it. Until there can be a freer expression of basic conflicts and divisions, it will be difficult to foster a climate in which individuals are free to make a choice. The paradox of any rigid and dualistic system is that it inhibits, rather than encourages, change. The necessary dialogue is blocked.

The second guideline follows logically. It suggests that if a correctional program is to be successful, it must develop a relatively unified and co-hesive social system. As Cartwright (1951: 389) put it in group terms, "if the group is to be used effectively as a medium of change, those people who are to be changed and those who are to exert influence for change must have a strong sense of belonging to the same group."

In spite of whatever status differences may exist between the correctional worker and the delinquent, they must develop a common sense of purpose, feel that they are members of one group, and participate in a system in which they have common objectives. Two pitfalls must also be avoided: (*a*) establishing authorities as "rejectors" and making inevitable the creation of two social systems within a program; and (*b*) institutionalizing means by which skilled offenders can evade dealing with the norms and expecta-tions of non-delinquent behavior. The chances for change will be increased if both offenders and officials can develop a common "we-feeling."

Third, says Cartwright (1951: 391), "information relating to the need for change, plans for change, and consequences of change must be shared by all relevant people in the group." Until the structural restraints that block communication and a common sense of purpose are removed, there can be little hope that the necessary alterations will come about. The guideline implies that any correctional program cannot expect to ameliorate strain for delinquents simply by placing and keeping them in a captive or patient role. No one has a greater stake than the delinquent in resolving the strains of a delinquent status and the stigma associated with it. But until he can participate meaningfully in the resolution of those strains and can occupy new and legitimate positions for which rewards are available, he will be inclined to stick to his older forms of adjustment.

The achievement of this solution, however, implies a fourth and extremely important guideline (*cf.* Cartwright, 1951: 391–392): "Changes in one part of a group produce strain in other related parts which can be reduced only by eliminating the change or by bringing about readjustments in the related parts." In other words, in the interest of reducing strain in the long run, strain, even conflict, will be produced in the short run. The reason, of course, is that delinquents cannot resolve their simultaneous internalization of deviant and conformist norms, cannot achieve open communication with staff, cannot learn to share in decisions which affect their lives and the lives of others without considerable tension.

The same is true for staff members. Significant changes in the status and role of the delinquent in the correctional organization cannot be achieved without significant alteration in the status and role of the correctional worker. In the process of making these changes, therefore, considerable conflict, pain, and fear will be engendered. The group on occasion may seem to be falling apart. Yet, such consequences should not be surprising, nor can they be avoided. If the changing of caste-relationships in correctional organizations is to occur, the inevitable pains of developing a new system will have to be suffered. Out of conflict, hopefully, will develop new structural forms which can be of greater utility than those of the past in changing offenders.

The reduction of delinquent strain in the long run, however, is also contingent upon the capacity of any program to deal with the failure of delinquents to achieve in a success-oriented, status-conscious society. Any thorough resolution of the total problem implies the necessity of considering what to do about the achievement issue as implied by the next causation statement and principle.

Causation Priority 3: *Decreased achievement results in delinquency.*
Intervention Principle 3: *Means for legitimate achievement should be made available.*

The interrelatedness among such factors as peer identification, strain, and lack of achievement becomes more and more obvious as this analysis proceeds and as an attempt is made to determine what should be done about each one of them. At the same time, it is also obvious that as one moves backward in time from delinquency, first to identification with peers, then to strain, and then to lack of achievement, the issues relative to correctional intervention become more and more global. That is, the question as to what should be done about identification with delinquent peers is not so broad as to what should be done about strain, and the problem of dealing with strain is not so complex as that having to do with the lack of achievement. The lack of achievement, for example, stems from the whole constellation of familial, educational, and cultural deficiencies faced by the lower-class child. The issue as to what should be done about them is tremendously complex.

One frame of reference suggests that the ideal correctional program should attempt to address the whole constellation of problems which the lower-class delinquent faces. This would be accomplished in an expensive, closed system operating upon the premise that the delinquent's problems are so great that they must be addressed in a protected environment. The ideal correctional program must provide means by which to make up for all of the delinquent's deficiencies—emotional, educational, social, recreational, and religious. But is this the case?

Quite aside from all of the possible problems of the total institution described above, there exists a whole list of additional questions which must be asked. Can correctional programs assume responsibility for dealing with *all* of the delinquent's problems? Even more important, is it necessary to correct all of them in the interest of changing *delinquent* behavior? Should the delinquent have to remain under legal and correctional jurisdiction, perhaps in custody, until all of these problems are corrected? If so, is it not possible that a whole set of new problems might result from the deprivation of liberty and socialization in an artificial environment?

These are difficult questions involving both ethical and practical issues. Perhaps the most efficient way to address them is to note two things. First, it seems certain that one of the most serious impediments to increasing the educational and interpersonal skills of the offender is his alienation from the school and other important middle-class institutions. Before he can be re-engaged with these institutions, before he can be reintegrated into their activities, his alienation must be decreased and his motivation increased to want to return. But this is not the only problem.

The delinquent is also stigmatized by virtue of his delinquent status. He is often rejected by society at large. Not only is he resistant to returning to the pains of involvement in community institutions, but the gatekeepers of those institutions, especially the school, may not want him to return. Yet, before he can be helped to achieve, both of these obstructions must be removed. Let us consider them separately.

THE PROBLEM OF MOTIVATION

Earlier in this chapter it was suggested that the motivation to change might be increased if the offender could become an active participant in the resolution of his own problems and those of his peers. By helping others to achieve, the offender might himself be motivated to achieve.

There is some evidence that this is a relevant possibility. The recent stress by black people on the importance of racial pride and black self-determination is some confirmation of this interpretation. The powerlessness of black people is not unlike that of the powerlessness of offenders. However, with a growing sense of group cohesion and self-pride, black people have developed a sense of capacity to do more about the control of their own destinies. The same might be accomplished among a group of offenders, providing correctional structures would permit it. Group techniques might be used by which offenders could be motivated to do something more about their lack of achievement, their lack of capacity to compete in an open society.

The problem with achievement *within* a correctional setting, however, is its insularity. Achievement in a total institution, for example, is not the same thing as achievement in the open community. It is not always easy for delinquents to see a direct relationship between isolated correctional activities and the realities and frustrations of the "outside" world from which they come. Correctional practices that do nothing by way of building a bridge between the correctional and the larger communities are inadequate. This leads us, then, to the problems of stigma, indeed to the task of providing a rite-of-passage back for the offender from a delinquent to a non-delinquent status.

THE PROBLEM OF STIGMA

From a humanitarian standpoint, society has long been aware of the stigmatizing effects of a delinquent status. Pleas are repeatedly made that the offender, once he has "paid his debt to society," be permitted to take his place once more among non-delinquent groups and activities. But these pleas are made without much attention either to the competing forces which inhibit the de-stigmatizing process or the societal reconstruction that will be required if reintegrative efforts are to be effective. As Erikson (1964: 16) points out,

> The community's decision to bring deviant sanctions against an individual is not a simple act of censure. It is a sharp rite of transition, at once moving him out of his normal position in society and transferring him into a distinct deviant role. . . . Perhaps the most obvious example of a commitment ceremony is the [delinquent] trial, with its elaborate formality and ritual pageantry. . . .
>
> Now an important feature of these ceremonies in our own culture is that they are almost irreversible. Most provisional roles conferred by society—like those of the student or conscripted soldier, for example,—include some kind of terminal ceremony to mark the individual's movement back out of the role once its temporary advantages have been exhausted. But the roles allotted to the deviant seldom make allowance for this type of passage. He is ushered into the deviant position by a decisive and often dramatic ceremony, yet is retired from it with hardly a word of public notice. . . . Nothing has happened to cancel out the stigmas imposed upon him by earlier commitment ceremonies.

The task of cancelling out the stigmas imposed by commitment ceremonies is not a simple one. We have two alternatives: either we can find ways for lessening the impact of the dramatic rite-of-passage from non-delinquent to a delinquent status or we can do more to develop the rite-of-passage in the opposite direction—from the status of delinquent to the status of non-delinquent.

Actually, there has been some limited effort to try both alternatives. On one hand, the need for reintegration has stimulated the development of community programs, like this one, designed to avoid ever separating the offender from the community. On the other, the New Careers movement has attempted to develop a rite-of-passage back for the offender by making use of his knowledge, once he is released, in poverty programs, gang work, and related activities (*cf.* Grant and Grant, 1967; Joint Commission on Correctional Manpower and Training, 1968). Both have attempted to avoid the repressive practices of the past by using potentially useful and new approaches to rehabilitation and destigmatization.

Even so, both kinds of efforts have been halting and uneven at best, primarily because the vital task of providing a destigmatizing ritual equivalent in impact to the ritual of arrest and trial or in developing new careers that are socially, politically, and bureaucratically acceptable has scarcely begun. The primary burden, therefore, still rests on the reformed offender to hide his stigmatizing past as the best way of dealing with it. Relatively few efforts have been made to dramatize a return to a non-delinquent status or to make the necessary institutional changes by which that return rite-of-passage can be made effective. Thus, conditions are such as to underscore the extent to which the problem of reintegration for offenders is a problem in cultural and societal, as well as offender, reconstruction. The success of any correctional endeavor will be dependent upon its capacity not only to elicit the cooperation of the offender (and that may be the easiest task), but also to elicit the cooperation of both officials and the public in finding ways by which to build the offender into a non-delinquent, non-stigmatizing role. In a very real sense, achievement does not even exist unless it is validated by conventional people as a part of the non-delinquent community. Given these problems, then, what guidelines might be cited relative to achievement?

OPPORTUNITY FOR ACHIEVEMENT: EMERGENT GUIDELINES

Two guidelines have already been suggested that would apply to the implementation of this principle. First, it has been suggested that a correctional program should provide ways by which to motivate delinquents to want to achieve. This would be accomplished largely through the use of group techniques and the alteration of correctional structures so as to give delinquents a stake in what happens to them in the correctional process. These matters were discussed earlier.

The second guideline implies the need for correctional programs to do a better job of providing legitimate alternatives which, in fact, are relevant to the problems of achievement outside the correctional community. The offender should be able to recognize a direct and acceptable connection between his correctional experience and his ultimate adjustment in the community. Assuming that the offender could be motivated to learn new skills and to develop new social relationships, the job is still only half done. He needs effective linkage with the non-delinquent world. This is obviously a problem that he cannot handle by himself and which has not adequately been addressed in correctional programs.

At the same time, this guideline suggests that it might not only be difficult, but unwise, for any correctional program to attempt to remedy, by itself, all of the disabilities that have led to the delinquent's lack of achievement in the first place. Even if it were successful in increasing some of his abilities, this would not be enough. Objective opportunities in the community would be needed also. Therefore, it would seem theoretically consistent to suggest some division of responsibility between corrections and the community in dealing with the achievement, indeed the whole correctional, problem.

The rite-of-passage problem for the delinquent is so important that any new achievement would be most meaningful if it were ratified not only by his peers and correctional associates, but non-delinquent peers and adults as well. Furthermore, such an approach would place the burden upon those institutions in the community whose regular responsibility it is to provide resources for child development. Such a burden would not be left solely upon the artificial environment of the correctional organization. Consequently, although any correctional organization should seek a group climate conducive to offender change, it must also seek help from the community for means by which the delinquent can be reintroduced into conventional institutions.

With that conclusion, we are led to a consideration of the final factor, social class, which was defined by the causation theory as being important in the genesis of delinquency. Let us consider it before summarizing the principles and guidelines for intervention that have been developed.

Causation Priority 4: *The lower the social class, the higher the subsequent delinquency.* (Theorem VI)

It will be recalled that social class was defined as having low priority in the definition of an intervention strategy. The reasons are two. First, in terms of its temporal proximity to actual delinquent behavior, social class was the most distant of all the major variables that relate to delinquency. Second, and beyond the proximity issues, social class membership confers upon a youngster an *ascribed status* that is acquired largely through no action of his own or that of corrections. He inherits this status because of the position of his parents in the class structure. In one sense, therefore, such status, although it relates to subsequent causal phases, is relatively impervious to change by correctional organizations. It would be neither realistic nor feasible for a correctional program to assume responsibility for making all lower-class delinquents members of the middle or upper class.

In the first place, it is not only questionable whether such a change is possible, but whether it is desirable. The theory advanced so far by no means implies that a change in social class is necessary in order to help offenders stop violating the law. But beyond that, the delinquent should have some say in the matter. Hopefully, the correctional techniques implied by the foregoing theory could help him to make a realistic assessment of his life's chances. Following that assessment, he should be free, in fact encouraged, to choose the life adjustment he desires.

Some offenders may continue to aspire upward and may seek the kind of education and work experience that would lead to upward mobility. Others may be more comfortable in pursuing a blue-collar job and in remaining among their peers in a lower-class environment where they feel the most comfortable. The most important things would be to reduce the functionality of delinquent behavior as a major adjustment for the delinquent and to provide him with personal and social resources to achieve an alternative, conventional adjustment. For those reasons, efforts to deal with class as a variable in any change process would be important only insofar as they relate to reduction of excessive strain and the need for the offender to achieve more effectively in community institutions. Those efforts could never hope to remove all strain for delinquents (even if they were middle rather than lower class) nor to insure their successful achievement of the American dream. For these reasons, no special intervention principle was advanced in response to the social class level of the offender.

Summary and Conclusions

The theory of causation for the Silverlake Experiment was used as the foundation upon which principles and guidelines for intervention were based. They were as follows:

Principle 1: *The delinquent group should be made the target of change.*
A. Delinquents should be assimilated into groups that emphasize law-abiding behavior and, concurrently, alienated from groups which favor delinquent behavior.
B. When the delinquent group is made the target of change, strong pressure for change can be achieved by making the group itself the *medium* of change. Unless pressures for change are generated *within* the group, then pressures exerted by outsiders will have little impact.

C. The overriding purpose of any group should be seen by members as that of changing delinquent behavior. Other purposes are of a secondary nature.

D. The delinquent should be sponsored in a reformation role. The most effective mechanism for exerting group pressure on members will occur in groups in which delinquents are induced to join with non-delinquents for the purpose of changing other delinquents.

Principle 2: *Social strain among delinquents should be reduced.*

A. Delinquent ambivalence can be most effectively utilized in a setting conducive to the free expression of feelings. The protection and rewards provided by any program for candor must exceed those provided either by delinquents for adherence to delinquent roles or by officials for adherence to custodial requirements.

B. If the group is to be used as the medium of change, the delinquents who are to be changed and the correctional workers who are to exert influence for change must have a strong sense of belonging to the same group.

C. The structural restraints that have traditionally blocked communication in correctional organizations should be removed. All information relating to the need for change, the methods to be used, and the consequences of change must be shared by all relevant people.

D. Efforts to reduce strain in the long run will inevitably produce strain in the short run. Organizational and personal changes cannot occur without conflict and tension.

Principle 3: *Means for legitimate achievement by delinquents should be made available.*

A. The delinquent must be motivated to want to achieve. This can be accomplished if he is sponsored in a reformation role, as described above, and if there are incentives in the correctional process for a heavy degree of involvement.

B. A rite-of-passage for the offender from a delinquent to a non-delinquent status is necessary. He needs effective linkage with the non-delinquent world. This will require community involvement and a ratification of achievement by non-delinquent peers and adults.

Beyond these intervention principles, and their attendant guidelines, no special principle was suggested as a means of responding to the class memberships of delinquents. Except for efforts to reduce strain or enhance achievement, attempts to change class identities and memberships were not implied.

References

ABEL, THEODORE. 1951. The sociology of concentration camps. *Social Forces*, XXX (December): 150–161.

BLALOCK, HUBERT M., JR. 1964. *Causal Inferences in Non-experimental Research*. Chapel Hill: University of North Carolina Press.

BORDUA, DAVID J. 1962. Some comments on theories of group delinquency. *Sociological Inquiry* XXXII, 2 (Spring): 245–260.

CARTWRIGHT, DORWIN. 1951. Achieving change in people: some applications of group dynamics theory. *Human Relations*, 4: 381–401.

CLEMMER, DONALD. 1940. *The Prison Community*. New York: Rinehart.

CLOWARD, RICHARD A., and LLOYD E. OHLIN. 1960. *Delinquency and Opportunity: A Theory of Delinquent Gangs*. New York: The Free Press.

COHEN, ALBERT K. 1955. *Delinquent Boys*. The Free Press.

CRESSEY, DONALD R. 1955. Changing the Criminal: the application of theory to differential association. *American Journal of Sociology*, LXI (September): 116–120.

CRESSEY, DONALD R., Ed. 1961. *The Prison*. New York: Holt, Rinehart and Winston.

EMPEY, LaMAR T. 1968a. Offender participation in the correctional process: general theoretical issues. *Offenders as a Correctional Manpower Resource*. Washington, D.C.: Joint Commission on Correctional Manpower and Training.

EMPEY, LaMAR T., and JEROME RABOW. 1961. The Provo experiment in delinquency rehabilitation. *American Sociological Review*, 26 (October): 679–696.

ERIKSON, KAI T. 1964. Notes on the sociology of deviance. In Howard S. Becker, Ed., *The Other Side*. New York: The Free Press.

GIBBONS, DON C. 1965. *Changing the Lawbreaker: The Treatment of Delinquents and Criminals*. Englewood Cliffs, N.J.: Prentice-Hall.

GLASER, DANIEL. 1964. *The Effectiveness of a Prison and Parole System*. Indianapolis: Bobbs–Merrill.

GOFFMAN, ERVING. 1961. *Asylums*. New York: Doubleday.

GRANT, J. DOUGLAS, and JOAN GRANT. 1967. *New Careers Development Project: Final Report*. Sacramento, Calif.: Institute for the Study of Crime and Delinquency.

Joint Commission on Correctional Manpower and Training. 1968. *Offenders as a Correctional Manpower Resource*. Washington, D.C.: Joint Commission on Correctional Manpower and Training.

KLEIN, MALCOLM W., and LOIS Y. CRAWFORD. 1967. Groups, gangs and cohesiveness. *Journal of Research in Crime and Delinquency*, 4 (January): 63–75.

LEWIN, KURT. 1947. Frontiers of group dynamics. *Human Relations*, 1 (June): 2–38.

MATZA, DAVID. 1964. *Delinquency and Drift*. New York: John Wiley.

MILLER, WALTER B. 1958. Lower-class culture as a generating milieu of gang delinquency. *Journal of Social Issues*, 14, 3 (Summer): 5–19.

MORRIS, T., and P. MORRIS. 1963. *Pentonville: A Sociological Study of an English Prison*. London: Routledge and Kegan Paul.

SCHRAG, CLARENCE. 1954. Leadership among prison inmates. *American Sociological Review*, 19 (February): 37–42.

——— 1961. Some foundations for a theory of corrections. Donald R. Cressey, Ed., *The Prison: Studies in Institutional Organization and Change*. New York: Holt, Rinehart and Winston.

SHORT, JAMES F., JR., and FRED L. STRODTBECK. 1965. *Group Process and Gang Delinquency*. Chicago: University of Chicago Press.

SIMON, HERBERT A. 1957. *Models of Man*. New York: John Wiley.

STREET, DAVID, ROBERT D. VINTER, and CHARLES PERROW. 1966. *Organization for Treatment*. New York: The Free Press.

SYKES, GRESHAM M. 1965. *The Society of Captives*. New York: Atheneum.

SYKES, GRESHAM M., and DAVID MATZA. 1957. Techniques of neutralization: a theory of delinquency. *American Sociological Review,* 22 (December): 664–670.

SYKES, GRESHAM M., and SHELDON MESSINGER. 1960. The inmate social system. *Theoretical Studies in Social Organization of the Prison*. Social Science Research Council Pamphlet No. 15 (March): 5–19.

THRASHER, FREDERIC M. 1927. *The Gang*. Chicago: University of Chicago Press.

CHAPTER FOUR

Operational Guidelines: Intervention

The assumption that it is entirely up to the inmate to take advantage of treatment opportunities if he is so inclined is still an important feature of treatment philosophy. Behavior is still regarded as primarily a matter of personal volition. Reorganization of attitudes and modification of affective attachments to objects and persons in the social environment are generally viewed as personal issues over which prison policies have little control. The possibility of redefining the roles and changing the social positions of inmates by means of administrative procedures receives relatively little consideration, although some efforts along these lines are being initiated through various forms of group therapy. In other words, a systematic and convincing rationale for the use of modern methods of therapy has not yet made its way very effectively into the philosophy of correctional administration (Schrag, 1961: 335).

Prior chapters in this book have attempted to correct one of the problems mentioned in the foregoing statement; namely, that of providing a rationale for the use of a particular set of intervention techniques at Silverlake. A second major problem remains, however; that of translating the rationale from theoretical to operational terms. Before the Silverlake Experiment could be implemented, the principles and guidelines developed in Chapter Three had to be stated in organizational terms.

These guidelines suggested the need for an organization possessed of three major characteristics: (1) an organization that would enhance the use of group techniques in the changing of delinquents; (2) an organization whose structure would help to remove some of the obstructions and strains which have made collaboration between delinquents and correctional workers difficult; and (3) an organization that could provide an effective linkage with the non-delinquent community and its institutions. The major objective of such an organization would not be the mere reduction of isolation and belligerence among delinquents, but the provision of opportunities by which they might become agents in their own behalf and experience positive contacts with non-delinquent persons and activities.

One further consideration had to be kept in mind as well; namely, that the subjects of the experiment *would not* be first-time offenders, but would be delinquents for whom the ordinary alternative would be institutional placement. Therefore, whatever program was developed would be constrained by judicial and community expectations that something more than minimal controls would be exercised. The past delinquent histories of the boys to be assigned to the program had to be kept in mind.

Given these background considerations, then, the first step was to consider approaches that have utilized group techniques in the past as a primary mode of intervention. It was felt that they might provide some clues as to the type of program to be set up at Silverlake. Their potential utility could be assessed in terms of the organizational needs just defined, especially in terms of the principles and guidelines for intervention developed in Chapter Three.

Prior Group Approaches

Despite many variations on the group theme, it would not be entirely inaccurate to suggest that the use of groups has been based upon four major frames of reference: (1) the *cultural transmission model*, which seeks through traditional educational techniques to train groups of offenders in obedience and socially approved behavior; (2) the *group psychotherapy model*, which focuses upon individual psychodynamics and the introduction of change that is theoretically independent for each actor; (3) the *group-centered model*, which suggests that change proceeds concurrently with and is the function of the effective development of the group; and (4) the *therapeutic milieu model*, which emphasizes the manipulation of the total milieu of an institution as the means for altering offender behavior. Each of these approaches was assessed in terms of its relevance for Silverlake.

CULTURAL TRANSMISSION MODEL

The cultural transmission model is the oldest of the four approaches. It is based on the general assumption that offenders lack adequate socialization and that the goal of corrections, therefore, is to indoctrinate the offender with the need for constructive citizenship, obedience to authority, and the problems of social adjustment. The approach is usually very formal and uses classroom procedures, lectures, orientation sessions, and highly structured activities as its main means of intervention. Vestiges of this approach remain in many correctional organizations today. Yet, despite its age, there are many problems associated with it.

In the first place, the group activities in which offenders participate do not really make much use of group phenomena, *per se*, offenders are treated as isolated atoms, and the results are disappointing. As Sarri and Vinter (1965: 330) point out,

> Clients often see little connection between the group sessions and their own life situations. Seldom is there any explicit concern with the mobilization of group forces, and interactional processes are not utilized to achieve or sustain changes in clients' attitudes and behaviors.

What is more, the formal character of this approach only seems to increase the offender's sense of alienation, not decrease it. Seeman (1959: 784–786) points out that if a group of persons who share common problems are convinced that learning will help them to achieve some goal, they will value that learning. But if they are impressed, instead, with a sense of powerlessness and if they feel they cannot exercise some control over the major factors that influence their lives, then learning is blocked. Instead of motivating the offender to change, the authoritarian character and didactic methods of the cultural transmission model may only enhance opposition. Certainly it would not seem to encourage collaboration between offenders and staff.

The final and perhaps most devastating criticism of the cultural transmission model is its failure to address the problems of providing an effective linkage with the non-delinquent community. It assumes, apparently, that deviant behavior is due almost solely to the delinquent's lack of acceptance of societal rules and authority. As a consequence, it overlooks the importance of providing structures in which a conventional rather than a deviant choice is available for the delinquent. The transmission of prevailing patterns to any group of persons is meaningful only if it is successful in addressing the major life problems that confront them. If it does not address them, it can at best, have only partial success. This model, then, seemed to lack the organizational characteristics necessary for the implementation of basic principles and guidelines at Silverlake: it failed to provide for an effective linkage of delinquents with the non-delinquent community; it did not allow for an effective use of group; and it did not seem conducive to the development of a collaborative social system in which staff and inmates would work together to solve problems.

GROUP PSYCHOTHERAPY MODEL

The group psychotherapy model, although of more recent vintage, is probably the oldest of the techniques designed to provide therapeutic treatment in a group. It was adapted from the mental health field and assumes that the basic problems of the offender are primarily psychogenic in character. Although psychotherapists traditionally have varied in their definition of the factors within the individual that produce his difficulties, they have tended to agree that his basic problem is some form of psychopathology.

In applying treatment, the usual technique involves efforts to help the client achieve insight into the concealed forces at the root of his disorder. Attention is focused upon psychodynamics and upon treating the individual *in* the group rather than *through* it. Although other group members are present, they are viewed as an audience who can benefit more from observation than from active participation in the treatment process. For example, Slavson (1943) suggested that

> By and large it is an error to speak of the group as an entity in therapy. It is always the individual and not the group as such, that remains the center of the therapeutic attention. . . . . The greatest single therapeutic value of such groups is the very absence of group formations.

In other words, therapy is viewed as a private phenomenon with very little recognition or concern for the effects of the group on the individual (*cf.* Harper, 1959: 132). It would seem that the objective is simultaneous individual therapy. Such therapy in the group may have the virtue of being more economical than individual therapy (Klapman, 1959: 6–7); it may provide a permissive setting in which the offender can ventilate hostile feelings (Cressey, 1954: 22); and it is probably a means of reducing social isolation and egocentricity (Slavson, 1943: 1). But it also possesses many limitations in terms of the model needed for this study.

In the first place, any attempt to make the group the target of change would have to pay considerable attention to the nature of group phenomena, not only the group phenomena of which delinquency is comprised, but the group phenomena of which correctional activities are comprised as well. Everyone, officials as well as offenders, is involved in activities that may be understood in terms of existing but often unrecognized group rules for behavior. Under many conditions, such rules hinder rather than facilitate the correctional task. Consequently, the experimental model would require group techniques concerned with more than the individual actor. Collective solutions, and collective techniques by which to pursue them, were needed.

Second, serious questions have been raised about the traditional emphasis in group psychotherapy upon insight. For example, Bandura (1967: 78) notes that studies have indicated that a client's insights and emergent "unconscious" might be predicted more accurately from a knowledge of his therapist's theoretical system than from his actual developmental history. That is, his acquisition of "insight" may better represent a conversion to his therapist's point of view than a process of self-discovery. But perhaps even more important is the issue as to whether insight, even if based on self-discovery, is adequate to deal with collective group problems and community linkage. For example, events occurring outside of the group psychotherapy session are considered significant only insofar as they are reflected in the group operation. Even though the role of the social milieu in the genesis of a problem may be recognized, its role in the resolution of that problem is minimal. By contrast, it would seem that, in addition to self-understanding, delinquents need the opportunity to learn new skills and ways of behaving. Too much group insularity and emphasis upon insight might neglect the problems of providing other kinds of experience by which new behavioral patterns could be acquired. Delinquents need reinforcement in non-group settings for attempts on their parts to try out new role behaviors. They need reasonable ties to non-therapy settings.

Thus, this model seemed to have relatively little utility, first, because its goals are limited to the individual, and, second, because it is too insular. It is not designed to address either the hypothesized group aspects of delinquency or the need for correctional activities to involve organizational and community, as well as offender, change.

THE GROUP-CENTERED MODEL

The group-centered model is marked by some sharp theoretical differences from the group psychotherapy model just described. It is based upon principles similar in part to those developed above for the Silverlake Experiment. For example, with regard to the genesis of delinquent problems, the group-centered approach assumes that the traits of the individual are very much the property of groups and are not uniquely psychodynamic in character. The aggressiveness of an individual (Lewin, Lippitt, and White, 1939), his personal values (Roethilsberger and Dickson, 1939), his willingness to change (Lewin, 1953), his sense of security (Seashore, 1954), indeed his self-concept, are thought to be group related. As a consequence, proponents of the group-centered approach make two important distinctions in their use of groups: they maintain (1) that the processes occurring in the group cannot be explained from an individual frame-of-reference and (2) that the treatment of individuals proceeds concurrently with, and is the function of, the effective development of a group (*cf.* Bach, 1954: 4–5; Hill, 1961). They argue, in fact, that, since groups are inevitable and ubiquitous, it is incorrect to assume that change can occur without taking them into account. As Cartwright and Lippitt (1957: 90) put it: "Groups exist; they are inevitable and ubiquitous; they mobilize powerful forces having profound effects upon individuals; these effects may be good or bad; and through a knowledge of group dynamics, there lies the possibility of maximizing their good value."

In terms of enhancing collaboration between offenders and staff, this model also had the virtue of implying a redefinition of offender and official rules As Benne and Sheats (1948: 43) point out, the distinction between the leadership role (the staff member) and the member role (the delinquent) is not so great. "The group-centered view is in direct opposition to the idea that the leader is solely responsible for the quality and quantity of work achieved in the group" (Scott, 1965: 37). In fact, leadership in such an approach is relative to the situation (*a*) in terms of the particular problem being addressed and (*b*) in terms of the particular goals of the group (*cf.* Gibb, 1947). It is conceivable that under many circumstances a group member, even in the delinquent group, might assume an anti-delinquent leadership role. If such an adoption were to occur, it would be highly desirable in terms of modifying the traditional character of correctional organizations, of extending offender involvement and of sponsoring offenders in reformation roles. In summary, then, the group-centered approach had much to offer when judged by theoretical guidelines. But, by the same standard, it also had some serious limitations.

In the first place, there is little in the group-centered literature that indicates how one should go about setting up a total organization designed to maximize the effectiveness of a group-centered approach. Other than restructuring relationships *within* the group, it does not specify how they should be restructured outside of it. And since group meetings, at best, can occupy only a small portion of the life space of all people in a correctional organization, the transfer of these restructured relationships to other activities must be specified. In what ways would relationships between staff and delinquents be restructured outside of group meetings?

A second glaring problem has been the tendency for clinical people, even some who utilize the group-centered approach, to adopt a neutral role with respect to everything that goes on in a correctional organization, outside of the group or "treatment" session. This has tended to emasculate "treatment" in terms of its impact upon the total life of the organization. To make matters worse, offenders are often selected individually for group participation on the basis of some personal diagnostic characteristic, something that is peculiar to each of them. Meanwhile, natural groupings within the organization—work groups, living units, etc.—are ignored. Consequently, as Cressey (1954: 24) observes, "Attitudes and values acquired from taking the role of law-abiding person in the group sessions may receive little support in the general prison community." Even though group members may develop keen interest in correctional problems and express a resolve to do something about them, their enthusiasm is usually dampened when they find that people outside their group—offenders as well as staff—do not share their enthusiasm. They learn quickly that the task of changing the personal and organizational patterns of others is discouragingly difficult (*cf.* Cartwright, 1951: 387).

By the same token, the problem is further enhanced by the usual isolation of the correctional organization itself from linkage with the non-delinquent community. The group member is twice removed, structurally, from effective participation in ordinary activities. Even though he might feel that it would make all the difference in the world if that which he has learned in the group could be translated into activities outside of it, he is still without the structural means to make such a translation. Thus, without attention to these kinds of problems, the group-centered approach would have little utility at Silverlake. Something would have to be added to the model.

THERAPEUTIC-MILIEU MODEL

The therapeutic-milieu model, the fourth to be considered, seemed to promise some of the solutions that the group-centered approach omitted. In a very real sense, a therapeutic-milieu model is the group-centered approach extended to a total organization. Contrary to the insularity of the small group, an attempt is made to manipulate the total environment in the interests of changing the offender and his relationships to others. The roles of staff members, as well as offenders, are radically altered. Treatment is not seen as an isolated phenomenon, separate and apart from the operation of the total institution. Quite the contrary. Open communication is defined as an absolute necessity. Consequently, everyone participates in daily group meetings, and power, at least theoretically, is widely shared. In some settings, custodial officers might carry out counseling. If psychiatrists are involved, an effort is made to dissuade others from seeing them as all-knowing persons having a monopoly on answers to all problems. And everyone, staff as well as inmates, may be subjected to criticism and group decision.

There are, however, some wide variations on this general theme. With respect to causation, law-violating behavior in the therapeutic community of Maxwell Jones (1953) is seen as a personality disorder manifesting itself in defective performance of social roles. In contrast, McCorkle, Elias, and Bixby (1958), at Highfields, see law-violating behavior as occurring among relatively normal individuals who have anti-social attitudes and delinquent self-images. Meanwhile, at Synanon, perhaps because it is concerned only with addicts and alcoholics, the basic problem is defined as extreme immaturity: addicts and alcoholics are emotional infants (*cf.* Yablonsky, 1965).

Because of these wide variations, therefore, there are wide variations when it comes to treatment. In the Jones therapeutic community, an effort is made to make wide usage of interdisciplinary professionals—anthropologists and sociologists—as well as the usual psychologists, psychiatrists, and other institutional personnel. At Highfields, the unit is small, including no more than twenty offenders and a minimum number of staff. At Synanon, representatives of the correctional structure are not permitted an official role. Synanon is an organization run *by* addicts *for* addicts. The group relations principle is carried to the ultimate extreme.

Similarly, objectives are different. In the Jones therapeutic community, the objective is more traditional in character—*i.e.*, to use group therapy in the interest of remaking the personality. Special effort is concentrated upon increasing the social "maturity" of the offender so as to make him more aware of his relationships to others and in that way to decrease his problematic behavior. At Highfields, objectives are more consonant with the group relations principle of sponsoring the delinquent in a reformation role and in having him adopt a non-delinquent set of values. At Synanon, the incoming addict is treated as a fetus who must become attached to the therapeutic womb and nurtured to a point of adult maturity. The task is not so much that of remaking the personality as it is in developing it in the first place.

Given these disparate points of view and objectives, it is difficult to evaluate the therapeutic-milieu model as a unity. However, in terms of the organizational needs at Silverlake, the general model had several things to suggest.

First, it implied the importance of paying attention to total organizational structure. It is conceivable that a correctional organization could be developed in which offenders became more aware of the dynamics of interpersonal and group forces and learned how to deal more effectively with them. It would be important if they could learn how such forces are generated, how others view them, and how other views can depart from their own. An increased ability to diagnose social situations could be very valuable. Offenders might become more able to deal effectively with others, to build up or modify their own implicit theories of why people do what they do, and to carry their new-found ability with them to other settings in which some interpersonal skills were needed.

On the other hand, the therapeutic-milieu model had little to suggest relative to the problems of reintegrating offenders into the community and of providing the necessary instrumental skills which delinquents so badly need. The problem with the model is that it has been implemented most commonly in total institutions and thus has tended to ignore the community linkage principle. Yet adjustment to a total institution is not the same as adjustment to the free community. As Sternberg (1963) points out, a therapeutic milieu may end up offering *protection* to the offender rather than reintegration. He may become so conditioned to life in the therapeutic milieu that it is only in such a milieu that he can function effectively. He is rendered incapable of community adjustment where different sets of pressures operate. With respect to Synanon, Gibbons (1965: 507) has pointed out that

> Persons who succeed in the Synanon system tend to become members of an ex-addict social system, living in a Synanon residence, and working for the organization. In short, they become professional ex-addicts. There are serious doubts about the extent to which official corrections can or will be made in the direction of long-term protection of offenders.

In contrast, if the Silverlake operation were to be consistent with its principles, it would have to take a different approach. It would have to extend its operation so as to be able to influence the external as well as the internal environment and, further, to make external issues an integral part of the problem resolution process.

Utility of Prior Approaches

By way of assessing the utility of prior approaches for the Silverlake Experiment, Table 4.1 was developed and used as a training device. It indicates graphically why the cultural transmission and group psychotherapy models were inappropriate, in terms of basic intervention principles, and why the group-centered and therapeutic community models could be of utility. Even so, neither of the latter two models were capable of addressing other issues:

1. *The Community Linkage Problem.* Neither approach was of much utility in suggesting ways of linking the offender with the community.

2. *Organizational Structure.* Neither approach provided much information on the structural characteristics of an organization built on the group relations principle. What are its subparts, its norms, its positions, its role expectations? If one is setting up a new correctional organization, and wishes to provide guidelines for staff and offenders, he needs some specific directives as to the organization he must start with.

3. *Organization Evolution.* Neither the group-centered nor the therapeutic-milieu approaches speak to the problems of organizational development in evolutionary terms. Any collaborative organization does not emerge full-blown; it evolves. Consequently, some kind of a theory of group development was needed at Silverlake, especially if offenders were to participate with staff in the development of the organization. Many of its

characteristics would emerge in a process of interaction; they would not be created by fiat. The basic question, therefore, was whether principles could be provided by which to help staff guide interaction within the organization in the interest of having its emergent character conform as closely as possible to theoretical expectations.

The remainder of the chapter is devoted to the way these three issues were addressed.

Community Linkage

The theoretical principles of this study, combined with the limitations of prior approaches, all seemed to lead to one inevitable conclusion: the experimental program should be located in the community. No matter what its components might be, it should be related to the task of community reintegration. Its success would depend upon community as well as offender reconstruction. The decision was made, therefore, to establish a community program.

Once this decision was made, a difficult practical problem had to be addressed: Would the program be residential with delinquents living at an experimental facility, or would it be non-residential with delinquents continuing to live in their own homes? There was something to be said for either alternative.

The *non*-residential alternative seemed preferable for theoretical reasons. There is reason to question the traditional belief that rehabilitation should be a two-step process: (1) residential supervision until the offender is somehow made more capable of full adjustment in the community, followed by (2) some kind of extended, community supervision. Experimentation is needed, instead, with techniques that would cause minimal disruption of the offender's contact with the community. Furthermore, the *non*-residential alternative is by far the cheaper of the two. Funds that might be required for feeding and lodging offenders, or consumed in the complex tasks of institutional management, could be used for other purposes more directly related to the task of reintegration.

Practical reasons, however, overruled the theoretical for this particular experiment. The physical size of Los Angeles, and its lack of adequate public transportation, made it impossible for boys both to live at home and to attend a daily program. Since the homes of experimental subjects were widely scattered throughout Los Angeles County, a non-residential program was not feasible. The program would have to be residential.

Consistent with this need, property was leased that was admirably suited for the purposes of the experiment. A sprawling, single-level home was acquired that was built in 1957 as a small orphanage for Japanese–

Table 4.1. Characteristics of Alternative Correctional Models

	Cultural Transmission Model	Group Psychotherapy Model	Group-centered Model	Therapeutic-milieu Model
Programmatic Assumptions	1. Offenders lack adequate socialization. 2. Deviant behavior is due to the delinquent's lack of acceptance of social rules and authority.	1. Basic problems of the offender are primarily psychogenic in character and unique to each individual.	1. Deviant behavior and self-concept are a product of offender's group associations. 2. Groups have profound impact on the individual.	1. Mixed assumptions, ranging from personal immaturity and pathology to deviant behaviour as product of group socialization.
Programmatic Objectives	1. Training in values and skills of predominant culture, acceptance of authority.	1. Correction of individual psychopathology.	1. Help offender recognize and deal effectively with his behavior in a group context.	1. Manipulate total milieu of institution to alter offender behavior. 2. Teach offender to use interpersonal skills in a variety of different situations.
Programmatic Techniques	1. Didactic method. 2. Offenders dealt with on individualistic basis in a group setting.	1. Simultaneous individual therapy in group setting. 2. Emphasis on individual insight.	1. Offenders are involved in their own reformation. 2. Change in individual is concurrent with, and product of, group development.	1. Emphasis upon change through group activity. 2. Emphasis on importance of altering total organizational structure based upon collective analysis.
Role of Staff or Therapist	1. Authoritarian leadership style.	1. Permissive atmosphere yet with heavy reliance, ultimately, upon group therapist.	1. Democratic leadership style. 2. Leadership role optimally shared by both staff and inmates.	1. Same as group-centered model but with changes to carry outside of group setting.

Prior Program Characteristics

Relation to Characteristics sought by Silverlake Experiment

Characteristic				
Type of Social System	1. Caste system with division into staff and inmate groups. 2. Emphasis on obedience and conformity.	1. Little attention to organizational phenomena, per se. Unspecified.	1. Implied alteration of staff-inmate relations but little specification outside of group setting.	1. Emphasis on total, open communication. 2. Hypothetically, power widely shared.
Effective Use of Group Techniques	1. Heavy structural emphasis, little attention to group phenomena per se.	1. Lack of attention to group dynamics or processes. 2. Group provides a setting, but not a mechanism for treatment.	1. Use of group dynamics potentially applicable.	1. Use of group dynamics potentially applicable.
Development of Collaborative Social System	1. Little apparent concern with collaboration between offenders and staff. Communications are directive.	1. Little concern with collaboration; change a private transaction between therapist and client.	1. Separation of group session from institutional life. 2. Lack of guidelines in placing group interaction in larger institutional context. 3. Little attention to problems of relating group interaction to matters of shared power and decision-making.	1. Hypothetically, power within the institution is shared. 2. Group activities not isolated, but integrated with all programmatic elements and decision-making.
Linkage with Community	1. Little or no linkage with community.	1. Little or no linkage with community.	1. Little or no linkage with community.	1. Little or no linkage with community.

American children. It contained all of the essential characteristics needed for a small operational facility. In addition, there was a separate, smaller building on the property, which was used to accommodate the research staff and their necessary equipment. The property was in a quiet neighborhood and the buildings forming the facility were very much like other homes in the area.

The Organizational Structure

After deciding upon a community locale, the second issue involved the definition of organizational structure for the experimental program. Three major elements of structure required definition: staff and offender positions, major program components, and basic program norms.

STAFF AND OFFENDER POSITIONS

It was felt that if lines of communication were to be kept open and if the division of staff and offenders into competing groups was to be avoided, organizational structure should be simple. Consequently, the number of staff and offender positions was kept small. The maximum number of delinquents assigned to the program at any one time did not exceed twenty. Likewise, the number of staff members was also kept small. It included only a program director, an assistant director, a part-time cook, and a part-time work supervisor and tutor. The program director, his assistant, and the work supervisor-tutor filled the major staff roles. The cook was present only to prepare breakfast and serve the evening meal.

In searching for staff members to fill these positions, the concern was far less with the specific professional training of candidates than with finding persons who were interested in innovation and experimentation. Their skills would be judged not only by their professional backgrounds, but their capacity and willingness to implement the principles of this particular study. In other words, they would be required to have a serious commitment to knowledge-building as well as to older standards of practice and definitions of professionalism.

The key person, of course, was the residence director. His ultimate selection came as a result of collaborative search conducted by the director of Boys Republic and the research director for the experiment. The formal training of the residence director who was ultimately selected had been in criminology and his background consisted of considerable working experience in group programs with juvenile and adult offenders. He was a bachelor, was able to live at the residence, and agreed to remain throughout the life of the experiment. It was a fortunate choice. He not only fulfilled his obligations, but did so in an exemplary manner. His was a difficult job and, as he describes it, it had many of the characteristics of life in a fish bowl with a school of barracuda. He might be chewed up on the inside, and while that was happening, others would research his activities from the outside.

The other professional position was filled by a young person with considerable group experience. The work supervisor and tutor roles were filled by part-time college students. The way in which these staff members worked with offenders is best understood in terms of the program com-components that were developed. They are discussed in the next section.

PROGRAM COMPONENTS

The number of program components was likewise kept small. It included a daily group meeting, attendance at school, and limited work and tutorial activities. No special arrangements were made for recreational and religious pursuits. Instead, boys were permitted, indeed encouraged, to go home on weekends. Each of these components is discussed below.

Group Meeting

The first major component was a group meeting held five times a week, Monday through Friday. This group meeting, conducted at the end of each day, became the primary mechanism through which attempts at collaboration and problem-solving were implemented. The resident population of twenty boys was broken into two groups of approximately ten each, each of which was led by one of the professional staff members, and each of which met for one and one-half hours daily.

The principles and guidelines upon which group sessions were based have already been discussed in Chapter Three. However, a few points merit review. First, the form of interaction that was used in these meetings possessed many features similar to the "guided group interaction" pioneered in the U.S. Army (Bixby and McCorkle, 1951), at Highfields (McCorkle *et al.*, 1958), and at the Provo Experiment (Empey and Rabow, 1961).

This approach utilizes techniques that are not commonly associated with traditional group psychotherapy. Guided group interaction attempts to make the group both the target and the medium of change. It emphasizes the development of the group as being productive of change for its members.

The role of the adult leader in these daily group meetings is extremely important. The ultimate development of the group depends in large part on his particular skills. He seeks to become a functional rather than an authoritarian member of the group, a task that is difficult in any correctional setting. His objective is not that of always imposing his will on the group, but of increasing the capacity of the group to analyze its own problems and to resolve its own difficulties.

Discussions in any single group meeting may center around a variety of different topics: family problems, school difficulties, personal inadequacies, delinquent activities, or discussion as to when a particular boy is ready to be released. Any group tends to go through a series of stages from one in which there is considerable testing and distrust to one in which boys carry an increasingly heavy responsibility for analyzing problems, making decisions, and helping to prevent difficulties. This evolutionary development will be the subject of later discussion in this chapter. Suffice it to say that the fundamental objectives of the group meetings are to elicit and document the problems group members face, to search for and find adequate alternatives, and to provide group support and personal rewards for the adoption of these other alternatives. By relating the pain and difficulties of group analysis to the larger setting of the community, it is possible for boys to try out new ways of behaving and to reality-test the consequences of doing so.

School Attendance

School attendance was the second major program component. In addition to location in the community, the new program needed institutional linkage. School attendance was chosen as the primary linkage (1) because of the obvious and ever-increasing need for academic and vocational skills; (2) because of the fact that employment with any career potential is extremely difficult for a teenage adolescent without formal education to obtain; and (3) because of the importance of the school as the major societal institution for adolescents.

It was our experience in the Provo Experiment (Empey and Rabow, 1961) that delinquent boys, perhaps even more than staff, were supportive of the importance of school for the delinquent. This support came as some surprise, but after discussion was easily understandable. The school, from these delinquents' view, is where the action is. It is less boring than the street; it is where members of the opposite sex can be found, and after all, education is important. Thus, delinquents in that experiment seemed to feel that if they could find some way to avoid the pains of the past and could somehow fit in, they would prefer to stay in school.

In order to establish school contacts, a series of meetings was held with school officials and arrangements were eventually made to enroll all experimental subjects in the neighborhood high school. Most of these meetings involved the principal and his staff, rather than people in the office of superintendent, the reason being that local cooperation was so important to the experiment. Even though approval was obtained from higher administration, the success or failure of the venture would depend upon the actions of local administrators and teachers.

There was considerable resistance to the proposal. School people were primarily concerned with two things: narcotics and the possibility of violence. They feared that delinquents would bring both to the school. Quite frankly, they saw the boys as outsiders who were being imposed upon them, as people who simply should not be a part of their local constituency. Secondarily, they felt that the delinquent group would not only disrupt the classroom, but would draw excessively upon already limited counseling, teaching, and administrative resources.

They suggested, as an alternative, that boys from the experiment be transported to special adjustment schools that exist in Los Angeles to receive students who have had disciplinary or other serious problems. This proposal was rejected because it was precisely opposite to the kind of community linkage that was desired. Delinquents need ties with successful people in "normal" schools, not with unsuccessful people in "abnormal" schools. What is more, it seemed certain that if the delinquent group was to become an integral element in the reformation process, all boys would have to go to the same neighborhood school so that they could know what was going on and could develop a group culture that would assist in the reintegration process.

In order to overcome the objections of the school, two points of agreement were reached: (1) that the experiment would not take delinquents who were confirmed addicts or proven violent, or sex offenders and (2) that the experiment would provide counseling and tutorial help to assist both with control and academic problems. Nevertheless, officials remained uneasy and reluctant. Innumerable relationship problems remained throughout the life of the experiment.

The daily schedule of the experimental subjects was similar to that of other students. They walked to school, leaving at approximately 7:30 in the morning and returning between 3:00 and 4:00 in the afternoon. They received lunch money and bought their own lunches at the school. They also carried on other routine activities in the community—shopping, getting hair cuts, etc.

A tutor was hired to assist the boys with their academic subjects, in addition to which the group meeting became a forum in which school problems, collective and private, academic and behavioral, were discussed. As a part of the group-centered approach, efforts were made to help the group assume both a control and a problem-solving function. Realistically speaking, staff members could rarely, if ever, be present when school difficulties occurred. As a consequence, the solution of many of these (and other community) problems was actually dependent on whatever feedback, assistance, and support could be provided by the delinquent boys themselves. The eventual consequences of efforts to relate group techniques and institutional linkage were many and provocative and will be analyzed in later chapters.

Work Activities

The third program component involved work and housekeeping activities. The boys at the experiment were responsible for maintaining the home and grounds in which they lived: cleaning, maintaining the yard, washing dishes, and so on.

There were two major reasons for having boys carry out these activities rather than hiring someone to do them: to improve their work skills and to use work activities as a basis for understanding personal and group problems. Emergent difficulties became grist for the group discussions. The idea was to use actual behavior, rather than subjective estimates, as the basis for understanding different people and working out their problems.

Work also provided the opportunity for boys to try out new roles in contrast to the ones which they had occupied heretofore. In order to encourage this kind of activity, two paid work positions were created as formalized devices for learning and reward. The occupants of these positions were known as "resident workers" who, in addition to receiving a regular allowance of $15, received an additional $45 per month. This extra pay was a means of enhancing the prestige of work positions and the responsibilities that were associated with them. These work supervisors, and not the staff, were responsible for carrying out the daily work functions of the residence. As might be expected, a number of problems and manipulations developed around these work roles. But rather than viewing them as problems to be controlled solely by staff, they became the basis for discussion and problem resolution by the daily groups.

Weekend Activities

The program design called for boys to spend weekends at home or with relatives. The intent was not simply to provide recreation or to maintain home ties, but to utilize home and community visits as a source of information. If the program were to succeed with the problems of community adjustment, it had to have behavioral indicators of family disruption, persistence in delinquent activities, association with delinquent peers, or, simply, a boy's ability to go and return on his own.

Every boy was faced with the dilemma of choosing between the demands of his friends and former environment outside the program and the demands of the program itself. The usual reaction is to test the situation by identifying with the former, but the complexities of a dual existence make it difficult to accomplish. A program in which there is daily interaction between staff and offenders in a group setting makes it difficult to retain two identities, two styles of operating over a prolonged period. And when boys themselves live with each other and participate in a daily group meeting, attempts at deceit by some of them often go awry. The daily group meeting is itself a collective board on delinquency; boys usually know what is going on and someone can be counted upon to discuss problems if he feels that serious efforts are being made to solve those problems rather than to punish people for having them. Therefore, the fact that the group is able to use actual behavior in the community to judge the extent to which a boy is involved with the program, to judge his progress, and even to judge his readiness for release means that there is no shortage of crucial material. One basic criterion for judging the relevance of any treatment program is not what an individual does while in it, but what he does while he is *not* in it. The program was designed to maximize the use of material that was external to, as well as within, the program itself.

NORMATIVE STRUCTURE

In addition to program components, some attention had to be given to the basic ground rules, the basic norms within which the program would operate. If attention is not devoted deliberately and consciously to the definition of norms for any organization, they will be derived informally, even inadvertently. In this particular case, the task of defining norms posed some difficult problems. First of all, theoretical guidelines called for the participation of offenders as well as staff in the definition of program norms. All information relating to the need for change, the methods to be used, and the consequences of change were to be shared by all relevant people.

At the same time, there were difficult constraints to be faced in attempting to derive new norms without starting with some ground rules in the beginning. No group, correctional or otherwise, is free to develop norms that are totally independent of the larger legal and cultural matrix of which they are a part. External constraints, especially for offenders, are always present. For example, any community program tends to raise fears that it will constitute a serious danger, that anything less than total confinement will be too unstructured. Consequently, it would be dishonest and misleading to cause delinquents to believe that all traditional controls and expectations could be ignored and that they were entirely free to define whatever norms they desired.

Beyond that, it is unlikely that any new program can function without ground rules. No social system can operate without limits, and complete permissiveness is certainly not the answer to the complete rigidity and authoritarian correctional structures of the past. Consequently, a basic step in setting up the new program required the development of two kinds of norms: (1) norms that would establish the basic ground rules within which everyone had to operate; and (2) norms designed to facilitate increasing collaboration between staff and offenders.

Ground rules—norms of the first type—would have to be stated at the outset. Like the basic framework of a new building, they would have to become the basis upon which a more elaborate structure could be built. Yet, while fundamental to the whole undertaking, such norms would not totally determine the final character and elaboration of the building. Norms of the second type—those concerned with collaboration—would fulfill this function. Emerging in the process of interaction between staff and offenders, they would add form and substance to the developing structure. Proceeding on this basis, then, steps were taken, first, to define basic ground rules and, second, to define a developmental procedure as a means of developing norms favorable to staff-offender collaboration.

Ground Rules

The basic ground rules were defined as follows:

1. Boys were required to live at the residence. Since they were assigned by the court, the only other alternative was return to court with the possible danger of incarceration.
2. Boys could not come and go as they pleased. They would have to meet some kind of a schedule, to be decided upon as the program developed.
3. School attendance was mandatory.
4. Physical assault would not be tolerated.
5. A decline in delinquent behavior was necessary. While it would be unrealistic to expect that boys could arbitrarily and immediately alter their life-styles, they would have to understand that the experimental program would not be a haven for persistent law violators. What they should understand is that a gradual diminution of law-violating behavior would be expected as they learned more about how to deal with it.
6. The new program was not a place to "do time." It was designed to return boys to the community as quickly as possible. However, no set length of stay was to be established and a given boy's release would be contingent upon his demonstrated changes in behavior and attitude.

While these ground rules seem restrictive, perhaps overly coercive, two things about them should be kept in mind. First, they were alternative to the physical controls, isolation, and restriction of an institution; second, they would be likely to produce anxiety as much for what they did not say as for what they did say. That is, they were *pro*scriptions, not *pre*scriptions. Their main function was to assert controls rather than to indicate solutions. Their ultimate utility, therefore, would depend upon the extent to which they could be joined effectively with a set of solution-giving prescriptions; that is, norms that would define the problem-solving procedures of the system, the things people should do.

Of the two, the task of defining prescriptions was the more difficult.

They could not be stated in advance and formalized like proscriptions because, as the guidelines for the experiment indicated, they were to be the product of collaborative interaction between staff and offenders. They would not be present at the outset; they would have to evolve.

This suggests that staff and offenders would be involved in nothing less than an attempt to build a new kind of anti-delinquent reformation culture. A major task for our planning, therefore, was to conceptualize and describe, in hypothetical terms, what kind of an evolutionary pattern might be anticipated. It would be unwise to expect staff and delinquents to engage in a prolonged dialogue and painful interaction without any prior notion as to what their objectives were and how progress toward them might be judged.

Suggesting a pattern for this endeavor was difficult because there was precious little theory and even less empirical evidence upon which to build. However, a statement by Cohen (1955: 61) provided the general background for what it was we were seeking:

> The crucial condition for the emergence of new cultural forms is the existence, in effective interaction with one another, of a number of actors with similar problems of adjustment. These may be the entire membership of a group or only certain members, similarly circumstanced, within the group. Among the conceivable solutions to their problems may be one which is not yet embodied in action and which does not, therefore, exist as a cultural model. . . .
>
> . . . For the actor with problems of adjustment which cannot be resolved within the frame of reference of the established culture, each response of the other to what the actor says and does is a clue to the directions in which change may proceed further in a way congenial to the other and to the direction in which change will lack social support. And if the probing gesture is motivated by tensions common to other participants, it is likely to initiate a process of mutual exploration and joint elaboration of a new solution. . . .
>
> . . . We may think of this process as one of mutual conversion. The important thing to remember is that we do not first convert ourselves and then others. The acceptability of an idea to oneself depends upon its acceptability to others. Converting the other is part of the process of converting oneself.

Using ideas implicit in this statement, with help from summaries of the literature on group development (*cf.* Martin and Hill, 1957; Tuchman, 1965) and from our experience in the Provo Experiment (Empey and Rabow, 1961; Scott, 1965), we proceeded to construct a highly speculative statement on the evolution of program culture. This statement posited a strong and intimate tie between interaction within the daily, small group meetings and the other components of the experimental program. The outlines of group and program development are summarized in Table 4.2.

Table 4.2. Summary Description of Stages of Group and Program Development at the Silverlake Experiment

	Stage 1: Search for structure	Stage 2: Stereotyped problem-solving	Stage 3: Awareness of individual differences and alternatives	Stage 4: Group awareness	Stage 5: Integration of group and program culture
Objectives	1. Foster and reward interaction 2. Teach members that the level of group performance depends heavily on them. 3. Instill confidence in the group.	1. Learn complexities of delinquent behavior. 2. Introduction of substantive problems. 3. Gather information on individual group members.	1. Clarify alternatives. 2. Make group members more aware of individual differences.	1. Increase understanding of group structure and process to maximize group problem-solving. 2. Increase capacity of offender to see himself in relation to group structure.	1. Link the operation of the small group with program and community activities. 2. Group members who have reached this stage become culture builders and maintainers for others.
Structural Context	1. Anomie expected. 2. Minimum of structure provided. 3. Group leader refrains from being authoritarian, does not foster dependency. *Transition* 1. Dissatisfaction with Stage 1. 2. Enforced attendance is galling and escape is sought. 3. Role of group leader emerges as important. He becomes functional in reducing anxiety by suggesting ways to proceed.	1. Some group members take risks—attempt to play leadership role. 2. Group leader poses problems for which solutions must be found, refuses to accept all responsibility for control function. 3. Delinquents experiment with decision-making. *Transition* 1. Dissatisfaction with stereotyping in Stage 2. 2. Group leader attempts to crystalize dilemmas and point out dysfunctions of type of interaction going on. 3. Explore alternative modes of interaction and behavior.	1. Two types of group members emerge: Resisters and Reformers. 2. Leader attempts to enrich interaction by providing involvement in complex decision-making. 3. Evidence of social control by the group. *Transition* 1. Increasing group awareness of the dysfunction of selfish individual pursuits. 2. Leader helps group become aware of consequences of factionalism	1. Group is seen as special entity. 2. Status of adult leader continues to change—his power and authority decreases and becomes shared by the group. 3. Leader continues to play teaching role. *Transition* 1. Group recognizes need to establish linkage for its members in the community and to extend its influence into other components of the program. 2. Achievement of this transition depends more than any other phase upon the readiness of group members to assist in the task.	1. Increased awareness of group as an entity. 2. Group members share power with leader in deciding when boys can be released from program and other important issues. 3. Adult leader is seen more as a group member. 4. Roles are assigned on the basis of competence.

	Stage 1	Stage 2	Stage 3	Stage 4	Stage 5
Group Process	1. Search for structure. 2. Testing. 3. Private search for meaning. 4. Leader sets stage for emergence of group culture.	1. Distrust of leader. 2. Testing continues. 3. Aggressive behavior, assertiveness. 4. Group members become aware of differences and problems they share with others. 4. Members more comfortable with leader and his role is better understood. 5. Candor is encouraged and rewarded.	1. Concern with conflicts between subgroups. 2. More free exchange than Stages 1 or 2. 3. Increased concern for welfare of group.	1. Interaction more candid and satisfying than at any previous stage. 2. Greater collaboration and cooperation than at earlier stages. 3. Conflict among sub groups still present, but to degree.	1. Periods of highly cooperative and motivated problem-solving. 2. Greater evidence of active reformation role than at any other time. 3. Greater trust and communication than earlier stages.
Discussion Content	1. "Safe", nonthreatening material.f 2. Leader does not provide conclusive answers, but sponsors discussion matter of interest to boys. 3. Interaction wandering and idiosyncratic. 4. Recitation of delinquent histories and personal problems.	1. Same as Stage 1 except for introduction of substantive problems: school problems, new delinquent acts, family problems, gripes about program demands.	1. Involves more sensitive and personal problems and feelings than prior stages. 2. Considerable amount of personal information is exchanged. 3. A more involved and persistent examination of problems and decisions.	1. Same as Stage 3 except that content is put more in context of group phenomena and their relation to total program and community.	1. Same as other stages except there is greater concern for total program operation, maintaining a collaborative system and addressing problems of boys in the community.

Briefly, the developmental process was hypothesized to occur in five different stages: (1) a search for structure within the small group; (2) a period of stereotyped problem-solving; (3) an awareness of individual differences and alternatives; (4) an awareness of group structure and processes; and (5) an integration of group and program culture. Each of these stages, in turn, was described in terms of the objectives for that stage, the structural characteristics of the group, the nature of the group process, and the kinds of discussion content that should be encouraged. From an early stage of development in which there is considerable resistance and testing, it was hypothesized that the overall process would work toward a stage in which delinquents would carry increasingly heavy responsibilities: analyzing problems, making plans, preventing difficulties, making decisions and sharing with staff the rewards, as well as the pains of the reformation endeavor.

The Training Function

The delinquency theory described in Chapter One, the intervention principles described in Chapter Two, and the operational guidelines presented above were used as the substantive material for staff training, both written and verbal. Involved in that training were all of the principal actors: the director of Boys Republic, the research director, the operational and research staffs. No one was excused or excluded from these sessions. "Training" was broadly conceived, and was an ongoing process rather than a one-shot experience; that is, sessions were held regularly throughout the life of the experiment rather than just preceding it. The tasks of explaining and becoming familiar with all of the theoretical and operational principles are not easily accomplished. They require repeated analysis and exploration; they involve an attempt to relate daily experiences to the theoretical structure as a means of insuring conformity to experimental design.

Because of the attempt that was made to coalesce administrative, action, and research people into an effective field experimental unit, relationships were generally good. However, certain deficiencies are worth noting. Training could have been far more effective had an attempt been made to conduct a pilot study of the experimental intervention for at least a year preceding the actual implementation of the overall design. Only when staff members are confronted with the problems of implementation are they placed in the position of having to reality-test theoretical abstractions. Theoretical and intervention statements are skeletal structures at best, and the task of operationalizing them requires considerable interaction, restatement and filling out. The task is analogous to that of the research person who must spend endless hours refining and pretesting his instruments before they become valid and reliable in measuring what he wants to measure. Without this initial preparation, an experiment such as this does not really begin to approximate theoretical design until well into the operational test of it.

This is not an inconsequential problem, but one that funding agencies and administrative, action, and research people must be more willing to confront. As it was, the experimental program operated for the better part of four years with additional time necessary for follow-up, analysis, and writing. Yet, with all this time, this field study was but a tiny segment of the total body of research that is needed. It would seem, therefore, that provision must be made for programs of research in which the problems of conceptualization, training, pilot operation, and testing might be conducted on a more comprehensive and systematic basis. All of these components should become an integral part of operations in corrections rather than an occasional, and often disliked, appendage. In this case, the implementation of the experiment suffered from the necessity of trying to collapse all of these steps into far too short a period of time.

References

BACH, GEORGE R. 1954. *Intensive Group Psychotherapy*. New York: Ronald Press.

BANDURA, ALBERT. 1967. Behavioral psychotherapy. *Scientific American*, 216 (March): 78–86.

BENNE, KENNETH D., and PAUL SHEATS. 1948. Functional Roles of Group Members. *Journal of Social Issues*, 4 (April): 41–49.

BIXBY, F. LOVELL, and LLOYD W. McCORKLE. 1951. Guided group interaction in correctional work. *American Sociological Review*, 16 (August): 455–459.

CARTWRIGHT, DORWIN. 1951. Achieving change in people: Some applications of group dynamics theory. *Human Relations*, 4: 381–401.

CARTWRIGHT, DORWIN, and RONALD LIPPITT. 1957. group dynamics and the individual. *International Journal of Group Psychotherapy*, VII (January): 86–102.

COHEN, ALBERT K. 1955. *Delinquent Boys: The Culture of the Gang*. Blencoe, Ill.: The Free Press.

CRESSEY, DONALD R. 1954. Contradictory theories in correctional group therapy programs. *Federal Probation*, 18 (June): 20–26.

EMPEY, LAMAR T., and JEROME RABOW. 1961. The Provo experiment in delinquency rehabilitation. *American Sociological Review*, 26 (October): 679–696.

GIBB, CECIL A. 1947. The principles and traits of leadership. *Journal of Abnormal and Social Psychology*, 42: 267–284.

GIBBONS, DON C. 1965. *Changing the Lawbreaker: The Treatment of Delinquents and Criminals*. Englewood Cliffs, N.J.: Prentice–Hall.

HARPER, ROBERT A. 1959. *Psychoanalysis and Psychotherapy*. Englewood Cliffs, N.J.: Prentice–Hall.

HILL, WILLIAM F., Ed. 1961. *Collected Papers in Group Psychotherapy*. Provo: Utah State Hospital.

JONES, MAXWELL. 1953. *The Therapeutic Community: A New Treatment Method in Psychiatry.* New York: Basic Books.

KLAPMAN, J. W. 1959. *Group Psychotherapy: Theory and Practice.* New York: Grune and Stratton.

LEWIN, KURT. 1953. Studies in group decision. In D. Cartwright and A. Zander, Eds., *Group Dynamics.* Evanston, Ill.: Row, Peterson.

LEWIN, KURT, R. LIPPITT, and R. WHITE. 1939. Patterns of aggressive behavior in experimentally created "social climates". *Journal of Social Psychology,* 10: 271–299.

McCORKLE, LLOYD W., ALBERT ELIAS, and F. LOVELL BIXBY. 1958. *The Highfields Story.* New York: Holt, Rinehart and Winston.

MARTIN, ELMORE A., and WILLIAM F. HILL. 1957. Toward a theory of group development. *International Journal of Group Psychotherapy,* 7: 20–30.

ROETHILSBERGER, F. J., and W. J. DICKSON. 1939. *Management and the Worker.* Cambridge, Mass.: Harvard University Press.

SARRI, ROSEMARY C., and ROBERT D. VINTER. 1965. New treatment strategies in juvenile correctional programs. *Crime and Delinquency,* 11 (October): 326–340.

SCHRAG, CLARENCE. 1961. dome foundations for a theory of correction. In Donald R. Cressey, Ed., *The Prison.* New York: Holt, Rinehart and Winston.

SCOTT, MAX L. 1965. Group development: an exploratory study of small group growth patterns. Unpublished master's thesis, Department of Sociology, Brigham Young University.

SEASHORE, S. E. 1954. *Group Cohesiveness in the Industrial Group.* Ann Arbor: University of Michigan. Institute for Social Research.

SEEMAN, MELVIN. 1959. On the meaning of alienation. *American Sociological Review,* 24 (December): 783–791.

SLAVSON, S. R. 1943. *An Introduction to Group Therapy.* New York: Commonwealth Fund.

STERNBERG, DAVID. 1963. Synanon House—A consideration of its implications for American correction. *Journal of Criminal Law, Criminology and Police Science,* LIV (December): 447–455.

TUCHMAN, BRUCE W. 1965. Developmental sequence in small groups. *Psychological Bulletin,* 3: 384–399.

YABLONSKY, LEWIS. 1965. *The Tunnel Back: Synanon.* New York: Macmillan.

CHAPTER FIVE

Operational Guidelines: Research

All man's disciplined creations have form. Architecture, poetry, music, painting, mathematics, scientific research—all have form. Man puts great stress on the content of his creations, often not realizing that without strong structure, no matter how rich and how significant the content, the creations may be weak and sterile.

So it is with scientific research. The scientist needs viable and plastic form with which to express his scientific aims. Without content—without good theory, good hypotheses, good problems—the design of research is empty. But without form, without structure adequately conceived and created for the research purpose, little of value can be accomplished. Indeed, it is no exaggeration to say that many of the failures of behavioral research have been failures of disciplined and imaginative form (Kerlinger, 1965: 290).

The foregoing chapters of this book have been devoted largely to the theoretical structure of the Silverlake Experiment. As Kerlinger's quotation implies, however, provocative theory is not enough. Any scientific investigation is dependent, as well, upon the soundness of its research design. This chapter is devoted, therefore, to a presentation of that design.

Its development required attention to two major issues (1) developing a body of research capable of addressing the two major objectives of testing delinquency theory and learning about the problems of delinquency reduction and (2) studying the problems of the FEM as a knowledge-generating device. These two issues will be treated separately.

Examining Theory and Delinquency Reduction

With regard to the task of examining theory and program operation, there were two problems with which the research design had to be concerned:

internal and external validity (*cf.* Campbell, 1957; Wiggins, 1968).

Internal validity refers to the ability of an investigator to exercise direct control over the variables he is studying and to determine whether his empirical conclusions are directly attributable to demonstrated relationships among those variables; in this case, to the variables involved in understanding and changing delinquents.

External validity, on the other hand, refers to the representativeness or generalizability of a given study. In this study, for example, concern would be with the extent to which one could generalize from its findings to some larger population of delinquents and other correctional programs. Unless the study involved some definable and representative group, the external validity of the study would be low.

Although both types of validity present important requirements for any scientific study, it most often turns out that they are incompatible. If one is to optimize internal validity through the use of stringent controls, as is often found in laboratory experiments, the meaningful generalization of results to the behavior of people in nonlaboratory settings becomes problematic. On the other hand, if one is to optimize external validity by selecting representative samples in real life settings, the task of exercising rigid internal controls becomes extremely difficult.

There is no easy solution to these problems and often the researcher must make a choice as to which type of validity is most important for his particular study. However, since a field experimental model was chosen in this case, this study fell somewhere between the horns of the internal and external dilemma. It would attempt to maximize internal validity through the application of some experimental controls and, at the same time, to maximize external validity by studying the behavior of people in their "natural" settings. Even so, some compromises were necessary which affected all aspects of the overall design.

POPULATION AND SAMPLE SELECTION

It will be recalled that two groups of subjects were randomly selected and assigned to experimental and control programs. The method of selection was relatively simple. The counselor of intake at Boys Republic, after determining whether a boy met the criteria for selection, used an assignment schedule provided for him by the research staff to assign the boy either to the experimental or control group. On occasion, some problems were encountered with this method, but in general it was followed. The few problems that were encountered with the method are discussed in Chapter Fourteen.

The manner in which subjects were chosen directly affected the generalizability, and thus the external validity, of the study. In ideal terms, subjects should have been randomly chosen in such a manner that they represented some larger population, such as all delinquents in a given city, county, or state. Practical considerations, however, made this difficult.

In order to achieve cooperation with Boys Republic as the sponsoring agency, it was necessary to choose experimental and control groups from the available populations being assigned there. That population was state-wide, but because the experiment was to be located near the delinquents' home community, the population source for the study had to be restricted. Eventually, it was chosen from Los Angeles County and included the following characteristics: (1) the ethnic breakdown corresponded closely to that of the county—three-quarters Caucasian, one-tenth Negro, one-tenth Mexican–American, and a tiny group of Orientals; (2) the age range was from $15\frac{1}{2}$ to 18 years; and (3) no psychotics, mentally retarded boys, addicts, or serious sex offenders were included. Other than these characteristics, the experiment had no control over the kinds of offenders assigned by the court to Boys Republic. Thus, the external validity of the study is limited, making it impossible to generalize with certainty to any larger population of delinquents.

On the other hand, the problems of internal validity are less serious. The reason is that the total population of offenders from Los Angeles County, assigned to the Boys Republic, were randomly assigned either to the experimental or the control program. An analysis of these two groups on a host of variables—age, mobility, family structure, social status, parental harmony, boy–parent relations, school interests, school participation, grades, aspirations, work experience, religious preference, ethnicity, offense history, and psychological characteristics—revealed very few differences. In fact, only 6 out of nearly 100 comparisons achieved statistical significance past the 0.05 level.[1]

The strongest of these six differences ($P<0.001$) had to do with the types of previous court dispositions encountered by subjects before their assignment to one of the two groups. Three things are of importance:

1. About one-third of the boys assigned to the experimental program had previously been incarcerated in a county probation camp while at the control institution the figure was much smaller, 7 per cent.
2. The majority of the boys assigned to the control institution, 54 per cent, had previously been on probation, while the figure for the mediatory program was only 35 per cent.
3. The control program was more likely than the experimental program to receive boys without *any* record of probation or previous incarceration.

Thus, on the basis of prior disposition, it seems that the experimental

1. In assessing sample comparability, *chi*-square or *t*-tests were used, depending on the level of measurement involved in the comparison.

community program inadvertently may have been assigned more serious, or at least more experienced, offenders. Whether this had a biasing effect on outcome will be examined in later chapters.

It was also found that a higher proportion of boys from the control group claimed to be more interested in school ($P<0.01$), were younger in age if and when they left school ($P<0.05$), had a job when they were assigned to Boys Republic ($P<0.05$), and were more likely to have participated in extracurricular school activities of a nonathletic nature ($P<0.05$). Finally, although both groups tended to come from disrupted families, a higher proportion of experimental boys came from divorced families, while the controls were more likely to have parents who were either separated or widowed ($P<0.05$). Nevertheless, given the number of variables that were examined, and given the laws of probability, one might expect this many differences to occur by chance. In the main, therefore, the groups appeared to be very much alike.

This finding is reassuring. It suggests that the use of randomization was a means of insuring the internal validity of the experiment because it served to control the effects of a large number of individual differences, and thus provided some assurance that emergent differences between experimental and control groups might be attributed to differences between the two programs.

Measurement Design: Input

The actual collection of data relative to the examination of delinquency theory and program operation was divided into three parts: (1) data on program *input* having to do with the characteristics of offenders at the time of their assignment to experimental and control programs, which could be used to classify them and to examine the causation theory; (2) data on program *process*, which could be used to examine the attempts that were made to implement the change postulates of the experiment and to explore the problems that emerged; and (3) data on program *outcome*, which could be used to measure the impact of the program on the boys, the staff, and the community.

The first major objective of input research was to examine the basic theoretical assumptions made about delinquents. Efforts to locate the reasons for the successes or failures of the experimental or control programs could not really be conclusive until it was known whether offenders actually possessed the characteristics postulated for them. To ignore basic assumptions and to limit the evaluation of these programs solely to an examination of their operational components or their outcomes would be like evaluating a surgical operation without knowing for sure why the operation was performed. It would do little good to worry about the skill of the surgeon or why the patient died unless one were sure of the accuracy of the diagnosis. The same was true at Silverlake. The validity of causal assumptions would have to be tested.

Second, input research was used as the first basic step in providing definitive information on the effects of the experimental and control programs on particular types of individuals. By carefully documenting the offense histories, the personality profiles, the peer group relationships, and other characteristics of offenders as they were introduced into both programs, input research could provide a basis for isolating the kinds of people with whom each program was successful and with whom they failed. It could then begin to indicate what changes might be required in terms of both selection criteria and program operation to make either or both of them more successful.

DEVELOPMENT OF SCALES AND TYPOLOGIES

In order to accomplish these objectives, many separate items of input information were collected. It was then necessary to find parsimonious means for displaying and using them. Consequently, the many items were divided into four major families of variables, and scales and typologies constructed for each of them. Those families and scales are as follows:

1. *Offense Scales.* The task of relating the official offense patterns of delinquents to other forms of behavior is a difficult one, largely because the official records are like the tip of an iceberg. They may or may not represent the kinds of offense the offender most often commits. Therefore, an attempt was made to develop several offense scales that might combine offense patterns into some helpful typologies. Data for the analysis were collected from two major sources: Los Angeles County Probation records and the Central Juvenile Index, an information center for law enforcement officials administered by the sheriff of Los Angeles County. It was felt that the data collected from these two sources provided as accurate and comprehensive a picture of *official* delinquent histories as could be obtained.

The methodological process involved in attempting to develop these typologies, briefly, was as follows: First, a factor analysis was performed on selected combinations of offenses. Some of the offenses clustered together in discernable patterns. This was an encouraging development and led to a second major step.

Next, an attempt was made to use Guttman scaling to see if the individual offenses that clustered together in the factor analysis could be further confirmed by the scaling process. If it was confirmed, then the behavior of each boy, in each offense category, could be represented and reproduced by knowledge of a single score. This analysis also proved successful.

As a result of the scaling efforts, five different scales were developed and are presented in Table 5.1. Arbitrary names have been assigned to these scales. It will be observed that some scales include offenses that seem to be logically related such as theft of various types, while others include a variety of different offenses that are not necessarily bound by logic, only by their empirical relationship to each other. See Appendix II for further detail.

There are always scientific questions regarding the validity of such scales. Some of the scales are methodologically weak because they only include as few as two offenses. It remains to be seen, therefore, when given a pragmatic test, whether they will relate with other variables in explaining or predicting behavior.

Table 5.1. Types of Behavior included in Offense Scales

Scale Name	Offenses included in Scale
I. Theft Scale	Petty Theft, Grand Theft, Breaking and Entering, or Burglary
II. Personal Disorganization Scale	Runaway from Institution, Destitution, or Bad Companions
III. Street Corner Scale	Fighting or Aggravated Assault, Curfew, Alcohol
IV. Automobile Scale	Auto Theft, Joyriding, Other Traffic Offenses
V. Family Problems Scale	Incorrigibility, Runaway from Home

In addition to the general offense scales just described, an attempt was made also to develop a scale of offense seriousness. This scale was designed to obtain some measure of the way the official agents of society—in this case, law enforcement agencies and the juvenile courts—view different offenses. Nothing inherent in a given act makes it illegal. Rather, the criminality of that act is defined by society and by law in action (*cf.* Becker, 1963: 9; Durkheim, 1962: 170; Erikson, 1962: 307–314; Kitsuse, 1962: 247–256). Thus, in addition to knowing what offenses boys commit, we are also in need of some idea of the way the law enforcement and the courts view them.

In order to construct the Seriousness scale, the following steps were taken. First, official records were carefully studied and a list was made of thirty-one selected offenses with which juveniles are most commonly charged. This list was then submitted to officers of the Juvenile Division of the Los Angeles Police Department, officers of the Juvenile Division of the Los Angeles Sheriff's Department, and thirteen judges and referees of the Los Angeles County Juvenile Court.

Each official was asked to rate the thirty-one selected offenses along a continuum of seriousness, 0 representing the least serious category into which an offense could be placed and 5 the most serious. The result of the ratings may be found in Table 5.2. In that table, offenses are ranked in the order in which all officials, as a group, rated them.

Parenthetically, it might be noted that some differences occurred. Judges and referees, for example, appeared to be more tolerant than the law enforcement agents. Nevertheless, there was a reasonably high degree of agreement among the rankings. Using Robinson's A (1957: 17–25), the measurement of agreement among the three groups was 0.91.

2. *Peer Commitment Scales.* Heavy emphasis was placed in the theory chapters on the peer associations of delinquents. In order to measure this dimension of behavior for the purposes of testing the causation theory and measuring change, a special questionnaire was developed (Appendix II). This questionnaire attempted to assess how respondents react to peers in a variety of different situations. It was then submitted to boys as they entered both the control and experimental programs. Responses were then factor-analyzed. The analysis revealed that boys tended to respond to the question-naire in distinctly patterned ways. Based upon these patternings, four Guttman scales, with high coefficients of reproducibility, were developed.

The first scale, labeled the Ratfink scale, had to do with the extent to which boys would give information to parents, teachers, or police if their friends were in trouble. The scale divided boys into four types, extending from those who would give information to all officials to those who would not give information to anyone.

The second scale, called the Ace-in-the-Hole scale, was comprised of only two items but dealt with the question of whether boys would hide their friends if they had run away from home or if they were in trouble with the law. It divided boys into three types, from those who would hide their friends under both circumstances to those who would not hide their friends under either circumstance.

The third scale had to do with the way boys would respond to their peers in a number of non-delinquent social situations. It was comprised of three items and was entitled the Sociability scale. It divided boys into four types extending from those who would stop watching TV, doing homework, or going to church in order to "mess around" with friends to those who would not miss any of these activities in order to go with friends.

The fourth scale, called the Deviancy scale, was composed of five items and had to do with the way boys would respond to their peers in a number of delinquent situations. At one extreme, it included boys who would follow their friends in any of a number of delinquent situations. In between were those who would participate in only some of the acts, while at the other extreme were those who would engage in none of them.

Table 5.2. Offense Seriousness Judgments

Offense	City Police N = 17	County Sheriff N = 20	Juvenile Court N = 13	Total N = 50
Aggravated assault; possibility of great harm; use of weapons	4.9	4.8	4.5	4.7
Child molesting	5.0	4.7	4.5	4.7
Forceable rape	5.0	4.6	4.6	4.7
Arson	4.9	4.6	4.5	4.7
Narcotics use (excluding glue)	4.8	4.5	4.5	4.6
Robbery	4.7	4.8	4.5	4.6
Drunk driving	4.0	3.6	3.8	3.7
Possession of dangerous weapons	3.9	3.6	3.5	3.7
Breaking and entering; burglary	4.4	3.7	2.7	3.7
Glue sniffing	4.0	3.5	2.8	3.5
Association with known narcotics users	3.9	3.4	2.9	3.4
Automobile theft	4.1	3.4	2.8	3.4
Non-forceable homosexual behavior	3.7	3.6	2.7	3.4
Probation violation; i.e., ineffective rehabilitation	3.7	3.6	2.5	3.3
Grand theft (greater than $50 and excluding auto)	3.7	3.4	2.5	3.3
Forgery (re: fictitious checks)	3.6	2.9	3.0	3.1
Runaway from correctional program	3.5	3.0	2.8	3.0
Assault and battery	3.5	2.7	2.9	3.0
Incorrigibility: defiance of teachers, parents and others	3.7	2.7	2.7	3.0
Damaging property; malicious mischief	2.8	2.4	2.3	2.5
Non-forceable heterosexual behavior	2.1	2.6	1.8	2.2
Liquor violations (possession, drinking)	2.4	2.2	2.2	2.2
Fighting: disturbing the peace	2.6	2.0	2.0	2.1
Runaway from home	2.6	1.8	1.8	2.1
Petty theft	2.8	1.7	1.9	2.1
Truancy from school	2.3	1.6	2.0	2.0
Gambling, loitering, improper companions	2.2	2.0	1.5	1.9
Driving without a license	1.5	1.8	1.8	1.7
Other traffic violations	1.8	1.2	1.6	1.5
Curfew violations	1.7	1.2	1.1	1.4
Smoking	1.1	0.5	0.3	0.7

An additional Kicks scale was developed which did not emerge from the factor analysis. In this scale, several items from the other four scales were combined to measure commitment toward activities, some of which were delinquent and some of which were non-delinquent, but all of which were concerned with pleasure-seeking.

The development of these scales seemed to bear considerable promise. The same data were collected from delinquents and non-delinquents in Utah and virtually identical clusterings of items were found (*cf.* Empey and Lubeck, 1968: 760–774). This was an important development because it implied some universality of response to peer activities in sharply different urban and rural situations. Comparisons on these scales revealed that the peer commitment items distinguished between delinquents and non-delinquents much more effectively than they distinguished between urban and rural boys in general, giving further substantiation to their possible relevance for the study of differences between delinquents and non-delinquents.

3. *Background Scales.* The large number of items of information collected on the social backgrounds of boys were also organized into various scales and indexes. In all, six different background scales were developed which covered a variety of different areas: school interest, academic performance, self-concept, aspirations, family relations, and work experience. Appendix II presents a detailed description of these scales and the methodology used in developing them.

In the main, these scales were used in much the same way as those that have already been described. For example, the School scale divided boys into different types based upon their interest in school, the grades they obtained, the extent to which they participated in extracurricular activities, their educational aspirations, and so on. These different types included, at one extreme, boys who were relatively successful and had high aspirations and, at the other extreme, boys who exhibited none of these characteristics. The other scales provided similar kinds of information in other areas.

Thus, the six background scales, in addition to those on offense history and peer influence, provided means by which to classify offenders and to determine in what ways background information might reflect upon the delinquency theory being tested and the programs under study.

4. *Personality Characteristics.* The Jesness Personality Inventory (1963), developed on California Youth Authority wards, was used as a fourth source of input data and served as a means of measuring the personality attributes of experimental and control boys. Efforts were made to determine whether these attributes were related in some way to past delinquent history, if they were helpful in measuring change, or if they were predictive in any way of those who succeed or fail in the experiment.

The inventory is comprised of nine basic scales that measure different dimensions of personality attributes. Jesness describes them as follows:

1. *Social Maladjustment* refers to a set of attitudes associated with unfulfilled needs, as defined by the extent to which an individual shares the attitudes of persons who demonstrate an ability to meet, in socially approved ways, the demands of their environment.
2. *Value Orientation* refers to a tendency to hold values characteristic of persons in a lower class.
3. *Autism* refers to a tendency in thinking to distort reality according to one's personal desires and needs.
4. *Alienation* refers to the presence of distrust and estrangement in a person's attitude toward others, especially toward persons representing authority.
5. *Affect* refers to an awareness of unpleasant feelings, especially of anger and frustration, a tendency to react readily with emotion, and perceived discomfort concerning the presence and control of these feelings.
6. *Withdrawal* involves a perceived lack of satisfaction with self and others and a tendency toward passive escape or isolation from others.
7. *Social Anxiety* is defined as the perceived emotional discomfort associated with interpersonal relationships.
8. *Repression* refers to the exclusion from conscious awareness of feelings and emotions that the individual would normally be expected to experience, or his failure to label these emotions.
9. *Asocialization* refers to a generalized disposition to resolve problems in social and personal adjustment in ways ordinarily regarded as showing a disregard for social customs or rules.

SELECTION OF A NON-DELINQUENT SAMPLE

As a means of assisting in the task of testing the causation theory, many of these input data were collected from a group of eighty-five non-delinquents who were students in a local high school in Los Angeles County. This sample of non-delinquents was selected because an examination of the causation theory simply could not be conducted on the delinquent sample alone. Before it could be said that theoretically defined variables were, in fact, related to the emergence of delinquent behavior, two things had to be demonstrated: (1) that the theoretically important variables were in fact exhibited by delinquents and (2) that these same factors did not occur as frequently or in the same patterned sequence among non-delinquents. It was for this latter reason that the non-delinquent sample was selected.

The non-delinquent sample was purposive rather than representative of all non-delinquents in Los Angeles County, since it was taken from a single high school. An effort was made, however, to make age, personal attributes, and racial breakdown similar to the delinquent population. All non-delinquents were 15½ to 18 years of age; 83 per cent were Caucasian, 15 per cent were Mexican–American, and 2 per cent were Oriental. No one was psychotic or seriously retarded. However, no Negroes were in attendance, limiting the sample in this respect.

The design used in this particular phase of the study was obviously non-experimental in nature. Since the propositions of the causation theory were stated in axiomatic form and since their test required comparisons between delinquent and non-delinquent groups, statistical rather than experimental controls were required. The non-delinquent sample suffered, however, from the same lack of external validity described earlier for the delinquent sample, since it was not randomly selected from some well-defined and larger population.

Measurement Design: Process

Research on *process* was the second major element of the measurement design. It had two fundamental contributions to make. First, it was a form of quality control. It provided a means of determining whether the experimental and control programs actually operated the way they were described on paper. Unless operation and design are consistent with each other, there would be no test of the actual change postulates.

The second contribution process research had to make was program description. Even though a concentration upon quality control might reveal whether or not a rigorous effort was made to implement the program, consistent with its conceptual design, it was also deemed important to have a careful understanding of the problems that were encountered and the issues that emerged. Furthermore, the experimental program was not a static and uniform entity, but was dynamic and changing in nature. It was important to document, as precisely as possible, the type of program that evolved.

In order to meet the need for quality control, a special social systems questionnaire was administered to staff and boys at both the experimental and the control programs. This questionnaire was designed to elicit the perceptions of boys and staff in both programs and whether they were consistent with theoretical design.

A second measure of quality control was conducted by means of a critical incident analysis. This analysis focused upon any significant incident arising in the experimental program: reports of actual delinquency, trouble at school, fights in the house, the administration of sanctions by staff or groups, or any other incident. The analysis sought to determine the nature of these incidents, how they were handled, whether staff and boys were able to collaborate or remained wide apart in their interpretations of them, and whether the program changed over time in its capacity to deal with these incidents. If, as hypothesized, the program were able to build a unified and cohesive social system, then there should be some evidence that boys and staff, working as a group, were able to develop new relationships for solving problems, exerting controls, and making decisions.

Closely related to the study of critical incidents was a study of sociometric relationships in the experiment: the way each boy was viewed by everyone else. The analysis examined the extent to which there were isolates and to which there were boys who were well accepted. The goal was to determine whether the position of an individual in the experimental program had any relationship to his perception of it and what impact it had upon him.

Finally, care was taken to provide a detailed description of the experimental program, not only internally but as it related to external systems such as families, the school, the courts and probation department, and to the community as a whole. One of the complaints heard most frequently is that experimental programs are not described in sufficient detail to permit their replication by others. Potentially valuable ideas and procedures are lost.

Measurement Design: Outcome

The third major element of the measurement design was a study of program *outcome*. As a first step in measuring outcome, recidivism rates were gathered. The official files of both the Central Juvenile Index of the Los Angeles County Sheriff's Department and the Los Angeles County Probation Department were used as a means of measuring law violations after release. Each source served as a check on the other and provided information on both "technical" (probation-office reported) and police arrests. This check of official files was conducted for a period of one year after all boys had been released from either program.

Recidivism rates were examined even though one school of thought suggests that their use at present is premature. The argument is that we have neither the knowledge to insure correctional success nor the ability to control the "categoric risks" (*cf.* Reckless, 1955: Chap. III); *i.e.*, the race, social class, or other community factors that are so crucial to the life of an offender after he leaves a program. Correctional outcome should not be measured in terms of recidivism simply because programs have so little direct control over the factors that determine correctional success.

There is also a persuasive counter argument. This argument points out that the reduction of delinquent behavior is the purpose for which correctional organizations exist. To ignore it, therefore, would be to ignore basic questions that would inevitably be raised about the experimental and control programs. Did they reduce delinquent behavior? Furthermore, joined with input and process, data on recidivism could help to indicate whether outcome rates were a function of the accuracy or inaccuracy of the basic assumptions made about delinquents (input) or the failure or the success of the staff in implementing the intervention strategy (process). Taken as a whole, therefore, recidivism rates as a part of the larger research package might have an important contribution to make.

The overall measurement design was such as to permit combined, as well as separate, analyses of input, process, and outcome data. As depicted in Figure 5.1, it was possible to determine whether there were any input or process variables that were related separately to outcome or whether there were chains of relationships that proceeded from input through process to outcome. Hopefully, the design would provide findings that would aid considerably in explaining the behavior of experimental and control subjects.

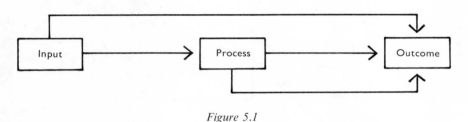

Figure 5.1

Finally, an analysis was made of the impact of the program upon the community. This analysis was largely descriptive and was concerned primarily with indicating the ways in which the program and its emergent problems were greeted by a number of external systems: the family, school, neighborhood, police, court and probation departments.

Summary of Research on Theory and Program

Figure 5.2 presents a summary of the research that was devoted to the two major objectives of examining delinquency theory and program operation. It will be observed, first, that offenders from Los Angeles County assigned to Boys Republic for institutional services constituted the population for the study. Second, in order to avoid the biasing effects of initial sample differences, this population was divided into experimental

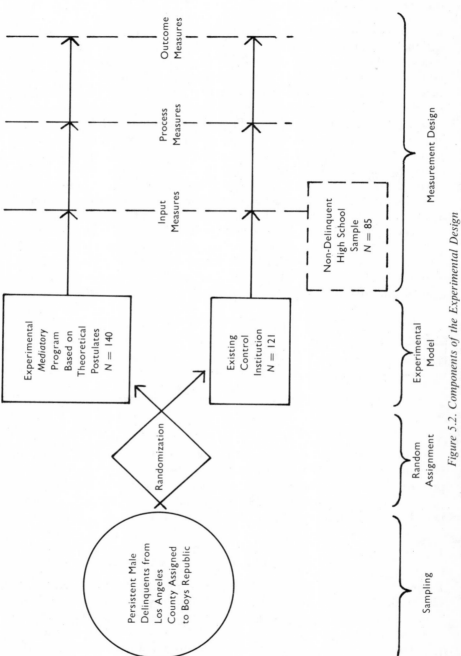

Figure 5.2. Components of the Experimental Design

and control groups through random selection. Third, three different kinds of data were collected: input data to reflect upon the assumptions made about offenders, process data to reflect upon the nature of the program itself, and outcome data to reflect upon its eventual impact. Input data were also collected from non-delinquents as a means of examining causation postulates.

Now, let us pay attention briefly to the steps that were taken to realize the third experimental objective of providing information on the problems and prospects of the FEM.

Information on FEM

The conduct of this experiment, it will be recalled, was concerned not only with the study of delinquency theory and control but also with the use of the FEM as a research tool. Let us consider this matter, first, in specific terms relative to the implementation of the measurement design just described and then in a more generic sense.

Insofar as the measurement design was concerned, a data collection schedule was set up much like the schedule for program operation. By adhering to it, it became a regular part of the operation of the FEM, a part about which delinquents as well as staff became aware. Just as an effort was made to develop a new set of norms regarding intervention, so an effort was made to develop a new set of norms regarding research. However, there was one important distinction between them.

While program operation had obvious and immediate consequences, especially for the boys, the consequences of research were longer-range in character. For that reason, the overall objectives of the experiment were shared with offenders and the problems that could occur were discussed. They were given to understand that research would play a neutral role. Because of the need for better knowledge, the objectives of research were to study the problems and processes of intervention, not to act as a judge or censor over whatever went on. Above all, what was desired was accurate information. While research was concerned with determining whether the intervention program could operate according to hypothesized design, it was not interested in interfering directly in individual cases. It was admitted that very serious problems might conceivably arise in which research people might have to intervene (*e.g.*, a serious crime or an obvious injustice), but such intervention was not their primary concern.

There is no way of knowing, of course, how completely delinquents accepted this point of view. However, there were some clues. Delinquents sometimes discussed the conduct of research in group meetings and it was not uncommon for boys who had been in the program for some time to explain the research schedule and procedures to new boys. In many ways, boys seemed to derive some pleasure from knowing that their points of view were important and that they might be able to contribute, even in the future, to the development of better programs. Furthermore, as will be seen in Chapter Eight, delinquents found themselves, along with research and other staff, defending the need for the experiment in public meetings. Experiences such as these, over time, tended to lead to rather substantial support by delinquents for the research effort. At least, it can be reported that throughout the life of the experiment there were no overt conflicts between research people and boys, and no instance in which there was outright refusal by a boy to participate in the research process.

In fact, problems of a reverse character sometimes occurred. Boys sometimes came to the research staff with problems for which they were seeking help. There were a few instances where boys approached researchers with the hope that they might sponsor them in group meetings and help to effect their release from the program. When events such as this occurred, research people were instructed to do two things: first, to avoid rejecting the boy, but, second, to explore with him the structure of the intervention program to see if the problem could not be handled there. Given the delicate nature of the relations between research and action, research people could not become "treaters" but only suggest ways for getting at basic problems. This was not always satisfying to the boy, of course, but it did help over time to define the position of relative neutrality that research had to occupy. While research people might join with boys and action staff to defend the importance of experimentation in the community, they could not become heavily involved in the internal workings of the program, *per se*, if they were to do a decent job of monitoring it.

Such problems were a part of the more generic issue of determining whether, given the overall structure of the FEM, action and research people, along with delinquents, could collaborate successfully in implementing the overall design. This was a complex task, involving not only the internal relations of people in the action-research unit itself, like those just described, but their relations to important external systems as well.

In the foregoing description of the research design in this chapter, reference was made on several occasions to research that would reflect not only upon the examination of theory and program but upon the adequacy of the FEM also. However, for the purposes of better understanding the problems of the FEM, two additional steps were taken: (1) a diary was kept on the problems that emerged and (2) an assessment was made of how they were handled. The data relative to these steps are presented in relevant chapters throughout the book and their implications examined. The concluding chapter is also devoted to that task.

A Concluding Comment

The role played by research in the conduct of this field experiment might best be summarized by repeating certain key distinctions. For those people, on one hand, who have been used to having research personnel play a totally detached role in planning and obtaining support for an innovation, it should be noted, in this case, that pattern was not followed. The research director, along with the director of Boys Republic participated in the hiring of personnel, in negotiations with external systems for support, in community meetings where opposition was encountered, and in feedback sessions to external as well as internal people. Thus, in addition to all of the technical, and more traditional, aspects of conceptualizing and conducting research, the conduct of the study involved participation by research personnel in many other activities as well.

On the other hand, when it came to the actual conduct of research, an attempt was made to have research people play a more traditional neutral role. But rather than leaving the conduct of that role to the vagaries of fortune, an effort was made to include it as an important part of the overall model. This involved plans to develop and structure it in much the same way as any other program component is structured, except that in this case it was an integral, rather than vestigal, part of the total experimental mosaic.

It is for these reasons that some attention was paid in this report to a long list of traditional problems which included whether the research could be conducted objectively; whether conflicts between action and research were disruptive; how the research may have posed insoluble conflicts for delinquents; and the ways in which external pressures may have thwarted the objectives of the FEM.

References

BECKER, HOWARD S. 1963. *Outsiders: Studies in the Sociology of Deviance.* New York: The Free Press.

CAMPBELL, DONALD T. 1957. Factors relevant to the validity of experiments in social settings. *Psychological Bulletin,* 54, 4 (July): 297–312.

DURKHEIM, EMILE. 1962. *The Rules of Sociological Method.* New York: The Free Press.

EMPEY, LAMAR T., and STEVEN G. LUBECK. 1968. Conformity and deviance in the "situation of company." *American Sociological Review,* 33, 5: (October) 760–774.

ERIKSON, KAI. 1962. Notes on the sociology of deviance. *Social Problems,* 9 (Spring): 307–314.

JESNESS, CARL F. 1963. Redevelopment and revalidation of the Jesness Inventory. Research Report Number 35, California Youth Authority (November).

KERLINGER, FRED N. 1965. *Foundations of Behavioral Research.* New York: Holt, Rinehart and Winston.

KITSUSE, JOHN. 1962. Societal reaction to deviant behavior. *Social Problems,* 9 (Winter): 247–256.

RECKLESS, WALTER. 1955. *The Crime Problem,* 2nd ed. New York: Appleton–Century–Crofts.

ROBINSON, W. S. 1957. The statistical measurement of agreement. *American Sociological Review,* 22 (February): 17–25.

WIGGINS, JAMES A. 1968. Hypothesis validity and experimental laboratory methods. In Hubert M. Blalock and Ann B. Blalock, Eds., *Methodology in Social Research.* New York: McGraw–Hill.

PART III

Results: Testing Theory and Strategy

CHAPTER SIX

Examination of Delinquency Theory

Three things can legitimately be asked of any empirical theory. First, the theory should have sound logical structure. That is, its postulates should be connected in such a manner that a number of claims or assertions can be derived from them by means of logical inference or deduction. Second, the theory should have operational significance. Some of its terms should be related by rule to observable data so that its meaning is clear and its claims can be tested by evidence and experience. Third, the theory should have high congruence with the world of experience. Its major claims should be generally consistent with the preponderance of relevant factual evidence. When these three requirements are met, the theory can be used successfully for pragmatic purposes (Schrag, 1962: 167).

Schrag's criteria for assessing the adequacy of any theory are highly relevant to a field experiment of this type. In prior chapters we have been concerned with both the logical and pragmatic adequacy of the theory upon which the experiment was based. In this chapter, we intended to go into its operational and empirical adequacy.

Our examination of the theory was cast into a framework of exploration rather than justification. Had we employed a stringent justificatory stance, our sole concern would have been with testing the truthfulness or falsity of the theory, and our evaluative choices in examining each of the postulates and theorems would have been virtually dichotomous: reject or fail to reject. But, by adopting an exploratory stance, our strategy was much less restricted. It permitted greater choice with respect to our concern for developing theory as well as testing it. If certain aspects of the theory were not corroborated by our data, then we might want to devote our attention later to a reformulation of it.

Such an exploratory stance has implications for delinquency control as well as for the more academic task of building knowledge. As indicated in Chapter One, it is rare that the underlying assumptions of any given correctional program are subjected to logical and empirical scrutiny. The lamentable consequence is that programs continue to operate even though their practices may be unrelated to the problems they are supposed to correct. Thus, in terms of this experiment, or any other correctional program, an examination of basic assumptions is highly important because it might (1) indicate inaccuracies in the assumptions upon which the program was based and (2) suggest new assumptions which might be productive of program improvement.

The examination of theory is also important from a broader scientific perspective. Even the most grandiose and elegant theories are useless if they do not correspond to empirical fact. Although both theory and fact are important to the acquisition of knowledge, neither is sufficient by itself. Just as it is possible to produce a morass of empirical facts that are not in any way connected by deductive logic, it is also possible to produce highly logical theories which are untrue in relation to available evidence. In the interest of general, scientific knowledge, therefore, it was deemed important in this study to examine the correspondence of the causation theory with the characteristics of the delinquent and non-delinquent samples that were involved in it. It was hoped that our exploratory stance might not only pave the way for more effective intervention by correctional programs, but might also contribute to the more general goal of scientific knowledge and theory-building.

Use of Non-Delinquent Sample

Before proceeding to the examination of the theory, one further point needs mention. It will be recalled that, in order to examine the causation theory, data were collected from a sample of eighty-five non-delinquents in a local high school as well as from the delinquent subjects in the experiment. Although it would have been desirable to have had a larger and more representative sample of non-delinquents, the available resources—staff, time, and money—simply did not permit its acquisition. Consequently, we took the next best step and purposively selected a sample of non-delinquents whose age distribution corresponded generally to our delinquent sample. This, at least, provided a comparison group with which to examine our theoretical statements. The characteristics of the non-delinquent sample and the procedure by which it was selected will not be repeated here since both areas were discussed in Chapter Five.

Operationalization of Basic Concepts

The first step in examining the theory was the development of operational definitions for its basic concepts. It will be recalled that the five major concepts used to construct the theory were: "social class," "achievement," "strain," "identification with delinquent peers," and "delinquency." Definitions were needed by which these concepts could be operationalized in concrete terms.

Social class was defined as an ordinal concept, used to denote groups of individuals who share similar attributes along a socioeconomic continuum. In operational terms, our measure of social class consisted of a scale with ten categories on which the prestige of each subject's father's occupation was ranked. The ascribed or inherited social class of each boy, as defined by his father's occupational prestige, was measured in this way.[1]

Achievement was defined as the attainment of goals, through legitimate means, that are endorsed and defined as important by society. For the adolescent, achievement in school is of primary importance. For that reason, achievement was measured in terms of school grades, awards at school, and participation in extracurricular activities. Work achievement was also measured. The number of jobs each subject had held during his lifetime was enumerated.

In precise operational terms, our measures of achievement were as follows:

A. Did subject ever win an award at school?
    1. No
    2. Yes
B. Number of extracurricular activities participated in at school.
    1. None
    2. One
    3. Two or more
C. Grade point average at school.
    1. Less than average grades, D or F.
    2. Average and above average grades, A, B, or C.
D. Number of jobs held during lifetime.
    1. None
    2. One or two
    3. Three or more

Strain was the third major concept. It was defined earlier as having two major components: (1) a detachment or disaffection from societal institutions and (2) a dynamic state of tension that involves a need for resolution.

1. For a precise description of this operational measure, as well as the steps taken to construct it, see Empey, 1956: 703–709.

However, because of the complexities inherent in attempting to define and measure strain couched in intrapsychic terms, we chose largely to use behavioral indicators. We attempted to measure strain in relation to school and work. In operational terms, our measures were as follows:

A. Did subject ever drop out of school?
   1. No
   2. Yes
B. Was subject ever fired from a job?
   1. No
   2. Yes
C. How smart did subject feel in comparison with others his own age?
   1. Smarter than average
   2. Average
   3. Less smart than average
D. What were the subject's perceived chances of attaining his vocational aspirations?
   1. Better than average
   2. Average
   3. Less than average

Identification with delinquent peers was the fourth concept. It referred to the process of internalizing the norms and beliefs, the subcultural standards of specific delinquent groups. Identification occurs when the individual makes the delinquent aggregate a primary reference group. Scales were constructed to measure peer group identification along the following four dimensions:

A. A *Ratfink* scale measured whether boys would inform on their friends to teachers, parents, or the police
B. An *Ace-in-the-Hole* scale measured whether boys would hide their friends in time of trouble
C. A *Deviancy* scale measured whether boys would go with friends to participate in activities of a delinquent nature
D. A *Sociability* scale measured whether boys would go with friends to participate in activities that were of a social but non-delinquent nature.

A detailed operational definition of these scales may be found in Appendix II and Chapter Five.

Delinquency was defined as the commission of an illegal act (or acts) which resulted in the official adjudication of the actor as delinquent. For the purposes of examining the theory, boys were divided into two groups: those who were officially adjudicated as delinquents and those who were not. Thus, our operational definition of delinquency was a simple dichotomy, based on official definition.

Measurement of Relationships

Goodman and Kruskal's *Gamma* (Goodman and Kruskal, 1954: 732–764; Costner, 1965: 347) was used to measure the relationships among the operational measures of the theory. The absolute value of *gamma* has a "proportional reduction in error" interpretation that enables the researcher to determine how much error is eliminated in predicting the rankings of a given variable through knowledge of the rankings of a second variable. For example, social class was postulated as an important determinant of adolescent achievement. How accurate is that postulate? *Gamma* helps to answer that question by indicating how much error is elimated in predicting rankings of achievement for a group if their class levels are known. It will also provide some indication of the degree to which achievement remains unexplained, even if class levels are known.

In terms of its other values as a measure of association, *gamma* was also chosen (1) because all of our operational measures were dichotomous or in rank-order form, and (2) because the *gamma* coefficient yields a relatively clear and unambiguous operational meaning when compared with other ordinal-based measures of association.

Examination of Postulates

The examination of empirical findings will be assisted by first recalling the theory in its entirety. As stated in Chapter Two, it was as follows:
Postulates:
I.   The lower the social class, the lower the subsequent achievement.
II.   Decreased achievement results in increased strain.
III. Increased strain results in high identification with delinquent peers.
IV.   Identification with delinquent peers results in delinquency.
Theorems:
I.   The lower the social class, the higher the subsequent strain.
II.   Decreased achievement results in increased identification with delinquent peers.
III. Increased strain results in delinquency.
IV.   The lower the social class, the higher the subsequent identification with delinquent peers.
V.   Decreased achievement results in delinquency.
VI.   The lower the social class, the higher the subsequent delinquency.

The findings regarding these postulates and theorems are presented in two ways. First, they are presented in their entirety in Table 6.1. This table is a correlation matrix showing all of the *gamma* coefficients used to measure each relationship expressed in each statement of the theory. As an aid to the reader in examining this table, the following things should be noted:

Table 6.1. Correlation Matrix for Total Set of Operational Measures

	ACHIEVEMENT				STRAIN				PEER IDENTIFICATION				
	2 School grades	3 School awards	4 School activities	5 Number of jobs	6 School dropout	7 Fired from job	8 Smartness	9 Vocational chances	10 Ratfink	11 Ace-in-the-hole	12 Sociability	13 Deviancy	14 Delinquency
1. Social class	−.02*	.01	.15	−.15*	−.10	.13*	.00	.19	.08	.04*	−.01	.01*	−.07
2. School grades					−.76	−.29	.51	.23	.03	.26*	−.06	−.09	−.72
3. School awards					−.15	.10*	.41	.28	−.03*	−.13	.00	.02*	.02*
4. School activities					−.29	.05*	.30	.15	.01	.04*	−.03	.06*	.01*
5. Number of jobs					.46*	.57*	.04	.16	.15	.23*	.22*	.24*	.45*
6. School dropout									−.12	.31	.23	.22	.76
7. Fired from job									−.21	−.03*	−.08*	−.12*	.61
8. Smartness									−.07*	−.16	−.19	−.06	−.26
9. Vocational chances									.03	−.10	.01	−.06	−.31
10. Ratfink													.15
11. Ace-in-the-hole													.60
12. Sociability													.28
13. Deviancy													.49

Block theory labels (as positioned in the matrix):
(Postulate I) — row 1 × Achievement (cols 2–5)
(Theorem I) — Achievement × Strain, upper; (Postulate II) — Achievement × Strain, lower (cols 6–9)
(Theorem IV) — row 1 × Peer Identification; (Theorem II) — Achievement × Peer Identification (cols 10–13)
(Postulate III) — Strain × Peer Identification (rows 6–9, cols 10–13)
(T VI) — row 1, col 14; (T V) — row 5, col 14; (T III) — row 9, col 14; (P IV) — rows 10–13, col 14

P = Postulate.
T = Theorem.
* = gammas whose directions (or signs) are contrary to theoretical expectations.

1. The total set of coefficients used to represent each postulate and theorem in the table are enclosed within double lines.
2. A negative sign in front of a coefficient indicates an *inverse* relationship; *i.e.*, a high value on one measure is associated with a low value on the other. The absence of a negative sign indicates the reverse; *i.e.*, a *direct* relationship in which high values are positively related.
3. An asterisk (*) following a coefficient indicates that its sign was contrary to theoretical expectations; *i.e.*, an inverse relationship was observed when the theory led us to expect a direct one, or *vice versa*.

Second, the specific findings regarding each postulate and theorem are taken from Table 6.1 and presented separately. The following are the criteria that were used in determining whether any particular theoretical statement was supported, or not supported, by the data.

1. The sign of each coefficient was examined to see whether it was commensurate with, or contrary to, theoretical expectations. If, for example, the theory specified that a given relationship should be inverse and its respective coefficient was direct or positive, then the coefficient would not be supportive of the theory.
2. An arbitrary cutting point of .20 was used in deciding whether any particular *gamma* coefficient was acceptable, by itself, as supporting a particular postulate or theorem. If the absolute value of any single coefficient did not exceed this figure, it was not considered supportive of the theory.
3. The total context of the findings, however, was also considered. That is, both the signs and magnitudes of all coefficients used to test a particular statement were taken into account. For example, in some cases the magnitudes of the various *gamma*s taken singly, did not reach the acceptable cutting point of .20. However, when they were considered in total, it was often the case that all, or most, of their signs conformed to theoretical expectations. When this occurred, it could not be ignored. The total configuration of both sign and magnitude for a series of coefficients had to be taken into account.

The following examination of each theoretical statement will take these three criteria into account.

Postulate I: The lower the social class, the lower the subsequent achievement.
This postulate received virtually no support from the data. It specified that social class and achievement are directly or positively correlated; that is, the lower the social class, the lower the achievement and vice versa. The findings, however, revealed two serious flaws in this postulate. First, the signs of only two of the four *gamma* coefficients conformed to expectations; social class was directly associated with "number of extra-

curricular school activities" (*gamma* = .15) and with "school awards" (*gamma* = .01). Contrary to expectation, however, there was a slight inverse relationship between social class and "school grades" (*gamma* = −.02) and between social class and "number of jobs" (*gamma* = −.15).

Second, and perhaps more important, all *gamma* coefficients failed to exceed the arbitrarily selected cutting point of .20. They were so low that the explanatory value of social class in accounting for differential levels of achievement was extremely limited.

Finally, the overall configuration combining both the signs and magnitudes of the coefficients was ambiguous, certainly not in support of the postulate. Thus, the data for the samples included in the experiment did not support the statement that lower social class results in decreased achievement. Furthermore, it should be noted that this finding is not due to some peculiar quirk in the class distribution of this delinquent population. The class level was weighted toward the bottom of the status ladder. About one-half of the subjects came from families in which the occupation of the father was an unskilled, semiskilled, or service worker, approximately a third from families of skilled workers (electricians, carpenters, machinists), small businessmen, and clerical jobs, and only about one-fifth from families of parents who were from the more prestigious business and professional occupations. The non-delinquent sample included about 7 per cent fewer in the lower status group, 10 per cent more in the middle group, and about the same in the upper group.

Postulate II: Decreased achievement results in increased strain.

This postulate received moderately high empirical support. The signs of twelve of the sixteen *gamma*s used to test it were in the direction specified by the postulate, while the signs of the remaining four *gamma*s were opposite to theoretical expectations. Of the twelve *gamma*s whose signs were commensurate with expectations, eight had absolute values that exceeded the .20 cutting point. These eight coefficients, ranked in order of magnitude, were as follows:

School Grades and School Dropout	= −.76
School Grades and "Smartness"	= .51
School Awards and "Smartness"	= .41
School Activities and "Smartness"	= .30
School Grades and Fired from Job	= −.29
School Activities and School Dropout	= −.29
School Awards and Vocational Chances	= .28
School Grades and Vocational Chances	= .23

These eight coefficients tended to support the postulate by indicating that boys who made low school grades were most likely (1) to have dropped out of school, (2) to have low self-evaluations in terms of smartness as compared to their peers, (3) to have been fired from a job, and (4) to have felt that their chances for achieving their vocational aspirations were low. Boys who had never won an award at school were also likely to have a low smartness self-evaluation and to have felt that their vocational aspirations would not be fulfilled. Boys who were less likely to have participated in extracurricular school activities had lower smartness self-evaluations and were likely to have dropped out of school. The evidence suggested, therefore, that lack of achievement was related to certain types of strain.

There were four coefficients whose signs did not violate theoretical expectations, but whose values were under .20. They were as follows:

Number of Jobs and Vocational Chances = .16
School Activities and Vocational Chances = .15
School Awards and School Dropout = −.15
Number of Jobs and Smartness = .04

Although some of these coefficients came close to the cutting point, they were not sufficiently high to meet the .20 criterion. However, the fact that their signs conformed to expectations could not be ignored in terms of the overall configuration criterion.

On the other hand, two *gamma* coefficients, each dealing with job stability, had signs that were not only *contrary* to theoretical expectations but exceeded the .20 cutting point. They were:

Number of Jobs and Fired from Job = .57
Number of Jobs and School Dropout = .46

The provocative thing about these two *gamma*s is that they involve "number of jobs," which was used as a measure of achievement. But contrary to expectation, a history of having held jobs seemed to be associated, *not* with achievement, but a failure to achieve. Rather than revealing a success pattern, those boys who had held large numbers of jobs were most likely to have been fired from a job, and to have dropped out of school. Thus these data seem to reflect less on the postulate that decreased achievement leads to strain than on the invalidity of using "number of jobs" as an operational measure of achievement. They seem to suggest that "number of jobs" may be more an indicator of strain than of achievement; namely, that boys who dropped out of school were also more likely to have worked. Furthermore, the fact that having held a number of jobs was correlated rather highly with being fired from a job may indicate that this was but another arena in which they had failed rather than achieved. The use of "number of jobs" as a measure of achievement is apparently inappropriate.

There were two remaining coefficients whose signs were also contrary to expectations, although their magnitudes were less than .20. They were:

School Awards and Fired from Job = .10

School Activities and Fired from Job   =   .05
Yet, even though these *gamma*s offered no support for the theory, their
coefficients were so low that they did not tend to constitute a major
contradiction to it either.

In terms of all three criteria, then, there was greater rather than less
support for the postulate that decreased achievement results in increased
strain. It seemed to have moderate support.

*Postulate III: Increased strain results in increased identification with
         delinquent peers.*

This postulate received a somewhat lower degree of empirical support.
Only four of the sixteen *gamma* coefficients between our operational
measures of strain and the peer identification scales—Ratfink, Ace-in-the-
Hole, Deviancy, and Sociability—were above the .20 cutting point and
possessed signs that did not contradict the postulate. These correlations,
ranked in order of their absolute magnitudes, are:
School Dropout and Ace-in-the-Hole   =   .31
School Dropout and Sociability   =   .23
School Dropout and Deviancy   =   .22
Fired from Job and Ratfink   =   −.21
Dropping out of school, as an indicator of strain, was the measure most
consistently related to peer identification. Those boys who had dropped out
of school tended to have the highest scores on the Ace-in-the-Hole,
Sociability, and Deviancy peer scales. Those boys who had been fired
from a job were also among those least inclined to "rat" on their peers.

Despite being low, however, eight additional coefficients had signs that
were commensurate with theoretical expectations. Since these coefficients
did not contradict the postulate, they might be of some value in reflecting
upon its accuracy in terms of the total configuration criterion. They were
as follows:
Smartness and Sociability   =   −.19
Smartness and Ace-in-the-Hole   =   −.16
School Dropout and Ratfink   =   −.12
Vocational Chances and Ace-in-the-Hole   =   −.10
Smartness and Deviancy   =   −.06
Vocational Chances and Deviancy   =   −.06
Vocational Chances and Ratfink   =   .03
Vocational Chances and Sociability   =   −.01
The value of the total configuration criterion is illustrated when these co-
efficients are considered with others. First, the signs of twelve of the sixteen
coefficients are supportive of it. Second, two of the eight coefficients were
near to the .20 cutting point, lending some further support to the postulate.

Finally, those coefficients that made the cutting point, when combined with those that did not, reveal certain substantive configurations that help to clarify the factors that seem to be related to peer identification. Three of the four *gammas* above the cutting point had to do with dropping out of school, suggesting that separation from school may contribute heavily to peer identification. Those boys who were separated from the atmosphere of this basic institution were more likely to identify with peer norms and activities that were of a deviant nature.

Strain produced through poor work adjustment ranked a weak second as a factor related to peer identification. Having been fired from a job was predictive of relatively high scores on the Ratfink scale. However, the questionable utility of work experience as a predictor in this theoretical framework is again illustrated, since three of the four relationships whose signs were contrary to theoretical expectation had to do with being fired from a job:

Fired from Job and Deviancy $= -.12$
Fired from Job and Sociability $= -.08$
Smartness and Ratfink $= -.07$
Fired from Job and Ace-in-the-Hole $= -.03$

The magnitude of all four of these relationships was slight and thus do not provide a major contradiction to the theory. Nevertheless, the anomalous character of poor work experience for this particular group, perhaps because of their age, is illustrated once again. Coupled with data presented earlier, these findings may indicate the presence of a group of boys among these delinquents who are unsuccessful at every endeavor: at school, at work, and with peers. The subject would seem to need further investigation.

In summary, the findings on this postulate suggest that the strain produced by poor institutional ties with school and work are an antecedent to peer identification. However, it is our feeling that the lack of definitiveness in these findings may be due as much to weaknesses inherent in the operational indicators of peer identification we used as to the lack of strong relationships. At least, the postulate should not be discarded until two weaknesses in these indicators are considered.

First, the measures could be seen as indicators of high peer identification without necessarily indicating high identification with delinquent peers. The fact that some of the indicators tend to reflect norms that are general in the adolescent population—*i.e.*, an unwillingness to fink on peers or a willingness to interact socially with friends—may diminish their utility as measures of delinquent identification.

A second problem with the indicators was their failure to separate the constraining influence of peers from the intrinsic appeal of the activities themselves—riding around, drinking, or stealing. The use of future indicators should take that fact into account. Thus, although the findings were supportive in a general way of the postulate that strain results in identification with peers, it could have received a better test.

Postulate IV: Identification with delinquent peers results in delinquency.

This postulate received a relatively high degree of confirmation. The *gamma* coefficients between the peer scales and delinquency were as follow:

Ace-in-the-Hole and Delinquency	=	.60
Deviancy and Delinquency	=	.49
Sociability and Delinquency	=	.28
Ratfink and Delinquency	=	−.15

Three of these coefficients were well above the cutting point and the signs of none of them contradicted the basic postulate. Boys who were most likely to predict they would hide a friend in trouble (Ace-in-the-Hole), go along with friends in committing delinquent acts (Deviancy), engage merely in group activities of a social nature (Sociability), and refuse to "rat" on a friend (Ratfink) were those who had actually been in the most recorded difficulty.

Examinations of Theorems

Having exhaustively examined the relationships expressed in the basic postulates of the theory, we proceed to the next step, which involves examining the relationships expressed in the derived theorems.

Theorem I: The lower the social class, the higher the subsequent strain.

This theorem did not receive much empirical support. None of the four *gamma* coefficients exceeded the 0.20 cutting point, although two of them conformed to the sign expressed in the theorem:

Social Class and Vocational Chances	=	.19
Social Class and School Dropouts	=	−.10
Social Class and Smartness	=	.00

The *gamma* between social class and perceived chances of attaining vocational aspirations (.19) almost met the acceptable cutting point, but the magnitudes and signs of this set of coefficients taken as a whole were not supportive of Theorem I.

To this finding must be added the fact that the sign of one of the four *gammas* was opposite to theoretical expectation:

Social Class and Fired from a Job	=	.13

Thus, the evidence regarding this particular theorem does not meet any of the criteria defined as acceptable for a particular statement. What is perhaps of greater significance is the emergence of a trend in which social class, at least for this particular population, turns out to be a relatively poor predictor. It was a poor predictor of decreased achievement in Postulate I; it was a poor predictor here; and, as will be seen later, it is a poor predictor of other factors as well.

Theorem II: Decreased achievement results in increased identification with delinquent peers.

This theorem received very little, if any, empirical support. The signs of only eight of sixteen *gammas* used to examine it were in support of it. However, as will be observed, none of them exceeded the acceptable cutting point:

Number of Jobs and Ratfink	=	.15
School Awards and Ace-in-the-Hole	=	−.13
School Grades and Deviancy	=	−.09
School Grades and Sociability	=	−.06
School Grades and Ratfink	=	.03
School Activities and Sociability	=	−.03
School Activities and Ratfink	=	.01
School Awards and Sociability	=	.00

Of the remaining eight coefficients, whose signs were contrary, four did exceed the acceptable cutting point. They were:

School Grades and Ace-in-the-Hole	=	.26
Number of Jobs and Deviancy	=	.24
Number of Jobs and Ace-in-the-Hole	=	.23
Number of Jobs and Sociability	=	.22

The *gamma* coefficient involving school grades is difficult to explain, but the three coefficients involving "number of jobs" is but another reflection of the problems of using this measure as an indicator of achievement. It is further confirmation of the conclusion that having held a large number of jobs is more likely a symptom of strain than of achievement for this group of boys.

The remaining four coefficients had signs that contradicted the theorem but possessed extremely low coefficients:

School Activities and Deviancy	=	.06
School Activities and Ace-in-the-Hole	=	.04
School Awards and Ratfink	=	−.03
School Awards and Deviancy	=	.02

Thus, in summary, the contradictory nature of many of these signs, the low levels of the coefficients, and the anomalous character of the "number of jobs" variable provide a configuration that provided little support for the theorem. By itself, decreased achievement seems to have little direct relationship to increased identification with delinquent peers.

Theorem III: Increased strain results in delinquency.

This theorem received a high degree of support. All of the four *gamma* coefficients used to examine it exceeded the .20 cutting point and none of their coefficients contradicted theoretical expectations.

The coefficients, listed in decreasing order of magnitude, were:

School Dropout and Delinquency   =   .76
Fired from Job and Delinquency   =   .61
Vocational Chances and Delinquency   =   .31
Smartness Self-evaluation and Delinquency   = − .26

These coefficients provide the highest empirical support of any proposition in the theory. Along with evidence in support of Postulate II, "strain" appears to be crucial factor leading to delinquency for this particular population.

Theorem IV: The lower the social class, the higher the subsequent identi-
             fication with delinquent peers.

As was the case with other propositions involving social class, this theorem was not supported by the data. Only two of the four coefficients used to measure relationships between social class and the peer scales conformed to theoretical expectation and all coefficients were extremely low, ranging from .08 to .01. The highest coefficient, that between Social Class and the Ratfink Scale, favored the theorem; the lowest, between Social Class and the Deviancy Scale, was contrary. Thus, social class seemed to have little relevance, one way or the other, for peer identification.

Theorem V: Decreased achievement results in delinquency.

This theorem received questionable empirical support. Two of the four correlations used to examine it were well above the .20 cutting point:

School Grades and Delinquency   = − .72
Number of Jobs and Delinquency   =   .45

However, only the high relationship between school grades and delinquency conformed to theoretical expectation. The sign of the relationship between number of jobs and delinquency was contrary. This contradiction again reflects the operational difficulties stemming from using "number of jobs" as an indicator of achievement. Its inadequacies have been observed previously and will be observed later.

The signs of the remaining relationships contradicted theoretical expectations, but their coefficients were so low as to be of little relevance:

School Awards and Delinquency   =   .02
School Activities and Delinquency   =   .01

Thus, the single significant finding relative to this theorem is the strong and negative relationship between school grades and delinquent behavior. The lower the grades, the greater the delinquency.

Theorem VI: The lower the social class, the higher the subsequent delinquency.

The findings relative to this theorem were consistent with prior ones in which social class was involved: social class was a poor predictor. Although the coefficient used to measure the relationship of class to delinquency was consistent with theoretical expectation, its magnitude was only $-.07$, way below the acceptable cutting point of .20. This and similar findings on other postulates and theorems may be due to the measure of social class that was used; namely, the occupational status of the delinquent's father. But given the utility of this measure in the past, it is difficult to dismiss these findings totally because of it. The finding could also be due to the particular population of offenders included in this study, but the finding is of such consistency throughout that it merits further investigation elsewhere.

Recapitulation of Findings

The causation theory, as originally stated, received only partial support. The findings may be summarized as follows:
1. Social class was of little explanatory value (Postulate I and Theorems I, IV, and VI).
2. Decreased achievement was associated with increased strain (Postulate II), but there was little support for the idea that it is directly related, either to identification with delinquent peers (Theorem II) or to delinquency itself (Theorem V).
3. Increased strain was related rather strongly to identification with delinquent peers (Postulate III) and, what is more, the relationship of strain to delinquency received the greatest support of any proposition in the theory (Theorem III).
4. The relationship between peer identification and delinquency was also strong (Postulate IV). It was second in magnitude only to the relationship between strain and delinquency.

These findings are summarized graphically in Figures 6.1 and 6.2. In Figure 6.1 the *four* major postulates of the theory are displayed and with them are shown the correlations whose magnitudes exceeded the .20 cutting point. It will be observed that, except for the failure of social class to correlate with achievement, there is some support for the sequential steps postulated in the theory. Success or failure in school was associated with the presence or absence of social strain, social strain was associated with peer identification, and peer identification was associated with delinquency. However, it is obvious that some reorganization of the theory may be in order since so many of the operational measures had to be discarded because they failed to meet the minimal cutting point.

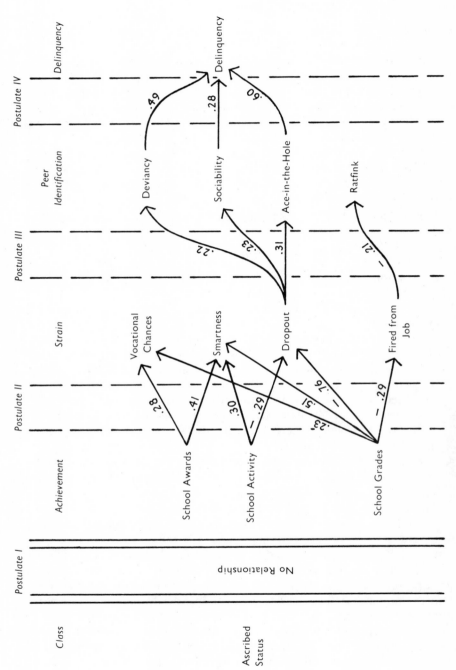

Figure 6.1. Summary of Correlations Supportive of Causation Postulates

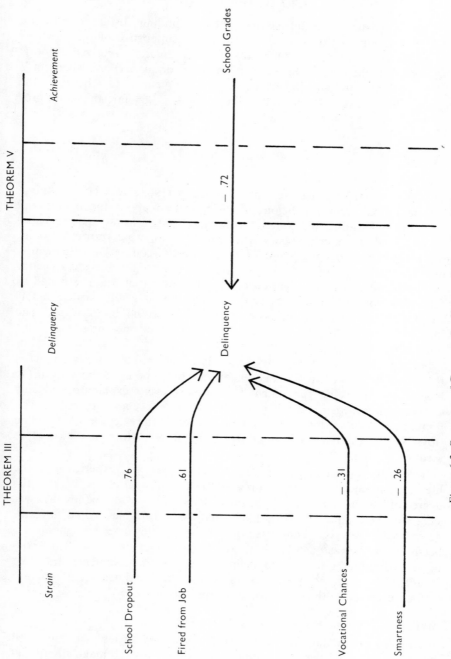

Figure 6.2. Summary of Gamma Coefficients Supportive of Theorems

This conclusion is strongly supported by the findings displayed in Figure 6.2. It summarizes the correlations that were supportive of the *theorems* above the .20 cutting point. Only two of the six theorems received support: Theorem III (the relation between strain and delinquency) and Theorem V (the relation between achievement and delinquency). Of the two, the relationship between strain and delinquency was, by far, the most pronounced.

Implications

IMPLICATIONS FOR THEORY

This theory did not meet several of Schrag's (1962: 167) criteria. First, in operational terms, questions might be raised about the operational measures of "strain" that were used. Because we had to test the sequential process leading to delinquency after the fact, we were restricted to indicators such as dropping out of school or self-concept. Consequently, our test was bereft of psychological indexes that might provide a clearer picture of the sense of alienation or powerlessness that was postulated as following from a lack of achievement. Likewise, as was indicated in this chapter, better measures of peer identification would be desirable. The inadequacy of these, and perhaps other operational measures, may have diminished the utility of the test.

Second, the test of the theory seriously questioned the heavy emphasis that has been placed in the theoretical literature upon membership in the lower class as being fundamental to almost every explanatory theme. Class membership in this analysis was of little explanatory value. The findings, of course, may be a function of characteristics peculiar to the Boys Republic population, but there were other factors that bear close scrutiny as well.

If delinquency is the cumulative product of a series of experiences in the life of the offender, as most theories suggest, then we could expect that the degree of association between class and delinquency would be low. As was suggested in Chapter III, it is likely that other variables would have far more predictive value. That was not only true in this case, but class membership, *per se*, was of little use in predicting any of the subsequent series of factors thought to lead to delinquency: low achievement, strain, or identification with delinquent peers. Thus, such findings seem to merit further attention both in constructing and testing theory.

IMPLICATIONS FOR CORRECTIONS

In terms of pragmatic adequacy, this test of theory strongly corroborated the argument that the assumption correctional people make about delinquents should be subjected to empirical test. If, as in this case, basic assumptions are faulty, then the failure of correctional programs to realize their objectives may be due to this condition. Before program operation could be improved, a better understanding of the problem would be required. Furthermore, the test of basic assumptions is important in a specific sense as well; that is, assumptions that may be appropriate for one particular group of offenders may not be appropriate for another. Some empirical verification would be important in almost every instance, not just in one or two isolated cases. The findings, then, illustrate the importance of making research a much greater part of operational strategies, not just on program operation and outcome but on basic assumptions as well.

IMPLICATIONS FOR FEM

This conclusion also suggests the likelihood that this particular field experiment could have been made far more efficient had a test of theoretical assumptions been conducted on the target population *prior* to the conduct of the experiment rather than as a part of it. The reasons are compelling. Since the number of subjects was small, basic assumptions could not be subjected to empirical test until all of the subjects had been processed and the experimental intervention completed. By that time, it was too late to revise the program strategy to make it more consistent with the problems that were being addressed. A pilot study prior to the experiment could have provided a much stronger empirical base upon which to build. Intervention principles could have been revised accordingly.

Because of the importance of reformulating both theory and strategy to make them more consonant with fact, that task will be undertaken after the rest of the findings have been presented. The reformulation will be presented in Chapters Seven and Eight.

References

COSTNER, HERBERT L. 1965. Criteria for measures of association. *American Sociological Review,* 30, 3 (June): 341–353.

EMPEY, LAMAR T. 1956. Social class and occupational aspiration: a comparison of absolute and relative measurement. *American Sociological Review,* 21 (December): 703–709.

GOODMAN, LEO A., and WILLIAM K. KRUSKAL. 1954. Measures of association for cross classification. *Journal of the American Statistical Association,* 49 (December): 732–764.

SCHRAG, CLARENCE. 1962. Delinquency and opportunity: analysis of a theory. *Sociology and Social Research,* 46, 2 (January): 167–175.

Implementation:
Consistency of Program Operation
with Theoretical Design

> The goal of social innovative experiments is to compare the effectiveness of new social sub-systems in solving a selected social problem. The social sub-system, which is the unit of research in experimental social innovation, can only be clearly understood in terms of its functional properties [e.g.] . . . the outcome of a sub-system is dependent upon the individuals who participate in it and the social context in which it is operative (Fairweather, 1968: 77).

This chapter is concerned with the operational aspects of the experimental program, whether it conformed to theoretical design, and what its basic problems were. It is often characteristic of correctional organizations that while staff members see themselves as operating consistently with their intervention guidelines, neither the offender population nor outsiders agree with that perception. It is also true that, without careful study of program operation, correctional organizations remain mysterious black boxes about which amazingly little is known. Consequently, the primary focus of this chapter will be upon the extent to which staff and offenders perceived the experimental program as operating according to theoretical design.

In order to conduct this analysis, a special questionnaire[1] was constructed

1. The questionnaire was based in part upon items developed and used initially by Wheeler (1961) in his study of socialization in correctional communities. We greatly appreciate the help his work provided.

and administered to staff and boys in both the experimental and control programs. The comparison of similarities and differences would help to indicate whether the experimental and control programs actually produced different perceptions and, further, whether those perceptions seemed consistent with program blueprints.

Measurement of Perception

The research questionnaire was designed to examine five major content areas, all of which reflected on the way in which basic intervention strategies were perceived.

1. The way the basic goals of experimental and control programs were seen, and whether they were concerned primarily with punishment, changing fundamental attitudes and values, education, discipline, or protecting the outside community.
2. Relationships between staff and offenders, and whether there was evidence of open communication and collaboration or whether relationships were characterized by social distance and unilateral staff decision-making.
3. The extent to which delinquent boys were inclined to play a reformation role, to indicate a willingness to help each other, and to adopt an anti-delinquent stance.
4. The way in which the rules and expectations of the two programs were seen and whether they were perceived as functional and helpful or arbitrary and meaningless.
5. Some perception of program sanctions, whether they were largely positive in character, emphasizing reward for desired behavior, or whether they were negative and focused primarily upon punishment.

The questionnaire was administered to 42 staff members and 127 boys at the control program at about the midpoint of the study. It was administered at approximately the same time to 8 staff members and 42 boys at the experimental program, except that it had to be administered on three successive occasions because not enough boys were in the program at any one time to obtain a sample of sufficient size for comparison with the control group.

This approach was possessed of all the problems inherent in any attempt to describe an organization, and interaction within it, by means of a questionnaire. Yet, more complex kinds of measures were difficult because this particular body of research was but one of a larger number of studies being conducted at the experiment. And, as mentioned in the chapter on research design, existing resources and competing demands made more elaborate methods infeasible. However, despite potential weaknesses, the findings of this chapter are suggestive and provide some corroboration for the findings of three successive chapters that utilize other methods for determining whether both programs operated according to design and what their problems were.

Perceptions of Goals

Boys and staff were asked to indicate how they perceived a series of abstractly stated correctional goals as these goals related to their respective programs. They were asked to indicate whether each goal was "important," "unimportant," or whether they were "undecided" regarding it. Their responses are displayed in Table 7.1 in terms of the percentage of each group that rated a given goal as "important." Several things about the findings are of significance.

Table 7.1. Perceptions of Correctional Goals

	Experimentals, %		Controls, %	
	Staff	Boys	Staff	Boys
1. To change the feelings or attitudes of boys so they can understand themselves better	100	91	98	71
2. To punish boys who have violated the law so they will not do it again	0	24	33	40
3. To provide training in discipline so that boys will learn to do what others want them to do	25	48	55	42
4. To protect the outside community	50	36	32	28
5. To train boys through education or work so that they will learn things they can use after their release	50	83	83	80

CHANGE *vs.* PUNISHMENT

First, although almost all staff members were in agreement in both programs regarding the importance of changing the feelings and attitudes of delinquents, more experimental than control boys rated this goal as "important." Thus, boys and staff in the experimental program were in greater agreement on this issue than were controls. Meanwhile, both staff and boys in the control program attributed greater importance to the goal of punishment than did those in the experimental program. The differences on this issue were even more striking than on the first, with none of the experimental staff *vs.* one-third of the control staff rating punishment as important, and only 24 per cent of the experimental boys *vs.* 40 per cent of the control boys so doing.

These two differences tend to conform to theoretical expectation, since by design there was greater emphasis in the experimental program on change and self-understanding, and since that program endeavored as well to reduce the strain produced by punishment when it becomes a major correctional goal. However, experimental boys did not always see the community program as a place in which change would be a goal they could adapt. If there was one thing they did agree upon, it was that when they entered the program, they did so with extreme resentment. They were very candid in testifying to that fact.

Said one, "When I first came here, I thought I was being shit on. I had already made up my mind that I was not going to let it affect me." Said another, "I thought it was just a place to serve your time. It was not until I had been here four months that I began to change my thinking." Their remarks all testify to the difficulties of obtaining collaboration from offenders and suggest that any ratification of change goals is likely to be a function of socialization in the program if it is to occur at all.

For that reason, it is worth noting that, although fewer control boys felt that a major objective of that program was change, seven out of ten did feel that way and, further, less than half of them (40 per cent) saw punishment as a major goal of their control program.

IMPORTANCE OF DISCIPLINE

The second interesting finding has to do with the disparity between boys and staff at both programs regarding the extent to which the learning of discipline is a major objective. While one-fourth of the experimental staff rated this objective as important, almost half of the boys did so. It seems likely that staff members may have underestimated the extent to which boys see staff emphasizing the importance of control and discipline and the extent to which the daily groups themselves emphasize this matter. This conclusion anticipates later findings, but it is one that will recur repeatedly in later chapters! Meanwhile, the figures were generally reversed for the control program, with more staff (55 per cent) than boys (42 per cent) rating this objective as important. Consequently, even though staff members in each program tend to vary between themselves on this matter, they also differ with the boys in their own programs as well.

If one looks at the daily routine that ultimately evolved in the experimental program, he may discover why almost half of the boys felt that discipline was an important objective. A tight and demanding schedule, not physical controls, may have been the reason. A group leader describes the program routine.

This may be a community program, but it does not provide a "normal" life, if by contrast one thinks of a total institution as "abnormal." We are somewhat more natural, but definitely not "normal."

The boys have breakfast here at 6:05 in the morning. It used to be later, but there was so much primping and hair combing that we had to make it earlier so they could leave for school at 7:30. They have to be there at 8:00. They also have some menial tasks to perform. Such tasks don't take more than 15 minutes, but it takes a helluva effort to get some of them done before the boys leave.

They buy their own lunches at school and stay there until they begin arriving home between 3:30 and 4:00. There is a supervised work period between 4:00 and 5:00. Not all boys work, however; often it is only those whom the group has put on work detail. Other boys have the hour free. In any event, there is a certain amount of work that must be done with this many people living together.

Then the group meeting is held from 5:00 to 6:30. This is the place where the greatest action is, where outside behavior is examined, problems, progress, and change are discussed. Sometimes it's a pressure cooker. This is one of the times boys have a chance to demonstrate that they mean what they say, because whatever goes on is the responsibility of all.

Dinner is at 6:30. Then nothing is scheduled on most nights until 8:00, when study period begins, and it lasts until 9:30. The tutor works here during that period. However, on Tuesday evenings, we have a group meeting for the whole house, which lasts from 7:15 to 8:15. Both small groups are brought together in an effort to maintain the house culture and to deal with whatever problems there are that involve everyone.

On Wednesday evenings, we also have a family group for those boys, and their families, who are having a lot of trouble. The boys who do not have family problems attend to their studies. Interestingly enough, we have had a lot of interest in these family groups, but I'm not sure whether it is because boys are interested in the groups or simply want to get out of studying. Some family problems were so great, though, that we just could not ignore them.

On Friday nights, right after dinner, boys who have not been restricted leave for the weekend. Those boys who are restricted are restricted for a number of reasons: failing in school, delinquency, or trouble at the house. They have a Friday night study session, and Saturday morning work. They leave when their work is done. It's their choice; it takes some of them until 5:00 P.M. Then everyone must return by 8:00 P.M. Sunday. Then the whole routine begins again.

One is struck by the high degree of regimentation in the program schedule that developed. But there are two sides to the question. On one hand, as the residence director argued,

I don't really see these demands as excessive. Oh, they're demands all right, but nothing like a prison or Marine Corps boot camp. Boys can, and do, make decisions; they are about as free as any other student who attends school; they do not march to and from school or any other activity; and they have their weekends at home. Remember also that our goal is to have boys out of here in a few months; this doesn't last forever. Beyond that, unless we can somehow get the whole society to change, the facts are that if boys are going to make it in school, or later at work, they're going to have to put up with routine. Who doesn't have routine?

What the residence director did not mention, however, is the problems that are introduced when one attempts to manage the lives of even twenty offenders in a common residence. They lead inevitably to greater regimentation, even in a setting like this. When asked about this he said,

> I do think you need to separate what I see as the reality of the daily routine that faces everyone, from the problems that correctional institutions create. I think, for example, that we create more problems than we can solve by having a residential program. Unless there is a compelling reason for such a program, such as dangerous offenders or psychotics, boys should live at home and come here each day on their own, and for a much shorter period of time. Then we could avoid some of this regimentation and, better still, do a better job of separating the problems involved in helping delinquents.

PROTECTION OF COMMUNITY

It seems likely that the differences between boys and staff regarding disciplined control, especially among experimentals, is also related to the issue of community protection. While boys see the issue in personal terms, staff define it in community terms. As one of the group workers put it:

> One thing I've thought a lot about recently is the fact that we did not anticipate the problems we were going to have. As time went on, we got more and more involved in outside forces. Community forces impinged on us and limited our own desires and needs, our desires to operate in an open way. This is particularly evident in our relations with the school. We have had to go more and more into the control function and less and less into what we said we were going to do originally.

Thus, more than any other group, the staff in the community program perceived "community protection" as an important goal. Further, experimental boys ranked second in this category.

The concern of experimental personnel with this matter, here and later, suggests somewhat paradoxically that community programs may, in the long run, develop greater concern for community protection than isolated places of incarceration which so often become preoccupied with institutional rather than community life. Whether this is "good" or not is another issue, but as one staff member put it, "It is realistic. It is not so much that we are asking for greater conformity by these boys, but that we are asking them to meet realistic problems that they will have to meet, wherever they are." This emphasis has merit in the sense that the problems about which he was speaking were almost always community-related. What his remarks do not reflect is the extent to which community demands may not always be the most "realistic" in terms of helping delinquents.

IMPORTANCE OF EDUCATION

Finally, Table 7.1 shows that, while everyone else (eight out of ten) ranks educational goals as important, only half of the experimental *staff* do. This general concern with education, except for experimental staff, is understandable in light of the emphasis placed upon school attendance by both programs. Yet the lesser concern by experimental staff probably reflects their tendency to become preoccupied (often overwhelmed) by the problems of maintaining controls in the open community and of changing delinquent points of view. In their concern for such matters, staff members, like teachers and parents, often become so involved that they tend to forget stated educational objectives. As one staff member put it, his concern was with "helping kids examine their behavior, how they get in trouble, what's behind getting in trouble, so that they have a chance to make some decisions as to whether or not they really want to go on getting into trouble or to make the kinds of changes that would help them stay out of trouble."

His comments are symptomatic, less of a conflict with the overall goals of the intervention strategy than of a conflict of subgoals within it. As originally stated, those goals emphasized both attitudinal and educational changes, as well as community linkage. Therefore, it appears that staff members may have been focusing differentially upon the first. In their concern for delinquent behavior, *per se*, they may have tended to forget the importance of other objectives. The delinquents, meanwhile, who found themselves in the school, and whose behavior while there was a focus of attention, found school hard to forget. Thus, for them, educational objectives seem to have taken on a different character. They were much more conerned about such matters.

Staff-Offender Collaboration

There was greater theoretical emphasis in the experimental program than in the control program upon removing the structural restraints that had traditionally blocked communication and collaboration between staff and offenders. Therefore, if that intervention guideline were implemented, there should have been greater evidence of collaboration and joint decision-making in the experimental program. Table 7.2, supplemented by additional data, presents the evidence regarding that issue.

There are two kinds of evidence in the table. The first is inherent in the

Table 7.2. Perceptions of Staff-offender Collaboration

	Experimentals, %		Controls, %	
	Staff	Boys	Staff	Boys
1. Staff personally keep boys informed about the operation of the program	88	63	66	54
2. Staff make changes in the program without consulting boys	75	33	57	38
3. If guys really want to, they can share in decisions about how this place is run	100	73	68	61
4. This place is pretty much split into two different groups with staff in one and boys in the other	0	17	42	46
5. The boys around this place have pretty much their own private set of rules	12	26	58	44

initial three items, which suggest a rather small but consistent tendency for staff and offenders in the experimental program to perceive a greater sharing of information and decision-making than those in the control program. The only exception is among experimental staff who feel that *they* make too many changes without consulting boys. A guess would be that this belief is a function of higher expectations, among control staff that this is what *should* be done. Overall, however, this finding is buttressed by four additional questionnaire items (not included in Table 7.2) of a different order.

1. Who makes most of the rules around here?

	Experimentals, %		Controls, %	
	Staff	Boys	Staff	Boys
Mostly staff	25	33	46	44
Mostly boys	0	7	0	11
Staff and boys together	75	57	54	32
Undecided	0	4	0	14

2. Who decides when a boy goes home?

	Experimentals, %		Controls, %	
	Staff	Boys	Staff	Boys
Mostly staff	25	6	45	25
Mostly boys	0	26	2	13
Staff and boys together	75	66	50	53
Undecided	0	2	2	9

The first two are concerned with the making of rules and decisions, and both conform to theoretical expectation. There is added support in the questionnaire responses for the notion that staff and boys in the experimental program perceived greater sharing of responsibility than in the control program.

Two related items are also supportive of this general picture. They suggest that both staff and offenders in the experimental program are more inclined to express a greater overall interest in boys than at the control program and that, when rules are made, they are made for the benefit of all, not just staff.

1. Do you feel that members of the staff are really interested in boys or are they just doing their job?

	Experimentals %		Controls %	
	Staff	Boys	Staff	Boys
Really interested	75	54	49	32
Only some interested	25	39	51	50
Just doing their jobs	0	7	0	18

2. When decisions and rules are made, who usually benefits from them?

	Experimentals %		Controls %	
	Staff	Boys	Staff	Boys
Mostly staff	0	7	15	24
Mostly boys	12	33	37	36
Staff and boys	88	54	49	30
No one	0	7	0	10

These findings lend support to the notion that experimental guidelines favoring collaboration and the reduction of strain for delinquents were actually implemented, at least to some degree. Furthermore, they are strongly reinforced by the last two items of Table 7.2, which may be the most significant items of all. These items indicate that, in sharp contrast to staff and boys in the control program, far fewer experimentals perceived that their organization was split into two different and competing groups or that boys in the experimental program had a private set of rules that would indicate the existence of a deviant inmate subsystem. In other words, there was far less evidence of competing inmate and official systems in the experimental program.

One might conclude, as a result, that in contrast to the control program, significant movement was made in the experimental program toward the achievement of a more collaborative and unified system. Yet a note of caution is in order. Although there were greater signs of collaboration and shared decision-making in the experimental program (Table 7.2), such findings are not especially surprising in light of both the size and traditional character of the control program. As one boy at the control program put it,

> At Boys Republic you could . . . Jesus Christ, you could have a serious problem, but with only one counselor for twenty or thirty guys and one psychiatrist for 130 guys, you know they can't get around to you. They don't have time to talk to you. They just jack you up and they don't help you with your problems or anything. You could go all the way through Republic easily and never have your problem solved. All you'd have to do is act pretty good and get around 80 progress reports, pass in school, maybe play a sport or two, and you would get out pretty easy. Your problem would have never had to be solved at all. You'd have the same problem when you got out.

Under such conditions, one would expect evidence of less communication and greater social distance in a total institution of larger size. At the same time, an experimental boy put his finger on one of the benefits that would seem to be inherent in a smaller system.

> I thought when I first came in this program that the supervisors and the older boys acted like a bunch of pricks. Now I see there is really a lot of human in them.
> I also found out why they seemed to have something going together that I couldn't understand at first. I found out that it is one of the hardest things to do to change. There are so many things to overcome and it gets too discouraging if no one knows you are changing day and night and you need the other guys to do it.

Closer relationships in the experimental program did turn out to be of benefit to this boy, but the basic question still remains as to whether it was helpful for all. This part of the analysis cannot answer that question, but subsequent chapters do speak to it and they indicate that much more must be achieved before joint problem-solving in the experimental program can be made more effective for all boys. Even though there was evidence that the experimental system conformed in some general ways to theoretical design, it was considerably less than perfect in achieving desired outcome.

The Reformation Role

A related question asks whether experimentals, more than controls, were willing to play a reformation role. Besides seeming to enjoy greater communication with staff, were experimentals also more willing to act as reformers with their peers? Were they willing to play the more difficult role of trying to change and help others? Developing a system in which delinquents played a more active role was every bit as important, theoretically, as developing one in which communication was increased.

The evidence in Table 7.3, while supporting an affirmative answer, is not as strong in that support as it might be. Instead, it suggests that while experimental boys seemed much less likely than controls to try to beat the system or to play a delinquent role in the organization (items 4–5), they were not more strongly inclined to play a reformation role (items 1–3). In other words, while the experimental program seems to have diminished the tendency for an inmate system to develop, it did not seem to be exceptionally more successful than the control program in involving boys in a mutual reformation process.

Table 7.3. Perceptions of Reformation Role played by Boys

	Experimentals %		Controls %	
	Staff	Boys	Staff	Boys
1. Boys personally keep other boys informed about the operation of the program	88	78	95	72
2. Boys talk to other boys about personal matters such as the way they behave, talk, dress	100	83	93	65
3. Boys personally tell other boys when they disapprove of what they have done	75	80	74	73
4. There are too many boys here who push other boys around	0	28	36	62
5. Most boys here are interested in just getting by while they are here	12	24	38	53

One difficulty with this conclusion, however, has to do with the nature of the items in Table 7.3. On such issues as keeping other boys informed about the operation of the program or disapproving of them when they do something you don't like, it could be that the general similarities between experimental and control boys were due to entirely different conditions. If, as Table 7.2 indicates, there was a stronger inmate system at the control program, then it may be that when controls indicated that they let other boys know when they disapprove of them or that they keep them informed on program operation, they are often doing so for delinquent rather than reformation purposes. Such could easily be possible in a total institution where inmate rather than official norms predominate. If that occurred, it would not be inconsistent with the finding that more control than experimental boys were inclined to push other guys around or to try just to "get by."

In contrast, since there was less evidence of an inmate system at the experimental program, it could be that the involvement of boys with each other took on a more positive character. It could be that when they informed each other about program operation, talked to each other about matters of behavior and dress, or expressed disapproval, they were doing so more from a reformist than a delinquent stance. If this were the case, then the findings would take on a much different tone.

By way of illustrating this possibility, consider the following two items:

1. How much do boys tell each other things they should do to stay out of trouble?

	Experimentals %		Controls %	
	Staff	Boys	Staff	Boys
A great deal	38	35	44	36
Some	62	48	44	39
Little or none	0	17	12	25

2. How much do boys put pressure on other boys to cover up trouble?

	Experimentals %		Controls %	
	Staff	Boys	Staff	Boys
A great deal	0	9	43	23
Some	63	18	43	40
Little or none	37	73	14	37

In much the same way as Table 7.3 results suggest, responses to the first of these two questions suggest that when boys (and staff) are asked how much boys do to help others stay out of trouble, few differences appear. But when they are asked how much pressure boys put on each other to *cover up* trouble, then the differences are great. The experimentals are less inclined to do so. It may be, therefore, that there are a number of control boys who, when they do work to help boys stay out of trouble, do so more from a manipulative than a reform standpoint.

An alternative interpretation would simply be that boys in both settings do relatively little by way of becoming active reformers. As a boy from the experimental program suggested, it is a tough thing to do.

Trying to help a guy is where . . . like you warned him, you know. I mean you just don't go and rat on him. You know what I mean? Like if I see a guy getting in trouble at school I'll probably tell him, 'You better hold that down.' But if I see him doing it again, I'm going to bring it up in group. But I mean just to go out and rat on someone, I don't go for that.

At the same time, there is no denying the persistence with which experimentals indicated an unwillingness to foster a delinquent subsystem or to cover up trouble, a tendency experimental staff may have underestimated. As an experimental boy put it,

> I've learned that withholding information like that [covering up a theft] hurts the other guys, and you get hurt too. It doesn't help at all if you hold information like that; it hurts everyone all the way around. Actually, if you are protecting the other guy because he's your friend, you're really not his friend. Because if he's your friend, you would give up that information and try to get him out of here as soon as possible and try to get yourself out of here sooner. I think most of the guys here now realize that because I know I do. From now on, if I find out anything I'm going to bring it up in group.

Despite such individual remarks, however, these data simply cannot answer the questions that have been raised. While the data suggest that experimentals were less willing than controls to foster an inmate subsystem, it is not clear that they were substantially more willing to perform strongly in a reformation role.

Perceptions of Rules

Part of the task of assessing the nature and influence of an organization has to do with the perceptions its members have of its norms and expectations. In this particular study, intervention guidelines suggested that experimental delinquents would be more inclined than controls to accept and reinforce norms if they had helped to develop them and thus would be perceived as more cooperative than authoritarian. Consequently, one aspect of this comparative study involved determining (*a*) whether, in fact, boys in the experimental organization perceived that they had participated in developing organizational norms and (*b*) whether they accepted those norms more readily than controls.

THE MAKING OF NORMS

The comments of the residence director regarding these issues help to clarify how norms were developed:

> When we first started, we didn't impose many rules. Most of them simply evolved, and those that did evolve tended to come as a result of problems. In some cases boys imposed their own norms and in others the staff tried to impose theirs. Then we began to find that this was not going to work too well because the problems simply did not go away. For example, right after we started this place, it became a hangout for all of the marginal girls in the whole damn region. It got so we couldn't eat our meals without interruption, some guys were on the phone constantly, and then Karl got in trouble at school with this girl who was about to be kicked out anyway. So what happened was we all finally concluded that if

we were going to stay in this neighborhood and get any work done, the parade of women had to stop. The place could not look like a male whorehouse. This kind of experience was repeated over and over and resulted in the kind of program we have today.

The responses to questionnaire items tend to confirm the director's description. More experimental than control boys not only perceived that they had participated in the development of organizational norms, but that they had shared in enforcing them.

1. Who makes most of the rules around here?

	Experimentals %		Controls %	
	Staff	Boys	Staff	Boys
Mostly staff	25	33	46	44
Mostly boys	0	7	0	11
Staff and boys together	75	57	54	32
Undecided	0	4	0	14

2. How much do boys in this program have to say about the kinds of rules that are made?

	Experimentals %		Controls %	
	Staff	Boys	Staff	Boys
A great deal	43	39	14	21
Some	57	45	64	47
Little or none	0	16	21	33

3. Who enforces the rules here?

	Experimentals %		Controls %	
	Staff	Boys	Staff	Boys
Staff	12	9	19	22
Boys	0	9	0	17
Staff and Boys	88	83	81	61
Undecided	0	0	0	2

Besides these differences between experimental and control boys, two other findings are worth noting. First, experimental staff also differed from control staff. They were more inclined than the latter to support the notion of cooperative norm-building and enforcement. Although significant numbers of the control staff said control boys had some say in the making of norms, their participation was apparently less active than in the experimental program.

Second, it is noteworthy that in two of the items, control boys, more than either their staff counterparts or experimental boys, said that they alone both made rules and enforced them. One cannot be certain as to the reason for this minority perception, but it is consistent with the previous

finding that there was a greater tendency in the control than in the experimental program for boys to be split into separate groups. The finding
suggests that at least a minority of control boys felt that it was they, and
not staff or staff and boys together, who made and enforced norms. Once
again, there seems to be evidence of an inmate system in the control
program.

ACCEPTANCE OF NORMS

Table 7.4 presents the data on the extent to which rules were perceived
negatively or positively. Several things are apparent. First, experimental
boys were more inclined than controls to view organizational norms in a
positive light and to reject the notion that those norms were nonsensical or
designed primarily to maintain control. The majority saw them as helpful.

Table 7.4. Perceptions of Program Rules

	Experimentals %		Controls %	
	Staff	Boys	Staff	Boys
1. Most of the rules here are helpful	75	63	92	46
2. This place seems concerned more with keeping boys under control than with helping them with their problems	0	15	10	31
3. Most of the rules around here don't make much sense to me	0	15	12	28

The picture for staff members, while essentially the same, had some
interesting variations. Nine out of ten of the control staff saw organizational
rules as being primarily helpful, with only one-tenth rejecting them as
nonsensical or concerned primarily with control. Experimental staff, by
contrast, while refusing totally to accept the idea that norms were negative,
still seemed to imply that more could be done to improve them, since only
three-quarters of them accepted existing norms as helpful. In this matter,
their replies were more mixed than control staff and may reflect the dynamic
and volatile character of the experimental system and perhaps a lack of
satisfaction with what they considered to be a disparity between theoretical
design and actual operation.

Finally, the fact should not go unnoticed that less than half of the
control boys perceived existing rules as helpful and that almost one-third
of them viewed rules negatively. They differed far more with control staff
on this issue than they did with experimental boys. Only half as many

control boys as staff felt that organizational rules were helpful. Such vast differences between experimental staff and boys did not appear.

Evidence of dissatisfaction with existing rules is relevant for two of the most difficult problems that confront correctional organizations. The first has to do with the general inability of programs to provide rules that are essentially *pre*scriptive in character—*i.e.*, rules that help people to know what they should *do* to deal with their problems—rather than rules that are essentially *pro*scriptive—*i.e.*, rules that tell them solely what they *should not* do. The former are solution-oriented, the latter control-oriented. Second, any set of rules requires an effective body of sanctions—rewards and punishments—by which those rules can be reinforced. Perhaps one of the reasons that the experimental staff was somewhat dissatisfied with existing rules, and both sets of boys were somewhat disinclined to play a strong reformation role, was due to these two sets of problems. As will be seen in the following section, for example, one of the most serious deficiencies of both experimental and control groups was their lack of positive re-inforcers, their lack of rewards for boys for new kinds of behavior. While both society and correctional programs stand ready with time-honored methods for punishing boys for any new trouble they get into, neither of them has rewards for *not* being delinquent. This could be a serious in-stitutional deficiency and will be discussed repeatedly in this and subsequent chapters.

Perceptions of Rewards and Punishments

As may be seen in Table 7.5, the data support strongly the conclusion just reached. Staff as well as boys were in virtual agreement that both stood ready to punish offenders for bad behavior but were much less inclined to reward them for good behavior. What is significant further is that, while staff were inclined to see themselves, if not boys, as rewarding good be-havior, the boys simply did not agree. Half or less of them perceived the existence of staff rewards for desirable activity, and, what may be worse, they perceived even fewer rewards from their peers.

These findings are especially significant for the experimental program because its intervention guidelines suggested that the development of a collaborative system—one in which boys have a significant voice—would not only reduce strain for them but would be intrinsically more rewarding. There would be positive support for any legitimate and helping behavior on their parts. Yet this goal was not achieved. Not only were experimental boys no more inclined than control boys to perceive the existence of staff rewards but perceived few rewards from their peers for non-delinquent activity. Their peers were even less inclined than staff to reward good behavior.

Table 7.5. Perceptions of Rewards and Punishments

	Experimentals %		Controls %	
	Staff	Boys	Staff	Boys
1. Staff punish boys for bad behavior	88	70	88	76
2. Boys punish other boys for bad behavior	75	85	69	75
3. Staff personally tells boys when they disapprove of what boys have done	100	74	86	67
4. Boys personally tell other boys when they disapprove of what they have done	75	80	74	73
5. Staff rewards boys for good behavior	63	50	83	43
6. Boys reward other boys for good behavior	37	30	33	25
7. Staff personally tells boys when they approve of what boys have done	75	48	86	50
8. Boys personally tell other boys when they approve of what they have done	67	51	62	50

As one reviews the unstructured comments of boys on their reactions to the major components of the program, he is struck by a series of ambivalent themes.

With regard to the group process: "I like it. Everyone has a responsibility in there. The guys make their own decisions. Yet, I'm kinda mixed. I didn't like it when the group was riding me, when they called me a liar. I disliked it, but it helped me."

With regard to the work: "The work helped me to stay out of trouble but it didn't help me solve my problems. I thought it was a chickenshit deal, especially when a work supervisor or the group put me on special work detail for something I did wrong. I think it's good when kids get caught for the things they do wrong, but the punishment bit don't make no sense to me."

With regard to school: "There are two things about this place that make me want to stay, freedom and broads. Anytime you get locked up, you don't have either. And school is a part of the whole scene; a guy needs an education and that's where the action is. The trouble is, I always feel like they're looking down on me at school. I know that Mr. A. don't want us there. We're a pain in the ass to him. And having to study every night is just too much. I'll never catch up."

Since staff members agreed with boys that there was little reward for good behavior, this set of findings is generally damning because it constitutes evidence of a failure on the part of the experimental system to implement a vital part of its intervention guidelines. Rewards for boys from delinquent peers for legitimate behavior were defined as one of the most important elements to be fostered.

This lack of peer support may explain the apparent unwillingness among many experimentals to play a stronger reformation role. There was not enough in such a role for them. While the experimental organization seems to have developed a more collaborative system than the control organization, to have avoided the development of a delinquent inmate system, and to have engendered greater support for organizational norms, its failure to cultivate a broader set of rewards for such activities as school and work constituted a serious failure.

Such a failure merits special attention because of its universality in correctional organizations. While it may seem logical that offenders should not receive rewards for not being delinquent—after all, no one else receives such rewards—that logic may need reexamination so long as there is a subculture of delinquency that can provide positive rewards for those who belong to it. It would appear, therefore, that some consideration might be given to the possibility of providing two kinds of rewards in correctional programs and of conceiving of them as occurring in sequential order: first, rewards for non-delinquent behavior and, second, rewards for achievement in legitimate pursuits. It seems likely that the first would be necessary only for a transitional period, provided delinquents could be introduced gradually into legitimate institutional activities, such as school and work. Assuming that this were possible, once delinquents were involved in legitimate activities, the first kind of reward would assume less importance. The legitimate satisfactions and new relationships associated with more common activities would assume preeminence.

A second consideration in seeking ways to provide positive as well as negative reinforcement in correctional programs involves offender types. As a method of considering this problem briefly, consider sociometric relationships. From daily observations made at the experimental program, it became obvious that cliques and isolates were in existence and that unless some way could be found to institutionalize a differential set of rewards that could somehow better suit the various types involved, many boys would fail the program simply because of their sociometric standings and not simply because they were more delinquent.

In order to examine this problem, a method was set up to determine the sociometric standing of each boy in the program. This method involved asking each boy to rate how well he liked other boys in the program. From these ratings, two sources of data were generated: (1) how much a given boy liked others and (2) how much he was liked in return.

On the basis of the findings, a four-fold typology was developed. The first type was labeled the *Aloofs* because it consisted of boys who were well liked by others but who did not like other people. The second type was called the *Loved-Ones* because it was comprised of boys who were well liked themselves and who liked others. The third type was labeled the *Beggars*. These were boys who liked others but were not well liked in return. The fourth type consisted of the *Isolates*, boys who not only did not like others but received dislike from others in response.

A breakdown of the experimental population into these different types may be found in Table 7.6. This table reveals that 10 per cent of the population were *Aloofs*, 53 per cent were *Loved-Ones*, 21 per cent were *Beggars*, and 17 per cent were *Isolates*.

Table 7.6. Sociometric Types

Type	Frequency	%
Aloofs	13	10
Loved-Ones	72	53
Beggars	28	21
Isolates	23	17
Totals	136	101

Staff as well as offenders tended to agree with these ratings. Sixty-three per cent of all responses received by the *Aloofs* and 55 per cent received by the *Loved-Ones* were favorable responses. On the other hand, only 19 per cent of the *Beggars* and *none* of the *Isolates* received favorable responses. In terms of their responses to others, 64 per cent of the *Loved-Ones* and 57 per cent of the *Beggars* gave favorable responses, while only 21 per cent of the *Aloofs* and 26 per cent of the *Isolates* did so.

Obviously, the characteristics of these different types could seriously affect the nature of rewards and punishments that individuals would be willing to grant one another, staff included, and would require attention in developing any new sanctioning system designed to overcome some of the problems that were described above. In later chapters, for example, it will be shown that sociometric (and other personal differences) are associated with in-program success and failure—and that these successes and failures were not always a function of new delinquent acts. Whatever happened to individuals was very much a product of interaction between the personal systems of individuals and the social system of the experimental program.

Implications for Theory and Intervention

In summary, this analysis has lent partial support to the notion that the experimental program was successful in implementing its intervention guidelines. In comparison with the control group, relatively more experimentals than controls favored change objectives, there was greater evidence of open communication and collaboration in the experimental program, there was less evidence of separation of staff and offenders into competing groups, and experimentals were more inclined to perceive organizational rules as helpful.

The major exceptions to this picture had to do, first, with the relative strengths of these differences and, second, with the inability of the experimental program to provide more rewards for non-delinquent behavior. Had the experimental program been able to conform more closely to ideal expectations, the differences on all the above items might have been greater. Further, the inability of the experimental system to provide more rewards, as opposed to punishments, as a means of reinforcing desired behavior probably was at the root of many of its difficulties. Despite possessing few of the more negative signs of traditional correctional organizations— caste relationships between staff and offenders and a rejection of institutional norms and expectations by offenders—there was too little evidence of a positively oriented reformation culture at the experiment for one to say that it had realized the ideals expressed for it in its theoretical guidelines.

Implications for FEM

Besides examining the consistency of program operation with theoretical design, it is important to consider the extent to which the conduct of research also conformed to its role in the overall FEM. Three matters bear discussion: (1) the degree to which research was accepted as a legitimate part of the enterprise; (2) the problems that were encountered in trying to implement all of the research originally planned; and (3) the problems of providing feedback to action people on the success of their efforts in implementing the intervention strategy.

With regard to the first matter, relatively few problems were encountered. The fact that research was defined as a vital part of the endeavor from the outset, that staff were hired with that as a precondition, and that staff meetings always involved both action and research people resulted in a surprisingly cooperative relationship. The fact that roles and expectations were clearly defined from the beginning seems to have helped a great deal.

Insofar as delinquents were concerned, their reactions can best be summarized by repeating rather typical comments from a research interview and by providing summary data on the views of boys as to whether respondents were being honest in their interactions with research people.

Interviewer: If a new boy came in and asked you what my job is, what would you tell him?

Respondent: I'd probably say he is the one who gives all the interviews around here. More or less asks you questions about the residence. Finds out your opinion about things around here, what's good and bad.

Interviewer: That may be all right. But what about the bigger question of your being part of an experiment? How do you feel about that?

Respondent: I think it's about time somebody studied the problems delinquents have. I kinda like the idea of doing something new. I guess I'd tell him the same thing that somebody told me when I asked him who the hell you were—that you are trying to get honest opinions from boys so we can improve this place.

Experimentals and controls were also asked in an anonymous questionnaire whether they thought others were being honest with research. Their replies are presented in Table 7.7. Experimentals were far more inclined than controls to believe that respondents were honest (59 *vs.* 28 per cent), and while significant numbers were undecided (39 *vs.* 52 per cent), only 2 per cent of the experimentals *vs.* 20 per cent of the controls thought they were dishonest.

Table 7.7. Statement: Boys in the program are honest with research

Statement: Boys in the program are honest with research.

	Experimentals %	Controls %
Agree	59	28
Undecided	39	52
Disagree	2	20
Totals	100	100

This response is understandable in light of the fact that experimentals participated much more in the research process and had much more contact with research staff than controls. Thus, the actual legitimation of research, at least among experimentals, seemed to be far less a problem than the fact that research plans for this phase of the study were overly ambitious.

Besides the data already presented in this chapter, original plans called for a far more comprehensive study of program operation than that which was actually conducted. This was to be accomplished by (*a*) using a complex scheme for typing each boy who entered the program according to his amenability to participate in a group-oriented program, followed by (*b*) a day-to-day recording of each of the two group sessions. These group sessions were to have been rated according to the Hill Interaction Matrix (Hill, 1955) in order to discover the relation of individual types to the group process and to discover whether groups evolved according to the scheme presented in Chapter Three. However, when it came to the actual conduct of this complex research, there was a lack of adequate research resources and the research itself tended to place too great a burden on boys and action staff. Research began to interfere with program operation. Consequently, initial attempts to monitor group processes were cancelled.

Looking back, this seems to have constituted a serious omission. Such research, had it been conducted, might have provided more information on specific matters than that presented here. This matter and other alternatives for studying program process will be discussed in Chapter Nine on critical incidents.

Finally, a serious problem developed relative to the feedback of research information to action staff regarding their implementation of the intervention strategy. Although regularly scheduled meetings were held little by way of empirical data were presented. Instead, most of the discussions were based on subjective observation. The reason was that, in an experiment so small as this, the accumulation of data in terms of any significant numbers is so slow that statistical information was unreliable. Thus, the staff was presented with a dilemma: Should research people present incomplete findings and run the risk of having the action staff revise their practices on the basis of them? Or should they withhold that information until more definite conclusions could be reached?

Although the latter course was followed, in retrospect we feel that it was the wrong one. A greater sharing of preliminary information, although risky, would certainly have been no worse than the subjective impressions that were given anyway. Furthermore, it may have improved relations between action and research people as well as provided a sounder basis upon which to make decisions.

Since the stance of the study was exploratory anyway, empirical findings could have been used for greater experimentation with program structure. Such experimentation need not have violated the basic principles upon which intervention was based but could have operated easily within them. We were too cautious. We could have experimented, for example, with the group process or with a different use of rewards and punishments in the interest of providing a more effective role for offenders. Furthermore, such experimentation need not have proceeded without their counsel and collaboration. Since a primary objective of the study was to increase that collaboration, there is no reason why an effort should not have been made to involve offenders in the use of empirical findings and the search for better alternatives. Indeed, it would not have been a denial of basic intervention principles, but perhaps a better implementation of them.

Thus, the findings in this chapter that reveal a failure to fully implement the intervention strategy reflect less upon the failures of the action staff alone than upon the failure of both research and action people to take full advantage of the more general characteristics of the FEM. More attention to the interaction among action, research, and offender groups and to the dynamic examination and reformulation of program operation should have been included as an integral component of the model.

References

FAIRWEATHER, GEORGE W. 1968. *Methods for Experimental Social Innovation*. New York: John Wiley.

HILL, WILLIAM F. 1955. *HIM: Hill Interaction Matrix*. Los Angeles: Youth Studies Center, University of Southern California.

WHEELER, STANTON. 1951. Socialization in correctional communities. *American Sociological Review*, 26 (October): 697–712.

CHAPTER EIGHT

Implementation:
Relation of Experiment to
External Systems

When we study a group, one of the first observations we can make is that the group is surviving in an environment, and therefore we say of the group, as of other organisms, that it is, for the moment at least, adapted to its environment. But this word *adaption* is ambiguous. Does it mean that the characteristics of the group are determined by the environment? No it does not, for the second observation we can make is that the characteristics of the group are determined by two classes of factors and not one only. These characteristics are determined by the environment, in greater or lesser degree according to the nature of the environment and of the group in question, and also by what we shall call for the time being the internal development of the group. But we are not yet at the end of our difficulties, for the third observation we can make is that the two classes of factors are not independent of one another. . . .

Thus the external system first gives a set of initial conditions from which our exposition can take its departure and then takes account of the fact that the adaption of the group to its environment is partly determined by the nature of the environment, while leaving us free later to show how this adaption is also in part determined by the internal development of the group (Homans, 1950: 90–91, 94).

In setting up the Silverlake Experiment, it was concluded that a mediatory community program for delinquents would be more consistent with intervention guidelines than confinement in an institution. Not only would a mediatory program hope to avoid some of the negative aspects of institutional life, but it would be in a far better position to link offenders with

161

non-delinquent activities in institutions. The success of the program would depend, in part, upon community as well as offender reconstruction.

This chapter is a descriptive account of the attempts that were made to establish community linkage. However, as Homans points out above, the success of that endeavor may be evaluated in terms of the interaction between the experiment as the "internal" system and the community environment around it. However, rather than referring to that environment as a single "external" system, we will conduct this analysis as though it were comprised of four external *systems*—those systems most likely, in our opinion, to affect the internal experimental system: the legal system, the neighborhood, the school, and the family.

The success of the endeavor to link the experiment to these external systems may be evaluated in terms of two major issues. The first had to do with the problems of establishing a community program. Attempts to organize new programs may fail not only because they raise fears that the community will be endangered but because they demand new institutional arrangements and accommodations, not only within the juvenile justice system but between the new program and such systems as the school and family. Therefore, one criterion as to whether intervention guidelines were implemented is whether the program was actually organized according to design while at the same time adapting to the ongoing activities of external systems.

The second issue goes beyond mere survival. It asks whether changes occurred within external systems that were sufficient to enhance better institutional linkage and reintegration for the offender. Beyond mere tolerance, was there enough accommodation on the parts of community systems to permit a new adjustment for offenders?

It should be noted that negotiations relative to these two issues involved research as well as action personnel. In the interest of seeing a thorough implementation of the total FEM, it was necessary for research personnel to participate. Key decision-makers in external systems tended inevitably to view the experiment as a delinquency reduction effort. It was necessary, therefore, to help them understand its broader implications.

The Legal System

RELATIONS WITH THE PROBATION DEPARTMENT

The Los Angeles County Probation Department was that segment of the legal system with which the experiment had most to deal. Since that department, in conjunction with the court, was responsible for the placement of offenders in local correctional agencies, its cooperation was vital.

According to experimental design, it was necessary for the Probation

Department to agree to two things: 1. to continue placing offenders at Boys Republic using the criteria it had always used, but also 2. that, after placement had been accepted by Boys Republic, random procedures could then be used to assign boys to the new experimental program as well as to the regular institutional program.

On an administrative level, department officials were not only willing to cooperate but were helpful and supportive. Because they felt that something be learned from the experiment that would be of interest to them, they were consistently available to render assistance.

On an operational level, some problems were encountered. As the resident director put it,

> Some probation officers don't believe either in short-term programs or offender decision-making. They prefer long-term placement. The result has been that those who are for us are really for us, and those who are against us are really against us. However, since the system is large enough to accommodate both types, we haven't had serious problems. At the present time, we now have boys in the program who were referred by eighteen different probation officers!

The way these problems were dealt with was to invite case workers and their supervisors to spend time at the residence, both at the beginning of the program and throughout its life, to discuss it in theoretical terms and to see it in operation. Research as well as action people participated. The climates of these meetings were enhanced by conducting them informally and by having refreshments available. Probation people were encouraged to, and did, raise important questions.

It was not always possible to provide conclusive answers, but by dealing candidly with them and discussing the lack of knowledge in the area of corrections, more than sufficient administrative and caseworker support was gained to make the experiment operationally feasible. In some cases, the staff of the experiment were also able to assist with the probation officer problems. For example, in the cases of two rather mature boys who were approaching 18 and who had poor relationships with their families, the staff recommended that the court be approached for permission to let the boys rent their own apartment and to support themselves. The court agreed to this proposal, and the step was taken. The boys were successful and have not been in trouble since.

Not all cases turned out this well, of course, and all differences of opinion were not resolved easily. Nevertheless, because probation and experimental staffs were generally willing to accommodate, a functional relationship was maintained. Overall, that relationship would have to be considered an excellent one.

Finally, one other step taken to establish linkage with external systems should be mentioned. Luncheons were held periodically at the experimental residence to which were invited not only representatives of the Probation Department, but the juvenile court, the police, the schools, the funding agencies, the members of the Board of Boys Republic, and university people. A detailed progress report was given to these people, describing both the action and research activities of the preceding period and the findings to date. The sessions were useful not only as a source of public relations but as a means of going deeper into the problems of experimentation. No attempt was made to gloss over the difficulties that were being encountered or to minimize the cases of failure that were occurring.

Candid report sessions of this type were undoubtedly trying to the board and officials of Boys Republic because they are so uncommon generally. These people must have felt as though they were washing their dirty linen in public. Yet it was our distinct impression that candor in these meetings was helpful, not harmful. There is a growing dissatisfaction with current practices and a growing respect for those organizations willing to evaluate their programs. All too rarely do correctional agencies, the courts or police have empirical findings upon which to base decision-making. Consequently, new information is welcomed. Likewise, the funding agencies were appreciative of efforts to conduct research and provide objective findings. Because they have also seen many cases in which promised research was not forthcoming, they welcomed it.

Incidentally, it should be mentioned that factors other than research data also helped these meetings, such as good food in a pleasant setting. The residence director, who prepared the luncheons, was an excellent cook and served vintage wines. His abilities contributed immeasurably to the creation of a mellow environment that helped to soften the inevitable questions raised by the research findings.

RELATIONS WITH THE JUVENILE COURT

Relationships with the Juvenile Court were characterized by distance and impersonalness. This impersonalness had nothing to do with the personal characteristics of the presiding judge nor with those under him. The judge, in fact, attended all of the briefing sessions just mentioned and exhibited considerable interest in them. The distance, instead, was a function primarily of the vast size of the Los Angeles court, which deals with thousands of cases annually. The number of cases involved in the Silverlake Experiment, by contrast, was a pittance. Consequently, the experiment did not, or could not, be expected to have much impact on the overall operation of such a system or to receive much attention in return.

This state of affairs could be perceived as desirable or undesirable, depending upon one's point of view. On one hand, the traditional separation of the judicial function from the correctional function did not constitute a barrier to setting up and operating the experiment so long as it operated within the law. The role of the court, in this case, was not inconsistent with its larger role as an impartial arbiter. It could, and did, retain a position of aloofness, one that reflected a concern for the rights of the offender as well as the community.

On the other hand, experiments such as this raise problems which have legal as well as correctional implications—problems which demonstrate once more that, however much one might like it otherwise, there is an interdependence of legal and correctional functions that cannot be ignored. The juvenile who continued to get into trouble was a case in point. One of the objectives of the Silverlake Experiment was to pose as clearly as possible for such offenders the limited alternatives open to them. Their continued freedom in the community, restricted though it was, was a tenuous thing. It depended, in large part, upon their willingness to examine and consider changing their delinquent behavior. If they would not change that behavior, they probably would have to face further legal involvement and possible long-term incarceration. The task of making these points clear, however, was not a simple one, for it is the nature of people in general, and delinquents in particular, to believe that the worst can never happen to them.

According to present legal practice, the alternatives for dealing with a difficult case are extreme. Either the juvenile must remain free in the community or be incarcerated on a permanent basis. Temporary detention as a correctional resource for the experiment was not a realistic alternative. Not only were facilities in Los Angeles extremely overcrowded, but the procedures for obtaining an order for detention were highly complicated, involving the processing of legal papers by the Probation Department and subsequent court action.

Such procedures helped to protect the legal rights of the juvenile. Yet there was need for other options. There were cases in this experiment where a boy was not only a threat to the community and program because he continued to violate the law, but who was probably lost to the program because he could not be detained temporarily. The legal processing was simply too cumbersome to control him physically for a short period as a part of program operation. Conversely, there were a few cases in which court action was taken and boys were removed from the program where such removal was considered unwise. In these cases, more flexible detention procedures, accompanied by regular program activities, might have worked to spare a boy permanent incarceration.

Such procedures were used in both the Provo Experiment (Empey and Rabow, 1961) and the Community Treatment Program of the California

Youth Authority (Adams and Grant, 1961: 8). In both cases, an offender was not incarcerated and then left there, as though incarceration was an end in itself. In the Provo Experiment, for example, a boy who was detained at night at Juvenile Hall was free during the day to participate in the work, school, and group activities of the program. Learning on his part, and that of his peers, was facilitated by a group analysis of why he had been incarcerated and what would be necessary to get and keep him out. Everyone became involved in the task of seeking an answer. Under such circumstances, the period of detention for any individual was usually short, only a few days. Yet both those who had been detained and those who had not quite been detained commonly reported that the temporary loss of freedom for someone, coupled with the task of searching for a solution, had been of extreme benefit.

It should not be forgotten, further, that this procedure has programmatic and organizational implications. The boy who continues to get into trouble without sanction can be a threat not only to himself and the community but to the normative stability of the program itself. It will be recalled that one of the ground rules for remaining in the community experiment was that delinquent behavior should decline over time. The program could not become a haven for the persistent lawbreaker; it would be unwise theoretically or practically to appear in any way to reward the persistent lawbreaker. The continued presence of such a person in the program was a living denial of the objectives sought by the organization. At the same time, the removal of a boy from the program by legal action, when everybody thought he could be helped, was likewise a denial of the norm that the new program could help people.

Going further, the action staff of the experiment were distressed on those infrequent occasions when, after returning a boy to court for continuing to get into trouble, the boy was set free. They were as concerned with its impact on other boys as on the delinquent in question. Extreme cases not only threatened to disrupt relationships with the school and community, but made the maintenance of an anti-delinquent culture difficult.

Thus, linkage with the Juvenile Court was not adequate. While the court did not oppose the experiment in any way and while the presiding judge was supportive of it, the experiment had virtually no impact on the court. The very size and impersonalness of the court system made difficult the kind of liaison that might have resulted in a more flexible and responsive correctional system.

RELATIONS WITH POLICE

Before the experiment was undertaken, its directors met with the captain of the Metropolitan Police Division in which the experiment was to be located. The purpose was to inform the captain, as with other officials, of the existing plans and to see if he had any qualms or suggestions. He accepted the idea with no reservations and replied that boys in the experiment would be treated as anyone else in the neighborhood. He kept his word. Never was there evidence of undue concern that the boys would be out of control and, consequently, no undue attention from the police. The police went to the residence on occasion, on official matters, but were always courteous and helpful. If a boy was picked up by the police, the staff, like parents, would be notified. Most of the time the boy would be turned over to the staff.

The captain of the Juvenile Bureau of the Los Angeles Police, a separate unit of the department, was also informed of the experiment. He, likewise, was an interested but non-intrusive participant. Along with a representative of the Metropolitan Division, he always attended the progress-report sessions described above and was well informed on the experiment. On those few occasions in which boys were involved with the police in serious matters, they were kind enough to call and inform the staff of the charges or other circumstances surrounding the case in question.

On one occasion, the captain of the neighborhood division proved to be of inestimable service to the experiment. After the experiment had been operating for almost two years, some local residents circulated a petition making a long list of complaints against it, charged that crime rates in the neighborhood had skyrocketed, and demanded that the project be eliminated. (More details on this incident will be described in the following section on community relations.)

The local Community Coordinating Council arranged two well-attended public meetings at which these charges were aired. Besides interested members of the community, these meetings were attended by boys and staff from the experiment, representatives from the local City Council, the Police Department, the Probation Department, and others. In all, over 200 people were present.

Because the charges were extremely serious, and because they had generated considerable fear and excitement, they might have resulted in the elimination of the experiment had they been substantiated by fact. However, the captain of the local division, hearing of the charges, took time from a busy schedule to attend both meetings. And when he was asked to respond to the charges, he quietly dispelled the fears that had been generated. Contrary to allegations, he said, there had been no increase in crime. In fact, for some reasons, rates had dropped in the neighborhood, making it one of the few places in the city where this had occurred. His factual and businesslike manner proved to be a turning point from which better relations were established. Had it not been for his appearance, however, the consequences for the experiment might have been extremely serious.

Thus, relationships with the police were constructive and helpful, even though it is conceivable that the police might be asked in some other experiment to perform a more active role in the reformation and reintegrative processes. In this case, the police seemed to have played the kind of role that was most helpful: detached and businesslike when needed, but unobtrusive when their presence was not required. From the standpoint of this particular study, therefore, interaction between the two systems was excellent.

Neighborhood Relationships

It will be recalled from previous chapters that the experiment was located in a large home in a middle-class neighborhood on the periphery of the down town area of Los Angeles. When the decision was made to locate in that area, some consideration was given to the possibility of announcing it publicly in order to generate neighborhood support. However, because of the possible resistance that might have been encountered if this approach were taken, it was decided instead to take a calculated risk. Rather than arousing fears about the experiment which could not possibly be based on evidence, it was decided instead to establish the residence first and then hope to demonstrate through actual experience that such a community program could be run without jeopardy to the neighborhood.

Interested officials, of course, knew about the study, as did the owners of the home that was leased. The latter, in fact, would not agree to sell the home until it could be demonstrated that trouble would not result. In addition, steps were taken to become acquainted informally, rather than formally, with immediate neighbors. This approach was generally successful over the life of the experiment.

Relationships with immediate neighbors were quite cordial. To the left of the residence was a vacant lot; the neighbor on the right made only one complaint, and that was that the boys were sometimes too noisy when they played touch football on the lawn. From time to time, however, various neighbors did complain of minor infractions by the boys such as cutting through private property on their way to school.

There was also some evidence of fear among some neighbors not so much because of what boys had done but because neighbors expected them to cause trouble. For example, during the first year, one man called the residence and asked, "Isn't it rather dangerous to have these kinds of boys in the neighborhood?" When the director asked him what he meant, had the boys done anything, his response was, "Oh, they haven't done anything, but they just don't look right to me." He was expressing the expectations that people ordinarily associate with a deviant role. Because the boys were officially defined as delinquent, he expected delinquency from them.

Another potential problem developed during the first year. A young girl in the neighborhood was molested by an unknown assailant. The mother, knowing about the experiment, suggested that the boys at the residence had been responsible. A subsequent investigation by the police, however, cleared the boys of any responsibility. Nothing came of this incident.

In was shortly after the publication of the second annual progress report that the most serious incident occurred. At the time of that report, the experiment had been running a sufficient length of time to enable a preliminary assessment of its effectiveness. Although better results might have been hoped for, the board of directors of Boys Republic were sufficiently satisfied with the results that they wished to insure that they could continue correctional activities in the community by purchasing the property on which the experiment was located. This decision led to the crisis.

A local attorney, hearing that the property had been placed in escrow, formed a Homeowner's Protective Association to block purchase of the property. This committee circulated a petition against the new program listing several serious charges, although they had never complained directly either to the director of Boys Republic nor to the staff of the experiment. The latter learned about the committee only through a friendly neighbor who had been asked to sign the petition. When this occurred, staff attempted to obtain a copy of the petition in order to learn of the charges being made against them, but all their efforts were in vain. The association would not release a copy.

A number of local neighbors, however, came forward in support of the experiment and were instrumental in arranging for the local Community Coordinating Council to hold two public meetings at which both sides could be heard. As explained earlier, these meetings were attended by boys and staff from the experiment and various city and county officials as well as by local residents. Three things, generally, were significant about these meetings.

The first was the successful refutation by the police of the charge that the experiment was contributing to an increased crime rate in the neighborhood. The charges made by the Homeowner's Protective Association could not be substantiated by police data.

The second was the fact that the chairman of the association, when denied the support of police evidence, used the second annual progress report of the experiment as factual evidence against it. By using data from the report, he reviewed the delinquent histories of the boys in the experiment, the initial findings of the critical incident study reported in this work, the theoretical references to the boys in the experiment as "offenders" rather than "children," and to a number of other details (many taken out of context) that he said were evidence that the experiment constituted a menace to the community. He concluded with the legal argument that, while local zoning regulations would permit the location of a "children's" home in the neighborhood, it would not permit the location of a "correctional facility" there.

The way in which the language and findings of this study were turned upon the staff and boys of the experiment was a distressing experience. It was distressing, in the first place, because the research data which had been openly published on the study might be the very ammunition that could result in its demise. But even more distressing was a recognition of the extent to which the language of corrections and social science is itself a form of labeling that may be very destructive of the objectives of both. It was clear that many people in the audience placed a much different interpretation upon concepts common to corrections than did correctional and research people. Such terms as "offenders," "critical incidents," or "delinquent acts" were sinister and frightening terms, much more sinister and frightening in the abstract, perhaps, than in reality. While "critical incidents," for example, are common occurrences in any social setting, not just correctional, people in the audience responded as though these were uncommon, as though they were not a part of everyday life. Their responses were naive but were, nevertheless, characteristic of the beliefs that delinquents are a breed apart and that their presence brings with it serious and immediate danger.

With regard to the implications of these reactions, two things were apparent. First, it might be argued that such problems could be avoided in scientific writings if new terms were adopted that would be less traumatizing to lay people, less likely to arouse unfounded and unrealistic opposition, both to the offender and to the correctional work that must be accomplished in the community. This use of alternative terms, however, would not really be new. The word "client" has often been substituted for the word "delinquent," the word "sickness" for "delinquency," and the word "cure" for the "correctional process." But these substitutions have not really eliminated the problem, only redefined it. Such words as "sickness" and "cure" still carry with them an undesirable connotation and provide the grounds for specialized treatment, set apart from the everyday life of the community.

It would seem, therefore, that a more likely approach would involve some attention to the relative merits of redefining terms as well as those of reducing the social distance between delinquent and non-delinquent groups. These particular community meetings, for example, were the first time that most of those in attendance had ever been confronted with this set of problems, or with "real-life delinquents," for that matter. The irony is that they may have been passing these same "delinquents" on the streets of their neighborhood every day. Yet it was only when the term "delinquent" was applied to the boys in question that a hideous specter was raised. The audience needed to recognize that fact. Thus, while the meetings were painful, in one sense, they may have been prototypical in another of the kinds of sessions that should be the rule rather than the exception when community programs exist. The reintegration process will probably require greater personal contact between the ordinary citizen and the delinquent. The citizen may have to struggle with basic issues as well as staff and offenders. Some evidence in support of this conclusion was provided by the events that followed the arguments of the chairman of the Homeowner's Protective Association at the meeting.

After he had concluded, the staff and boys of the experiment were permitted to explain their side of the question: the background and nature of the study, its emphasis upon the importance of community help for delinquents, and the findings of the study to date. It was pointed out by research people that the progress report was an honest attempt to highlight problems as well as progress. Hopefully, a factual account could serve as a basis to improve not only this program but programs for other young people in which the community would be involved. The accounts of the program by staff were supplemented by remarks from some of the boys who described the experiment from their points of view. Their personal descriptions of the problems they had encountered, their reactions to the meeting itself, were both illuminating and often poignant.

Incidentally, the reasons for having delinquent boys attend these meetings should be mentioned. As has been suggested, it was a difficult and sometimes denigrating experience for them to hear themselves described impersonally as though they were people from some other planet. The experience was not one to lift their sense of self-esteem and satisfaction. Yet it was felt that if the reintegration process is to have any meaning, interaction between delinquents and conventional people must take place. Offenders cannot be treated as hothouse plants, totally separated from confrontations of this type, in the name of protecting both them and the community. To do so is to retain that aura of mystery, that separation of the offender from the public, that makes reintegration so difficult.

As it turned out, there were many people in the audience, apparently, who had not made up their minds on the basic issues of the meeting. Consequently, in addition to the police evidence, the report by staff and boys seemed to have a salutory effect. Many listeners responded favorably to honest admissions by staff and boys that, while they had many problems, they were making a serious attempt to accomplish something worthwhile. Even though the experiment might not be a success, the opportunity to try should not be thwarted. The consequence was an increase of support for the experiment.

Aside from the reporting issue, one final aspect of the meeting was significant. A surprising number of people in attendance expressed surprise that the program even existed. Some had passed it every day on their way to work but had not even known of its presence. They found it difficult, therefore, to be indignant when they personally had seen little trouble. They expressed interest in learning more about it.

In order to accommodate and inform these and other interested people, an open house was arranged at the residence on two successive Sundays. Attendance at these gatherings was rather good and permitted a wide range of people to become acquainted with both boys and staff. The outcome was probably healthy, engendering support in at least some segments of the community.

Perhaps symbolic of the times, however, the issue over which the confrontation was generated—namely, the desire of Boys Republic to buy the property for correctional purposes—was not resolved by community action, open houses, or democratic decision-making, but by legal criteria. The whole matter was referred to the Zoning Commission in Los Angeles and placed in the hands of legal staffs representing both sides. By the time the matter was decided, however, it had assumed significance that transcended the experiment itself, because the final decision would constitute a precedent that could affect other community correctional programs, current and future. The Zoning Commission delayed an opinion for approximately ten months, perhaps to let the matter cool off. But when the decision was finally made, it was in favor of the experiment. Zoning regulations were interpreted to permit the program to continue and Boys Republic to purchase the property in question.

Other than this zoning incident, there were few other incidents to mar experiment-community relations. In fact, in a few cases relationships went beyond mere accommodation. A few neighbors made it a habit to employ boys from the experiment for landscaping and other work at their homes. Beyond the money that the boys earned and the pleasant associations they had, there was an occasional high spot. For example, one woman gave a boy an envelope that contained not only his pay, but a pen and pencil set. She also included a note thanking him for his services and explained that he was one of the best workers that she had ever had. This pleased the boy, of course, and helped to raise his self-esteem. But, for the most part, relationships in the community were impersonal, rather than conflicted. Boys were more detached from intimate involvement in neighborhood affairs than involved.

Whether this condition differs widely from the general situation in Los

Angeles is difficult to say. Urban neighborhood relationships are not overly personal in any event. What this reflects is the necessity for us to reconsider our rather romantic belief that urban neighborhoods can somehow approximate the cherished qualities of small towns and to seek new forms by which interpersonal relations can somehow be improved.

Beyond that, part of the impersonalness was undoubtedly attributable to the nature of the experiment itself. The average length of stay was only six months and boys usually went to their own homes on weekends. Their contacts through the school, furthermore, were not especially helpful in the reintegration process, not only because of the difficulties they experienced in the school but, again, because the length of stay was short. Neighborhood acquaintances and friendships could not be built up on that basis.

Many of these limitations might have been addressed on a more lasting basis had the program permitted boys to live in their own homes. While it is true that delinquents may have difficulty adjusting to their own neighborhoods, it is also true that any efforts by a program to effect reintegration may have more lasting impact if they operate there. Whatever success is realized in linking a boy with non-delinquent elements in the neighborhood and school is not lost when the boy completes his stay in the program. This was not true in the Silverlake Experiment where the transition still had to be made back into a boy's own neighborhood and school after he was released. Even though the Silverlake program was located in the community, reentry problems for many of the boys remained.

This condition speaks to one of the perpetual limitations of *residential* programs, which, even though located in the community, still cannot really be an integral part of the *boy's* community life. It leaves both boys and staff with a very real gap when it comes to dealing with the neighborhoods, the families, the peers, and the schools with which the delinquent must eventually come to terms. It would seem wise, therefore, to locate community programs in such a way that they can address the delinquent's ordinary community relations more effectively.

Relations with School

The task of establishing and maintaining effective linkage with the school created one of the most difficult problems encountered by the experiment. The problem had many dimensions. To begin with, it was difficult to enroll the boys. The officials of the local high school, in a middle-class white neighborhood, were asked to enroll the twenty boys from the experiment. This request made them highly apprehensive. They were fearful that the boys would hang out together as a group, constitute a collective menace, and become a source of "infection" for other students, bringing with them drugs and other delinquent activities.

Second, the school, like all schools in Los Angeles, had a severe shortage of counselors and special programs. Therefore, there was extreme concern that the experimental boys would put a severe strain on currently inadequate resources. Officials argued that many of the students already in the school who were not delinquent would not receive the attention they needed.

As an alternative, school officials suggested that the delinquent boys be enrolled in Special Adjustment Schools. Such schools, they argued, had been set up for the very purpose of dealing with the kinds of boys in the experiment. It was logical from their standpoint that use should be made of them.

These problems made necessary a long series of negotiations with school officials because the notion of enrolling boys in Special Adjustment Schools was not acceptable, theoretically or practically. In a practical sense, the task of transporting twenty boys to and from distant special schools each day was almost insurmountable. But, theoretically and even more important, it was linkage with the conventional community that experimental subjects needed, not more contact with marginal or deviant groups. Thus, a different solution was needed.

It should be noted, incidentally, that these negotiations were carried out with the principal of the local high school rather than with people in the superintendent's office. This may have been a debatable procedure, but local administrators enjoy considerable autonomy in the vast Los Angeles school system. Their attitudes toward any local innovation, as a result, can mean the difference between success or failure. It was felt, therefore, that close liaison with the principal was a necessity. If arrangements could not be worked out with him, then appeal could be made to higher authority, but it would be preferable in the long run to have his sanction and support without coercion from above.

After prolonged and often tense discussion, the school agreed, albeit reluctantly, to enroll the experimental subjects based upon the following conditions: no known sex offenders, no severely disturbed boys, and no narcotics addicts would be enrolled. However, when it came time to enroll the first group of boys, it was discovered that serious differences existed over the ground rule having to do with narcotics "addiction." To people in the experiment, "addiction" meant the habitual use of heroin or some other addicting drug; to school officials, the term meant the use of any drug: pills, marijuana, or even glue. They were resistant to accept any boy whose record reflected such use.

This reluctance, on one hand, was understandable. Drug use in Los

Angeles schools was just emerging at that time as a widespread phenomenon, not only in ghetto schools but in well-to-do schools such as this one. On the other hand, it was pointed out to them that, in many ways their argument was academic since the official court record rarely paints an accurate picture of a boy's history of delinquency. Studies of undetected delinquency, for example, suggest that the court record may not be an accurate index of the kinds of delinquency in which an individual most often engages. Thus, in the case of drugs, the court record may not reflect any use on the parts of some individuals even though they are heavy users, while it could list the only case in which another boy might be involved. The first type, as a consequence, would be accepted in the school, but the second rejected.

What was needed, it was argued, was not a rejection of drug users out of hand, but more effective programs in connection with the school, such as this one. The experiment could help to monitor and control boys and need not constitute a danger to the school. In contrast, the arbitrary denial of any boy who had used drugs could actually hinder the search for a solution. Drug use was becoming so widespread that all youngsters could not be locked up. There was a serious need to look for alternatives such as this one. But despite this argument, the issue was never really resolved and tension persisted over the matter, with an occasional boy being rejected because of a history of drug use, while others with longer histories were included simply because their records did not reflect it. Fortunately, at that time, the number of boys with *official* records of drug use was very small and it was usually possible to enroll them.

Another problem was bureaucratic. In order to enroll new boys, it was necessary to locate and obtain their school records. This was not an easy task in a vast system, especially for dropouts. As a result, much of the time of a Welfare and Attendance Officer was required. This was not only an additional burden on the school, which complained about the matter, but often hindered enrollment for a number of weeks.

In summary, the task of even reinstating the experimental subjects in school was a difficult one, to say nothing of the problems of keeping them there. The endeavor was made worse by the generally negative and resistive attitudes of the local officials. While one can easily appreciate their concern, their attitudes made cordial relations impossible.

As for the task of keeping boys in school, the list of problems was even greater. The first had to do with matters of dress and deportment. In terms of dress, school officials complained about long hair and sloppy clothes. In terms of deportment, there were cases in which boys from the experiment were seen smoking on or near the school grounds, in which they talked back to teachers, in which they slept in school or, in one case, where a boy was over-affectionate towards his girl friend. Although these are not atypical problems in the sense that they occur among the non-delinquents as well as delinquents, the school felt that a disproportionate amount of them were being created by the experimental boys.

Truancy was an even more serious problem. The school took the position that any boy who was absent from school for longer than one day without permission or excuse would be suspended—an action that would prevent the boy from returning to this particular school but would permit him to enroll in a Special Adjustment School. Undoubtedly, this penalty was far more extreme than that imposed on students who were not in the experimental program, but the school remained adamant about it. The irony was that far more contacts between the school and experiment were over these issues than over academic problems. Reports of academic failure, for example, came to light only at report card time, but violations of the dress or deportment codes would be reported immediately.

Steps were taken at the program to deal with these problems. Matters both of dress and behavior became topics for group discussion and solution. As the residence director noted,

> They did help some. Some kids needed to learn to bathe; others needed either a full-time dermatologist or a change in diet. The mere analysis of different life styles and personal idiosyncracies helped. It was good for boys to recognize that such things as speech habits or dress could hinder adjustment. At the same time, the necessary accommodations between school and experiment was far too one-sided.
>
> The boys got so they were spending a hell of a lot of time pressing shirts and trousers so they would look nice. Thus, many problems persisted not so much through a lasting unwillingness on the parts of delinquents to change as it did in the school's arbitrariness and preoccupation with control.

School officials took the position that boys from the experiment could not expect special treatment. They would have to be treated like everyone else, neither favored nor disfavored. Existing standards and rules would be applied to them in an objective and consistent fashion. If they could adhere to these standards, they were welcome; if they could not, they were not welcome.

Without doubt, there were tremendous frustrations on both sides over these matters. As Kvaraceus (1966: 139) has noted, the schools now hold and are likely to hold the largest segment of the nation's disturbed and disturbing youth population. Thus, the school is in the unenviable position of attempting to deal with a tremendous number of conflicting expectations. While the family and the community have tended to expect more and more from the school, they have not provided it with the moral, financial, and instrumental support to carry out all of these functions. It is in the position of trying to reconcile the demands of some for traditional approaches to education with more recent demands for counseling, vocational training, discipline, and health for all young people, many of whom have backgrounds of cultural deprivation and poverty which have not prepared them to make effective use of the school (*cf.* Woodworth, 1965: 11–12).

Conversely, as later chapters will indicate, there is evidence that school pressures may have contributed considerably to a high runaway rate at the experiment. Staff members were frustrated because they felt that, with greater understanding, the school and the experiment were in an ideal position to collaborate. On one hand, the experiment was designed to provide the kinds of supervision and support for educational achievement that delinquent school failures had not had before. It was in a position to provide some of the back-up support—counseling, direction, and tutoring —that is not always available in the school. The school, on the other hand, had the educational and social resources the delinquent boys needed badly. It was potentially capable not only of providing academic and vocational training but of adding adult role models and satisfying relationships with peers, things that conventional correctional programs could not hope to duplicate. However, because relationships were poor, activities at the experiment ended up placing far more responsibilities upon boys for making the necessary adaptions than upon the school. Undoubtedly, some of the heavy regimen at the experiment described in the previous chapter was due to this effort. The linkage effort was largely a failure. Not all the results were bad, however.

The average grade received by all boys at the residence improved from a D during the first year, to a C during the second year, and then to a C+ during the third year. Furthermore, unsatisfactory grades and behavioral problems went down markedly. This apparent change in performance was, in part, deceptive, because as the program progressed, many new boys tended either to fail early in their stay or to run away. Thus, the grades reflected the performance of only about 50 per cent of the experimental group. (See Chapter Ten for statistical details.)

The problems that were generated both for some boys and the school is best illustrated by a tragic event that occurred during the second year of operation. Two weeks before the end of school, there were five boys at the residence who, for various reasons, were not attending school. Three had not been admitted because they were glue sniffers and two others had been suspended for behavioral problems. Two of these boys went to the school, in violation of school and residence rules, to see another boy when they were supposed to have been downtown on an errand. They were observed by the vice-principal who asked them to leave. They did so but later returned. Again, they were seen by the vice-principal who followed them to the edge of the campus where an argument ensued.

One of the boys started to walk away, but the other became involved in a physical altercation with the vice-principal who was subsequently struck and hospitalized. The boy involved in the assault and his companion insisted that the vice-principal had become very angry and had struck the first blow. The vice-principal insisted that the opposite was true. The reports of witnesses, meanwhile, were similarly contradictory, one blaming the boy, one blaming the vice-principal. In any event, the boys were returned to court where one was made a ward of the California Youth Authority (which means incarceration in the state system) and the other was sent to a County Probation Camp.

The impact of that incident was considerable. Other boys in the program, as well as staff and school people, were shocked and disbelieving. Contrary to general opinion, this violence and its consequences were as upsetting to most boys as to staff. However, in contrast to fears that the event would result in a severance of relationships with the school, that did not happen.

Along with staff, the boys at the residence purchased a gift for the vice-principal that was presented to him at the hospital the day after the accident. He expressed regret in return and indicated that he did not wish the incident to have a lasting harmful affect. It did not, except for the not inconsequential fact that two boys involved in the incident were incarcerated. Thus, although relationships with the school, such as they were, were not disrupted, such relationships did not become more functional.

While this was gratifying in the sense that school relations were not severed, conditions still remained much less than ideal. The problem is well summarized in a general sense by Witt (1964: 4), who suggested that much confusion, chagrin, and wheel-spinning occur in that educational setting where the school is not "tooled up" to deal with the problem student. The result for the student is ego-deflation, withdrawal into apathy, or "acting out," which, as in this case, can be very destructive. Because he is keenly sensitive to the low image of himself he sees reflected in the school, this youngster may seek escape from the pain of low self-esteem by withdrawing or fighting back.

The solution for such problems will not be easy to find. Attempts by the school in this instance to treat serious delinquents like any other student had many drawbacks. Its approach simply beclouded a number of significant issues. One very real obstacle had to do with the fact that boys from the experiment were known as delinquents to school officials, and as a consequence each incident of problem behavior was not associated just with the individual who precipitated it, but with the whole group. It was a source of a stigma for all of them. Problems tended to snowball and resulted in difficulties for all of the boys from the residence rather than the minority who were involved.

Beyond that, the problems of academic retardation were even more serious. Boys in the experiment, like many other young people, needed special attention. The school in this instance, even if its attitude had been different, did not have special programmed instruction, special learning devices, and individualized help that might have been more effective.

Since the Silverlake Experiment relied so heavily upon linkage with the school, that linkage might have been more effective had some of the recent innovations in learning theory and education been applied in this instance. A significant omission of the experiment seems to have been its failure to approach the school in advance to build techniques more consistent with educational problems. It now seems clear that much more preparation, in conjunction with the school, was needed.

Relations with Families

It will be recalled that the delinquency theory and intervention guidelines of the Silverlake Experiment did not specify direct and systematic intervention with families. This did not mean that "bad" homes were viewed as unimportant at some time in the genesis of delinquency. Instead, it was suggested that negative family influences occur very early in the chain of variables leading to delinquency. Consequently, although a "bad" home may have been instrumental at some early phase in the genesis of a boy's delinquency, it must be recognized that it is now other delinquent boys, not his parents, who are current sources of support and identification. Any attempts to change him, therefore, would be more fruitful if they concentrated upon those factors instead of parental relations.

In implementing this approach, it was felt that whatever problems a delinquent was having with his family might best be addressed through weekend visits at home in combination with the problem-solving processes of the small group. This group might be in a better position to assist in the transition from childhood to adulthood than the family. To the extent that intrafamily changes were needed, resources would be better expended on helping the boy deal with his family rather than the reverse. Parental problems are often worse than his.

Once the experiment was begun, however, it soon became apparent that some revision in strategy would be required. Although the original plans seemed adequate for most delinquents, there were a number for whom special attention to family matters was necessary. On one hand, there were parents whose resistances to the program dissipated its effectiveness. When asked about his parents' reactions, for example, one boy replied, "My dad thinks the program is punishment and my mom thinks it's a pain in the ass." On the other, there were others whose relations were such that while they could not live successfully together, neither could they stand the thought of permanent emotional or physical separation. If the program were to help, therefore, some modification in family intervention would be required.

Family problems came to light in a number of ways. In most cases, they surfaced in group meetings. In the process of discussing unsuccessful weekends at home or the tendencies of some boys always to attribute their basic difficulties to family relations, it became apparent that some problems could not be resolved until all sides of the matter were heard. In other cases, parents came to the residence requesting help. In any event, the pressures were such that staff members felt that something had to be done.

In response to those feelings, the decision was made to address family problems in a way as consistent as possible with the original design, especially with the notion that problems are a function largely of interactional patterns rather than strictly private or personal disabilities. If there is a lack of communication or unresolved tensions in a family, for example, these are matters for which everyone in the family may be responsible, not just the delinquent member. Following these notions, therefore, two basic ground rules for dealing with families were set up.

First, both the delinquent and his parents had to be willing to deal as a group with their problems. Staff members refused to see either of these parties privately on the grounds that families had to see themselves in total context and to work as a group in addressing their difficulties.

Second, both boys and parents had to recognize that family problems could not be treated in isolation, as though they had no effect on relationships outside the family. For example, a boy's problems at home would be reflected in his relationships with staff and boys in the experimental residence or at school. These problems, therefore, could not be swept under the rug but would have to be addressed openly. Since family information could not be kept entirely secret, staff members, boys, and families would have to feel free to allude to these problems whenever appropriate in groups or other meetings at the residence.

Although there was some reluctance to accept these ground rules, they did not, in the main, constitute a serious problem. As a result, linkage with families at the experiment was carried out principally in the following ways. First, some conferences involving only a staff member, a delinquent, and his family were held. In most of these cases, these conferences were initiated by the boy or his family. Second, there were times when a boy's family would be requested by his small group to attend one or more of the group's meetings. Problems would sometimes arise with the boy which required information from the family. The facts of a particularly difficult problem could not be elicited and dealt with unless the family's side of the matter could be heard. Finally, because the number of families requesting help grew to be fairly large, it was decided to hold meetings at the residence in which all families experiencing problems were invited to attend. Such meetings included not only interested parents and their older children, but all the boys at the residence who were interested.

To the considerable surprise of both staff and boys, these meetings were well attended. At first they were held infrequently, but then grew to a point where they met on a regular basis each week. The result was that families not only became much better informed as to the nature of the overall program itself, but became involved in working on mutual problems. These family groups operated on the same self-help principle as the delinquent groups. This meant that staff members did not serve as the only resource but encouraged families to help each other. These families in turn were aided considerably by the delinquents themselves, most of whom were far more skilled than their parents in the operation of a group.

Unfortunately, the family groups were not studied systematically so that "hard" data can be provided on them. As a matter of fact, the amount of research being conducted in the experiment had already reached a saturation point, making it infeasible to institute any new data-gathering endeavor. It is impossible, therefore, to speak with certainty about the nature or success of these efforts. However, as with most activities of this type, whether in this experiment or elsewhere, there were some striking examples of success—examples that are always easier to remember than the failures.

One boy, who of the 261 experimental and control subjects in this study had the longest record of offenses, became involved with his family in the family groups. In addition to his long delinquent history, he was sloppy in his dress, lazy in his work, failing in school, negative and hard to reach. His mother was a domineering, complaining woman, constantly telling of her woeful situation in life. The father, in contrast, was a mild, unobtrusive person who had a pronounced stutter.

After five months in the group sessions, the whole family experienced what can only be described as an amazing transformation. The boy became concerned with his appearance, began to perform well in school, became helpful with other boys, and after release from the program did not recidivate. The mother, after considerable painful attack and discussion by others in the group, became less domineering and complaining. The other members of the family seemed better able to breathe. The father, meanwhile, made perhaps the most significant change. He exhibited a dramatic loss of his stutter and began to assert himself in a more effective manner. In sum, for this particular boy and his family the family meetings were probably the most significant aspect of the program. But since the inclusion of family intervention was omitted for theoretical reasons and came late in the program, its overall impact cannot be assessed. In fact, too little systematic attention to family linkage seems to have been a major omission in the design of this study.

Implications for Program Operation

This chapter has shown that the operation and survival of the Silverlake Experiment were highly dependent upon and intricately related to a number of important external systems. The findings indicated that it was far easier to establish the experimental program and to have it survive physically than it was to integrate it as an effective element of the community.

It is significant that the most effective relationships of the experiment were with legal systems: the police, the courts, and probation. Of these relationships, those with the police and probation were most effective. The police did not oppose the experiment, remained detached and professional in their relationship to it, and effectively defended it in public meetings. The Probation Department was both an ally and an interested observer. It was willing to make whatever sensible adjustments were needed in order to establish and maintain the study. Little more could have been asked of it. The court, meanwhile, was simply too detached to provide either help or opposition. This detachment is probably of value in maintaining the role of the court as a disinterested arbiter, but it also reflects a legal and bureaucratic maze that may have to be altered if correctional activities in the community are extended.

It is also important to note that while relationships with legal systems were generally good, they are probably the least important of all such relationships when it comes to ultimate adjustment by youth in the community. If they are to be successful, their linkage with family, schools, and peers will probably be more crucial in the long run than their linkage with police, courts, and correctional agencies. It is only when all others have failed that the latter come into action.

The least effective linkage during the experiment was with the school. Although the importance of such linkage was emphasized in the intervention strategy of the experiment, that linkage was never made functional. This failure was probably due to three things: (1) the response of the school to delinquents as a control rather than an educational problem; (2) the lack of resources in the school to provide additional attention to this problem population; and (3) the design and conduct of the experiment itself.

Because the latter was residential in character and because boys remained in residence only a relatively short time, they either failed to become established in the school or, having done so, had to disrupt that relationship at an early stage in order to return to their own homes. In addition, once subjects were assigned to the experiment and admitted to the school (a significant but not sufficient achievement), staff attention then shifted to other matters. Both research and action people became preoccupied with internal matters—the conduct of research, the development of an anti-delinquent culture, or the handling of difficult cases. There was neither enough attention nor available staff to deal adequately with the linkage issue.

Problems of family linkage were of a different character. By design, the experiment did not emphasize the need for special program components to deal with family relationships. For some delinquents, this seems to have been a mistake. The experiment was forced to make some rather drastic revisions in order to deal more directly with family problems, both by way of understanding what those problems were and of seeking solutions. However, since such revisions were incomplete at best, it would appear that family linkage remained inadequate.

Implications for FEM

Future field experiments might make significant contributions if they could devote further study to linkage problems. In seeking reconciliation between offenders and others, mediatory institutions imply the need for bilateral, not unilateral, change. Yet, as this study has exhibited, we know next to nothing about ways to bring it about. The failure to establish effective linkage for offenders with external systems was perhaps its most significant failure.

Several major areas were suggested in which significant experimentation might take place. The first had to do with the problem of reconciling court and correctional processes. While the court must retain its independence, it cannot ignore the impact of its own decisions, and the welter of legal and bureaucratic practices surrounding it, upon a growing number of community programs. The difficulty, for example, of obtaining temporary detention for an occasional offender or of bringing correctional knowledge to bear upon court decisions speaks to the necessity for more effective linkage. The problem is one of altering current complexities in the interest of improving the functions of both the court and correctional programs. Field experimentation designed to study these problems could be extremely useful.

The same is true for the neighborhood, family, and school. One obvious alternative would be to experiment with mediatory programs that are non-residential in character. Such programs might be located in local neighborhoods so that linkage with family, friends, and school, once established, could be maintained. Rather than struggling, as did the Silverlake Experiment, to develop rather artificial bonds of short duration, such local programs might establish bonds of a more lasting character.

It is quite clear, as well, that future field experimentation should pay greater attention to the role of the school. One of the greatest problems of the Silverlake Experiment was its inability to establish effective linkage with the school not only as an institutional entity but as an effective learning environment for its delinquent population. There developed too heavy a reliance upon control and punishment and too little an emphasis upon learning and reward. It would seem, as a result, that efforts to redesign educational and reward systems within the school might well be an important component of any future FEM. Effective linkage would involve the application of new resources and approaches within the school as well as outside of it (for example, *cf*. Cohen *et al*., 1968). If the school is to become a more effective resource, it must have a more intimate involvement in the planning and developmental process.

Finally, the failure of this experiment to address family problems directly also seems to have been a serious omission. The findings of other chapters, as well as this one, suggest the need for FEMs that could better answer such questions as the following:

1. What is an efficient method for identifying the family difficulties that must be addressed?
2. What are the relative merits of using group techniques to address total family constellations as contrasted with the more traditional casework approach?
3. What special benefits might be gained from a self-help approach in which the families of delinquents, as well as delinquents themselves, are sponsored in a reformation role?

Hopefully, greater systematic attention to family problems, in addition to linkage problems with the school, community, and legal system, would result in a more effective use of future FEMs.

References

ADAMS, STUART, and MARGUERITE Q. GRANT. 1961. *A Demonstration Project: An Evaluation of Community Located Treatment for Delinquents*. State of California Department of Youth Authority (March 1).

COHEN, HAROLD L., JAMES A. FILIPEZAK, JOHN S. BIS, and JOAN E. COHEN. 1968. Case II: model project. *Research in Psychotherapy*, 3: 42–53.

EMPEY, LAMAR T., and JEROME RABOW. 1961. The Provo experiment in delinquency rehabilitation. *American Sociological Review*, 27 (April): 256–358.

HOMANS, GEORGE C. 1950. *The Human Group*. New York: Harcourt, Brace.

KVARACEUS, WILLIAM C. 1966. *Anxious Youth: Dynamics of Delinquency*. Columbus, Ohio: Charles E. Merrill Books.

WITT, LEONARD A. 1964. *The Need for Improving the Employability of Offenders.* Boston: Boston University Training Center in Youth Development. (Mimeo.).

WOODWORTH, DONALD G. 1965. *The Effects of Laws Governing Youth Employment and School Attendance on Youth Offenses and Delinquency.* Prepared for the Office of Juvenile Delinquency and Youth Development, Stanford Research Institute, Menlo Park, California.

CHAPTER NINE

Implementation:
Critical Incidents[1]

. . . there is a basic split between a large class of individuals . . . , conveniently called inmates and the small class that supervises them, conveniently called staff. . . . Each group tends to conceive of members of the other in terms of narrow hostile stereotypes, staff often seeing inmates as bitter, secretive, and un- trustworthy, while inmates often see staff as condescending, high-handed and mean (Goffman, 1957: 46–47).

Restriction of communication between staff and inmates maintain the formal authority of the staff and is presumed to reduce the possibility of their being corrupted by inmates. However, it increases the possibility of inmates corrupting other inmates (Glaser, 1964: 129).

This chapter is concerned with the efforts that were made at Silverlake to increase communication and collaboration between staff and offenders. It will, it is hoped, shed some light upon the extent to which program princi- ples and guidelines were successfully implemented. Of specific concern were such guidelines as the following:

1. The delinquent should be sponsored in a reformation role. The most effective mechanism for exerting group pressure on members will occur in groups in which delinquents are induced to join with non-delinquents for the purpose of changing other delinquents.

1. This chapter is based in part upon findings reported earlier in an article by LaMar T. Empey and George E. Newland, "Staff-Inmate Collaboration: A Study of Critical Incidents and Consequences in the Silverlake Experiment," *Journal of Research in Crime and Delin- quency*, 3 (January, 1967b): 1–17. Printed by permission of the authors and the publisher.

2. Delinquent ambivalence can be utilized most effectively in a setting conducive to the free expression of feelings.
3. If the group is to be used as the medium of change, the delinquents who are to be changed and the correctional workers who are to exert influence for change must have a strong sense of belonging to the same group.
4. All information relating to the need for change, the methods to be used, and the consequences of change must be shared by all relevant people.

In designing process research to determine whether these guidelines had been implemented, one additional guideline was kept in mind; namely, that altered relationships between staff and offenders of the type implied here would likely be characterized by crisis and conflict. In the process of attempting to develop a new program culture, many difficulties would be expected. Delinquent behavior and standards would inevitably come into conflict with the conformist and official standards of the staff, especially since the program was located in the community where delinquent as well as conventional alternatives were omnipresent. Consequently, research designed to focus upon difficult problems and the way they were resolved would be one of the most effective methods of determining whether a new and collaborative arrangement had actually been achieved. If the guidelines had been successfully implemented, there would be evidence of candor, sharing of information, and collaborative problem-solving in the system.

There is little reason to argue the need for this kind of process research. It is a form of quality control that is desperately needed in corrections, especially since program objectives and actual practices often differ so widely (*cf.* Street, Vinter, and Perrow, 1966: 177–187). It is important to learn whether program design is ever implemented. Evaluation of program success will be meaningless so long as correctional design remains inconsistent with practice.

Data Gathering

A modified critical incident technique was used as a method of highlighting and exploring the points of crisis that emerged (*cf.* Flanagan, 1954). Since it was difficult to pinpoint in advance what these points might be, "critical incidents" were defined in a generic way to include any behavior that might disrupt the internal or external stability of the experimental program. Such incidents would include not only clear-cut violations of the law but any acts that precipitated interpersonal conflict within the system or any conflict between the program and the community that might threaten the continued existence of the program. It was hoped that information of two types might be gleaned: (1) the extent to which there was a general sharing of information regarding difficult incidents as contrasted to a high degree of secrecy and deceit; and (2) the way in which difficult incidents were handled by boys and staff.

Data regarding critical incidents were obtained by means of a specially designed interview schedule. A total of 157 incidents, involving 591 interviews with 99 boys and 5 staff members, were studied over a two-year period. Interviews were conducted in the following manner: First, when information regarding a critical incident became a matter of concern either to the daily group meeting or to the staff (*i.e.,* an arrest, a fight, or trouble at school); attention was focused on it and interviews were conducted. Second, since interviews on other topics were conducted on a systematic basis, it was common practice to query boys during those interviews about incidents which had not come to the attention of staff or group. If one was volunteered or a lead given, it was followed up and interviews with other relevant persons were conducted. Third, periodic informal interviews were conducted with boys regarding their own and others' undetected incidents. From the information thus obtained, it was often possible to piece together incidents that had remained generally undetected. In addition, group sessions were monitored to determine if incidents known only to research staff eventually came to the attention of both boys and staff.

Since there are always questions regarding the validity of findings in sensitive areas such as this, the following steps were taken to deal with the problem: (1) members of the research staff were separate from the treatment staff; (2) information was privileged and responses were anonymous; (3) information supplied by one individual was checked against that supplied by others; and (4) responses were checked against official records.

There is no sure way of indicating the extent to which these steps were successful, but it is our impression that there was little deliberate distortion by respondents. Once boys understood the research role, they seemed more willing than reluctant to discuss critical incidents. In many cases, information was volunteered rather than hidden.

Nature of Incidents

All of the incidents cannot be categorized neatly, but in general they broke down into six major categories. They are displayed in Table 9.1. The first category was *assault,* which comprised about 12 per cent of the total. Eight incidents occurred in the community and eleven at the residence. Mostly they involved fights between individuals at the residence. However, in three cases, there were fights between boys from the residence and boys in the community, and, in one case, a boy attacked a homosexual. In only one case, that of the homosexual, were the police involved.

The second major category was *theft,* which constituted 14 per cent of the total. Fifteen incidents occurred in the community and seven at the residence. Most thefts were highly situational and apparently unpremeditated. Within the residence, they had to do primarily with the kinds of theft that occur when people live together in formal settings, such as theft of food, clothing, and money. In the community, the primary problem was with automobiles. In three cases, cars were taken outright. In two additional cases, a boy took his family car and remained away overnight, and in a final case, boys went joyriding in a "stolen" car. The interesting thing about these theft incidents is that they were much more likely to be detected by group discussion at the residence than by the police. Boys either confessed to or were detected by the group. Furthermore, the group sometimes took remedial action. For example, one boy who had taken a car and kept it parked on a side street so he could use it when he wanted, was required by the group to return it to its owner. He received a $5 reward from the startled owner for his efforts.

Table 9.1. Kinds of Critical Incidents

Type of incident	N	% of total
Assault	19	12
Theft	22	14
Pleasure-seeking	39	25
School	14	9
Unauthorized absences	41	26
Miscellaneous	22	14
Totals	157	100

The third category was *deviant pleasure-seeking*—pleasure-seeking that, in the main, if it occurred among adults, would not constitute illegal behavior. A total of 39 such incidents, constituting 25 per cent of the total, occurred. Twenty-four were in the community and fifteen at the residence. About half of these involved either the possession or drinking of beer and liquor. The remainder included sex activities, sniffing glue, an occasional use of drugs or marijuana, or posing illegally as an adult in order to enter "gay" bars or those served by topless waitresses. The police were responsible for detecting five of these incidents; the remaining 34 came to light through interviews and activities at the residence.

The fourth category had to do with *school problems,* which, although

representing less than 10 per cent of the total, were important and provocative. On one hand, the experiment had the rather surprising effect of raising
the grade-point average of boys from near failure (D) during the first year
to slightly above average (C+) the third year. Thus, rather than being
academic, virtually every school incident had to do with the violation of
school rules: smoking, unacceptable dress or haircuts, over-display of
affection with a girl friend, truancy, and, finally, a very serious incident
involving violence. In the latter incident, two boys from the experiment,
one of whom had been suspended from school and one of whom had not
yet been enrolled, went to the school grounds when they were supposed to
have been shopping. They were seen by the vice-principal who ordered them
to leave. They did so but returned later. Again, they were seen by the vice-
principal and a fight ensued. The vice-principal was struck and hospitalized.
The boys insisted that the vice-principal had initiated the attack. The vice-
principal insisted that the attack was unprovoked. The statements of witnesses to the police were contradictory, one indicating that the vice-principal
had struck the first blow, the other suggesting that the boys had initiated
the attack. In any event, the boys were charged with assault and institutionalized by the court.

Other boys at the residence were visibly shaken by the incident because
it was such an obvious threat to the stability of the experiment, from both a
personal and an organizational standpoint. However, the incident seemed
to precipitate a crisis from which somewhat better relations between school
and experiment emerged. Even so, the fundamental problem for both
organizations, quite aside from the violence *per se,* still remained: namely,
that of reconciling the conditions needed for correctional innovation with
the normative demands of the school. The problems with which the school
was preoccupied were control problems, while improved academic performance received little attention. More will be said regarding this problem
in another section.

Unauthorized absences made up the fifth major set of critical incidents
and constituted 26 per cent of the total. These absences extended all the
way from short-term truancy to permanent runaway. In many cases, boys
who sneaked away returned of their own volition to the house; in a few
cases they were picked up by the police.

The question of unauthorized absences in a community program is a
thorny one and will be dealt with in detail in the next chapter. It is not
always possible to distinguish among those boys whose absence signifies
an inability to succeed in the community from those whose absence does
not represent a serious problem. Furthermore, staff must be concerned not
only with the meaning of an absence to the runaway himself, but its meaning to other boys.

Shared Knowledge of Incidents

Effective collaboration between inmates and staff depends heavily upon the extent to which information is communicated among them regarding the kinds of incidents just described. If an anti-delinquent reformation culture is to be developed, it is as incumbent upon offenders as upon staff to share information regarding the need for and consequences of change.

Respondents in this study maintained that information regarding most critical incidents was shared. Knowledge about such acts, they said, was communicated rather quickly and boys were willing generally to discuss them with staff in group sessions. However, we were skeptical about these reports and especially concerned that, if information was being shared, it might be the result of research interviews rather than an open and candid program culture. We feared that even though an incident might remain generally hidden prior to an interview, the fact that the interview was held, rather than the program itself, might be the stimulus for discussions about it. Consequently, we kept careful track of the extent to which boys knew about incidents at the time we first discovered them.

In general, the findings, which are displayed in Table 9.2, support the boys' position that information was being shared. In 76 per cent of all incidents, boys who had not been participants in these incidents knew about them at the time they first came to our attention. Nevertheless, the fact that one-quarter remained hidden is significant; there are some interesting differences in the types of incidents which did, and did not, become common knowledge.

Knowledge about such acts as unauthorized absence, interpersonal friction, or trouble with neighbors was virtually complete, a finding that is not too surprising in light of the nature of the incidents. A finding that is somewhat more surprising is that acts of theft, which were clear-cut

Table 9.2. Incidents Detected

Type of incident	N	Detected prior to interview %	Total eventually detected %
Assault	19	42	70
Theft	22	82	91
Pleasure-seeking	39	55	72
School	14	70	100
Unauthorized absences	41	100	100
Miscellaneous	22	95	95
Totals	157	76	87

violations of the law, were detected in more than eight out of ten cases. More of these, one might have guessed, would have remained hidden. The fact that they were not may symbolize a desire on the parts of respondents to do something about them. School incidents ranked next and were detected in 70 per cent of the cases.

The acts least likely to be known at the time of interview were acts of assault, mostly fights, which were known in only 42 per cent of the cases, and acts of deviant pleasure-seeking, which were detected only 55 per cent of the time. Furthermore, even though Table 9.2 reveals that the number of undetected acts were decreased after the interviews, almost one-third of the incidents of assault and pleasure-seeking remained undetected to the end. The interviews, therefore, may have served as a stimulus for sharing knowledge about incidents, but it is clear that they did not result in the discovery of all deviant activities.

The fact that a number of incidents involving fights or pleasure-seeking, such as sex, alcohol, pills and marijuana, remained hidden is significant both because of the community's general concern with violence and narcotics and because violence, especially, is the means by which delinquent inmate leaders maintain control over others. This finding may represent a chink in the argument made by boys (and staff) that most critical incidents were known and being dealt with, especially since many of these acts occurred in and around the residence.

On the other hand, there is a striking similarity between the extent to which various types of acts remained hidden and the rankings of seriousness boys placed upon these acts. Both participants and nonparticipants were asked to rate each incident as serious or nonserious at the time it was reported. Their accumulated rankings, and the extent to which the acts were discovered, are displayed in Table 9.3.

It is noteworthy that the acts least likely to come to the attention of the program were those considered least serious. If the findings are valid, therefore, they may imply that the lack of attention to these matters—fighting, drinking, sex, and pills—comes less from sinister intent to deceive on the part of the actors involved than from a lack of concern with the acts. The finding does not lessen the problems staff members have in establishing effective communication with boys regarding these matters, but it does throw a different light on them. So long as the delinquents involved do not consider these acts especially serious, they will be less inclined to do anything about them. The data reflect the enduring problems of correctional programs called upon to "motivate" offenders to change various kinds of behavior that the offenders do not consider especially serious.

Yet, despite decreased communication regarding assault and pleasure-seeking, these findings, taken at face value, suggest that the efforts of the

Table 9.3. Seriousness and Detection Ranking of Incidents

Type of incident	Rating incidents serious		Incidents detected prior to interview		Incidents eventually detected	
	%	Rank	%	Rank	%	Rank
School	86	1	70	4	100	1.5
Theft	83	2	82	3	91	4
Miscellaneous	81	3	95	2	95	3
Unauthorized absence	78	4	100	1	100	1.5
Pleasure-seeking	66	5	55	5	72	5
Assault	45	6	42	6	70	6
Totals	73		76		87	

experiment to uncover and deal with difficult problems may have been reasonably successful. We definitely did not detect the shared paranoia against open and collective discussion that one finds so characteristic of the close-custody institution. Thus, extended knowledge about persistent behavioral problems at Silverlake could serve as a vital precedent to collaboration and constitute the basis upon which alternative forms of behavior could be built. This conclusion, however, was subject to a number of qualifications. Effective collaboration requires effective problem-solving, as well as problem identification. The latter is more difficult to achieve.

The Problem of Validity

The first qualification has to do with the lack of any independent means by which to validate what boys reported. It is impossible to say with certainty whether boys were reporting only those incidents to the research staff that had already become common knowledge and thus were safe to talk about; or whether they were being completely candid. It is obvious from the above tables that some unknown incidents were being reported and did remain unknown to other boys and staff. But beyond that, a check on validity must rely on a number of indirect findings.

First, a check of official records revealed that only 13 per cent of the many acts described above, which could have resulted in legal action, were detected by the police, to which could be added another 3 per cent if one counted school problems. Thus, there is a strong parallel between these findings and studies of self-reported delinquency among adolescents in general that indicates that less than one out of ten delinquent acts is detected by the police (*cf.* Empey, 1967). Thus, even though this subpopulation of offenders is scarcely representative of adolescents in general, the research interviews and, to a slightly lesser degree, the program itself seems to have been successful in tapping knowledge about the large reservoir of delinquent acts that ordinarily go undiscovered in the community, and perhaps by correctional people as well.

Second, an analysis was made of incidents committed both individually and in groups in an effort to determine whether both kinds of acts were represented in the data. One line of reasoning would be that individually committed acts might remain hidden while group acts would be discovered, since by their very nature such acts are more visible. If group acts are vastly over-represented in the data, therefore, one might be suspicious of the findings. (Group incidents in this context refer to those committed by two or more boys from the program while individual incidents involve only a single boy even though he may have been with companions from outside the program.)

Table 9.4. Individual and Group Incidents

Type of incident	N	Individual		Group	
		% of row total	% detected	% of row total	% detected
Assault	19	37	100	63	50
Theft	22	82	89	18	100
Pleasure-seeking	39	41	81	59	65
School	14	86	100	14	100
Unauthorized absence	41	80	100	20	100
Miscellaneous	22	45	100	55	92
Totals	157	61	95	39	75

Table 9.4 indicates the extent to which both kinds of acts ultimately came to the attention of boys and staff at the residence, either before or after the interview. The findings are surprising. They indicate, first, that six out of ten reported incidents were individually rather than group committed and, further, that individual incidents were more likely to be discovered, 95 *vs.* 75 per cent. The data, then, simply did not support the notion that group incidents were the most common or the most visible.

Increased Control

This seeming anomaly merited further attention because of its relevance for the efforts that were made at the experiment to build an anti-delinquent culture. Therefore, it was subjected to an analysis designed to look at the program in evolutionary terms. First, it was ascertained that the number of critical incidents had declined over the life of the experiment. During the first eight months of the program, the average number of critical incidents per boy was 4.2; during the second eight months, it declined to 1.23, and during the third to 0.88. Furthermore, along with this decline, proportionately fewer of the incidents were committed in the community, a goal for which the program was striving. These findings, then, were encouraging from the standpoint of delinquency control.

In addition to a decrease in the total number of incidents, there was also a decrease in the number of incidents committed in groups. During the first eight months, 61 per cent of the incidents were committed by groups, but these proportions declined to less than one-third in the second and third eight-month periods. Thus, at least for the incidents that were discovered, the sharing of delinquent acts became much less common, implying that group support for delinquency was on the decline and that, through the sharing of information, the program culture may have been exerting greater control.

Finally, it was found that almost one-half of all critical incidents were precipitated by only 11 per cent of the population. There was a second marginal group of about 14 per cent whose behavior was on the serious side because they participated in three or four incidents. But, in contrast to these two groups, 28 per cent of the population were not involved in any incident and the remaining 47 per cent were involved in only one or two incidents. Thus, three-quarters of the population were generally conformist with only a small proportion persistently deviant.

Once these findings had been uncovered, both action staff and boys were asked to comment on them. The residence director said,

> when the first group of boys came here, they were committed to protecting each other, certainly not to confronting one another; that is, unless they wanted some boy to get in trouble. They shared just enough information to make things look good. They never went so far as to force staff to remove someone from the program; yet they kept the program at a high level of critical incidents. Something was happening constantly.

> When something did happen, however, the boys always had beautiful rationalizations. It was always someone else's fault. Unless we had positive proof, they were always able to protect one another. Then about two months after the program started, the lid blew off.

> It turned out that about ten boys had been involved with a homosexual and had been financing the purchase of marijuana and other goodies through the services they rendered him. But as often happens in these cases, some of them ended up beating him up rather badly, so much so that the police got involved.

When this happened, it scared some of the boys so badly, they brought the matter up in group. There was an attempt to retrench, to clean house as it were. This wasn't the straw that broke the camel's back, but it certainly helped. From then on, discussions became a lot more open.

Another thing that happened was that I got wind of the fact that one guy, Vincent, was really preventing people from talking in the group. He was using strong-arm methods to keep them from getting involved, so I arbitrarily got rid of him. I think this act, plus the trouble they were already in, really dramatized the need for some kind of action. It was then that the boys really started breaking up their old gang.

One of the remaining leaders in this group, however, put the matter a lot more simply. "When I first came in," he said,

I thought I was screwed. I didn't know nothing , so I joined the nonsquealers club. I was leery as hell of that bit on sharin' information. I was brought up in a school where you didn't open your mouth. You got the hell beat out of you, and stuff like that. It's hard to tell on guys when you might be doing the same, or almost the same. I don't know, it kind of makes you insecure inside.

Then when that big blowup occurred, and the heat came on, I could see that Jack [the group leader] was trying to help me, so I started trying. I got so I even started to like this place. The thing I liked most was that the meeting had most of the say-so—the guys making their own decisions—even though the staff could have done things entirely their own way.

The task of putting the change culture in motion, however, was not a simple one, as witnessed by another boy's comments on the same series of events.

Boy: I felt the staff wanted us to change—I mean real fast! You know and I know that some guys don't want to change. For example, on our first Friday night out, some of us guys got together. We got on the freeway and these guys wanted to stop someplace, you know, to look for some pills. So we dropped by this place and made a connection.
Interviewer: Then where else did you go?
Boy: Oh, man, I don't feel like going into all this.
Interviewer: Well, go ahead.
Boy: Well, everybody in the house knows about it.
Interviewer: I don't.
Boy: You mean you don't know about *that* group?
Interviewer: Tell me.

Boy: Well, hell, the point is that these things we were doing all the
                time just seemed *natural*. It ain't easy to change them.

All of these events testify to the fact that in the early days of the program,
it was divided into official and inmate systems. And then, as the statistical
data indicated, there was a decline in the numbers of critical incidents and a
decrease in group delinquencies. The deviant system became more atten-
uated as the program culture emerged. There seemed to be less and less
group support for delinquent activities.

The process of change, however, was not without its ups and downs.
There were two kinds of problems: (1) the reassertion of delinquent norms
whenever a group of new boys entered the program and (2) the efforts of
some boys to develop a "duke" system within the program. Let us consider new boys first.

Said one of the staff leaders,

> We have to start rebuilding the culture every time we get a new group. When
> you have 30 per cent new boys, your delinquent culture is much stronger. For
> example, last summer, the first thing a group of new boys did was to sneak out
> at night to buy booze. But in contrast to the problems we had when the program
> first started, this only happened a couple of times until someone brought it up
> in the group. Within a week, it was pretty well all cleared up.

From the perspective of one of the older boys, however, it was not quite
that simple.

Danny: Remember when Bill and all those guys were here, all the stuff
                that was going on then? It's starting to get like that again.
                Guys are starting to get alliances going and they're not saying
                stuff, like, you know, Paul. They are dropping pills and not
                saying anything about it. And now the whole house is down
                on Don because he ratted on them. The whole house has
                started going like that again.

Interviewer: You see the house as going delinquent again? Why did it
                change, from when Bill was here, and become non-delinquent
                for a while?

Danny: Well, some guys would take a stand in group and tell what
                was happening. Now it's getting back, 'cause some of the
                new guys are scared of the others—like Larry's scared of
                Tom, and some other guys are scared of other guys and stuff
                like that.

Interviewer: Why do you think the house is going back to the delinquent
                way?

Danny: It's just mainly guys figuring they can get around the pro-
                gram, find some kind of an easier way out, without having to

change, or encounter any group pressure or anything. Most guys want to get out; they don't want to change. Take guys like Mario, they don't want to give anything at all. Some guys are really trying, and the ones that are, it really discourages them.

Interviewer: You're really saying that there are two or three guys that are really messing things up. Why isn't something being done about that?

Danny: I think some moving in on it was done; but it's just starting now.

Interviewer: In other words, you think that the house, the kids, will do something about Tom and Mario?

Danny: And a few other guys. Yeah, I think they will. But it's going to be hard; they are going to have to take strong pressure, 'cause the other guys, the ones who are doing the house wrong, are going to have other guys with them, and they are going to try to keep them from doing something about it. They are going to give a lot of pressure; call them "rat" and all that, and they are going to have to take it.

Interviewer: You mean some new boys are going to have to take an anti-delinquent stand?

Danny: Yeah . . . I think it's much easier to go along with the guys that are messing up. I think that the standard is going down, the standard of the house. Like when Bill and all those guys were here, the house went way down; everybody had booze and dope; and then it went up, cause more guys took a stand. But the more I see, now, it's starting to go back down again. But I think that I'll just try to take a stand to deal with it.

The "duke" system, by contrast, was less of a problem. "This was a big problem at first," noted a staff leader,

but ironically it was introduced as much by staff as boys who chose two of the strongest boys to become paid work supervisors. Without our knowing it, they were running this place by force for their own benefit. These two boys used the job much as they would in a prison. They had their own rules; they had their own room; they even conned us into allowing them into having their own telephone. They became very comfortable, all the while using their satellites to control others so they could keep their own noses clean. Fortunately for us, our own system saved us.

When we gave other boys an opportunity to talk about such things in group meetings, and did support our own norms against personal assault—no fight, period—the whole thing came to light. If you give boys, especially the victims, an opportunity to confront something like a duke system, there is a good chance you can control it. In fact, the group then insisted that they share in the selection of work supervisors and that everyone have a shot at it at some time during their stay. Thus, it has been damn hard for a duke system to continue with as strong a culture as we have developed against personal aggression and in favor of group control over it.

Despite evidence of some persistent problems, these interview data did tend to support statistical evidence that the experimental program may have been successful in achieving some of its program objectives. There is evidence that a considerable amount of information was shared between boys and staff, that boys who persistently perpetrated critical incidents were in the minority and that those who did offend repeatedly did not possess the kind of group solidarity indicative of a strong inmate subsystem. But this is evidence primarily of an increasing capacity in the experimental program to control behavior. The basic issue is whether there was also evidence of the ability of inmates and staff to collaborate in solving as well as controlling problems. As Jones (1964: 95) has suggested, compliance with prosocial norms may indicate submission to program authority but it need not signify a basic change in life style or an increased capacity to sustain law-abiding behavior after release. Likewise, Glaser's findings (1964: 97–99) suggest the possibility that offenders may reduce the pains of the correctional experience by becoming increasingly isolated, not only from staff but from each other. In this case, for example, increased sharing of information and heightened controls may have tended to isolate offenders rather than uniting them in an anti-delinquent yet supportive group culture. The basic issue, therefore, was whether the program culture was capable of uniting offenders and staff in providing constructive help or whether it tended only to isolate them.

Differences in Perception

The evidence is not too encouraging. In the first place, there were important differences in perception suggesting that, even after a considerable period of time, members of the system were not communicating well with each other. For example, when most boys were queried by research staff about their own feelings regarding a particular critical incident in which they had participated personally, they expressed concern and indicated some desire to change: "I knew I was doing wrong when I went with those guys and that I would be hurting the house as well as myself, but I went and did it anyway. What can I say?" Such remarks are reminiscent of a growing body of evidence that suggests that the delinquent is only casually and intermittently immersed in illegal behavior and that his investment in delinquent activities is not sufficient to render him unavailable for alternative courses of action. He is neither totally alienated from the goals of the larger society nor is he an adherent to an ethic characterized by total opposition to widely shared conceptions of the "good" life (*cf.* Matza, 1964: 28; Short and Strodtbeck, 1965: 59, 271).

Yet other boys and even staff members—those who were not participants in the incident—indicated little awareness of this possibility. Instead, their reactions were characterized by distrust of the offender. They did not readily accept his protestations that he was concerned about his behavior and wished to change it. Almost always, they were skeptical of him. "I think," said one boy, "that it is a good thing to put one of these guys in his place right away. Let him know he can't bullshit you along. I never believe their stories."

This particular reaction is difficult to evaluate. It may be that the perpetrators of critical incidents are correct, that they do experience concern, that they are amenable to change. In favor of their point of view is the evidence that about one-half of the boys studied were involved in either one or two incidents and that only about one in ten was in trouble repeatedly. If they had been in a total institution where they were not so free and the opportunities for deviance not so great, this evidence might be discounted. Because they were in the community where opportunities for trouble were constant, the evidence cannot be totally discounted. Boys who were involved in critical incidents may have learned something that decreased further violations.

On the other hand, relationships in most correctional organizations are characterized by suspicion and distrust, not only between offenders and staff but among offenders themselves. This cloud of distrust cannot be totally discounted, as many of the earlier quotations indicated, because there are always persons within such organizations—staff as well as offenders—who have no intention of changing. There are very real grounds, therefore, for remaining skeptical about any individual's protestations of innocence or his stated desire to become something else. This is especially true in light of our inability to classify persons in some way that would be helpful in reality-testing their verbal statements. What happens in the absence of such information is an indiscriminate tendency to stereotype everyone.

As Cloward (1956: 19) points out, there is a high degree of "pluralistic ignorance" in correctional organizations. "Because conforming prisoners feel constrained to pay lip-service to deviant norms, their visibility to conformists is obscured. The consequence of this is the fact that each conformist comes to believe that he is the only one who holds sentiments which support socially acceptable values."

Glaser (1964: 116) says his research supports Cloward's conclusion: "There is evidence from all components of our study . . . that most inmates are considerably concerned with trying to 'go straight.'" Not only inmates, but staff and research people commonly err in assuming that the inmate's primary reference group is the inmate group. For some, that is the case, but for many others it is not.

Finally, "pluralistic ignorance" or what Matza (1964: 35–36) calls "shared misunderstanding" is found among delinquents in the community. There is a tendency for them to attribute to their peers greater commitment to delinquent values than they actually feel. They fail to understand the mixed, rather than unitary motivations that accompany behavior. That this failure should occur among adolescents, however, should not come as any surprise because it is a failure that characterizes interaction in almost any human setting. People stereotype one another and continue to react to each other in terms of those stereotypes.

It seems almost certain that "pluralistic ignorance" was one basic problem encountered at Silverlake, one that prevented full implementation of the intervention guidelines. It would have to be overcome if the program culture were to become more effective. How that could be accomplished is not certain. The program principles emphasizing candor and trust seem to have pinpointed the problem; the difficulty was one of implementation.

It seems almost certain that pluralistic ignorance could never be completely overcome in an organization in which some members represent authority and others are legally deviant. But, if nothing else, a greater awareness of its presence might aid in the task of overcoming destructive stereotypes and dealing more directly with actual problems.

Responses to Critical Incidents

A second problem relative to the task of finding new solutions had to do with the deliberations of boys and staff as to what should be done when an incident occurred. How should the group respond? What action, if any, should be taken? Their responses are indicated in Table 9.5.

In two-thirds of the cases, boys who had not participated in an incident felt that the imposition of negative sanctions upon its perpetrators should be the first order of business: restrictions, extra work, or, in limited cases, even expulsion from the program. In only 14 per cent of the cases was the suggestion made that response should be limited to group analysis and decision-making, although in one-fifth of the cases it was recommended that the incident needed no special attention. In one sense, therefore, the majority of those not involved in an incident were extremely punitive, remarkably "square."

Table 9.5. Preferred Reactions to Incidents

Preference for action	Participants		Non-participants		Staff	
	N	%	N	%	N	%
No action needed	34	47	68	21	4	2
Group analysis	14	19	46	14	55	34
Negative sanctions	25	34	208	65	103	64
Totals	73	100	322	100	162	100

On the other hand, this majority did not see the imposition of sanctions as precluding attempts to understand the deviant or to seek solutions, but they felt that the setting of limits was a key step that should be taken at the outset. Only after this was done should causes and new alternatives be considered. They believed that the offender had to learn to comply.

In contrast, boys who had perpetrated critical incidents were understandably more lenient regarding themselves. Half of them saw little need for formal response since they had "learned their lesson," a third did see merit in formal action in the form of some sanction, but, surprisingly, only one-fifth suggested that attempts to analyze and to discuss problems should be the initial step.

Staff members, meanwhile, responded more like the nonparticipant than the deviant group of boys. As the residence director put it, boys have to learn to "buy into the system."

> Basically, some of these guys treat this place like a candy store, looking over all the chocolates and then deciding they don't want any. They look over the system and decide there is nothing they want: group, school, or work. They simply won't buy into it. Until they learn they have to pay the price demanded, we cannot do anything with them.

In two-thirds of the incidents, therefore, staff preferred some kind of formal action as a first step: restriction, loss of privilege, or some other sanction. They were different, however, in the sense that in one-third of the cases, they would have liked the first step to involve discussion and problem-solving. Nevertheless, their responses contributed to an overriding theme that emphasized that only after limits were set should inquiry into causes and solutions be pursued.

This obvious preoccupation with the functions of control and the utility of punishment is good documentation of the conclusion reached by Street *et al.* (1966: 159–177) that there is a general strain toward custodialism, even in treatment-oriented programs where such actions are inconsistent with stated goals. This documentation illustrates again the value conflict over punishment *vs.* reformation objectives that is likely to appear in any correctional setting. A belief in the efficacy of punishment, furthermore, is one shared by offenders as well as staff. If anything, offenders were more in favor of negative sanctions in this experiment than staff members.

On the other hand, one can ill afford to oversimplify the issues involved. A great disservice can be perpetrated by attributing these findings solely to staff and offender ignorance and inhumanity. In order to correct the problem, more than a permissive lifting of controls would be involved. In their analysis of a "therapeutic community" in England, Rapoport, Rapoport, and Rosow (1960: 135–142) noted that the community continually oscillates from a condition of high organization to one of near disorganization. In its highly organized phase, behavior tends to be consistent with ideals. It does not arouse anxiety because the amount of social deviance is small; staff and offenders can afford to be permissive. The social climate is relaxed and the amount of trust is enhanced. But when deviance increases, tension rises and problems exceed the capacity of staff-offender collaborative arrangements to deal with them. There is the threat of organizational disintegration.

When this occurs, ideals are discarded. The staff acts arbitrarily to remove or control the deviants. On occasion, exceptional leadership on the parts of inmates may stem the tide, but this is unusual. Many inmates, like staff, are frightened and anxious that controls be reasserted. Thus, staff members may be moved, as Street *et al.* (1966: 190) put it, "to the brink of despair." There is often evidence that permissiveness on their parts invites the "smuggling in of weapons, the creation of kangaroo courts, and other developments that often end in frightening staff members into taking strong and even frantic disciplinary action (*cf.* Street *et al.,* 1966: 183). Collaboration under such circumstances is discarded and the staff assumes control.

Once having done this, however, reparative forces soon come into play. Authorities feel guilty about their actions and the pendulum swings once more toward the pole of permissiveness and collaboration. Inmates feel reassured and more confident of their capacity to contribute to problem-solving objectives, but only after excessively deviant individuals are removed or controlled. Increased confidence is a function of the reassertion of social structure. Apparently the system can tolerate only so much tension before the need for conformity becomes paramount.

The same phenomena seem to have been operating in this study on occasion. Some forms of deviant behavior, some critical incidents, seem to have threatened personal and organizational needs above and beyond abstract philosophies of punishment or treatment. Demands for punishment and control were reflections in microcosm of the responses that seem to characterize the larger society when either the volume or seriousness of deviant behavior is perceived as reaching dangerous levels. Thus, when these problems are considered in light of program guidelines and principles they look as follows:

On one hand, the availability of a great deal of knowledge about the delinquent activities of some of the boys could constitute grist for the group discussions and point to changes the boys must make if they are to stay out of trouble. But, on the other hand, too much knowledge of this type at times may have been debilitating. Boys and staff may have become preoccupied with the critical incidents of a small minority of boys who repeatedly got into trouble. If this occurred, too much attention could have been devoted to punishment and control and far too little attention to self-understanding and rewards for constructive behavior.

Such problems raise questions as to how much information agents of social control should have and what they should do with it after they have it. Obviously, information about the delinquent activities of the small percentage of serious and persistent offenders in this experiment was important. But what are the most dangerous activities? How do staff and boys draw the line between acts that have little consequence and those that must be controlled? How do they avoid unreasonable tension and flights into unproductive and useless forms of control? Conversely, how do they balance personal and organizational needs? Acts of punishment and control, while possibly of little utility for the deviant, do have an important role to play in maintaining social solidarity. The basic issue, therefore—one pinpointed by this analysis but not solved—is in finding a better reconciliation of personal and systemic requirements.

Interestingly enough, not all innovative programs have moved in the direction of increased permissiveness. Perhaps the clearest example is Synanon, the program for drug addicts run by drug addicts (*cf.* Yablonsky, 1965). The kinds of acts tolerated there are highly qualified and do not run the entire gamut of deviance, especially where the basic problem—the use of drugs—is involved. Instead, a few fundamental rules are retained, which, if not obeyed, will result in expulsion, unqualified and irretrievable. Narcotics of any kind are not permitted on the premises and any individual who uses them, or associates with those who do, is booted out. The use of group discussion in behalf of this particular deviant is not even at issue. The feeling seems to be that those who will not abide adherence to basic norms are unlikely to change and, furthermore, that their presence constitutes a real danger to the welfare of others.

The responses of boys and staff at the Silverlake Experiment express a similar flavor. There is a seeming need, especially on the parts of boys who are attempting to play a reformation role, for a wall of solidarity against excessive deviancy. Psychologically, it seems difficult for them to maintain their own acceptance of prosocial norms, their own change in role, or their own ability to help others unless there is a program climate that is strong and supportive. They take what seems to them to be a very practical position—namely, that not every boy will be able to "make it"—and they feel that unless they and staff are willing to set limits, other boys will be lost also. It is not that offender-reformers are totally interested in punishment or that they are unwilling to help another offender, it is that they seem to demand that he adhere to certain expectations as behavioral evidence of a personal commitment to a change in standards. In evolving a new adjustment, there seems to be considerable need for peer group and program support.

Staff rigidities reflect a similar variety of pressures. In dealing with critical incidents, they feel, rightly or wrongly, that they are continually confronted with the problems of balancing the needs of an individual against the needs of the whole group. They are, indeed, driven to the brink of despair on occasion. They fear that a single bizarre incident or a boy who remains repeatedly deviant can undo many months of successful work in the neighborhood, at the school, and with the authorities. As a consequence, some of the personal insecurities of staff members are not greatly different from those of boys. They tend to seek structure through the imposition of sanctions as a means of preventing or dealing with critical problems.

The failure to resolve this basic issue seems to lie behind the sometimes contradictory findings of this study. And, what is of even greater significance, is the fact that public correctional agencies cannot always do what Synanon does or, for that matter, what society-at-large does; namely, boot out the people who will not conform. It seems apparent that boys and staff in this study were caught in the no-man's-land between the need, on one hand, for sufficient structure by which to meet organizational requirements and enough flexibility, on the other, to deal with exceptional problems. The requirements of personal and social systems do not always coincide. The conflict is one that has received little rational attention and for which empirical guidelines are lacking. In fact, it is not without paradox that subjects in a correctional study—staff and offenders—must set about trying to find solutions for problems that as yet others have failed to find. The paradox provides but a brief glimpse of the many complexities—ethical, organizational, and scientific—that are confronted in a field experiment of this type.

Prediction of Critical Incidents

In addition to the analysis of incidents, *per se*, an attempt was made to see whether such incidents might be predicted on the basis of personal and background characteristics. It would be important to learn whether certain types of boys are more predisposed to create critical incidents than others.

A variety of scales and indexes were developed by which to measure personal characteristics. The list falls generally into four major areas: personality, social background, peer relations, and offense history. Since all scales and indexes were described in detail in Chapter Six, that description will not be repeated here. Suffice it to say that a total of 29 complex measures of personal and background characteristics were developed: nine indexes of personality characteristics, eight social background scales, four peer relations scales, and eight offense scales. These scales, rather than a host of single-item variables, were used because of the need for a parsimonious system for classifying and analyzing offender characteristics.

A stepwise regression analysis (*cf.* Draper and Smith, 1966: Chap. 4) was used to examine the relationship of the thirty predictor variables to critical incidents. This technique involves the computation of a sequence of multiple linear regression equations in a stepwise manner (*cf.* Hirschi and Selvin, 1967: Chap. 9 for advantages and disadvantages). At each step, the variable added to the regression equation is the one that makes the next greatest reduction in the error sum of squares. Through the use of this technique, it is possible to examine the contribution of each variable when it is added to the regression equation and to determine which variables make the greatest contribution in understanding critical incident behavior. Runaways were not included in the analysis since they will be handled in a separate chapter.

Two findings of importance emerged. First, the amount of explained variance accounted for by all of the input scales was 54 per cent. Furthermore, the ten best predictors of the stepwise analysis accounted for 46 per cent of the variance. Not more than 8 per cent of the total variance was added by the remaining twenty variables. Both of these coefficients—54 and 46 per cent—are relatively high and indicate that involvement in critical incidents is predictable on the basis of input characteristics and is not determined solely by situational factors.

Second, when one considers the variables included in the list of ten best predictors, he finds some striking differences. As can be seen in Table 9.6, the peer influence and social background scales contributed nothing to the total *explained* variance. The personality scales, however, account for 68 per cent, or over two-thirds of the total *explained* variance, while the offense scales accounted for 32 per cent. Thus, involvement in critical incidents seems to be more closely related to personality traits first and to offense history second. Peer group relationships and social background did not emerge as predictive in the first ten steps of the stepwise regression.

This may be a significant finding in light of evidence provided earlier that

Table 9.6. Variance explained in predicting Critical Incidents

Variable category	Proportion of variance added to R²	% of explained variance
Peer influence	0.000	00.0
Personality	0.311	67.5
Offense	0.150	32.5
Background	0.000	00.0
Total R² after first 10 steps	0.461	100.0
Total R² after additional 19 steps	0.5435	

*Critical incidents that were *not* runaways.

six out of ten incidents were individually rather than group committed and, further, that the number of group incidents declined over the life of the experiment. In seeking an explanation, two possibilities emerge. First, this program, by virtue of its design, may have been more successful in controlling socially induced than personality-induced incidents; or, second, personality may be more closely related, in general, to deviant behavior in a correctional setting than group factors. Our data are too insufficient to enable any definite conclusions on this matter. However, given the likelihood that group-centered programs may not be appropriate for all offenders, it could be that group forces were better controlled in this setting than personality factors. The perpetrators of critical incidents may have been those least likely, for personal reasons, to become involved in the reformation subgroup of the program.

By way of information, the particular scales of the Jesness Personality Inventory that were most predictive of incidents, in order of importance, were:
1. *Social Maladjustment Scale.* A set of attitudes associated with unfulfilled needs, as defined by the extent to which an individual is unable to meet, in socially approved ways, the demands of their environment. (This scale added 17 per cent explained variance of the total figure of 46 per cent.)
2. *Repression Scale.* The exclusion from conscious awareness of feelings and emotions that the individual would normally be able to experience or his failure to label these emotions. (This scale added 8 per cent explained variance to the total).
3. *Alienation Scale.* The presence of distrust and estrangement in a person's

attitude toward others, especially those in authority. (This scale added 2 per cent explained variance to the total).
4. *Asociality Scale.* A generalized disposition to resolve problems of social and personal adjustment in ways ordinarily regarded as showing a disregard for social customs or rules. (This scale added 2 per cent explained variance to the total.)

Implications for Program Operation

This analysis has presented a mixed picture, and its implications are much like those of Chapter Seven. On one hand, there was evidence that some of the basic experimental guidelines and principles had been realized; namely, that there was considerable sharing of information regarding sensitive and difficult critical incidents, that the majority of these critical incidents were precipitated by a minority of the population, and that their number had declined over time. A program culture, shared by staff and most boys, seems to have developed that was increasingly efficient as a mechanism for social control, more effective in discovering problems than regular agencies already existing in the community. Furthermore, since personality was the best input predictor of critical incident behavior, it may be that the experimental program was more successful in dealing with and controlling group-related rather than personality-related difficulties.

On the other hand, there was some indication that, because of complex pressures, the approach to critical incidents by both staff and delinquents may have been overly formal, overly punitive. The data on the subject were limited but tended to confirm the findings from Chapter Seven, which suggested that programs such as this should experiment further with means by which they can deal more effectively with the deviant individual who is perceived as a threat to everyone. At the same time, they would also need to provide greater security and rewards for those who are not only making changes themselves but are seeking to help the persistent deviant.

These are not simple problems. In the first place, they are of the kind with which community and correctional agencies have already *failed.* Like everyone else, offenders and staff in the experimental program were made insecure by the deviant individual and were perhaps too ready to turn to traditional punitive methods to deal with him. At the same time, their behavior also suggests that a total absence of structure is not the answer either. Staff and offenders simply cannot operate effectively with too much uncertainty. Not only may the persistent deviant be encouraged by an overly permissive climate, but those former offenders who are trying to help him would be at a loss as to how to cope with the situation. The trick still remains that of helping staff and offenders to collaborate effectively within normative limits upon which they both agree. A climate in which there is an adequate mixing of both certainty and flexibility is not easy to develop. Such a climate requires the continued maintenance of a delicate equilibrium in which either too much normative certainty or too much flexibility can have disastrous results.

Implications for the FEM

A major implication of this chapter for the construction of improved FEMs has to do with the methodological techniques by which researchers attempt to document program processes. In this chapter, and throughout this book, two major techniques have been used: statistical analyses based on questionnaire data and the personal perceptions of delinquent and staff members obtained from periodic unstructured interviews. It is our feeling that, although both techniques provided important information on basic issues, neither provided sufficient description of what really went on in the minds of the individuals who participated in the experiment.

The design and conduct of many, perhaps most, sociological studies depend upon some knowledge of the subjective views of the actors to be investigated. To be able to ask relevant questions and to explore key issues, the sociologist must have some prior grasp of the way those issues look to the persons who are to be studied, what they contend with, and why they believe as they do. There is nothing quite so difficult as attempting to gather data on the nature and subjective side of institutional patterns and pro- cesses without such information. The systematic collection of such sub- jective data was not included as a component of the present FEM, and, as it turns out, this may have been a significant omission.

As a means of rectifying this deficiency, we suggest that future studies of this nature institute the writing of personal diaries by selected participants. If such diaries were kept continuously by key individuals and if these individuals structured their perceptions around a common framework of incidents, a wealth of important descriptive information pertaining to program operation could be the result. A much clearer and more compre- hensive picture of program process might then be gleaned.

For example, in the present study we might have randomly selected a small number of delinquents and staff members for this purpose. The individuals selected could then have been paid a special salary to record their impressions of day-to-day events and routines. The daily recording of personal diaries could then have been instituted as a part of regular data collection procedures.

One important byproduct of keeping diaries, in addition to improved documentation of program processes, could be a detailed record of the subjective viewpoints of boys who might not complete the experiment. As will be seen in the the next chapter, a significant number of boys (about half of the total population) either ran away or were failed and, because these individuals did not finish the program, we were unable to obtain much information from them. This means that our description of process is seriously incomplete. If some of these individuals had been involved in keeping personal diaries up to the point of their departures (and even after they left), then valuable data might have been obtained concerning their particular problems and perceptions of the program. This information could then have been used both to assess the adequacy of program operation and to suggest needed improvement in program design.

References

CLOWARD, RICHARD A. 1956. Concluding comments and an example of research. In Helen L. Witmer and Ruth Kotinsky, eds., *New Perspectives for Research on Juvenile Delinquency*. Washington, D.C.: U.S. Government Printing Office.

DRAPER, N. R., and H. SMITH. 1966. *Applied Regression Analysis*. New York: John Wiley.

EMPEY, LAMAR T. 1967b. Delinquency theory and recent research. *Journal of Research in Crime and Delinquency*, 4 (January): 28–42.

FLANAGAN, JOHN C. 1954. The critical incident technique. *Psychological Bulletin*, 51 (July): 327–358.

GLASER, DANIEL. 1964. *The Effectiveness of a Prison and Parole System*. Indianapolis: Bobbs–Merrill.

GOFFMAN, ERVING. 1957. *Characteristics of Total Institutions*. Symposium on preventative and social psychiatry. Washington, D.C.; Walter Reed Army Institute of Research.

HIRSCHI, TRAVIS, and HANAN C. SELVIN. 1967. *Delinquency Research: An Appraisal of Analytic Methods*. New York: The Free Press.

JONES, JAMES A. 1964. The nature of compliance in correctional institutions for juvenile offenders. *Journal of Research in Crime and Delinquency*, 1 (July): 83–95.

MATZA, DAVID. 1964. *Delinquency and Drift*. New York: John Wiley.

RAPOPORT, R. N., R. RAPOPORT, and I. ROSOW. 1960. *Community as Doctor: New Perspective on a Therapeutic Community*. London: Tavistock Publications.

SHORT, JAMES F., JR., and FRED L. STRODTBECK. 1965. *Group Process and Gang Delinquency*. Chicago: University of Chicago Press.

STREET, DAVID, ROBERT D. VINTER, and CHARLES PERROW. 1966. *Organization for Treatment*. New York: The Free Press.

YABLONSKY, LEWIS. 1965. *Synanon: The Tunnel Back*. New York: Macmillan.

CHAPTER TEN

Implementation: Runaways[1]

Deviance is not a quality that lies in behavior itself, but in the interaction between the person who commits an act and those who respond to it (Becker, 1963: 14).

As discussed earlier, the Silverlake Experiment reflected a recent trend in corrections to develop a new institutional form—a *mediatory* institution whose major function would be to reverse the processes of stigmatization for the serious offender and to develop a rite-of-passage for him back into a non-delinquent status. Yet, despite a growing interest in this new institutional form, it possesses a number of problems associated with society's vestigal interest in punishment and coercive restraint.

The first is theoretical. Functionalists (Coser, 1962: 172–174; Erikson, 1964: 13–14) have suggested that the offender may be of greater worth to society as a deviant than as a nondeviant; that is, by maintaining him in his deviant status, especially under strong physical controls, society can use him as a reference point by which it can deter others and perpetuate its normative boundaries against deviance. To change his role would be to obscure such boundaries.

Second, the loss of coercive restraint over the deviant is regarded as a threat to community safety; the community is legitimately concerned with its own protection as well as with the offender's reintegration. Thus, by implication, the mediatory institution, as contrasted with the total institution, may be seen as blocking these two major functions. By failing to punish the serious offender in a closed setting, it (*a*) threatens to destroy

1. The analysis of runaways in this chapter is based in part upon findings reported earlier in an article by Steven G. Lubeck and LaMar T. Empey, "Mediatory *vs.* Total Institution: The Case of the Runaway" *Social Problems*, 16 (Fall, 1968): 242–260. Reprinted by permission of the publisher.

the boundary-maintaining function he performs and (*b*) decreases the security of the community.

The behavior of staff members in a number of open correctional settings is indicative of their awareness of this possible blockage. Fears of community reaction are omnipresent and there is a constant trend toward custodialism, especially when crises occur. New and innovative methods are dropped and a general, sometimes frantic, reassertion of controls by staff develops (*cf.* Street, Vinter, and Perrow, 1966: 159–190). Even in the "treatment-oriented" therapeutic community, there is a continual oscillation from a condition of permissiveness to one in which staff discards its own ideals and acts arbitrarily to remove or control the deviant (Rapoport, Rapoport, and Rasow, 1960: 135–142).

These problems are symbolic, of course, of the kinds of problems that were anticipated for the Silverlake Experiment and would pose a serious test for the whole intervention strategy. As a consequence, process research was designed to study two of the most persistent difficulties likely to be encountered: runaways and in-program failures. Such a study could help to shed further light on the adequacy of program design and implementation and to provide badly needed information on the relationship of personal to organizational characteristics.

Runaways

When physical controls over serious offenders are decreased and when isolation from the community no longer exists, as at Silverlake, the potential for runaways is increased. Yet, if mediatory institutions like Silverlake are to be effective, perhaps even to survive, they must find nonphysical means for preventing them. The point is that if the older functions of prison are to be replaced, the potential benfits must seem transcendent. As a consequence, it was necessary in designing the Silverlake Experiment to search for normative and psychological, rather than physical, means by which to maintain social control.

Unfortunately, studies dealing with runaways that might have been helpful were few in number and those that were available were concerned almost exclusively with individual characteristics (Cochrane, 1948: 3–5; Gunasekara, 1963: 145–151; Loving, Stockwell, and Dobbins, 1959: 49–51); that is, they revealed the traditional preoccupation of officials and society with the personal pathologies of offenders and showed very little concern with the organizational characteristics of the programs from which offenders run or with the interaction between personal and social systems. In light of organizational theory, these were important omissions since organizational phenomena may be as highly related to runaways as personal characteristics.

In their study of correctional organizations, for example, Street *et al.* (1966: 197) found a wide variation of runaway rates between six different juvenile correctional programs and interpreted the varied rates to be a function of differences in the organizations studied. They found that the two organizations that placed the highest emphasis on control and containment had relatively low runaway rates (16 per cent and 20 per cent), while the two organizations that emphasized "treatment" goals over those of control had relatively high runaway rates (50 per cent and 29 per cent).

In fact, Street, *et al.* (1966: 197) pointed out that, while the low runaway rates in the first two institutions reflected their concern with containment, the latter two considered runaways to be "irrelevant, unfortunate, symptomatic or even healthy." This relative lack of concern for the absconder undoubtedly contributed to the higher runaway rates. Yet, any mediatory institution that continually ignores runaways may be courting disaster. Community concern over the potential threat of the convicted offender, real or imagined, cannot be ignored.

One of the crucial tests for the intervention strategy at Silverlake was whether attempts to develop a reformation culture would be successful in dealing with these problems. Similarly, one of the tests of the research design was whether it could provide badly needed information relative to the impact of this design on runaway rates, especially to examine the ways in which the individual traits of offenders might interact with the characteristics of the experimental organization to produce or inhibit runaway behavior.

Definition and Measurement Issues

DEFINITION OF RUNAWAY

A rather stringent definition of runaways was adopted. A runaway was defined as any unauthorized leave of absence from either program that lasted longer than 24 hours. In general, this stringent definition was adopted because of its significance for the operation of the two programs. Not only did the absence of an offender from either program create considerable anxiety, but it also meant special problems at the experimental residence. It will be recalled from Chapter Eight that boys who were absent without leave for more than one day were suspended by officials from school. Consequently, such absences, even for a short period, had extremely important significance—a significance that added to the importance of conducting research on the subject.

It should be noted that all runaways did not result automatically in termination from either program. There were some boys who ran away and were accepted back. Furthermore, among those who were terminated, some ran away as many as three or four times before they were either dropped from a program or ended the runaway behavior. Even so, we felt it important to predict all occurrences of runaway behavior, even though that behavior did not always result in termination.

RUNAWAY RATES

Of particular importance to this study was the fact that the terminal runaway rates for both institutions covering a $2\frac{1}{2}$-year period were relatively high and strikingly similar—37 per cent at the experimental residence and 40 per cent at the control program. While these high and strikingly similar runaway rates were distressing, they did provide an excellent opportunity, given the initial similarity of the randomized samples and the large organizational differences between the two programs, to determine if the same sorts of variables were associated with running away at both places. They helped to indicate whether certain types of boys were predisposed to run away from one program and not the other and whether program characteristics could be linked to such differences.

MEASUREMENT PROBLEMS

It will be recalled that a variety of scales and indexes were developed by which to measure offender characteristics. In all, they include a total of 31 complex measures: 9 indexes of psychological characteristics, 8 social background scales, 4 peer relations scales, 8 offense scales, and 2 process measures that included sociometric standing and the number of critical incidents that were not runaways.

The same stepwise regression procedures that were used to predict critical incidents were used in this analysis. An advantage of the stepwise procedure is that it enables one to develop an optimal 10-variable regression model by selecting the best predictors from the group of 31 possible predictors. This is an important advantage because when a large number of variables (*i.e.*, 31) is used in multiple regression, the degree of error present may be magnified and the amount of explained variance might be spuriously high. Stepwise procedures do not necessarily eliminate problems of error or spuriously high explained variance, but they might help to reduce the problem by excluding variables whose potential contributions to the multiple regression might be small and possibly reflective of error.

Thus, stepwise procedures seemed particularly well suited to the task of determining how well we could predict variation in runaways. However, the very efficiency of stepwise procedures for prediction purposes limited its utility for the purpose of identifying which families of measures—*i.e.*, peer, offense, background, or personality—were the most efficient predictors. The reasons for this are complex and will not be given detailed discussion at this point. Suffice it to say that problems of "multicollinearity" (*cf.* Gordon, 1968) or high correlations among predictor variables might cast questions of doubt upon the effective use of stepwise procedures in determining how much families of measures or single measures contributed to the explained variance. Because of this, a series of multiple regression models using all 31 predictor variables were calculated in addition to the 10-variable stepwise models. The 31-variable regression models would certainly not eliminate multicollinearity problems but, when examined in conjunction with the 10-variable models, might give a better indication of how much variation could be legitimately attributed to families of measures. Even so, problems of error and multicollinearity may remain, problems that may or may not seriously affect the findings.

Prediction of Runaway Behavior

The first issue we looked at was the amount of explained variance provided by these families of variables. (By way of explanation, "explained variance" refers to the per cent of the total variation in runaway behavior that is explained by offender characteristics.) Unfortunately, the ability of these sets of variables to explain runaway behavior was not as great as we had hoped. The explained variance for the experimental sample was only 16 per cent in the 10-variable model and 17 per cent in the 29-variable model. However, it was nearly twice as high for the control sample, 30 and 36 per cent respectively. The analysis which follows will shed some light on the reasons for this low predictability.

THE BEST PREDICTORS

Since there were some differences in explained variance between the two programs, the next question asks what the most efficient predictors were. What personal factors were most closely associated with running away? In order to get at this issue, our analysis is described in terms of the per cent of the explained variance that any set of predictor variables contributes to the total. For example, in Table 10.1 it will be observed that for the experimentals the "total explained variance," using the first ten steps of the stepwise regression analysis, was 16 per cent. Meanwhile, of that total, the offense scales alone accounted for 8 per cent. Thus, they accounted for 50 per cent of the explained variance in the experimental program. In other words, the "per cent of explained variance" is a relative term designed to provide information on the proportions each type of measure—offense,

Table 10.1. Variance explained in predicting Runaways—Experimental and Control Institution

Variable category	Experimental institution				Control institution			
	10-Variable stepwise regression		31-Variable multiple regression		10-Variable stepwise regression		29-Variable[a] multiple regression	
	Proportion of variance added to R^2	Explained variance %	Proportion of variance added to R^2	Explained variance %	Proportion of variance added to R^2	Explained variance %	Proportion of variance added to R^2	Explained variance %
Peer identification	.033	21	.037	22	.000	0	.073	20
Personality	.015	9	.028	17	.065	21	.114	32
Offense	.080	50	.036	22	.125	41	.124	35
Background	.032	20	.056	33	.115	38	.046	13
Process	.000	0	.011	7	—	—	—	—
Total	.160	100	.168	101	.305	100	.357	100

[a] Only 29, as opposed to 31, predictors were used for the control group because measures of critical incidents and sociometric standing were not collected for this group.

personality, background, and peer—contributed to the total explained variance.

As will be observed in Table 10.1, offense history tended to be the best predictor for both experimental and control programs, but here the similarity ended. Peer influence at the experimental program accounted for a higher proportion of the total explained variance than at the control program. In fact, peer influence in the control setting was not among the ten most predictive variables to emerge in the stepwise regression analyses. By contrast, personality and background characteristics seemed to account for relatively higher proportions of the explained variance at the control than at the experimental program.

In light of the fact that the two samples were randomly assigned to either program and that they were essentially similar at the time of their assignment, these findings suggest the importance of organizational impact upon individual behavior. Those factors associated with runaway behavior in the total institution seemed to be different from those associated with it in the experimental setting.

In attempting to isolate the nature of these different patterns, we discovered that these general findings, complex as they are, actually understated the interactive effects of organizational and personal variables. We discovered that this overall analysis was actually masking more facts than it was revealing, the reason being that, as structural changes occurred within each of the organizations, the relationship of the four sets of predictor variables to running away changed also, *suggesting that there may be no uniform sets of personal variables that will be predictive of running away unless organizational characteristics are held constant.* By way of illustration, consider what happened when important programmatic changes occurred in the two institutions.

Effect of Program Changes on Predictability

At the approximate midpoint of the study, sixteenth months after it began, the staff of the experimental program was confronted with a serious dilemma because of the high runaway rate. On the one hand, if the high incidence of runaways persisted, the program risked serious reaction from the community and school. In fact, the runaway problem was paralleled by the development of the Homeowner's Protective Association mentioned in Chapter Eight and by the policy of the school to suspend any absentee. As a consequence, the staff of the program felt that something drastic had to be done.

On the other hand, any attempt by the staff to impose stringent surveillance and physical controls over the boys would risk the possibility of defeating the mediatory philosophy and goals of the program. They were confronted with the task of attempting to decrease runaways while, at the same time, finding social or psychological, as opposed to physical, means for doing so.

In order to deal with this problem, the action staff, in consultation with the research staff, decided to experiment with the imposition of a strong negative sanction against runaways. They called all of the boys together and announced arbitrarily that any boy who ran away would be automatically terminated from the program and recommended for incarceration. By treating the sanction experimentally, its impact could then be analyzed within the context of the FEM.

The reactions of the assembled boys were surprising. The announcement was greeted almost with a sense of relief. As one boy put it,

> It was getting so around here that everybody felt entitled to one runaway. In fact, the story was that you're safe until you split the third time. That's the one that gets you in real trouble. So whenever some cat got a little fed up, he just took off.

A second boy also made a significant point. It was his position that the group simply could not deal with some problems, such as runaways.

> There are some things this group is not going to do—and that is to put some kid out if he is likely to get locked up. The way I see it, that's staff's responsibility, not ours.
>
> But you know, man, that still leaves us in a bind because these dudes that just keep on fuckin' up, fuck us up too. They make it hard for guys that do want to change. Man, I just don't know. You can't win. Anyway, I guess I'm for it.

In any event, the impact of this arbitrary decision was dramatically demonstrated almost immediately. Within a few days after the sanction was imposed, four boys left and were summarily terminated. One boy, faced with the prospect of incarceration, returned to the residence and pleaded for leniency, but the staff remained adamant and he was incarcerated. The nature of the sanction was dramatically demonstrated.

The immediate impact of this action on other boys was great. During the two months following its imposition, there were *no* runaways.

One boy's view on this matter was short and to the point. He saw the AWOL sanction as a personal deterrent.

Interviewer: What do you think of the new AWOL restriction?
Kel: I think it's pretty good.
Interviewer: Why?
Kel: Because it's holding me back.
Interviewer: Otherwise you'd be gone?
Kel: Yep.

However, the effects of the sanction seemed to diminish over time: during the third month there were two runaways, and by the end of the fourth month there were five, making a total of seven in all. The runaway rate then continued to increase until it reached its prior level. Thus, the sanction had an immediate, but not a lasting effect.

In discussing phenomena of this type, Festinger (1957: Chap. IV) and Aronson (1966: 25–27) have argued that a severe negative sanction may be ineffective in producing personal change, although it may produce an initial "public compliance." Aronson, for example, contends that a "single mild threat" may produce more effective and more long-lasting changes than severe threats. He suggests that "one way to get a person to inhibit an activity is to get him to devalue it . . . and one way to get him to devalue it is to stop him in the first place with a mild threat rather than a severe one" (Aronson, 1966: 27).

If one accepts this point of view, then the runaway sanction may have been too severe. It may have produced initial public compliance with little change in the personal or subcultural norms and practices of delinquents. However, there is another viewpoint that one might take. It is possible that once the runaway norm was applied, not enough was done to keep it alive and meaningful. One of the things we observed in the program was that continual attention must be paid to the maintenance of key norms, attention that uses discussion and positive reinforcers as well as negative ones. The reascendancy of the runaway rate could have been due, at least in part, to this inadequacy. Unfortunately, we did not collect data that would bear directly on this issue, but some data were collected that deal with it indirectly.

In examining the factors associated with the runaway problem, two issues were considered: (1) the extent to which the personal factors associated with running away changed after the sanction; and (2) the kinds of problems encountered by a program in attempting to develop, impose, and maintain a norm absolutely opposed to running away.

Before and After Analysis. In order to determine the personal effects of the sanction, the experimental sample was divided into pre- and post-sanction groups and separate attempts at prediction made using personal factors as predictors. The findings may be found in Table 10.2. The explained variance for the pre-sanction group was 35 per cent for the 10-variable model and 40 per cent for the 31-variable model. For the post-sanction group it was 41 per cent and 56 per cent. This indicates a slight increase in the predictability of runaways after the sanction, but even more important, the analysis revealed some drastic shifts in the types of variables associated with running away.

Prior to the sanction, the peer influence scales accounted for 22 per cent

Table 10.2. Variance explained in predicting Runaways at the Experimental Program before and after the Runaway Sanction

Variable category	Before sanction				After sanction			
	10-Variable stepwise regression		31-Variable multiple regression		10-Variable stepwise regression		31-Variable multiple regression	
	Proportion of variance added to R²	Explained variance %	Proportion of variance added to R²	Explained variance %	Proportion of variance added to R²	Explained variance %	Proportion of variance added to R²	Explained variance %
Peer identification	.076	22	.062	16	.000	0	.074	13
Personality	.025	7	.054	14	.133	33	.167	30
Offense	.121	35	.055	14	.177	44	.241	43
Background	.124	36	.144	36	.096	24	.068	12
Process	.000	0	.081	20	.000	0	.013	2
Total	.346	100	.396	100	.406	100	.563	100

of the explained variance in the 10-variable model, and 16 per cent in the 31-variable model; yet after the sanction, their predictive power was much lower. Thus, the sanction may have diminished the effects of situational peer influence. At the same time, the predictive power of personality factors was greatly increased. Before the sanction, they accounted for 7 and 14 per cent of the explained variance; after the sanction this figure jumped to 33 and 30 per cent. The predictive capacity of the offense scales also increased after the sanction: from 35 and 14 per cent to 44 and 43 per cent, while the per cent of the explained variance accounted for by the background factors decreased from 36 per cent in both models to 24 per cent and 12 per cent.[2]

These findings seem to indicate a mutual influence between structural change, personal characteristics, and resulting behavior. In its attempts at control, the experimental program may have deterred certain types of individuals from running but at the same time may have created new problems for others. Before examining the implications of this finding, some significant changes that occurred at the institutional program will be examined because they bear so heavily on this issue. There are both some differences and similarities which merit special attention before any final assessment of implications can be made.

Effect of Changes at the Control Institution

At approximately the same time the runaway sanction was imposed at the experimental program, the program at the control institution underwent a series of major organizational changes as well. These changes were not directed specifically at the control of runaways but reflected an effort to revamp some of the older methods that had been used for "treating" delinquents. These changes resulted in major alterations in the general structure of the program with concomitant changes in the specific roles of staff and the specific roles of boys.

The most important change involved a shift from a concentration upon

2. The changes in the predictability of the offense, background, personality, and peer identification scales does not mean that the boys' actual personal characteristics changed over time. Analyses can only be interpreted to mean that the types of boys prone to running away changed over time.

Furthermore, it should be pointed out that if a group of scales is found to be predictive, this does not necessarily mean that high scores on the scales are associated with running away. For example, the finding that the predictability of the personality scales increased after the runaway sanction does not necessarily mean that only those boys with a high degree of personality maladjustment were most inclined to run away after the sanction. It could also be that low scores on certain personality factors might be related to the incidence of runaways. However, in the case of runaways at the experiment, it turned out that those boys with high personality problems were those most inclined to run. This issue will be the subject of further discussion later in this chapter.

one-to-one relationships between staff and boys to a more group-oriented form of treatment. As in the experimental program, an effort was made to involve boys more heavily in the counseling and decision-making processes. In order to enhance the effects of groups, therefore, certain other changes followed. For example, a boy's length of stay at the institution prior to this time had been predetermined; his length of sentence was relatively fixed. After the change, length of stay was made indeterminate. His release from the program was predicated upon his willingness to contribute to the reformation of others and to exhibit constructive behavioral changes to his peers as well as to staff.

Similarly, the furlough-granting policies of the control institution were changed. Prior to the change, passes to visit home or the nearby town were issued to boys at set intervals, the first one being issued three months after entrance into the program. After the change, passes were issued solely on the basis of merit as determined by the group. As a consequence, some boys remained within the confines of the institution for six months or longer without being granted a pass.

The introduction of the group techniques radically redefined a number of staff roles. Before the change, the power of sanction and control remained largely in the hands of a small custodial staff, while counselors were concerned primarily with "treatment" in the form of individual counseling. The new changes, however, resulted in a marked shift of power from custody to treatment staff. This shift was not without negative consequences. It generated considerable conflict between the counseling and custodial groups, with many of the latter keenly feeling their loss of power.

Alterations in the roles of certain inmates were greater than those already implied. Prior to the change, a formally elected boy government had existed. This government, involving all of the elective officers ordinarily found in a community—mayor, police chief, fire commissioner, councilman, etc.—was used ostensibly to fulfill two major functions: to teach responsible citizenship and to assist staff in maintaining control. This system granted considerable power to a small minority of elected officials. One major change was to restructure the boy government system and to distribute this power so that it might be used informally in small group decision-making. Hopefully, it would result in a more democratic method of examining problems and resolving issues by eliminating the granting of considerable power to an elite inmate group.

Before and After Analysis. The same procedure used for assessing the impact of change at the experimental institution was used at the control institution. The sample was divided into pre- and post-change groups and separate attempts at prediction made for each group. The results of the analysis may be found in Table 10.3.

Table 10.3. Variance explained in predicting Runaways at the Control Institution before and after Organizational Changes

| | Before changes | | | | After changes | | | |
| | 10-Variable stepwise regression | | 29-Variable multiple regression | | 10-Variable stepwise regression | | 29-Variable multiple regression | |
Variable category	Proportion of variance added to R^2	Explained variance %	Proportion of variance added to R^2	Explained variance %	Proportion of variance added to R^2	Explained variance %	Proportion of variance added to R^2	Explained variance %
Peer identification	.111	27	.136	24	.085	15	.110	16
Personality	.019	5	.222	39	.223	41	.147	22
Offense	.238	58	.138	24	.083	15	.240	35
Background	.043	11	.079	14	.161	29	.187	27
Total	.411	100	.575	101	.552	100	.684	100

The total explained variance before the change was 41 per cent in the 10-variable model and 58 per cent in the 29-variable model. After the change, it rose to 55 and 68 per cent. Some striking changes in the types of variables associated with running away also occurred. As was observed in the experimental setting, there was a decrease in the predictive contribution of the peer influence scales. Before the change, peer factors contributed 27 and 24 per cent of the explained variance but declined to 15 and 16 per cent.

Personality factors, meanwhile, increased from 5 per cent to 41 per cent in the 10-variable model and decreased from 39 to 22 per cent in the 29-variable model. The contributions of the offense scales in the 10-variable models decreased markedly, from 58 per cent before the change to 15 per cent after it. In the 29-variable model, they increased from 24 per cent to 35 per cent. Furthermore, the per cent of explained variance accounted for by background factors increased from 11 and 14 per cent to 29 and 27 per cent. Clearly, this is further documentation of the differential impact of organizational change upon personal characteristics as they are associated with behavior. In specific terms, it indicates that one could not assume a static relationship between the personal factors associated with running away without regard to either organizational structure or organizational change.

COMMON PREDICTOR VARIABLES

One additional issue needs consideration before the implications of these findings are discussed. It will be recalled that each of the four main measures —peer influence, personality, offense history, and social background—are comprised of several complex indexes. It is of importance to know whether any of the single indexes that make up these complex measures appear repeatedly as the most predictive, whether, for example, an offense pattern, a personality trait, or some other factor made its appearance in the stepwise analysis under a variety of organizational changes. If it did, it might constitute a reliable measure upon which to base correctional decisions. Single predictive measures could be of considerable use to correctional people in both classification and program operation.

In general, there were not many reliable single predictors, but a few exceptions were notable by their presence.[3] Table 10.4 shows how many times each scale was included in the stepwise regression runs and the nature of each scale's relationship to running away. A plus sign in the

3. One note of caution regarding the stepwise procedures. Only those predictor variables that correlate most highly with the dependent variable are initially included in any multiple regression model. If other variables are redundant with those that appear initially, they would not be included in the model. Thus, it is possible that some measures, because they correlate highly with those that are included, did not appear (*cf*. Gordon, 1968).

Table 10.4. Number of times Variables appeared in the Stepwise Regression Analyses—Predicting Runaways

	Experimental Program			Control program			Total N. of times included
	Total	Before	After	Total	Before	After	
Offense Scales							
Seriousness	[a]+	+		+	+	+	5
Family problems	+	−	+	+	+		5
Automobile	+		+	−	−		4
Habitualness		+	−				2
Theft					−	+	2
Personal disorganization	+						1
Street corner			−				1
Background Scales							
School interest	+	+		+	+	+	5
Self-concept	+		+	−		−	4
Age		−		−		−	3
Social class		+					1
Family disorganization			+				1
Work			+				1
Aspirations				+			1
School frustration						−	1
Personality Scales							
Autism		+	−	−		−	4
Social anxiety	+			+		−	3
Repression	+		+			+	3
Withdrawal				+	+		2
Affect			+				1
Asocial index						+	1
Peer Influence Scales							
Sociability	+	+		−			3
Deviancy	+	+					2
Ratfink				+	+		2
Ace-in-the-Hole			+	+			2

[a] The (+) and (−) signs indicate the directions of the *beta* weights for each scale in its respective regression model. A (+) sign indicates that high scores on a given scale were associated with a high incidence of runaway behavior. A (−) sign indicates that high scores on a given scale were associated with a low incidence of runaway behavior.

table indicates that high scores on a given scale were related to running, while a minus sign in the table indicates that low scores on a given scale were related to running.

The most efficient group of predictors included the offense seriousness scale, the family-related offenses scale, and the school interest scale. Each of these scales appeared in all but one of the six prediction models, including both the experimental and control groups. The offense scale that measures seriousness was positively related to running away in all instances. This means that offenders who had committed the most serious delinquent acts were the most prone to run from both programs. The scale that measures family-related offenses—incorrigibility, and running away from home—was, for the most part, positively related to running. The only exception was before the sanction at the experimental program, at which time low scores on this scale were associated with running away. A high degree of interest in school was also associated with running in all instances, a finding that is significant but for which we do not have an explanation.

The second most efficient group of predictors were the automobile offenses scale, the self-concept scale—a boy's view of his "smartness" compared to his peers—and the autism scale from the personality group. The specific manner in which each of these scales were related to runaways may be found in Table 10.4.

In summary, the factors that were most consistently associated with running away, no matter what the organizational circumstance, were a background of serious automobile and family-related offenses, interest in school, self-concept, and a tendency to be autistic. While a prior knowledge of these factors would leave much unknown, they might be of help to correctional staff, singly or in configuration, in anticipating runaway behavior.

Implications: Theoretical and Pragmatic

There seem to be at least three major issues contained in the overall findings just described: (1) the extent to which offense history remained relatively high in its relationship to running away; (2) the dynamic relationship between personal and social systems; and (3) the implications of these findings for correctional theory and control, both for mediatory and total institutions in general.

OFFENSE HISTORY

It is striking, and perhaps ironic, that offense history, with all the errors in record keeping and official subjectivity it implies, should have greater overall predictive value during the $2\frac{1}{2}$ years of the study than the several measures of background, peer influence, and personality characteristics that were used, especially since it is the latter that have received the greatest amount of attention from social scientists and clinicians. Offense history proved to have an overall higher predictability than any other category for nearly all of the six stepwise regression analyses. The only exception was with the post-sanction group at the control institution, where the contribution of offense scales was overshadowed by background and personality factors.

Such findings underscore both theoretical and methodological weaknesses in the field. For example, despite all the theoretical superstructures that have been built upon the notion that personality deviations and delinquent behavior are related, the conclusions one could reach from these findings are very similar to those reached by Hathaway, Monachesi, and Young (1960: 439) based upon a much more comprehensive study of the subject; namely, that personality factors by themselves are relatively weak predictors. They "are much less powerful and apply to fewer cases among the total samples than would be expected if one reads the literature on the subject."[4]

Actually, this study suggests a different kind of qualification than that suggested by Hathaway *et al.* The problem may lie not so much in the total lack of utility of personality measures as in the static classifications that personality and our other measures have supplied: that is, they have failed to account for the impact on personality of experience in different situational contexts. This study indicates that personal response will not be nonconditional but will vary as organizational structure varies.

When dramatic shifts occurred in the two institutions, the various measures of personality characteristics seemed to assume a greater predictive power. This was especially true at the experimental program. They seemed to reflect problems precipitated by structural changes. What is implied, therefore, is a need for theory and measurement that do a better job, first, of identifying various personal characteristics and, second, of explaining the ways in which those characteristics may influence or are affected by different organizational contexts. Since role expectations change from organization to organization, it would be important to know how those changes are reflected in psychological terms.

Insofar as the practical problems of corrections are concerned, there is a

---

4. Summaries of other studies on adult criminals suggest: (1) that the majority of offenders are more alike than different from the general population and (2) that measures of personality which yield deviancy variations reliability still do not distinguish among delinquent behaviour types (Lagache, 1950; Mensh, 1963: 21–28). However, one theoretical framework, which utilizes "maturity levels" rather than personality types, has resulted in an extremely complex linkage between a scheme for classifying delinquents and variations in treatment techniques (*cf.* Sullivan, Grant, and Grant, 1957; Warren, 1967).

tremendous lag between the amount of research which is concerned with the interaction between personal and social systems and the amount of general theory which posits a profound and complex relation between the two. Until more research is focused on this area, therefore, the findings of this study suggest that relatively simple measures of the past behavior of offenders may be of more immediate and practical utility in assigning offenders to different programs than measures of personality and background characteristics. They may still be the most stable indicators as to what should be done with offenders in a general way.

Once offenders are in the correctional system, however, administrators might be forewarned that the predictive efficiency of different characteristics will vary considerably, depending upon organizational changes that occur. The factors that were helpful in classifying offenders initially will not necessarily be the best indicators when change occurs.

On one hand, organizational changes in both institutions seemed to be followed by an increase in the predictive contribution of personality factors and a concomitant decrease in the effects of peer influence. And, to make matters more complex, the predictive contribution of background factors decreased in the community but increased in the institution.

All of this simply underscores the dynamic and mutually dependent relationship between personal and organizational systems, where dramatic changes in one seem to effect dramatic changes in the other. Perhaps the greatest certainty lies in the assumption that, where offenders do have personality difficulties, those difficulties can be expected to surface initially under the duress of structural change. But once new collective adjustments are worked out—deviant or otherwise—it is likely that a new configuration of predictive variables will emerge, likely with personality factors again decreasing in importance and others increasing.

IMPLICATIONS FOR COMMUNITY PROGRAMS

The interdependence of personal and organizational characteristics is best illustrated by the problems that were encountered in the experimental program, where change efforts were directed toward creating and maintaining a non-delinquent reformation culture and simultaneously confronting boys with the mediatory problems of school and community adjustment. This program, despite its concern for the offender, may have put those persons with the greatest number of personal disabilities in the most vulnerable position, especially after the runaway sanction was imposed. As substantiation for this notion, we discovered that as the normative structure of the experimental program was solidified by the sanction, it seemed to precipitate personal problems rather quickly and either rejected the people who had those problems or failed to develop adequate mechanisms by which to socialize and retain them.

The evidence is derived from additional analyses of runaways before and after the implementation of the runaway sanction. This analysis, covering a thirty-two-month period, revealed that early runaways became an increasing problem. An "early runaway" was defined as one occurring within two months after a boy's assignment to the program. During the 16 months before the sanction, when program norms were still in the process of being established, boys were as inclined to run away late in their stay as early. During this period, 37 per cent of the inmates ran away at some time or other, with only about 14 per cent of these runaways—about one-third of the total—occurring during the first two months of the inmates' stay. But, after the sanction, as normative expectations began to solidify, the number of early runaways began to increase.

During the first eight months after the sanction, even though the total number of runaways did not increase, the per cent of early runaways increased from one-third to more than half of the total. During the second eight-month period after the sanction, the overall runaway rate again remained about the same at 36 per cent, but the early runaway rate increased even further, to 77 per cent of all runaways. Thus, there was a dramatic increase in the per cent of early runaways, while at the same time the overall runaway rate remained fairly stable. These changes are graphically displayed in Figure 10.1.

The analysis of critical incidents, presented in the preceding chapter, revealed that, in contrast to those boys who entered the program before the sanction, boys who entered the system later in its life were increasingly confronted with a program culture in which their peers, as well as staff, began immediately to impose controls and scrutinize behavior. The following comments from one of the boys illustrates this condition and presents a theme that can be found in virtually every one of the interviews in which offenders were asked to speak to this issue.

> Right from the start I think I hated and resented this place. I thought I was unjustly put on, and I was all confused. So the first thing I tried to do was brownnose the staff, and act big among the boys. But no matter how it came out I was low man on the totem pole. I was nothin'.

Thus, it appears that as the culture developed, a pecking order emerged that left the new boy on a limb. Along with it seems to have been a diminishing tolerance for deviance.

An obvious remedy for this situation might have been a greater degree of tolerance and versatility on the part of the program. But more than manifest functions must be considered. On one hand, runaways clearly

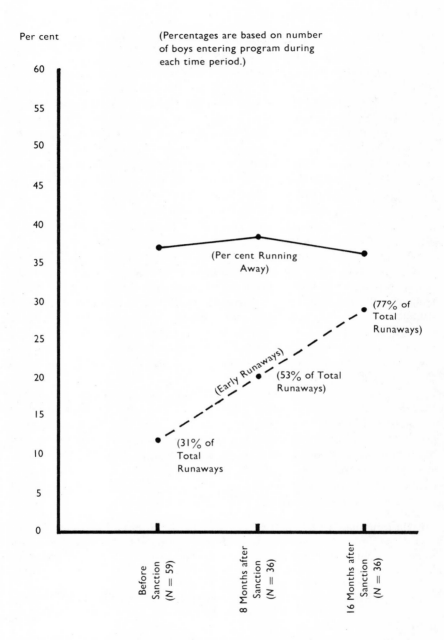

Per cent

(Percentages are based on number of boys entering program during each time period.)

60
55
50
45
40
35
30
25
20
15
10
5
0

(Per cent Running Away)

(Early Runaways)

(77% of Total Runaways)

(53% of Total Runaways)

(31% of Total Runaways

Before Sanction (N = 59)

8 Months after Sanction (N = 36)

16 Months after Sanction (N = 36)

Figure 10.1. Changes in Early Runaways at the Experimental Program Before and After the Sanction.

seem to thwart the manifest correctional objective of decreasing delinquent behavior. Obviously, it seems that boys who do not stay in the system cannot be changed by the system. Furthermore, runaways are perceived by the community and school as threatening, especially where the correctional program is located in a residential neighborhood. Manifest objectives, therefore, would seem to suggest the need for a radical alteration of organizational characteristics in order to retain and help the most difficult problem cases.

This conclusion seems especially pertinent when the "causes" for runaways are investigated. They reveal a high degree of situational, as contrasted with possibly "deep-seated" or premeditated, influences.

Interviewer: Pete, why don't you tell me why you went AWOL?

Pete: Well, I was just sitting in the classroom, and it was one of the classes that Sam was in, and he just walked up to me, said uh, "The car is downstairs, got a full tank of gas, let's split."

Interviewer: Did you give it any thought when you went AWOL?

Pete: No, I didn't even think of it as going AWOL.

Interviewer: How did you feel at the time?

Pete: At the time I was going?

Interviewer: Yes.

Pete: Nervous, I was scared.

Interviewer: Why were you scared?

Pete: It was a . . . I'd never done anything like this before.

Interviewer: Did you know about the sanction that when boys go AWOL, they can't come back to the residence?

Pete: Yeah.

Interviewer: How did you feel about it at the time?

Pete: I didn't think of it as going AWOL.

Interviewer: How did you feel about it afterwards?

Pete: I felt, ah, stupid. One of the stupidest things I've ever done. And I knew it.

Interviewer: Are you glad you went AWOL?

Pete: No.

Interviewer: Why not?

Pete: 'Cause, I coulda been, well, released, I mean I probably coulda been released by now.

Interviewer: What kinds of things could have prevented you from going AWOL?

Pete: If I wasn't so easily led at the time.

Interviewer: What do you mean by being easily led?

Pete: Well, that was one of my main problems, that they were trying to get at in group. That I was a follower. And, uh, I mean I just coulda said no without hurting either of us, but I just, I didn't want 'em to think me chicken . . . afraid to go so I just split.

Interviewer: In other words, you thought that Sam and the others thinking you chicken was more important than what the group had said?

Pete: Yeah, at the time.

It would seem that to react punitively to an act such as this would indeed be an unnecessary "dramatization of evil" (Tannenbaum, 1938: 21) and might end up evoking the very traits that are being complained of. On the other hand, the problem is that runaway behavior may have important consequences, not just for runaways but for other offenders in the system. By forcing nonconformists out of the system at an early stage, the task they have of maintaining a cohesive reformation culture may be facilitated. This is important because in addition to being concerned with those offenders who cannot deal with normative demands, a mediatory program must also be concerned with those who can. In this case, where offenders were sponsored in a reformation role, where they were expected to solve problems and make decisions, strains generated by the incoming deviant who does not conform rather quickly may be more of a threat than the system can tolerate. The adjustment for everyone, including the conformist, is tenuous.

Both offenders and staff tend to compartmentalize on this issue. For example, the boy who was cited earlier, and who complained about being low man on the totem pole, felt that the program should be tougher, not more lenient.

Jack: I think this place ought to be a lot more tough. Harder work and more of it. If staff let boys know where they stand, right from the beginning, a lot more would be accomplished.

Interviewer: I take it, then, that you are in favor of the AWOL restriction.

Jack: I think it had a good effect because then guys realized that they just couldn't go AWOL and then come back again. Well, they had more to risk, instead of just going AWOL and then knowing, you know, well, I'm coming back, maybe tomorrow or the next day. I won't get sent down.

Interviewer: How many times did guys think they could go AWOL before getting into serious trouble?

Jack: About three times. Everyone kind of felt that not until the third time would a guy get sent down. Now if you go AWOL once, you're gone, and I think it's good, 'cause it puts pressure on guys to stay in the house because nobody wants to leave here and serve time some place else.

As was pointed out in the chapter on critical incidents, the history of such social movements as Synanon provides some confirmation of this notion. It suggests that the personal and social adjustments of those who radically alter their roles are sufficiently threatening as to require strong, even rigid, in-group supports (Yablonsky, 1965). If this is the case, then one might anticipate considerable suspicion and intolerance by those who are converted to the system toward those who are unwilling to commit themselves religiously to it. Anyone who cannot accept membership zealously is not permitted to endanger those who can. "I think," said one boy, "that it is discouraging when a guy is changing and there are a few pricks around who are doing just the opposite. It gums the whole works up and the group spends all its time putting fires out."

In a similar way, Bullington, Mann, and Geis (1969: 456–463) report that ex-addicts who had been hired to work with practicing addicts in the community experienced considerable role conflict between their new-found inclination to adopt middle-class behavior and the job demands placed upon them as street workers. Their relationships with practicing addicts were such an intense and forceful reminder of what they had been, and could again become, that it seemed necessary for them "to put distance between themselves and their clients in order to secure a firm middle-class footing."

Evidence such as this suggests the possible need to redefine the reformation role for the ex-offender. How much protection and social distance does he need from his more delinquent peers? When does their behavior become a threat to his own tenuous adjustment. In the Silverlake Experiment, for example, it appears that while both staff and boys may have been overly rigid with runaways and other kinds of "troublemakers," any attempt to remedy that situation would require attention to the alternative costs for those delinquents who were playing an active reformation role. Besides considering what might be done to make life more comfortable for marginal people, one would also have to consider what such an alteration would do to those offenders who accept and reinforce the reformation culture. But rather than pursuing this issue here, let us postpone it because this is not the last we will see of it. It keeps reappearing, like a sore thumb, throughout the chapter.

IMPLICATIONS FOR TOTAL INSTITUTIONS

In contrast to the mediatory experimental program, the runaway problem at the total institution seems to require a different perspective. The experimental program was an emerging organization; the total institution was an organization of long standing. The problems at the experimental program were due to an effort to establish normative structure. The problems at the total institution were due to an effort to revise structure.

Thus, it could be anticipated that these changes would affect the offender population in the total institution in a way different from the population in the experimental program. And that is what our data suggested.

While changes in the experimental program seem to have had the greatest effect on the incoming deviant, as manifested by the increased trend toward early runaways, such a trend at the total institution was not present. Instead, the runaway problem was represented by a marked increase in overall runaway rates, rather than an increase in early runaways.

Figure 10.2 reveals that some drastic shifts occurred. The overall runaway rate before the organizational changes was about 25 per cent. But, in the first eight months following the changes, it increased to 41 per cent, and in the second eight months, to 59 per cent. Meanwhile, the early runaway rate remained at about the same proportion of the total. Therefore, it is clear that the runaway problems produced by the changes were of the kind that affected older role encumbents in the system, not just new ones.

This drastic increase in overall runaway rates, suggests that the control program may have been in an "anomie" state. Anomie, as conceptualized by Durkheim (1951), connotes a dynamic and drastic shift in the institutionalized norms of a social system. As a result of this shift, old normative patterns are no longer applicable to new situations.

The normative discontinuity that is produced was studied by Durkheim as one type of social condition contributing to suicide rates, but it could logically be related to other escapist phenomena such as runaways. In fact, runaway rates may be an important indicator of variations in the normative continuity or cohesiveness of any correctional institution.

By way of illustration, it will be recalled that the boy government system and all of its social positions were restructured by the changes at the total institution. This meant that certain boys, notably the elite group of governmental officials, lost the power and privileges associated with their former positions. This was combined with alternations in the old norms concerning length of sentence and furlough-granting. Instead of "doing time" according to preset conditions, boys were faced with an entirely new set of normative expectations. Under the new system, decisions to release a boy or to grant him furloughs were based entirely on meritorious performance, as evaluated within small-group settings. Our findings led us to believe that, as a consequence of these discontinuities, certain types of boys, notably ones with personality problems, may have chosen to escape the system by running instead of remaining in the system and coping with the new problems and strains engendered by the changes.

It is also significant that the structural changes affected staff subgroups. As mentioned earlier, the role of the custody staff was revised, and this particular subgroup underwent a considerable loss of power. This power

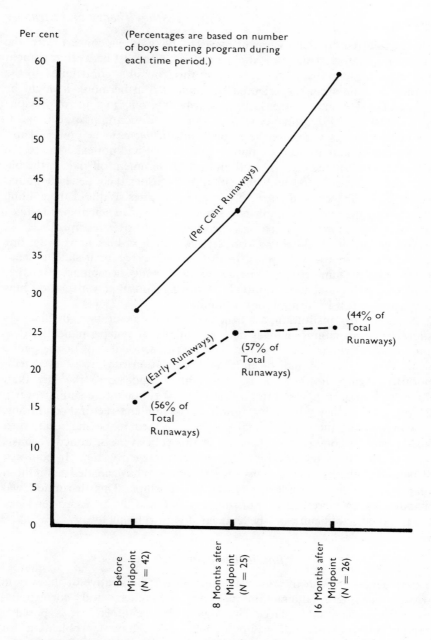

Per cent

(Percentages are based on number of boys entering program during each time period.)

(Per Cent Runaways)

(Early Runaways)

(44% of Total Runaways)

(57% of Total Runaways)

(56% of Total Runaways)

Before Midpoint (N = 42)

8 Months after Midpoint (N = 25)

16 Months after Midpoint (N = 26)

Figure 10.2. Changes in Early Runaways at the Control Institution Before and After Organizational Changes.

was transferred to the treatment staff, to be used in concert with the inmate population. This resulted in considerable conflict between treatment and custody subgroups. This conflict, in turn, possibly contributed to the already existing strain experienced by inmates. Furthermore, it might be pointed out that anomie does not necessarily refer only to a *loss* of previous social position. The same type of normative discontinuities can occur among subgroups who have received a drastic *increase* in power. Thus, the treatment staff and certain inmate groups who had not experienced the status enjoyed by the custody staff and boy government officials in the old system, were now faced with the situation of using their newly acquired power constructively and effectively in group settings. Without the guiding structure of the old system, this new situation may have heightened feelings of insecurity for many, which may also have led to overt escapism.

This possibility highlights a correctional paradox. In a naive way, one would expect that a willingness on the part of correctional staff to share power with all inmates would be greeted with ready acceptance. But that need not be the case, at least initially. A drastic shift in power relationships may easily result in turmoil, not tranquillity.

At the control institution, as at the experimental institution, the findings suggest that structural changes may be initially, if not permanently, dysfunctional. Certainly it is no joke to either correctional staff or the public if, in an open setting, half of an inmate population runs away, even temporarily. Again, however, it is important to underscore the fact that, although overall runaway rates at the two institutions were similar over a $2\frac{1}{2}$-year period, they were not symptomatic of similar structural conditions.

Runaways at the experimental program seemed to be the result of a high degree of cohesiveness. Because of this cohesiveness, nonconformists were forced out of the program at an increasingly early stage. In contrast, structural changes at the total institution appear to have created a condition of anomie disruptive of prior power relationships. This disruption was manifest by an increased overall runaway rate and an increased tendency for personality difficulties to be associated with running away.

Implications for FEM

Experimentation with the runaway sanction was illustrative of the way in which meaningful interaction between researchers and correctional practitioners can take place. The high incidence of runaways posed a serious problem for both groups of individuals. It was problematic for researchers because they needed an adequate number of successful graduates in order to assess the impact of the experiment. It was problematic for practitioners because they wanted to retain potential runaways but could find no effective means by which to do so. The runaway problem was every-one's problem and, consequently, everyone—researchers, practitioners, and administrators—collaborated experimentally in search of an effective solution. Thus, even though the long-range effects of the runaway sanction were minimal, it represented a joint effort to solve a critical problem. This type of interaction between action and research is a highly important aspect of the FEM, an aspect that was sadly lacking throughout this study on other issues. What is suggested, therefore, is the need for further experimentation of this type.

Another major implication of these findings is that research is badly needed on the relation between personal and social systems. For example, although this chapter has documented an important interactive effect between personal and social systems, it has provided very little information on the runaway problem as seen from the subjective perspective of the runaway. Since we were unable to identify runaways in advance and did not track them down after they ran, such information simply was not available. One important step, therefore, would be to have daily diaries kept by a randomly selected group of paid offenders whose comments and perspectives would at least be available prior to the time they ran. Such comments might be extremely important in shedding light on the reasons why some boys ran. What problems were they encountering? What was the source of those problems—school, group, family or friends?

By the same token, the use of diaries from offenders who did not run could be equally important. Did they see problems coming? Was the presence of runaways a hindrance to them, as some of them suggested? Information from them could provide some knowledge of both sides of the coin.

As for the study of social systems, it seems likely that experimentation with alternatives other than the runaway sanction used here could be highly important. For example, one issue has to do with the right of self-deter-mination among delinquents. When this experiment was set up, everyone except delinquents had some say in how the program was to be constructed and who was to be accepted as its subjects. If a delinquent did not want to be assigned to the experiment, he had no choice in the matter. The only way in which he could exercise his freedom of choice was to run away, as many did.

What about the possibility of allowing offenders, under experimental conditions, to have some say in the matter, to enter into some kind of a contract with staff and other offenders regarding the conditions under which he would stay in a given program? He might have the opportunity of trying it out for a few days before making his choice. Boys already in the program might also be expected to give their reactions to him—whether or not they wanted him. Then, once the decisions were made, there might be a better chance for success.

As another alternative, runaways could be dealt with in a nonpunitive manner and efforts could be made to retain those individuals who might try to escape from the program. The long-range consequences of keeping this particular type of deviant within the system could then be assessed. Would the retention and unconditional reacceptance of runaways back into the program seriously hinder program operation and goal accomplishment? Or would it increase the capacity of the program to deal with the problems of a wider range of individuals? Additional experimentation could have helped to answer questions such as these.

These are but a few of any number of new approaches that might be tried. But whatever is done, this study indicates the importance of studying it carefully. In that regard, it is necessary to note that such innovations might create important research problems. For example, if boys were permitted a choice, as suggested above, it might be incompatible with the traditional, experimental requirements of random assignment and make all the more necessary the careful study of those who did and did not enter a particular program and whether or not they eventually failed.

Thus, whatever might be done, new problems would be created, for research as well as action. Compromise would be required; *i.e.,* should the short-run issue of self-determination and possible reduction of runaways be permitted at the expense of not using random assignment? Although the former alternative might help to reduce a possible runaway problem, the latter might well provide important information on who does and who does not succeed in different kinds of programs. Thus, no matter what was done, serious dilemmas would be created, dilemmas that are inevitably inherent in the use of an FEM and that would require collaborative resolution.

References

ARONSON, ELIOT. 1966. Threat and obedience. *Trans-Action,* 3 (March–April): 25–27.

BECKER, HOWARD S. 1963. *Outsiders: Studies in the Sociology of Deviance.* New York: The Free Press.

BULLINGTON, BRUCE, JOHN G. MANNS, and GILBERT GEIS. 1969. Purchase of conformity: ex-narcotic addicts among the bourgeosie. *Social Problems,* 16, 4 (Spring): 456–463.

COCHRANE, N. M. 1948. Escapees and their control: a brief study of escape data. *Prison World,* 10: 3–5, 28–29.

COSER, LEWIS A. 1962. Some functions of deviant behavior and normative flexibility. *American Journal of Sociology,* 68 (September): 172–181.

ERIKSON, KAI T. 1964. Notes on the sociology of deviance. In Howard S. Becker, Ed., *The Other Side*. New York: The Free Press.

FESTINGER, LEON. 1957. *Theory of Cognitive Dissonance*. Stanford, Calif.: Stanford University Press.

GORDON, ROBERT A. 1968. Issues in multiple regression. *American Journal of Sociology*, 73, 5 (March): 592–616.

GUNASEKARA, M. G. S. 1963. The problem of absconding in boys' approved schools in England and Wales. *British Journal of Criminology*, 4 (October): 145–151.

HATHAWAY, STARKE R., ELIO D. MONACHESI, and LAURENCE A. YOUNG. 1960. Delinquency rates and personality. *Journal of Criminal Law, Criminology, and Police Science*, 50, 5 (February): 433–440.

LAGACHE, D. 1950. *Psycho-Criminogenese: Tenth General Report*. Paris: 2nd International Congress of Criminology.

LOVING, W. S., F. A. STOCKWELL, and D. A. DOBBINS. 1959. Factors associated with escape behavior of prison inmates. *Federal Probation*, 23 (September): 49–51.

MENSH, IVAN N. 1963. Personality studies of mentally ill offenders. 2nd Symposium, Atascadero (California) State Hospital.

RAPOPORT, R. N., R. RAPOPORT, and I. ROSOW. 1960. *Community as Doctor: New Perspectives on a Therapeutic Community*. London: Tavistock Publications.

STREET, DAVID, ROBERT D. VINTER, and CHARLES PERROW. 1966. *Organization for Treatment*. New York: The Free Press.

SULLIVAN, CLYDE, MARGUERITE Q. GRANT, and J. DOUGLAS GRANT. 1957. The development of interpersonal maturity: applications to delinquency. *Psychiatry*, 20 (November): 1–15.

TANNENBAUM, FRANK. 1938. *Crime and the Community*. New York: Columbia University Press.

WARREN, MARGUERITE Q. 1967. *Community Treatment Project, Progress Reports Nos. 1–7*. Sacramento: California Youth Authority, 1961–1967.

YABLONSKY, LEWIS. 1965. *The Tunnel Back: Synanon*. New York: Macmillan.

CHAPTER ELEVEN

Implementation: Program Failures

Imagine a society of saints, a perfect cloister of exemplary individuals. Crimes, properly so called, will there be unknown; but faults which appear venial to the layman will create the same scandal that the ordinary offense does in ordinary consciousness. If, then, this society has the power to judge and punish, it will treat them as such (Durkheim, 1951: 68–69).

The boys at Silverlake were not "saints," but there was some evidence that the processes to which Durkheim alludes were in operation there. Some boys were defined as "failures" and excluded not only from the experimental but the control program, and, as will be seen, they were not always the most serious delinquents.

Failures resulted from staff and group decisions to terminate boys from either of the two programs on the basis of what the former perceived as persistent incorrigibility or resistance to treatment. Rather than jeopardizing the stability of the whole, some boys were defined as troublemakers and excluded.

Like runaways, an analysis of these failures seemed to reflect a decreasing tolerance on the parts of staff members and reform-oriented delinquents toward persistent deviants. There are, however, two important ways in which the failure problem differed from the runaway problem. First, the failure rates at both programs were much lower than the runaway rates. At the experimental program, the overall runaway rate was 37 per cent, while the failure rate was less than half of that figure, or 17 per cent. Similarly, the failure rate at the control institution, 10 per cent, was less than one-fourth the size of its runaway rate, which was 40 per cent. Thus, in-program failures did not constitute as large a problem for either program as did runaways.

A second point of difference has to do with the fact that in-program

240

failures, unlike runaways, were nonvolitional acts on the part of those who were failed. Staff members, rather than the failures themselves, made the decisions for termination. Runaways, on the other hand, were volitional, a choice of the runaway himself.

This difference has important implications for prediction and control. With runaways, attempts at prediction were directed toward isolating the possible personal and organizational characteristics that may have led certain individuals to run. The problem of control was concerned with seeking effective means for deterring these individuals.

Since failures, on the other hand, were not based on the individual decisions of boys, the task of predictions would be more to discover which kinds of boys staff members and inmate reformers found undesirable or dysfunctional to their treatment programs. The problem of controlling failures would seem to require more tolerance on the part of staff members toward incorrigibles or else more effective selection criteria, rather than deterrence through the use of sanctions.

In order to predict in-program failures, a format identical to the one used in the analysis of runaways was used. Multiple regression techniques were employed to predict failures on the basis of the thirty social background, personality, offense, and peer influence scales. The results of the overall prediction attempts at both the control and experimental programs may be found in Table 11.1.

Perhaps the most interesting general finding to emerge from this analysis was the very high degree of similarity between the two programs. Based on the first ten variables of the stepwise regression, the explained variance at the control institution was 23 per cent and at the experimental program it was only slightly larger, 27 per cent. When all of the variables were included in the multiple regression analysis, the explained variance figures were only slightly higher, 29 and 39 per cent. These coefficients are relatively low but nevertheless indicate that failures can be predicted with about the same accuracy at either program. Furthermore, at both programs the offense scales seemed to account for most of the *explained* variance: 57 and 52 per cent at the control institution and 53 and 40 per cent at the experimental program. The personality scales were next in order, accounting for 33 and 21 per cent at the control institution and 43 and 42 per cent at the experimental program. The social background scales were third best in their ability to predict. They accounted for 10 and 24 per cent of the explained variances at the control program and 4 and 8 per cent at the experimental program. At neither program did the peer influence scales emerge as predictive in the first ten steps of the overall regression analyses, and at both programs they contributed only a small amount of variance to the full regression models.

Table 11.1. Variance explained in predicting Failures at the Control and Experimental Programs

Variable category	Experimental institution				Control institution			
	10-Variable stepwise regression		31-Variable multiple regression		10-Variable stepwise regression		29-Variable multiple regression	
	Proportion of variance added to R^2	Explained variance %	Proportion of variance added to R^2	Explained variance %	Proportion of variance added to R^2	Explained variance %	Proportion of variance added to R^2	Explained variance %
Peer identification	.000	0	.006	1	.000	0	.009	3
Personality	.116	43	.161	42	.077	33	.061	21
Offense	.142	53	.152	40	.134	57	.151	52
Background	.012	4	.032	8	.023	10	.069	24
Process	.000	0	.035	9	—	—	—	—
Total	.270	100	.386	100	.234	100	.290	100

These overall results suggest that the staff members and boy reformers at both programs may have employed similar sets of criteria upon which to base their decisions for failure and that similar types of offenders were the most problematic. Apparently, boys with the most persistent and serious offense backgrounds and boys with personality problems were least tolerated and most prone to failure. Peer influence and social background were relatively unimportant.

Failures and Organizational Change

In the section on runaways, documentation was made of the fact that structural changes in experimental and control programs had a profound effect on the personal factors associated with running away. Would the same be true of in-program failures?

In order to answer this question, the same kind of before-and-after analysis was conducted on in-program failures as on runaways. Two findings of importance were in evidence.

First, failures at the experimental program became more predictable over time. The explained variance rose from 36 and 56 per cent prior to the midpoint of the study to 55 and 61 per cent following it. This increase in predictability suggests that people in the experimental program may have become more consistent in their decisions to terminate certain types of boys.

Second, as can be seen in Table 11.2 the predictive capacities of the four different sets of variables, before and after the midpoint, did not change nearly so much as they did with runaways. Nevertheless, the changes that did occur followed very much the same pattern. Offense background was the highest and most stable predictor throughout, with the contribution of personality increasing after the change and social background and peer influence remaining about the same.

These findings suggest that both runaways and failures at the experimental program may have resulted from the same underlying forces, even though they were different types of acts. Whether these forces had to do with the emergence of the program culture or something else, they seem to have affected the relationship between personal and social systems in much the same way.

CHANGES AT CONTROL INSTITUTION

The pattern at the control institution differed somewhat. Again, predictability increased—from 39 and 57 per cent to 49 and 57 per cent—after organizational changes occurred (Table 11.3). But more important, the predictive efficiency of the offense scales rose markedly—from 36 and

Table 11.2. Variance explained in predicting Failures at the Experimental Program before and after Organizational Change

Variable category	Before midpoint				After midpoint			
	10-Variable stepwise regression		31-Variable multiple regression		10-Variable stepwise regression		31-Variable multiple regression	
	Proportion of variance added to R²	Explained variance %	Proportion of variance added to R²	Explained variance %	Proportion of variance added to R²	Explained variance %	Proportion of variance added to R²	Explained variance %
Peer identification	.021	6	.025	4	.000	0	.035	6
Personality	.115	32	.161	29	.222	40	.247	40
Offense	.177	49	.213	38	.269	49	.219	36
Background	.050	14	.084	15	.062	11	.083	13
Process	.000	0	.074	13	.000	0	.032	5
Total	.363	101	.557	99	.553	100	0.616	100

Table 11.3. Variance explained in predicting Failures at the Control Institution before and after Organizational Change

Variable category	Before midpoint				After midpoint			
	10-Variable stepwise regression		29-Variable multiple regression		10-Variable stepwise regression		29-Variable multiple regression	
	Proportion of variance added to R^2	Explained variance %	Proportion of variance added to R^2	Explained variance %	Proportion of variance added to R^2	Explained variance %	Proportion of variance added to R^2	Explained variance %
Peer identification	.046	12	.035	6	.000	0	.016	3
Personality	.092	24	.160	28	.140	29	.108	19
Offense	.141	36	.231	40	.253	52	.286	50
Background	.111	29	.144	25	.096	20	.162	28
Total	.390	101	.570	99	.489	101	.572	100

40 per cent to 50 and 52 per cent—with less pronounced changes in personality, background, and peer relations. Apparently the changes that occurred focused more strongly than they had previously on offense history.

That these changes occurred within the control institution and, equally important, that the configurations of variables were different for the experimental and control programs again dramatizes the possibility of a differential relationship of personal characteristics to behavior in different social systems. Furthermore, as with runaways, the patterns of dealing with in-program failures in the two programs differed markedly.

Experimental and Control Differences in Dealing with Failures

The highest failure rate for the experimental residence occurred at about the same time the runaway sanction was implemented. Prior to this time, the failure rate had been only 11 per cent, but during the eight months that followed it more than doubled to 25 per cent. And, though it declined during the final eight-month period to 18 per cent, it never reached its original level. Thus, there seems to be little doubt that intolerance for the boy defined as a "deviant" or "trouble-maker" reached its apex at about the same time the whole organization was highly concerned over the combined problems of runaways, the Homeowner's Protective Association, and the unwillingness of the school to tolerate behavior problems. Furthermore, as with runaways, in-program failures became increasingly a port-of-entry problem; that is, they occurred early in the stay of those defined as failures.

Before the time of the runaway sanction, only 14 per cent of the failures occurred within two months after admittance. During the eight-month period following the sanction, this figure rose to 40 per cent, and by the final eight-month period, over half, or 57 per cent, of the failures were terminated within the first two months of their stay.

In contrast, no such trend was in evidence at the control institution. Prior to the introduction of major programmatic changes, the failure rate there was about 13 per cent. During the eight-month period following these changes, the figure dropped to about 9 per cent and rose again to 12 per cent during the final eight months. Meanwhile, the early failure rates remained relatively low throughout all the time periods. In contrast to the experimental institution, it was older inmates—that is, inmates who had been in the program for a relatively long period of time—who continued to be those most likely to be defined as in-program failures.

Since these differences occurred, the next logical question is whether both programs were dismissing essentially different kinds of boys. That question is answered partially in Table 11.4, which provides a listing of

Table 11.4. Number of times Variables appeared in Stepwise Regression—Predicting Failures

	Experimental program			Control program			Total N. of times included
	Total	Before	After	Total	Before	After	
Offense Scales							
Theft	[a]+	+	+	+	+	+	6
Seriousness	−	−	−	−	−		5
Family problems	+		+		−	+	4
Personal disorganization	+	+			+	+	4
Number of prior incarcerations	−			−		−	3
Length of time between last offense and program entry			+			−	2
Automobile theft		−					1
Street corner		−					1
Background Scales							
Social class	+		+	+			3
Work		−		−			2
Self concept		−		+			2
Family disorganization			−		+		2
Age					+	−	2
Personality Scales							
Repression	+		+	+	+		4
Withdrawal	−		−		−	+	4
Social anxiety	+		+	+	+		4
Alienation	−	−				−	3
Autism	+			+			2
Affect				−		−	2
Value orientation		+					1
Social maladjustment						+	1
Peer Influence Scales							
Deviancy		−					1
Sociability					+		1

[a] The (+) and (−) signs indicate the directions of the beta weights for each scale in its respective regression model. A (+) sign indicates that high scores on a given scale were associated with a high incidence of failure. A (−) sign indicates that high scores on a given scale were associated with a low incidence of failure.

those *specific* scales from each of the four categories—offense, background, personality, and peer—that appeared one or more times as predictive of failure. The table reveals a different patterning of variables, especially over time, for the two programs but there were also some notable similarities.

The most consistent predictors for both programs were offense categories. The theft scale, from the offenses group, was the most consistent predictor and appeared in all of the six prediction models. In all instances, high scores on this scale were associated with running away. The theft scale was followed by the offense seriousness scale, which appeared in all but one of the prediction attempts.

Unlike the analysis of runaways, however, where it was found that the most serious offenders were likely to run, the relationship of seriousness to failing was inverse in all instances; that is, there was a tendency to fail the least, not the most, serious offenders. This sharp and consistent tendency in both programs would seem to be highly significant, especially since Table 11.4 also shows that failures were boys who had offense histories characterized by family problems and personal disorganization and who tended to be highly anxious, to have poor interpersonal relationships, and to repress their emotions rather than to act them out by running away. It seems quite clear that both programs were tending to fail boys with high degrees of personal difficulty.

This conclusion is partially confirmed by an analysis of the sociometric standing of both failures and runaways. It will be recalled from earlier chapters that four distinct types of sociometric types were found to exist in the program: *Aloofs*, who were liked by others but who in turn rejected others; *Loved-Ones*, who were well liked by others and who liked others in return; *Beggars*, who liked others but were intensely disliked in return; and *Isolates*, who neither liked nor were liked by others.

Table 11.5. Relationship between Sociometric Type and In-program Terminations at the Experimental Program[a]

| Type of Termination | Sociometric type | | | | | | | |
| | Aloof | | Loved-one | | Beggar | | Isolate | |
	Frequency	%	Frequency	%	Frequency	%	Frequency	%
In-program failure	1	8	9	13	5	18	5	22
Runaway	9	69	18	25	11	39	14	60
Successful graduation	3	23	45	63	12	43	4	17

Lambda (asymetric) = .22

[a] Four boys, all of whom were early failures, were not included in this table due to lack of sociometric.

As will be observed in Table 11.5, it was the least liked boys that were most likely to fail the program. For example, while 63 per cent of the *Loved-Ones* successfully completed the program, only 9 per cent were failed (with the remaining one-quarter running away). By contrast, only 17 per cent of the *Isolates* completed the program with 22 per cent failing and 60 per cent running away. The *Beggars* (43 per cent completion) and *Aloofs* (25 per cent completion), who were in between these two extremes, were also more inclined to terminate than complete. The moral seems clear enough: "Be a lover!"

The sociometric data, then, help to complete the total picture. Those boys who were the least liked, both by other boys and staff, were those who were most inclined either to be defined as failures or to run away. But, while those who chose the course of running away were likely to be the more serious group of offenders, the failures were those whose backgrounds were marked by a history of theft and personal disorganization. The only strong common tie between them was a history of family problems. Neither group had gotten along well with their families.

It is difficult to evaluate these findings without more specific information on the processes of interaction between failures and others, but one thing seems clear. Failure in both the experimental and control programs was associated more with personal disability than with serious criminal tendencies. This does not mean that failures did not create problems for their respective programs or that they had not been problematic for families and community, but it does seem likely that their difficulties were more of an interpersonal than a strictly criminal nature.

Implications for Program Operation

Such findings demonstrate just how complex the search for solutions in corrections is likely to be. First, along with the runaway chapter, it provides strong support for the point of view that offender behavior is very much a function of the character of correctional, as well as personal, systems. One thing that is badly needed, therefore, is more attention to the problems of constructing operational strategies that takes into account the dynamics of personal and organizational interaction rather than the singular characteristics of offenders as such.

Second, both this and the critical incident and runaway chapters documented a tendency on the part of the experimental program to become increasingly rigid in its dealings with "deviant" individuals, raising some important questions regarding the involvement of the offender in a reformation role. It was our distinct impression that a program climate developed, whether realistic or not, in which staff and the most successful boys felt threatened by others whom they viewed as unwilling to buy into the reformation culture. A kind of cohesion seems to have developed among them that suggested that even if only a few boys "made it," they would prefer this to a setting in which a wider range of behavior would be tolerated.

On one hand, such a phenomenon is not uncommon. Most social movements, and this seemed to be one on a microcosmic level, tend to develop strong in-group bonds. In the process of dealing with difficult problems, they develop rather narrow definitions of the kinds of behavior and people that will be tolerated. There is little respect for a wide range of individual differences, especially where a great deal is at stake. Either a person buys the whole package or he is out. The fundamental problem is that there are no conclusive answers regarding the kind of structure that is needed to balance competing individual and organizational needs in such movements. How much conflict can be tolerated? To what degree do marginal people threaten the stability of the whole? And, insofar as correctional organizations are concerned, how much latitude will external systems—legal, educational, and community—allow such organizations?

It must not be forgotten that the population of this study was comprised of individuals whom the larger society had already rejected. Therefore, it is little wonder that that population found it difficult to develop a substitute community, one that was more tolerant and capable of dealing with conflict and deviance than the larger community. There is no question that boys as well as staff felt a great deal of external as well as internal pressure.

The thing that makes these issues so critical is that our research findings indicate that the range of tolerance in the experimental program could have been extended without excessive danger to the community. The number of critical incidents not only declined over time (Chapter IX), but this chapter has indicated that those who were defined as "failures" were not the most serious delinquents but tended to be people with interpersonal problems. Obviously, the experimental program needed better criteria by which to distinguish between the two. Beyond that, if its structure was such that it could not deal with "failures," it needed viable alternatives for them. It did not have them.

Finally, one cannot ignore the fact that for some boys the experimental culture seems to have been functional. What would have happened to them, had it been otherwise, is difficult to say. Later chapters, however, will speak to that issue.

Implications for the FEM

This chapter illustrated the difficulty of replacing older institutional forms with new ones. If the findings are at all typical of other attempts at correctional innovations, one could not remain sanguine about the problems that were encountered. These problems indicated why the emergence of experimental programs are often resisted. The disadvantages may appear to outweigh the advantages.

What must not be overlooked, however, is the likelihood that some strain, both personal and social, will be the inevitable consequence of any attempt to change correctional practices, especially if that change is deliberate and purposive rather than evolutionary and long in coming. The creation of mediatory programs, furthermore, will not be the sole source of difficulty. Changes in total institutions will probably produce similar results. What is suggested, therefore, is the need for further experimentation in the context of the FEM.

Deutscher (1962: 468) has suggested a model that might be useful in experimenting with the best steps to be taken when deviance, such as running away or failing, and reactions to it are the principal variables. He points out that the perception of social deviance is influenced not only by the actual amount of deviance in any setting but also by the extent to which that deviance is tolerated. The relationship can be expressed in the following equation:

$$\text{Rate of in-program terminations} = \frac{\text{Number of runaways and boys perceived as failing to respond to program}}{\text{Tolerance of staff and reformers toward runaways and failures}}$$

According to this equation, termination rates—runaways and failures—could be influenced by several different alterations in the equation, examples of which are:

1. The incidence of deviant behavior by some boys could increase in any program, while the tolerance for that deviance by others remains relatively constant. Under such circumstances, the number of in-program terminations could be expected to increase.
2. The incidence of deviant behavior could remain constant but be accompanied by a decrease in tolerance. In this event, in-program terminations would also increase, even though the actual volume of deviant behavior remained the same.
3. An increase in deviancy might be accompanied by a decrease in tolerance. If this were the case, in-program terminations could be expected to rise even further.
4. Finally, one could have an equation in which deviance remained the same, in which it increased, or in which it decreased, while tolerance

for deviation followed exactly the same pattern. If this occurred, one would expect termination rates to remain about the same.

Using the Silverlake findings as an example, it seems that reactions were closest to the second equation; that is, even though the amount of deviation remained the same, or even declined over time, tolerance toward deviation also decreased, perhaps adding to the problem. The two most obvious alternatives for experimenting with the situation, therefore, might have involved (*a*) using research findings to screen out potential failures, if one desired tighter control; or (*b*) loosening controls and increasing tolerance in order to deal with a wider range of individuals. In either event, one might discover more about the impact of such changes on personal and organizational behavior.

It is obvious, for example, that program terminations could have been diminished considerably by broadening the degree of toleration among the reformation group so as to include boys who would not remain in school or who did not seem to have much commitment either to changing themselves or to helping others to change. But if this had been done, the nature of the program would have changed and with it the involvement and commitment of other boys who were struggling to improve. One could not have it both ways. Any alterations, therefore, could have been expected to provide new consequences, both good and bad. This suggests that solutions should not be provided without careful study.

References

DEUTSCHER, IRWIN. 1962. Some relevant directions for research in juvenile delinquency. In Arnold M. Rose, Ed., *Human Behavior and Social Processes*. Boston: Houghton Mifflin.

DURKHEIM, EMILE. 1951. *Suicide*. Trans. by John A. Spaulding and George Simpson. New York: The Free Press.

CHAPTER TWELVE

Results of Implementation:
Recidivism and its Correlates

It must be said [about our correctional agencies] that at best we have been inefficient, at worst we have been inhumane, and at all times we have been confused. We need to lessen the confusion by being more specific about our objectives and agreeing upon them. If we then can build some information bases that will provide a start toward evaluation of programs in terms of these objectives, we can only become more efficient. If we then can identify specific kinds of treatment which are helpful to certain kinds of offenders, our programs can be made more effective, more helpful to offenders and to the general public, and hence more humane (Gottfredson, 1967: 33).

In Chapter One it was argued that any evaluation of outcome for a delinquency reduction experiment should be based upon two kinds of measurement: (1) the extent to which the effects of basic factors thought to produce delinquency were altered; and (2) the extent to which law-violating behavior was decreased.

The first kind of measurement would seek to determine the degree to which the experiment was successful in producing the kinds of changes defined as important by its intervention theory—in this case, decreasing the negative effects of delinquent peer identification, reducing social strain, and providing legitimate means for achievement. The process analysis already conducted has helped in part to answer this particular question; that is, the analysis of critical incidents, runaways, in-program failures, and the impact of external systems helped to indicate something about the ability of the internal system to reduce basic problems.

253

While there was some evidence that the use of group techniques was successful in developing an anti-delinquent reformation culture, that culture was not always adaptable to many of the problems that arose. Furthermore, the strain produced by these problems was undoubtedly magnified in many cases because of the poor relationship the experiment had with the school and to a lesser degree with families and the community. These poor relationships not only decreased the opportunities of some delinquents for legitimate achievement but also probably increased the levels of strain that they were already experiencing.

This particular aspect of outcome evaluation as a result raised serious questions about the overall implementation of the experiment; questions that are well illustrated in Table 12.1. As a result of the problems that were encountered, the table indicates that no better than 46 per cent of the experimental subjects (as contrasted to 50 per cent of the controls)

Table 12.1. Experimental Outcome in terms of Program Graduates, Runaways and Failures

	Experimentals		Controls	
	N	%	N	%
Graduates	64	46	60	50
Runaways	52	37	48	39
Failures	24	17	13	11
Totals	140	100	121	100

successfully completed the program. The remainder were runaways or in-program terminees. As a consequence, if one used this single criterion as the basis for outcome evaluation, there would be some grounds for rejecting the experimental approach. However, there are other data to be presented in this chapter that are much more definitive than this general finding.

Besides providing various measures of recidivism—on runaways and failures as well as program graduates—these data indicate something about the impact of the experiment upon the personal characteristics of the delinquent subjects, the way in which those characteristics were related to future recidivistic behavior. Such information is of much greater value in suggesting whether the experiment had an impact than gross figures. As a consequence, the remainder of the chapter will be devoted to these issues.

Examination of Recidivism

Recidivism, for purposes of this analysis, was defined in stringent and official terms. Any new recorded arrest, no matter where it appeared—on the Central Juvenile Index for Los Angeles County or on Probation Department files—was defined as a recidivistic offense. This stringent definition was limited by the fact that it included offenses for which guilt was not always established in court. On the other hand, it provided perhaps the best general index of the delinquency rate for this particular population, since the value of any such index decreases as the distance from the delinquent act increases in terms of official decision-making (Sutherland and Cressy, 1955: 25–26). The further removed the index from the delinquent act, the greater the likelihood that official decisions, policies, and procedures will affect its accuracy.

In order to examine recidivism rates, all experimental and control subjects—runaways and failures as well as successful graduates—were followed through official records for a period of at least twelve months after their termination from either program. Recidivism was examined in three different ways: (1) in terms of individuals—that is, whether each subject recidivated and, if so, the frequency with which he did so; (2) in collective terms by comparing the total volume of delinquency committed by subjects twelve months before assignment to the experiment with their total volume committed twelve months after release; and (3) in terms of the seriousness of the recidivistic offenses.

RECIDIVISM IN INDIVIDUAL TERMS

Table 12.2 shows the frequency of recidivism for all experimental and control subjects, whether successful graduates or not. Two things about the

Table 12.2. Overall Recidivism Rates for Experimental and Control Subjects

Number of offenses	Experimentals		Controls	
	N	%	N	%
0	84	60	68	56
1	35	25	29	24
2	8	6	16	13
3	5	4	4	3
4 or more	8	6	4	3
Totals	140	101	121	99
Average number of offenses	0·73	—	0·87	—

table are significant. First, although only about half of all subjects successfully completed their respective programs, approximately six out of ten had no recidivistic offenses and eight out of ten had no more than one such offense. Furthermore, during the twelve-month follow-up period, the average number of offenses for experimentals was only 0.73 and for controls was 0.87. Thus, given the stringent definition of recidivism that was adopted, most subjects seemed to have been relatively free of delinquency.

The second significant thing about the table is the relative similarity in outcome when experimental and control programs are compared. Although the experimental group seems to have had a slightly higher success rate, that advantage was not very large and could easily have been due to chance. The experimental community program, then, did not seem to have had a more significant overall impact than longer-term treatment in the open educationally oriented control institution. It is tempting to explore these implications further at this time but, before doing so, let us analyze these rates in more specific terms, separating program graduates from runaways and failures to see what might then be revealed.

RECIDIVISM RATES FOR SUCCESSFUL GRADUATES

If one considers only successful program graduates, several specifics might be noted. First, 82 per cent of the control graduates remained totally arrest-free contrasted with only 73 per cent for the experimental group, suggesting that the control program may have been more effective for

Table 12.3. Recidivism rates comparing Graduates, In-program Failures, and Runaways within Experimental and Control Groups

Number of Recidivist Offenses	Experimentals						Controls					
	Graduates		In-program failures		Runaways		Graduates		In-program failures		Runaways	
	f	%	f	%	f	%	f	%	f	%	f	%
0	47	73	12	50	25	48	49	82	4	31	15	31
1	13	20	8	33	14	27	4	7	6	46	19	40
2	1	2			7	13	4	7	2	15	10	21
3	2	3	2	8	1	2	2	3			2	4
4			2	8	3	6			1	7	1	2
5					2	4	1	2				
6	1	2									1	2
Totals	64	100	24	99	52	100	60	101	13	99	48	100
Average number of offenses	0.42	—	0.92	—	1·02	—	0.40	—	1.08	—	1.15	—

successful graduates. However, as will be observed in Table 12.3, it is the similarities rather than the differences between the two programs that are striking. For example, since control graduates who did recidivate were more inclined than experimental graduates to be repeat offenders, the average number of recidivist offenses for both groups was approximately equal: 0.40 offenses per boy among the controls and 0.42 per boy among the experimentals. Likewise, if one compares graduates who had only one or fewer offenses, the figure for controls is 89 per cent and that for experimentals is 93 per cent. Thus, it would appear that for boys who are able to complete both programs, effectiveness is almost identical and is pleasingly high, especially in light of their rather long delinquent histories.

RECIDIVISM RATES FOR RUNAWAYS AND IN-PROGRAM FAILURES

When one considers those who did not successfully complete either program, the picture changes somewhat. First of all, any boy who failed to complete either program or was a runaway could be defined technically as a recidivist; that is, since he had failed to adhere to program demands and to adjust successfully to them, he could be defined as a law violator. Thus, if this technical definition were accepted, all such individuals would be defined as "recidivists." However, this is a highly debatable and rigid definition that does not take into account the possibility that the programs themselves may have been partially at fault in causing some boys to run away and in defining others as failures and that many such delinquents could live in the community without further violations. Consequently, it was rejected, and only arrest statistics for violations in addition to running or being failed were considered.

When this approach was taken, it was found that approximately half of all experimental failures and runaways did not commit additional offenses, with the average number of offenses per boy being 0.92 for in-program failures and 1.02 for runaways (see Table 12.3). Meanwhile, the success rate for failures and runaways in the control program was not so high, with slightly less than one-third remaining free of violations and with the average number of offenses per boy also being somewhat higher, 1.08 for in-program failures and 1.15 for runaways (see Table 12.3).

Since this was the first significant difference in outcome between the two programs, it was thought that it might be due to the many and complex vagaries of official processing, the most notable possibility being that more experimental than control boys, after committing an additional offense, might have been incarcerated. If this were the case, then the opportunity for further violations on their parts would have been deminished and their lower violation rates the function of official processing, not non-delinquent behavior.

As will be seen in Table 12.4, it may be that this was the case, although not likely. Only 24 per cent of the experimentals, as contrasted with 37 per cent of the controls, were incarcerated for additional offenses in the California Youth Authority, the placement in which security is the greatest and where the average length of stay is nine months. On the other hand, fewer experimentals than controls were left totally free in the community on probation or with cases dismissed, 35 *vs.* 46 per cent. The remainder, 42 per cent of the experimentals and 18 per cent of the controls, were placed in low-security probation camps and private community institutions where opportunities for violations are greater than in the California Youth Authority and where length of stay is often shorter. If any experimental or control subject recidivated after assignment to one of these programs, that act would be reflected in these figures.

Table 12.4. Dispositions of Runaways and In-program Failures at Experimental and Control Programs

	Experimentals		Controls	
	N	%	N	%
California Youth Authority	18	24	22	37
Probation camps and private institutions	32	42	11	18
Probation, dismissal, or moved	26	34	28	46
Totals	76	100	61	101

The other thing that is significant about these findings is that subjects who did not complete either program were much more likely to recidivate than those who did. Their higher rate of recidivism, of course, is also compatible with the findings of Chapters Ten and Eleven, where it was shown that failures and runaways were characterized by the most serious delinquent histories and problems of personal adjustment. Yet, while this is further documentation of the need for programs that can deal more effectively with such boys, it is tempered by the not insignificant finding that half of this portion of the experimental group was not arrested for any additional delinquent acts whatsoever and that the average number of offenses for controls as well as experimentals was low (an average of one offense per boy in a twelve-month period).

Before-and-After Recidivism Rates

A second way of reviewing recidivism rates is to consider them on a collective and before-and-after basis. Such an analysis provides a means of determining the capacity of the two programs to control delinquency in a general sense; that is, to determine whether they effected any reduction in the overall volume of delinquency. All too often, there is a tendency to evaluate programs solely in absolute terms rather than relative terms; that is, to ask whether offenders assigned to them recidivated or not, without due regard to the possibility that such programs, even if their subjects did recidivate, may have been successful in effecting a reduction in overall delinquency rates.

Table 12.5. Volume of Offenses before and after assignment: Experimental Group

Type of termination	Offenses 12 months before	Offenses 12 months after	% reduction
Successful graduates (N = 64)	173 ($\bar{x} = 2.70$)	27 ($\bar{x} = 0.42$)	84
Runaways (N = 52)	144 ($\bar{x} = 2.77$)	53 ($\bar{x} = 1.02$)	63
In-program failures (N = 24)	62 ($\bar{x} = 2.58$)	22 ($\bar{x} = 0.92$)	64
Totals (N = 140)	379 ($\bar{x} = 2.71$)	102 ($\bar{x} = 0.73$)	73

The findings which follow illustrate the importance of conducting this kind of analysis. As will be seen in Table 12.5, the total number of offenses committed by all experimental subjects during the twelve-month period prior to assignment was 379. During the twelve-month period after assignment, this figure declined significantly to only 102 offenses. This is a 73 per cent reduction in the volume of delinquency committed by these experimental subjects, a sizable decrease indeed! Furthermore, the reduction in overall volume for those who successfully completed the experimental program was even greater, 84 per cent. Meanwhile, the reduction rate for runaways and in-program failures, though lower, was still significant, with a 63 per cent reduction for runaways and a 64 per cent reduction for in-program failures.

The degree of reduction in volume for the controls was not greatly different (Table 12.6). The entire control group committed a total of 322 offenses during the twelve-month period prior to assignment and only 93 offenses during the twelve months following, an overall reduction of 71 per cent. Furthermore, the reduction in volume for control graduates was

85 per cent, for runaways was 52 per cent, and for in-program failures 64 per cent.

These figures are remarkably similar to those for the experimentals and suggest that both programs may have contributed significantly to a decline in the volume of delinquency committed by this particular population of offenders, including those who did not successfully complete their programs. However, the data are subject to more than one interpretation.

It is possible that these observed reductions may be not due to changes in the behavior of this group of delinquents but rather to the vagaries of chance, to what has been called a "regression effect" (*cf.* Campbell, 1957). Problems of regression might occur when experimental and control subjects have been selected for their extremity on a given variable. For example, they were selected in this case because they were repeat offenders with a considerable number of recorded offenses.

Table 12.6. Volume of Offenses before and after assignment: Control Group

Type of termination	Offenses 12 months before	Offenses 12 months after	% reduction
Successful graduates (N = 60)	164	24	85
	($\bar{x}$ = 2.90)	($\bar{x}$ = 0.40)	
Runaways (N = 48)	114	55	52
	($\bar{x}$ = 2.38)	($\bar{x}$ = 1.15)	
In-program failures (N = 13)	44	14	68
	($\bar{x}$ = 3.38)	($\bar{x}$ = 1.08)	
Total (N = 121)	322	93	71
	($\bar{x}$ = 2.66)	($\bar{x}$ = 0.74)	

Since it is likely that official records are subject to considerable error (*i.e.*, they do not represent a complete count of all of a boy's offenses) and since the recording of any single act may be largely fortuitous (*i.e.,* the probability that it will be recorded may be less than 0.10), then it may easily be that the official offenses for this particular group of extreme cases would decline over time. Given the fortuitous nature of detection, the chances of their offenses being detected on more than a few occasions would be very small. For example, the probability that these offenders would be detected both before and after their correctional experience might be very low ($0.10 \times 0.10 = 0.01$), while the probability that they would be recorded in the first period (as they were), but not in the second, might be much higher ($0.10 \times 0.90 = 0.09$). Thus, a reduction in the volume of recorded offenses for both experimental and control groups could be due to chance.

There is really no way of telling from these data whether the reduction was due to real or regression effects. The argument that it was due to regression could be countered by theory and evidence that repeat offenders and parolees are much better known to the police and, thus, are much more likely to be picked up than others. The fact that they have been labeled greatly increases their visibility and thus the chances that they will be rearrested. Even so, we are left without conclusive answers. Regression may or may not have affected the reductions noted above.

The importance of finding answers to this dilemma are considerable since, if the reductions are real, they may indicate that corrections have been far too insensitive to change as a transitional phenomenon, measured in degrees rather than absolutes. If the total volume of post-program offenses actually do decline, even though some such behavior occurs, better means are needed by which to take that into account. One alternative for answering the question would be to select an additional control group of repeat offenders, refrain from subjecting them to any treatment, and then compare the decline in the volume of their offenses with those who are treated. Another alternative would be to gather detailed information on undetected illegal acts, both before and after treatment. This information could then be used, along with official records, to assess the possibility of regression effects. The importance of finding some such methods is also illustrated by before-and-after measures of seriousness which we conducted. As with the measures of frequency, they also indicated a decrease in delinquent behavior.

Before-and-After Measures of Seriousness

In order to conduct this analysis, the offense seriousness scale presented in Chapter Five was divided into "low," "medium," and "serious" offense categories. "Low-serious" offenses ranged from 0 to 2 on the 5-point scale and included such offenses as driving without a license, gambling, curfew violations, and truancy. "Medium-serious" offenses ranged from 2.1 to 3.5 and included the largest number of offenses such as running away from home, damaging property, auto theft, and associating with known narcotics users. "Serious" offenses ranged from 3.6 on the scale to 5 and included a smaller list of offenses such as breaking and entering, robbery, child molesting, and violent assault. Tables 12.7 and 12.8 present the findings. Three things about them are significant.

First, the most significant comparisons for both experimentals and controls are on the "medium-serious" offenses, since this category included

Table 12.7. Volume of Offenses by Seriousness, before and after assignment: Experimental Group[a]

Seriousness categories for types of terminees		12 months before	12 months after	% reduction
Graduates	Low	20	12	40
	Medium	130	11	92
	High	20	4	80
Runaways	Low	15	4	74
	Medium	110	35	68
	High	19	10	47
In-program failures	Low	4	3	25
	Medium	48	14	71
	High	9	4	56
Total	Low	39	19	51
	Medium	288	60	79
	High	48	18	62

[a] 27 of the offenses appearing in Table 12.5 are not included because their recording in official records made them unclassifiable in terms of our seriousness index.

Table 12.8. Volume of Offenses by Seriousness before and after assignment: Control Group[a]

Seriousness categories for types of terminees		12 months before	12 months after	% reduction
Graduates	Low	20	5	75
	Medium	110	8	93
	High	29	8	72
Runaways	Low	18	4	78
	Medium	73	37	49
	High	17	14	18
In-program failures	Low	6	0	100
	Medium	32	10	69
	High	6	4	34
Total	Low	44	7	84
	Medium	215	55	74
	High	52	26	50

[a] 29 of the offenses appearing in Table 12.6 are not included because their recording in official records made them unclassifiable in terms of our seriousness index.

the largest number of kinds of offenses and since these kinds were the most often committed. Furthermore, the number of "high-serious" offenses for both groups, both before and after, was greater than the "low-serious" offenses, perhaps underscoring the kind of delinquent population under study and the kinds of offenses to which legal authorities are most likely to respond.

Second, the findings tend to underscore the conclusions reached in the previous section; namely, that if one looks at decreases in the volume of offenses, he finds marked changes on a before-and-after basis. Among the experimentals, overall, there was a decline of 51 per cent in "low-serious" offenses, 79 per cent in "medium-serious" offenses, and 62 per cent in "high-serious" offenses. Among the controls, the figures were 84 per cent, 74 per cent, and 50 per cent, respectively. The changes, again, were most marked for successful graduates: 40 per cent, 92 per cent, and 80 per cent for experimentals and 75 per cent, 93 per cent, and 72 per cent for controls.

Third, it appears that the experimental program may have been slightly more successful than the control program in reducing the more serious offenses but less successful in reducing the least serious ones. This difference was most marked among runaways and in-program failures. Among runaways, the per cent reductions on "low-serious" offenses were 74 per cent for experimentals *vs.* 78 per cent for controls, on "medium-serious" offenses, 68 per cent *vs.* 49 per cent, and on "high-serious" offenses, 47 per cent *vs.* 18 per cent. The differences for in-program failures were not quite so great but tended in the same direction.

This finding is probably an important one because it supplements the findings presented in Table 12.3, indicating that those boys who did not complete the control program were more delinquent after termination than experimentals and that, as a consequence, this program may have had less impact that the experimental one on those boys who ran away or failed in it, even though they stayed for longer periods of time. But, perhaps even more important, the findings suggest that even if the two programs were equal in effect, the experimental community endeavor posed no greater danger to the community after release than the institutional, control program.

The importance of this finding is underscored by the fact that such differences were probably not due to regression effects since both groups were subject to the same effects. Furthermore, the major background differences between the two groups at the time of their assignment to the experimental and control programs might have led to predictions of success exactly opposite to these actual findings. It will be recalled from Chapter Five that the major difference between experimental and control groups, at time of assignment, had to do with the fact that the experimental group had encountered more stringent court dispositions prior to assignment than the control group. Almost one-third of the experimentals had been incarcerated prior to assignment *vs.* only 7 per cent for controls. The majority of the controls, instead, had either been on probation (54 *vs.* 35 per cent) or without previous probation (31 *vs.* 21 per cent). Thus, if prior court disposition means anything, these findings may indicate that the experimental subjects, because of their prior incarcerations, may have been a more difficult group to deal with. It might have been expected, therefore, that they would not have performed as well after release as the control group. Yet this was not the case. The community program did at least as well. In addition, it should not be forgotten that both programs brought about a significant reduction in the volume of serious offenses, suggesting that they were important sources of delinquency control.

Maturational Reform

Before reaching final conclusions on these findings, one note of caution is in order. That note of caution has to do with "maturational reform" (*cf.* Matza, 1964). Maturational reform refers to the fact that the law violations of most delinquents tend to diminish as the delinquents move from adolescence toward adulthood. Whether this is due to an increased sense of responsibility attendant on becoming an adult or to the fact that many juveniles are arrested for acts that would not be criminal if they were adults, the fact that age is inversely related to the chances of further law violation is a well-documented fact (Glaser, 1964: 36; Wilkins, 1969: 54–56). Consequently, it might be expected that the subjects of this study would undergo a certain degree of maturational reform, the effects of the experimental and control programs notwithstanding. To the extent that this was the case, it becomes important to separate the effects of experimental stimuli from the effects of maturational processes.

A simple analysis was performed in order to assess the possible effects of this phenomenon. The ages of subjects at the time of their entrance to either program were correlated with the following measures of recidivism: the total number of official recidivistic offenses per boy, the scale ranking of his most serious recidivist offense, the length of time after his termination before the first recidivist offense, and the number of incarcerations in a correctional institution that occurred after termination from either program. To the extent that maturational reform affected recidivism, negative correlations would be expected; that is, older boys would be expected to have lower scores on the recidivism measures and younger boys would be expected to have higher scores. Product-moment correlations were used to assess the relationship between age and recidivism. The results of the analysis may be found in Table 12.9.

As will be observed, the signs of all of the correlation coefficients were negative and thus tended to support the maturational-reform hypothesis. However, the magnitudes of the correlations were so low that they would be of scarce utility as predictive devices. The highest coefficient, −.15, was between age and number of incarcerations. The remaining coefficients were much lower: the correlation between age and total number of recidivist offenses being −.04, between age and seriousness, −.05, and between age and length of time before recidivism, −.04. Thus, although there seems to have been a slight tendency toward maturational reform among the subjects of this study, it appears to have had only a very slight effect.

Table 12.9. Correlations between age at time of entry to either Program and Measures of Recidivism (N = 257)

Variable correlated with age	Correlation coefficient
1. Total number of official offenses after release	− .04
2. Scale rating of most serious recidivist offense	− .05
3. Length of time after program release before first recidivist offense	− .04
4. Number of incarcerations after release	− .15

It is possible that had subjects been followed for a longer period of time, the effects of maturational reform might have been more pronounced; that is, since the follow-up period lasted for only twelve months, one might expect greater evidence of such reform over a longer period. However, since in this case the concern was with the effects of programming *vs.* maturation, it appears that the programming had the greater effect.

Prediction of Recidivism

While the foregoing analysis has been useful in indicating the extent and nature of recidivism, it has not indicated anything about the types of offenders most likely to recidivate. The remainder of the chapter will be devoted to that task.

A sampling of the literature concerned with predicting and explaining recidivism reveals that a long list of variables have been used: family problems (Gould and Beverly, 1963: 14–16; Wattenburg, 1953: 633); personality and maturity factors (Franks, 1956: 199; Gould and Beverly,

1963: 16; Grant and Grant, 1959: 133); physical appearance (Corsini, 1959: 49–51); school adjustment and education (Gould and Beverly, 1963: *iii*; Wattenburg, 1953: 634; Wattenburg and Saunders, 1954); age (England, 1962: 246; Glaser, 1964: 36–40; Glaser and O'Leary, 1968: 5–8; Thompson and Adams, 1963: 36; Wilkins, 1969: 55–56); work record (Kirby, 1954: 543); criminal record (England, 1962: 246; Glaser, 1964: 44–49; Glaser and O'Leary, 1968: 8–17; Kirby, 1954: 543) and a host of others. However, with a few exceptions, such as Glaser's, one of the problems with most prediction studies has been their failure to relate their predictor variables to any well-defined body of theory. Thus, although a given set of variables might yield a high degree of predictability, its explanatory worth might be limited because it has been derived outside of a theoretical context.

An attempt has been made in this chapter, as in prior chapters, to remedy this problem somewhat by relating the predictive models to those variables and concepts that were used in setting up the experiment. Such measures include social class, various background indicators of school performance, family situation, work behavior, and self-concept as measures of achievement and strain; the Jesness Personality Inventory as measures of personality and possible strain; the Peer Scales as measures of identification with delinquent standards; and the various scales used to measure offense backgrounds. The Sociometric Scale, length of time in treatment, and number of critical incidents were also included as possible indicators of process at the experimental program. Finally, as was done in prior chapters concerned with prediction, a series of 10-variable stepwise regression models and 32-variable multiple regression models were both used to assess the extent to which recidivism could be predicted by input and process variables.

Prediction of Recidivism Frequency

Two kinds of comparisons were important in assessing the predictability of recidivistic behavior for experimental and control groups: within-group comparisons, contrasting program graduates with runaways and failures, and between-group comparisons, contrasting both kinds of offenders from both kinds of programs. The basic data for these comparisons are supplied in Table 12.10 (for the experimental group), and Table 12.11 (for the control group). Let us begin with the within group-analysis.

COMPARISONS WITHIN EXPERIMENTAL GROUP

As may be seen in Table 12.10, the explained variance for the program graduates after the first ten steps of the stepwise analysis was 39 per cent

Table 12.10. Variance explained in predicting Frequency of Recidivism for the Experimental Program Graduates and Runaways and Failures

| Variable category | Program graduates (N = 62) | | | | Runaways and in-program failures (N = 73) | | | |
| | 10-Variable stepwise regression | | 32-Variable multiple regression | | 10-Variable stepwise regression | | 32-Variable multiple regression | |
	Proportion of variance added to R²	Explained variance %	Proportion of variance added to R²	Explained variance %	Proportion of variance added to R²	Explained variance %	Proportion of variance added to R²	Explained variance %
Peer identification	.0316	8	.0469	9	.0109	3	.0235	5
Personality	.1182	30	.1895	35	.0514	16	.1013	23
Offense	.0821	21	.1413	26	.1491	47	.1406	33
Background	.1437	36	.1435	26	.1089	34	.1097	25
Process	.0191	5	.0268	5	.0000	0	.0563	13
Total	.3947	100	.5480	101	.3204	100	.4314	99

and for the 32-variable multiple regression, it was 55 per cent. The figures for runaways and in-program failures were slightly lower at 32 and 43 per cent. When the explained variance, furthermore, was broken down into specific categories, both important similarities and differences between the two groups appeared.

With regard to similarities, the Peer Scales proved to have little predictive efficiency for either group, suggesting that the experimental program may have been successful in its endeavor to decrease the negative impact of this factor on boys. However, since that question can best be answered by between- rather than within-group comparisons, it will be reserved for later discussion.

Meanwhile, for both groups the explained variation contributed by background, personality, and offense history was relatively high. Of greatest significance was the fact that, of all these measures, family disorganization had the highest relationship to recidivism for both groups. In both instances, it was the first measure selected by the stepwise regression procedures and accounted for the greatest proportion of variance of all single measures in both 32-variable models. Thus, it was the best single predictor of recidivism for the experimentals.

This finding is provocative because family disorganization was not given much importance in the construction of the intervention guidelines for the experiment. Instead, attention was focused on changing peer relationships, decreasing strain, and increasing achievement, with the expectation that improvement in these areas would have the greatest chance of decreasing further delinquency. Furthermore, in reformulating the causation theory (see Chapter Thirteen), it will be shown that boys from disrupted family environments were most likely to be delinquent. Therefore, the finding that family disorganization was highly predictive of recidivism for both program graduates and failures may be a result of the experiment's inattention to family problems in its theory of causation and intervention strategy. If intervention priorities had been different and if more theoretical attention had been focused upon family disorganization, its relationship to recidivism might not have been so pronounced.

In addition to family disorganization, three other background scales were predictive. For both types of releasees, boys who had previously dropped out of school and had made failing grades were most likely to recidivate, indicating the persistent problems of achievement and lack of self-confidence for this particular group. As a corollary kind of corroboration, consider the fact that, for runaways and in-program failures only, a positive orientation toward work and high educational aspirations were associated with success rather than failure after leaving the program, even though these boys did not manage to complete it. By contrast, boys with poor work histories, in conjunction with poor school performance and low aspirations, were more likely to recidivate.

So much, then, for similarities within the experimental program. What about differences between graduates *vs.* runaways and failures? In pursuing this question, two things stand out.

First, personality was a more efficient predictor of recidivism for graduates (30 per cent of the explained variance in the 10-variable model and 35 per cent in the 32-variable model) than it was for runaways and failures (16 per cent and 23 per cent). Specific personality factors for graduates were predictive in two ways: (*a*) those who tended to be highly autistic and asocial were those most likely to recidivate; while (*b*) those who were socially anxious and more inclined to repress their difficulties were most likely to stay out of additional trouble.

Meanwhile, by far the most predictive set of scales for runaways and failures were Offense Scales, a finding that possessed some provocative characteristics. While high scores on the Theft Scales were associated with increased recidivism, previous histories of street-corner delinquency and previous incarcerations were associated with reduced recidivism. It seems, therefore, that while high scores on utilitarian, perhaps criminally oriented delinquency seem to have been associated with greater recidivism; the more common, street-corner activities were not. This may reflect the apparent decrease in delinquent peer identification that the experimental program seems to have effected.

Thus, when considered in light of the overall theory upon which the experiment was constructed, this set of within-group comparisons for the experimentals makes some sense. On one hand, they underline areas in which the theory was inadequate—*i.e.*, the failure to address family problems— and, on the other, they suggest areas in which the actual implementation of the theory itself may have been at fault—*i.e.*, the failure to reduce the strains produced by a lack of achievement at school and a poor work history for graduates as well as runaways and failures. At the same time, the evidence suggests that the effects of the important variable of peer identification were significantly decreased.

COMPARISONS WITHIN CONTROL GROUP

As may be seen in Table 12.11, the explained variances yielded by the regression analyses were relatively higher for the control group than for the experimental group: 43 and 56 per cent explained variance for graduates and 52 and 72 per cent for runaways and in-program failures.

Again, some major similarities were observed regarding the types of factors that were predictive of recidivism for graduates *vs.* runaways and in-program failures.

Table 12.11. Variance explained in predicting Frequency of Recidivism for the Control Program Graduates and Runaways and Failures

Variable category	Program graduates (N = 58)				Runaways and in-program failures (N = 44)			
	10-Variable stepwise regression		30-Variable multiple regression[a]		10-Variable stepwise regression		30-Variable multiple regression[a]	
	Proportion of variance added to R^2	Explained variance %	Proportion of variance added to R^2	Explained variance %	Proportion of variance added to R^2	Explained variance %	Proportion of variance added to R^2	Explained variance %
Peer identification	.1627	38	.1620	29	.1605	31	.0800	11
Personality	.0883	20	.1216	22	.2909	56	.4304	60
Offense	.1481	34	.1511	27	.0434	8	.0489	7
Background	.0327	8	.1091	19	.0219	4	.1335	19
Process	.0000	0	.0190	3	.0000	0	.0283	4
Total	.4317	100	.5628	100	.5168	99	.7211	101

[a]These models contain only 30, as opposed to 32 variables because measures of critical incidents and sociometric standing were not collected at the control program.

As was observed at the experimental program, the predictability of peer influence and background factors was about the same for both types of releasees. However, in contrast to the experimental program, peer identification was more highly predictive while background factors were relatively low in their predictive capacities, a pattern that is opposite to that shown for experimental subjects. For successful graduates at the control group, the Peer Deviancy Scale was directly related to recidivism, while the Peer Sociability Scale was inversely related to it. For program failures and runaways, the Deviancy and Ace-in-the-Hole Scales were both inversely related to recidivism. In the 10-variable stepwise models, the only background variable predictive of recidivism at the control program was the Family Disorganization Scale. It was directly associated with the recidivism of both types of releasees from this program. Thus, its emergence in these regression analyses may underscore the failure of both programs to address the family disorganization issue. Meanwhile, the high predictive efficiency of Peer Scales for the control group is significant.

Insofar as differences between control graduates *vs.* in-program failures and runaways are concerned, it was found that personality factors were highly, and much more, predictive of future recidivism for in-program failures and runaways than for graduates. Boys who did not complete this program and who then recidivated tended to reveal a high degree of affect, a value orientation that was delinquent, and to be socially maladjusted. In contrast, there was no single Personality Scale that ranked high as a predictor for graduates. Instead, the factors that predicted recidivism most efficiently for control graduates (in addition to peer identification) were the Offense Scales. High scores on Automobile and General Deviancy Scales were associated with high recidivism. Thus, this finding provided not only striking differences within the control program but also when compared with the experimental program. The patterns of factors that predicted recidivistic behavior was, in many cases, opposite for the two programs.

Our ability to conjecture about these patterned differences, for the control program, is somewhat more difficult than for the experimental program because its basic premises and specific activities were not as well described and documented. However, two things are significant.

First, it appears that the control program may have failed to deal with the personality problems of some boys—perhaps causing many not only to run away or to fail but to get into additional trouble. At the same time, it does not seem to have altered some of the specific offense patterns of its graduates.

Second, it is obvious that, since the nature of the explained variances for the experimental and control programs are opposite, these programs seem to have affected delinquents in much different ways. Such important differences are strong confirmation of conclusions reached in Chapters Ten and Eleven, which suggest that, if one wishes to predict behavior, he cannot rely solely on such static measures as personality, offense, peer, or background factors unless he holds organizational factors constant. When different organizations are involved, the differential interaction of personal and organizational characteristics are likely to create conditions that will alter significantly the capacity of any input factors to be universally predictable. By way of emphasizing that point, let us summarize the differences between the experimental and control groups.

BETWEEN-PROGRAM DIFFERENCES

Between-program differences suggest that even though the delinquent population assigned to the experimental and control programs were essentially similar at the time they entered those programs, the factors that predict their recidivism differ considerably.

1. Within the experimental program, the Peer Scales were not useful predictors for either graduates or runaways and failures, while the reverse was true for the control program. Thus, in light of the theoretical emphasis upon changing peer identification in the experimental program, this finding lends substance to the notion that it may have had a significant impact in altering the relationship of this factor to delinquency.

2. In contrast, the Background Scales were relatively efficient predictors for the experimental group but not for the controls. Since the most efficient predictors of recidivism at the experimental program were family disorganization and academic and work performance, these factors may have possessed a great debilitating effect upon the experimentals who remained in the community and who had to continue interacting in home and school. The controls, in contrast, were placed in a more sheltered environment, especially insofar as school was concerned. The control institution provided an enriched program and a setting in which competition with nondelinquents was not necessary. This finding may indicate that some delinquents, whose home and academic problems are the greatest, may need some kind of a moratorium in a sheltered environment to deal with them.

3. Differences between experimental and control programs on the personality scales were striking confirmation of the way in which the interaction between personal makeup and organizational character might be reflected in actual behavior. Among program graduates, personality scales were more predictive for experimentals than controls. However, the predictive efficiency of such scales was not always associated with future recidivism. For example, while autistic and asocial tendencies among experimentals were associated with recidivism, relatively high degrees of social anxiety and ability to repress problems were associated with success.

While such findings must be treated with caution because of their relatively low capacity to predict behavior, they are important because they indicate that different approaches to correctional intervention might be related to personal makeup in strikingly different ways.

As even greater confirmation of this conclusion, note that while personality was a relatively poor predictor for runaways and in-program failures in the experimental program, it possessed higher predictability for such people in the control program—by far the most efficient predictor of all. Specifically, recidivism was associated with a high degree of affect, social maladjustment, and a delinquent value orientation. Since these personality factors are so outstandingly significant for this particular group, it would seem that some investigation and alteration in control strategy might be important so as to lessen their effects.

4. Finally, it appears that a somewhat similar phenomenon was occurring in both programs with respect to offense history. While in the experimental program, offense history was a less efficient predictor of recidivism among *graduates* than in the control program, the reverse was true for in-program failures and runaways. Apparently, for those boys who successfully completed the experimental intervention, the effects of prior offense history were dissipated, but for those boys who did not, they remained highly important. Therefore, just as the control strategy might need change with respect to its effect on the personality problems of those who did not successfully complete treatment, so the experimental strategy would need alteration with respect to certain offense patterns for its runaways and failures. Conversely, it could also be said that for the control institution, the failure to alter specific offense patterns among graduates may have led to further delinquency on their parts.

Implications

IMPLICATIONS FOR PROGRAM OPERATION

The findings on the prediction of recidivism have provided strong confirmation of weaknesses in the theoretical and operational character of the experimental program—weaknesses that have constituted a dominant theme throughout the whole study. It was pointed out in earlier chapters of the book, as well as in this chapter, that neither the theory of causation nor the intervention principles took adequate account of the extent to which family disorganization was an important problem to be dealt with in the intervention strategy nor was that strategy adequately implemented insofar as establishing effective relationships with the school was concerned, even though such relationships were originally posited as extremely important. The high predictive power of family disorganization and school behavior in accounting for variations in recidivism suggest very strongly that these factors could have been dealt with much more effectively by the experimental program. Furthermore, since the work histories of boys also proved to be predictive of recidivism, this factor might also have been dealt with more adequately.

Similarly, the high predictive power of personality factors and peer identification at the control program suggests that its program strategy might have been more effective in mitigating these factors. However, it must also be recognized that no program can be expected to deal effectively with all types of delinquents or to construct strategies by which all types of problems might be ameliorated. There are probably an indefinite number of factors that might be predictive of recidivism for any given program.

This being the case, the overall findings of this chapter suggest that, since different kinds of boys reacted differently to the treatment programs of Boys Republic and Silverlake, a crucial issue for improving program operation has to do with providing a more efficient match between types of offenders and types of programs so that a more optimal use of correctional resources might be made. In Chapter Fifteen, a preliminary attempt at matching offenders to types of treatment will be made through the use of simulation techniques. It is hoped that the attempted simulation, although imperfect, will provide some direction for more efficient correctional practice and improved theory.

IMPLICATIONS FOR THE FEM

This chapter, in combination with earlier chapters, illustrates that even though the experimental program was not more effective than the control program in reducing delinquency, its major significance was that it provided a framework for understanding what occurred. Thus, in addition to evaluating the delinquency reduction effort, *per se*, the components of the FEM— the statement of causation theory, the intervention principles, the operational guidelines, and the empirical examination of these components— have contributed to our knowledge of the factors related to experimental outcomes.

One major inadequacy of the FEM, however, has been its failure to provide a framework for better understanding the outcomes of the control program. Limited interpretations have been made in this area, but, for the most part, the theoretical assumptions, intervention principles, and program operation of the control institution were not subjected to systematic study. Unfortunately, we did not have adequate resources to sponsor a more extensive examination of the control program, and future experiments of this nature should make a sufficient allowance of time and funds to do so.

Furthermore, the fact that experimental and control outcomes were so highly similar, regardless of the manner in which recidivism data were analyzed, suggests needed improvements in the designs of future FEMs. In most experimental research, significant differences are usually sought between experimental and control groups, and such differences are used as the ultimate criteria of a program's success. In the present case, however, it is difficult to draw conclusions on this matter.

First, we had no criteria by which to discern whether the experimental and control programs could be considered successful or unsuccessful in their attempts to deal with this particular population of offenders. No definitive conclusions could be made because we did not have a baseline for comparison. By studying similar types of offenders in other institutions, we might have been able to establish expectations concerning what might constitute successful outcome.

Second, as was pointed out earlier in this chapter, attempts should be made in future correctional experiments to assess the possible effects of regression. Since such effects might operate to make programs seem more successful in reducing delinquency than they actually are, efforts should be made to separate them from the actual results of programmatic stimuli.

Finally, this chapter has suggested the value of evaluating program effectiveness on a before and after basis. It is often the case that programs are assessed solely on the basis of recidivism rates, *per se*. An examination of before and after figures can reveal important information on the extent to which the law-violating activities of a given group of offenders have been reduced, provided, of course, it can be demonstrated that such delinquency reduction figures are not spuriously tied in with regression effects.

References

CAMPBELL, DONALD T. 1957. Factors relevant to the validity of experiments in social settings. *Psychological Bulletin,* 54 (July): 297–312.

CORSINI, RAYMOND J. 1959. Appearance and criminality. *American Journal of Sociology,* 65 (July): 49–51.

ENGLAND, RALPH W. 1962. A study of post probation recidivism among five hundred federal offenders. In Norman Johnston, Leonard Savitz and Marvin F. Wolfgang, Eds., *The Sociology of Punishment and Correction.* New York: John Wiley.

FRANKS, C. M. 1956. Recidivism, psychopathy and personality. *British Journal of Delinquency,* 6 (January): 192–201.

GLASER, DANIEL. 1964. *The Effectiveness of a Prison and Parole System.* Indianapolis, Ind.: Bobbs–Merrill.

GLASER, DANIEL, and VINCENT O'LEARY. 1968. *Personal Characteristics and Parole Outcome*. Washington, D.C.: U.S. Government Printing Office.

GOTTFREDSON, DONALD M. 1967. Current information bases for evaluating correctional programs. *Research in Correctional Rehabilitation*. Washington, D.C.: Joint Commission on Correctional Manpower and Training (December).

GOULD, DONNA E., and ROBERT F. BEVERLY. 1963. *The Initial Home Visit Research Schedule and its Relationship to Parole Performance*. Sacramento: California Department of Youth Corrections, Research Report No. 13.

GRANT, J. DOUGLAS, and MARGUERITE Q. GRANT. 1959. A group dynamics approach to nonconformists in the navy. *Annals of the American Academy of Political and Social Science*, 322: 126–135.

KIRBY, BERNARD C. 1954. Parole prediction using multiple correlation. *American Journal of Sociology*, LIX (May): 539–550.

MATZA, DAVID. 1964. *Delinquency and Drift*. New York: John Wiley.

SUTHERLAND, EDWIN H., and DONALD R. CRESSEY. 1955. *Principles of Criminology*. New York: J. B. Lippincott.

THOMPSON, MARGARET, and STUART ADAMS. 1963. *Probationer Characteristics and Probation Performance*. Report No. 10. Los Angeles: Los Angeles County Probation Department.

WATTENBURG, W. W. 1953. Juvenile repeaters from two viewpoints. *American Sociological Review*, 18 (December): 631–635.

WATTENBURG, W. W., and FRANK SAUNDERS. 1954. Factors related to repeating among girls in trouble with the police. *Journal of Abnormal and Social Psychology*, 50 (May): 405–406.

WILKINS, LESLIE T. 1969. *Evaluation of Penal Measures*. New York: Random House.

PART IV

Implications and Reformulations

CHAPTER THIRTEEN

Implications for Delinquency Theory

> It is my central thesis that empirical research goes far beyond the passive role of verifying and testing theory: it does more than confirm or refute hypotheses. Research plays an active role: it performs at least four major functions which help shape the development of theory. It *initiates*, it *reformulates*, it *deflects* and it *clarifies* theory (Merton, 1957: 103).

The final element of the FEM used in this study called for an assessment of implications. This is the first of three chapters concerned with that task. It is devoted to a review of the inadequacies of the delinquency theory upon which the experimental program was based, a reformulation of that theory, and an assessment of its implications both for further research and intervention.

By way of review, it will be recalled that the theory was originally stated as follows:

Postulates:

I. The lower the social class, the lower the subsequent achievement.
II. Decreased achievement results in increased strain.
III. Increased strain results in high identification with delinquent peers.
IV. Identification with delinquent peers results in delinquency.

Theorems:

I. The lower the social class, the higher the subsequent strain.
II. Decreased achievement results in increased identification with delinquent peers.
III. Increased strain results in delinquency.
IV. The lower the social class, the higher the subsequent identification with delinquent peers.
V. Decreased achievement results in delinquency.

VI. The lower the social class, the higher the subsequent delinquency.

When the theory was examined in Chapter Six, the following was revealed:

1. Social class was of little explanatory value (Postulate I and Theorems I, IV, and VI).
2. Decreased achievement was associated with increased strain (Postulate II), but there was little support for the idea that it is directly related, to either identification with delinquent peers (Theorem II) or delinquency itself (Theorem V).
3. Increased strain was related rather strongly to identification with delinquent peers (Postulate III) and, what is more, the relationship of strain to delinquency received the greatest support of any proposition in the theory (Theorem III).
4. The relationship between peer identification and delinquency was also strong (Postulate IV). It was second in magnitude only to the relationship between strain and delinquency.

Thus the findings provided a mixed picture, tending to deny the importance of some postulates and theorems, as originally stated, but affirming the importance of others. They provided grounds neither for totally rejecting nor for accepting the theory. Instead, they suggested the importance of reformulating it.

Reformulation of Theory

This reformulation was accomplished in five steps:

Step 1. Two basic theoretical concepts, "social class" and "achievement," were discarded since, in the original test of the theory (Chapter Six), their respective postulates and theorems received little empirical support. The remaining concepts—"strain," "identification with delinquent peers," and "delinquency"—were retained. Since this discarding of concepts was based on findings from this single study, however, it should be kept in mind that this step might not be applicable to another population of delinquents.

Step 2. Step 2 involved a reconsideration of family variables. Originally, family variables were omitted from the theory, but as it turned out, this may have been a serious omission. Not only was it found that the family constituted an important external system with which the experiment had to be concerned (see Chapter Eight), but family disorganization turned out to be predictive of in-program terminations and recidivism in certain instances (see Chapters Ten, Eleven, and Twelve). For this reason we decided to find out in what way relationships within the family might be related to the onset of delinquency as well as other important concepts within the theory.

The two following items were used to measure family relations:

A. Were subject's natural parents living together?
   1. Yes
   2. No (because of divorce, separation, or death)
B. How well did subject get along with his parents?
   1. Less than average
   2. Average
   3. Better than average

These indicators, it turned out, were highly related to official delinquency. The relationship between family separation and delinquency (using *gamma*) was .77, and between boy–parent harmony and delinquency it was −.49 Consequently, family variables were included in the reformulation as indicated in Step 3.

Step 3. A new theoretical concept was created in the hope that such antecedents to "strain" as poor family relations or school adjustment could be better conceptualized. This concept, labeled "institutional ties," was introduced into the theory in order to account for the kinds of institutional, familial, and educational problems that delinquents seem to have.

If an adolescent comes from a disrupted home environment, or does poorly in school, he is in danger of "getting off the institutional track," of suffering from a lack of meaningful interaction with the two most important socializing agents of society. For example, Short and Strodtbeck (1965: Chaps. 10, 12) found that, compared with others, gang boys were characterized by a long list of "social disabilities" which led to, or were caused by, their lack of meaningful and rewarding ties with major societal institutions. Their disabilities involved unsuccessful school adjustment, limited social and technical skills, a low capacity for self-assertion, lower intelligence scores, and even a tendency to hold their peers in low esteem. Consequently, their chances of encountering failure and strain in their attempts to participate in legitimate activities were extremely high.

In a similar way, Matza (1964: 51) also implies that a lack of institutional ties is directly related to the occurrence of delinquent acts. Although his theory is far less deterministic than the one developed by this study, and although it heavily emphasizes the importance of the immediate situation in the occurrence of delinquency, several of his ideas lend credence to the importance of institutional ties. He points out that "the delinquent, primarily because he is a juvenile but also because of the provinciality of his subculture, exists within a narrow life space centering around a local turf which includes school, family and peers." The delinquent's reference points for action stem primarily from these three sources.

But what happens if he is cut off from conventional institutions? What happens if he denies or, in Matza's terms, "neutralizes" the legitimacy of their institutional constraints? "Stripped of moral guidance . . . ," says Matza (1964: 89), "he momentarily exists in a stark and frightening isolation." He often turns to his peers for moral guidance, but they do not fulfill that function. Instead, "they function to exacerbate his mood of fatalism and to provide a context of mutual misconception." The result of this is continued strain and the likelihood of participation in law-violating acts.

The point is that the problems of the delinquent may stem as much or more from his divorcement from the moral constraints of conventional socializing institutions than from the singular lack of achievement that was so strongly emphasized in our original statement. Since the findings of this study seemed to point very strongly in that direction, there were grounds for concluding that one of the basic concepts of the theory should take institutional ties into account in a more comprehensive way.

Step 4 The basic theoretical statement was revised (*a*) because of its importance for general scientific investigation and (*b*) so it could be submitted to a more rigorous test. The revised statement of the basic postulates and theorems was as follows:

Postulates:
  I. Decreased institutional ties results in increased strain.
 II. Increased strain results in increased identification with delinquent peers.
III. Increased identification with delinquent peers results in delinquency.

Theorems:
  I. Decreased institutional ties results in increased identification with delinquent peers (deduced from Postulates I and II).
 II. Increased strain results in delinquency (deduced from Postulates II and III).
III. Decreased institutional ties results in delinquency (deduced from Postulate I and Theorem II).

Step 5 The final step in the restructuring process involved a redefinition of the operational measures used in the revised theory. They were operationalized as follows:

Institutional Ties—The measures of school grades and family separation were combined to form a single measure of this concept. In order to derive this new measure, grades in school were dichotomized into two categories: (1) average or above average grades (A's, B's and C's) and (2) below average grades (D's and F's). Family, separation was also dichotomized into (*a*) homes in which both parents were present and (*b*) homes in which both parents were not present. A new measure was then computed on which a score of 2 indicated that a given subject made average or better than average grades in school and came from a family in which both parents were present, a score of 1 indicated that only one of the above two conditions were present, and a score of 0 indicated that a given subject obtained less than average grades in school and came from a broken home. Thus, a score of 2 indicated relatively strong ties with the two major socializing institutions for children, a score of 1 indicated a tie with only one of those institutions, while a score of 0 indicated strong ties with neither of the two.

Strain—Six single items of information were combined to form a measure of strain. Each item was dichotomized as follows:
1. How well did subject get along with his parents?
   Less than average = 1   Average or above = 0
2. Did poor school ties result in dropping out of school?
   Yes = 1   No = 0
3. How smart did subject feel relative to others his age?
   Less smart than average = 1   Average or above = 0
4. How many jobs had subject held?
   Two or more = 1   None or 1 = 0
5. Was subject ever fired from a job?
   Yes = 1   No = 0
6. What were subject's perceived chances of obtaining his vocational aspirations?
   Less than average = 1   Average or better = 0

These dichotomies were then added together to form a single measure of strain, with a score of 6 indicating highest strain and a score of 0 indicating lowest strain.

Identification with Delinquent Peers. A measure of this concept was computed by adding together each boy's scores on the Ratfink, Ace-in-the-Hole, Sociability, and Deviancy scales. This yielded a single measure of peer identification that ranged from lowest peer identification, represented by a score of 0, to highest peer identification, represented by a score of 13.

Delinquency. The dichotomy used in the original theory was retained in the revision. In order to measure delinquency, boys were divided into two groups: (1) those who were officially delinquent and (2) those who were not.

Empirical Examination of Revised Theory

As was done with the original test of the causation theory, Goodman and Kruskal's *gamma* (1954) was used to measure the relationships between each of the revised operational measures. This time, however, only single measures of each concept were used in order to make the test as simple as possible and to reduce the complexity of interpretation.

The summarized results of the analysis in the form of a total correlation matrix may be found in Table 13.1. The findings are encouraging since they

Table 13.1. Correlation Matrix for Revised Causation Theory

	Strain	Identification with delinquent peers	Delinquency
Institutional ties	−.49 (Revised Postulate I)	−.30 (Revised Theorem I)	−.83 (Revised Theorem III)
Strain		.30 (Revised Postulate II)	.76 (Revised Theorem II)
Identification with delinquent peers			.49 (Revised Postulate III)

meet all three of the criteria mentioned earlier. The signs of all *gamma* coefficients were commensurate with the signs expressed in the theory; the absolute values of all *gamma* coefficients exceeded the .20 cutting point; and the total configuration of findings conformed to theoretical expectations.

In terms of the basic postulates:
1. Decreased institutional ties were related to increased strain (−.49)
2. Increased strain was related to increased identification with delinquent peers (.30)
3. Identification with delinquent peers was associated with delinquent behavior (.49)

   The theorems were also supported:
1. Decreased institutional ties were related to identification with delinquent peers (−.30)
2. Increased strain was strongly associated with delinquent behavior (.76)
3. Decreased institutional ties were also highly correlated with delinquency (−.83)

The results were sufficiently promising as to merit examination in a more rigorous fashion. This examination required consideration of each theorem separately.

Theorem I

Theorem I was deduced from Postulates I and II according to the following logical argument:

Postulate I: Decreased institutional ties result in increased strain.

Postulate II: Increased strain results in increased identification with delinquent peers.

            Therefore:

Theorem I: Decreased institutional ties result in increased identification with delinquent peers.

According to the "sign rule" outlined in Chapter Two, we would expect the relationship between institutional ties and identification with peers to be negative since the algebraic product of the sign of Postulate I (which was negative) and the sign of Postulate II (which was positive) would yield a negative sign. This expectation was supported by the data since the gamma coefficient for Postulate II was positive, .30, and the coefficients for Postulate I and Theorem I were negative, $-.49$ and $-.30$ respectively.

The conditions of the "transitivity rule," also outlined in Chapter Two, were also satisfied, since the premises of the argument were stated in asymmetric sequential form and since the middle term of the argument (which in this case was "strain") appeared at the end of the first premise and at the beginning of the second premise. By giving "strain" this position in the argument, we made it an intervening variable in the causal process. We were saying that *institutional ties are related to delinquent peer identification through the intervening variable of strain.* This is an important point and brings us to a discussion of a further condition necessary to validate the logical argument presented above.

Costner and Leik (1964: 819–835) have proposed that if the postulates of an axiomatic theory are stated in asymmetric causal form and if what we have called the "transitivity rule" is satisfied, then one additional requirement needs to be met before valid deductions using the sign rule can be made. This additional requirement states that one must "assume a 'closed system,' i.e., there is no 'connection' (causal or 'spurious') between the variables in the postulates except those stated or implied in the postulates" (Costner and Leik, 1964: 831).

Translated into statistical terms, this means that the relationship between institutional ties and peer identification, *controlling for strain*, should yield a partial correlation of zero, since in our argument we imply that institutional ties are related to peer identification through the intervening variable of strain. This means that, when we control for the effects of strain, we would expect any relationship between institutional ties and peer identification to disappear.

The empirical examination of the effects of an intervening variable like strain is relatively easy to conduct when cardinal measures and product moment correlations are used. However, we had only ordinal data and were using *gamma* coefficients. Since there are no well-accepted techniques for computing partial correlations with ordinal data, we had to find some means by which we could compensate for this limitation, even though they might be less than desirable. First, we computed a partial *gamma* coefficient developed by Davis (1967: 189–193). Although Costner and Leik (1964: 833–834) specifically point out that Davis's formula for partial *gamma* is not sufficient for validating the sign rule, we felt that it might be useful in giving an indication, albeit a limited one, of the effects of strain as an intervening variable. Second, we also computed a partial correlation coefficient using product moment correlation, recognizing that our ordinal data would limit its interpretation.

Our findings were these: When the Davis partial *gamma* was used to control for strain, the original correlation between institutional ties and peer identification decreased from $-.30$ to $-.16$. This finding did not entirely satisfy the condition proposed by Costner and Leik, that the partial should be zero, but it nevertheless reduced the absolute value of the original correlation by nearly one-half.

Similar results were observed when we used *product-moment* correlation. The original relationship between institutional ties and peer identification, using product-moment correlation, was $-.12$. When we controlled for strain, it declined to $-.06$. Again, a decrease in original value of one-half was observed. Thus, in both instances the partial correlations tended to support the role of strain as an intervening variable. Although in neither instance were they zero, they did suggest that strain may be an important intervening influence.

Theorem II

The second logical argument with which we were concerned had to do with the derivation of Theorem II:

Postulate II: Increased strain results in increased identification with delinquent peers.

Postulate III: Increased identification with delinquent peers results in delinquency;
                Therefore:

Theorem II: Increased strain results in increased delinquency.

An examination of the *gamma* coefficients for these postulates and theorem reveals that the deduction of the theorem conforms to the "sign" and "transitivity" rules, although the magnitude of the theorem is considerably higher than either of the two postulates from which it was derived. The original *gamma* coefficient for Postulate II was .30, for Postulate III it was .49, and for Theorem II it was .76.

In this particular argument, identification with delinquent peers is implied as the intervening variable. Therefore, we would expect the relationship expressed in Theorem II to disappear when we controlled for peer identification. However, the logic of the argument was not supported. When we controlled for the effects of peer identification using the Davis partial, the relationship between strain and delinquency, rather than decreasing, increased from .76 to .79. This was completely opposite to theoretical expectations.

When product-moment correlation was used, the picture did not change much. The partial correlation decreased only slightly from an original correlation of .31 to .29. Thus, these results did not enable us to conclude that peer identification is a necessary intervening variable between strain and delinquency. Although on the surface the "sign" and "transitivity" rules were satisfied, the assumption of "closed system" was not.

Theorem III

Finally, the logical argument in Theorem III was concerned with the relation between institutional ties and delinquency. The following deduction was used to arrive at this theorem:

Postulate I: Decreased institutional ties lead to increased strain.
Theorem II: Increased strain leads to delinquency.
                     Therefore:
Theorem III: Decreased institutional ties lead to delinquency.

Again, the "sign" and "transitivity" rules were satisfied, with strain appearing to be a necessary intervening variable in the argument. The *gamma* coefficient for Theorem III was −.49, for Theorem II it was .76, and for Theorem III it was −.83.

As was the case with the second argument, however, the assumption of "closed system" was not satisfied when the effects of strain were controlled. When the Davis partial *gamma* was used to control its effects, the correlation between institutional ties and delinquency did not change from its original value of −.83. When product-moment correlation was used, however, it did decline somewhat, from −.34 to −.22, but this decline was not sufficient to provide much support for the assumption of a "closed system."

In summary, the empirical examination of the revised causation theory

again provided a mixed picture. At face value, the *gamma* coefficients used
to measure the relationship expressed in each postulate and theorem seemed
to be supportive of the theory. The absolute value of each coefficient exceeded the .20 cutting point established earlier, and in no instance did
the signs of the coefficients contradict the signs expressed by the postulates
and theorems. However, when the assumption of a "closed system," as
proposed by Costner and Leik (1964) was examined, the results did not
confirm the theory. In the derivation of Theorem I, the assumption seemed
to be partially met, but in the derivation of Theorems II and III, the assumption was not met at all. Part of the problem may have stemmed from the
fact that, given our ordinal measures, we did not have adequate statistical
tools to examine this assumption. But even though we used statistical techniques that were not entirely satisfactory, the results were sufficient to con-
vince us that the "closed system" assumption was not met.

Theoretical Implications

If one considers both the original and revised statements of the theory, the
foregoing analyses can be characterized, in part, as a failure to confirm
either statement, especially if rigorous criteria are used. However, some
highly significant implications, both theoretical and practical, emerge from
the findings.

NON-UTILITY OF SOCIAL CLASS

Despite the overwhelming reliance most sociological theories have placed
upon social class as an explanatory variable, not a single one of the postulates or theorems that involved social class was supported by the data.
Social class was almost totally useless as an explanatory variable. This
result tends to support the findings of recent studies which seriously question
the existence of a universal causal relationship between social class and law-
violating behavior (Clark and Wenninger, 1962; Dentler and Monroe,
1961; Empey, 1967b; Empey and Erickson, 1966; Gold, 1966; Nye,
Short, and Olsen, 1958; Porterfield, 1946; Reiss and Rhodes, 1961). These
studies, using self-reports of undetected lawbreaking, have yielded very low
correlations between these two theoretical concepts. Yet, because we were
concerned with official delinquency in this case, we might have expected
different findings. That we did not would seem to be of special significance.

It is of further interest to note that our findings are also very similar to
those of Polk (1965) in his study of delinquency in Lane County, Oregon.
As was this case, Polk (1965: 14) found that delinquency was more highly
related to poor adjustment in school than it was to social class. He found

that "a comparison of the incidence of delinquency by academic grade and social class level shows virtually *no effect* being produced by economic status at the same time that rather striking relationships obtain between differing grade levels." Polk's (1967) results further suggest that social class, by itself, is simply too global a concept to be of much use as an explanatory variable. Models and theories are needed that take better account of the interlocking configurations of economic, ethnic, familial, and educational variables as they relate to different social strata. A better picture is needed of the way these factors, along with official processing, interact to produce delinquency.

DEFINITIONAL AND MEASUREMENT PROBLEMS

One basic issue has to do with a number of definitional and measurement problems ordinarily associated with the study of delinquency. "Delinquency" as a social fact does not exist until two things are present: (1) law-violating behavior occurs; and (2) an individual is adjudicated guilty of engaging in that behavior. The theory just examined was concerned far more with the former than the latter and as such may have overlooked many of the official processes that must be explained if "delinquency" is to be understood. Consider official processing. Much recent literature has focused attention on the importance of the discretionary powers of the juvenile court and police in determining who are to be officially adjudicated as delinquent and institutionalized and who are not (Matza, 1964: Chapter Four; Piliavin and Briar, 1964; Skolnick, 1966; Tappan, 1946). One major weakness of our theory was its failure to account for the interaction between various types of adolescents and the legal system itself.

For example, even such basic factors as a boy's demeanor and appearance upon apprehension by police might determine whether he will be arrested and officially labeled. Piliavin and Briar (1964) found that police were more likely to arrest or issue citations to juvenile law-violators who were Negro, uncooperative, unrepentant, or dressed in the style of "toughs." Those who were Caucasian, cooperative, well-mannered, well-dressed, and repentant were more likely to receive informal reprimands and admonishments. This led to the conclusion that the official delinquent "is the product of social judgment. He is a delinquent because someone in authority has defined him as one, often on the basis of the public face he has presented to officials than of the kind of offense he has committed."

Similarly, Myerhoff and Myerhoff (1964: 328–336) found that police officers and community officials were often highly tolerant toward the delinquent activities of middle-class adolescents and did not want to contaminate their future success with records of official delinquency. As a consequence, the less serious offenses of these youths were dealt with in an informal way, presumably in deference to factors that they felt argued for a future lack of delinquency.

The juvenile court must also deal with conflicting mandates. It must respond to conditions of dependency and neglect among juveniles as well as to their illegal behavior. Unlike adult courts, where there is much greater concern with due process, Matza (1964) points out that the juvenile court system operates much like the Moslem "Kadi" courts, where judges possess a wide range of discretionary power. They are not expected to try all offenders according to the same consistent criteria but are expected instead to take into consideration not only the crime committed but the needs of the defendant and the needs of the community.

Besides his task of assessing guilt or innocence, the juvenile judge is caught between the social control theory of punishment and the more humanitarian philosophy of reform. Thus he is in a very delicate situation in which the principle of "individualized justice" gives him incredibly wide discretion, yet provides him with incredibly few guidelines for action.

One of his major problems, according to Matza (1964), is to determine which clients are to be "rendered unto probation," thus satisfying the demands of professional underlings for mercy, and which are to be "rendered unto prison," thus satisfying those indignant persons who demand punishment. According to Matza, the manner in which the court makes its decisions depends on three major factors: risk of scandal, parental sponsorship, and availability of bed space in an institution. If a juvenile has committed a serious offense and risk of public scandal is high, he will likely be incarcerated. If, however, the risk of scandal is moderate, the decision will then depend on the nature of his parental sponsorship. If his sponsorship is adequate, then he will likely receive probation; if it is inadequate, the chances are increased that he will be incarcerated. Finally, if the risk of public scandal is low, then only those offenders with virtually no parental sponsorship will go to an institution, providing, of course, that bed space is available. The consequence of all of this is likely to be a great deal of judicial inconsistency, even for similar types of offenders.

With all of this in mind, it is not suprising to find that our measure of "institutional ties"—family stability and school performance—rather than other variables bears the highest relationship to being an officially defined incarcerated delinquent. It may easily be that such findings reflect not only the "etiological processes" involved in the genesis of law-breaking behavior but the kinds of factors upon which police and court decision-making is based. Those offenders who, besides being law-violators, are doing poorly in school and/or come from broken homes are more likely to be candidates for incarceration because of their lack of sponsorship in the community. Although we would need a control group of delinquents on probation to verify this notion, it seems highly plausible that our findings are as much reflective of official processing as of any unique characteristics delinquents possess.

It is of further interest to note that the information involved in our measure of "institutional ties" would be much more visible to the juvenile court and would provide a more obvious basis for decision-making than would the more amorphous characteristics of "class," "strain," or "peer identification." This may be an additional reason why the relationship between delinquency and institutional ties was greater than it was for other variables.

The foregoing discussion points out one of the many problems involved in using "official delinquency" as an indicator of "delinquent acts." While it is true that official records can be used as an indicator of illegal acts, they are at best a "diluted" indicator; that is, they vary in response to official activities as well as to whatever it is that causes juveniles to violate the law. This "dilution" is certainly not a fatal flaw, since most social indicators are diluted in one way or another, but it does highlight a fundamental issue. The issue has to do with the fact that if official measures are to be used in testing the causation theory, the following two assumptions must be made: (1) that "official delinquency" is positively correlated with the number of "delinquent acts" actually committed, and (2) that measurement errors (*i.e.*, regression errors of "official delinquency" regressed on "delinquent acts") are at most only weakly correlated with the other variables of the theory. If one or both of these assumptions are highly questionable, the validity of using "official delinquency" as an indicator of "delinquent acts" becomes subject to great doubt.

It is our contention that the first assumption is not as problematic as the second; that even though "official delinquency" may be positively correlated with delinquent acts, the discrepancy between official and undetected measures may well be related to other concepts of the theory. Costner (1969: 247–248) has represented this type of measurement problem in Figures 13.1 and 13.2.

In Figures 13.1 and 13.2, X and Y represent theoretical concepts and X^1 and Y^1 represent the respective indicators or measures of these concepts. In both figures, it is postulated that a change in X leads to a change in Y. The small letters a and c refer to what Costner (1969) calls "epistemic coefficients," or the correlations of the indicators with the theoretical concepts they are intended to measure. The letter b represents the "true" correlation coefficient between concepts X and Y, which is estimated by the correlation between the two indicators, X^1 and Y^1. If, in the case of Figure 13.1, the epistemic coefficients are high and if X is not uniquely correlated with Y^1, then a valid estimation of b might be obtained. If, however, X

is directly correlated with Y^1 (see Figure 13.2) in some unique way, then what Costner calls a "differential bias" is present and the test of the theoretical model becomes seriously confounded.

It is our feeling that the use of an official measure of delinquency contains the differential bias problem represented in Figure 13.2, thus negating the second assumption that measurement errors are only weakly correlated with other variables. To illustrate this point, let X in the model stand for the concept of "institutional ties," let Y stand for the concept of "delinquency," and let Y^1 stand for the indicator of delinquency as measured by official records. It is our contention—and the *gamma* coefficients presented

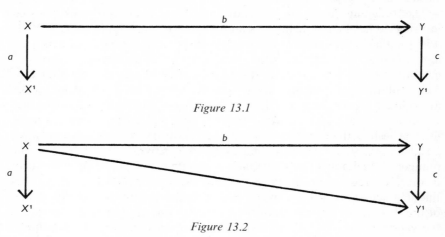

Figure 13.1

Figure 13.2

earlier seem to support it—that poor institutional ties not only affect delinquency in an etiological sense (*i.e.*, that their absences are related to the onset of law-violating behavior), but that they also affect the differential legal processes by which some law violators are officially defined as delinquent and others are not (*i.e.*, offenders lacking institutional ties are more likely to be dealt with formally). This being the case, X is related to Y and Y^1 in two very distinct ways, thus confounding the test of the theory.

This situation might be rectified, at least in part, by two things. First, by collecting measures of undetected, illegal acts, in addition to official measures, it would be possible to use both sets of information as a means of assessing the amount of "differential bias" introduced by using only official measures. Second, as Costner (1969: 255–261) has recently suggested, by having at least three indicators for each theoretical variable in a single theory, it is possible to check for errors such as the differential bias presented in Figure 13.2. This second step would aid considerably in the task of assessing the utility of official measures.

One other possible solution would be to create two theories, one to explain law-violating behavior and the other to explain official processing, and then to allow the two theories jointly to account for "official delinquency." However, if both theories include some of the same variables, a likely possibility, logical and measurement problems would be even more complicated.

CLOSED SYSTEM ASSUMPTION

Another problem highlighted by this analysis has to do with the failure of the revised theory to meet the "closed system" assumption. This was a significant finding because of the importance attached in the theoretical statement to the notion that delinquency is the product of a sequential series of variables or experiences. If the closed system assumption were true, we would have expected that the further a given variable is from delinquency in the etiological chain, the lower its relationship with delinquency would be. We implied in the theoretical statement that:

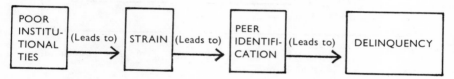

Following this chain, we would have expected peer identification to have the highest direct relationship to delinquency, strain the next highest and institutional ties the lowest. Contrary to this expectation, however, just the opposite occurred.

When the observed relationships between variables were plotted (see Figure 13.3), the variable that was furthest from delinquency in the sequential chain (institutional ties) also had the highest relationship to it ($-.83$); the variable that was closest (peer identification) had the lowest relationship to it (.49); while strain occupied a central position, possessing a relationship of .76 with delinquency.

On the other hand, there was some evidence that the "closed system" assumption was partially met when we examined the relationships between institutional ties and peer identification, controlling for strain. The original *gamma* coefficient of $-.30$ between institutional ties and peer identification declined by nearly one-half when the intervening influence of strain was controlled. However, this was not enough to alter the fact that the general model was not supported. Findings did not allow us to make the assumption of a closed system when actual delinquent behavior was considered as a part of the entire model.

In light of the stress placed in Chapter Two, indeed by sociological theory in general, upon the importance of peer identification leading to delinquency, these findings are highly significant. They underscore the profound need for a more definitive statement of the nature of the relationship between these two concepts. For example, if the theoretical concepts are reordered in such a way that those concepts with the highest correlations are placed closest together in the etiological sequence, then, as may be seen in Figure 3.4, the sequential ordering between peer identification and delinquency is altered drastically. This new ordering suggests very strongly that peer identification may result from, rather than lead to, delinquency:

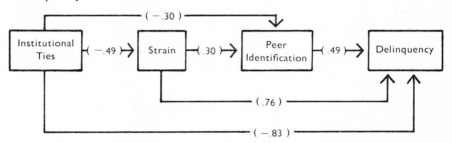

Figure 13.3. Relationships Among the Variables of the Revised Causation Theory. (As Measured by Gamma.)

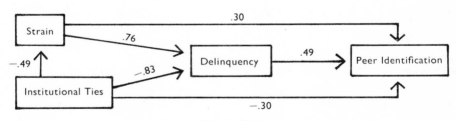

Figure 13.4

Furthermore, it might be noted that the relationships among strain, institutional ties and delinquency are made more complex than they were originally represented. Although additional research of a longitudinal nature would be needed to examine the validity of this causal chain, it is nevertheless highly suggestive of the need for reconceptualization in this area. This need is related to our use of axiomatic theory. Some important deficiencies were inherent in it.

THE UTILITY OF AXIOMATIC THEORY

The findings suggest that our use of axiomatization may have forced us into an oversimplification of our basic argument. There is a discontinuity between the narrative statement of the theory and its formalized version. Specifically, the interdependence of the relation between peer identification and delinquency is not represented in the formalized version of the theory (*i.e.,* the relationships may not be asymmetrical but may work both ways). Furthermore, certain steps connecting the variables alluded to in the narrative version do not appear at all in the formalized version. Most notable is the possibility that once an individual is officially processed, he is stigmatized. Stigma, then, may become an intervening variable that could contribute to further strain, greater identification with peers, and subsequent further delinquency. Thus, in attempting to present the theory in an elegant way, through the use of axiomatization, we did so at the expense of ignoring some important complexities. As it turns out, this may have been a very serious omission.

One plausible alternative to axiomatization that might rectify the above difficulties has to do with the use of causal models (*cf.* Blalock, 1964, 1969). The advantages of using causal models over axiomatization are: (1) a greater simplicity of presentation; (2) a greater ease and explicitness in representing symmetric and interdependent relations; and (3) an increasingly large body of literature in sociology that pertains to causal models, how to draw out their implications, and the assumptions necessary for such implications to be logically valid. For example, in causal model form, our revised theory might be presented as follows:

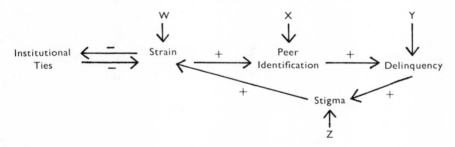

Figure 13.5

As in earlier figures, arrows have been used to specify the causal sequences among variables. Plus signs (+) have been used to indicate relationships that are direct, while minus signs (−) have been used to indicate inverse relationships. The letters *W, X, Y,* and *Z* indicate "exogenous" variables that have not been specified within the theory but that are assumed to affect theoretical variables directly. We will not elaborate here on what these "exogenous" variables might be, but, for methodological reasons, it would be important to specify their existence and to measure them before attempting to estimate the relationships among basic theoretical concepts (see Blalock, 1969: Chap. 4 for an elaborate discussion of this point).

It will be noted that in this revised statement there are two "feedback loops." The first involves a symmetrical and interdependent relationship between institutional ties and strain. The second involves a more complex loop in which strain may contribute initially to peer identification and subsequently to delinquency, but is further enhanced by official processing and stigma. If this loop does, in fact, exist, then it may contribute to a better understanding of official defining and labeling processes as well as to those factors that initially contribute to the law-violating behavior.

Implications of the Revised Theory for Experimental Alteration

The theoretical deficiencies just described illustrate the importance of utilizing an FEM in the conduct of correctional innovations. They indicate that an empirical examination of programmatic assumptions can be of immense value in pinpointing the areas in which correctional practices may be inconsistent with the problems they are supposed to address. Such was partially true in this case. If the intervention principles of the Silverlake Experiment were to be made more consistent with the problems possessed by the particular group of offenders with which it was concerned, then some revision would be in order.

The assumption was made in Chapter Three that the greater the temporal proximity between any factor in the etiological sequence leading to delinquency and delinquency itself, the greater would be its priority for intervention purposes. Consequently, the listing of factors to be addressed, in order of priority, were as follows: *identification with delinquent peers*, followed by *strain*, then by the *lack of achievement*, and, finally, by *social class*.

The intervention principles that were developed from this listing of priorities were as follows:
1. The delinquent group should be made the target of change.
2. Social strain among delinquents should be reduced.
3. Means for legitimate achievement by delinquents should be made available.
4. Except for efforts to reduce strain and enhance achievement, attempts to change class membership *per se* were not implied.

Actually the findings of this chapter do not so much discredit the principles that were set as they imply the need to revise and redefine their priorities. Even though the axiomatic model did not receive complete support from the data (*i.e.*, the "closed system" assumption was not met under rigorous test), the major variables upon which the intervention strategy was based were not entirely discredited. Although our theoretical model proved to be less than perfect in accounting for the sequential process that led to the commission of delinquent acts among this particular population, the variables it identified—the lack of institutional ties, strain, and peer identification—still retained considerable explanatory value. Thus, our intervention strategy was oriented toward dealing with some of the relevant factors even though the choice of theoretical models did not prove to be an optimal one.

If we used the findings that resulted from our initial reformulation of the theory, the intervention principles might be reordered in terms of those factors that had the highest direct relationships to delinquency. This revised ordering would then be as follows:

1. *Improve institutional ties*—The linkage of the offender with conventional institutions would become the first rather than the last order of business.
2. *Reduction of strain*—The reduction of strain would retain the same approximate priority.
3. *Decrease delinquent peer identification*—Attempts to make the delinquent group the target of change would occupy somewhat less attention than previously indicated.

However, if we used the more complex statement of the theory, as just discussed in Figure 13.5, strain would occupy the major focus of any intervention strategy. It occupies a pivotal position with respect either to the forces that lead to official processing in the first place or to the subsequent cycle of relationships introduced by official processing, *i.e.*, stigma and the likelihood of increased peer identification.

Whatever alternatives were chosen, however, the overall implications of this chapter strongly emphasize the need to pay attention to both institutional ties and the reduction of strain. Both factors seem to be crucial no matter which model is chosen.

References

BLALOCK, HUBERT M., JR. 1964. *Causal Inferences in Nonexperimental Research.* Chapel Hill: University of North Carolina Press.
1969. *Theory Construction: From Verbal to Mathematical Formulations.* Englewood Cliffs, N.J.: Prentice–Hall.

CLARK, JOHN P., and EUGENE P. WENNINGER. 1962. Socio-economic class and areas as correlates of illegal behavior among juveniles. *American Sociological Review,* 26 (December): 826–834.

COSTNER, HERBERT L. 1969. Theory, deduction and rules of correspondence. *American Journal of Sociology,* 75 (September): 245–263.

COSTNER, HERBERT L., and ROBERT K. LEIK. 1964. Deductions from axiomatic theory. *American Sociological Review,* 29 (December): 819–835.

DAVIS, JAMES A. 1967. A partial coefficient for Goodman and Kruskal's gamma. *Journal of the American Statistical Association,* 62 (March): 189–193.

DENTLER, ROBERT, and LAWRENCE J. MONROE. 1961. Early adolescent theft. *American Sociological Review,* 26 (October): 733–743.

EMPEY, LAMAR T. 1967b. Delinquency theory and recent research. *Journal of Research in Crime and Delinquency,* 4 (January): 28–42.

EMPEY, LAMAR T., and MAYNARD L. ERICKSON. 1966. Hidden delinquency and social status. *Social Forces,* 44 (June): 546–554.

GOLD, MARTIN. 1966. Undetected delinquent behavior. *Journal of Research in Crime and Delinquency,* 3 (January): 27–46.

GOODMAN, LEO A., and WILLIAM K. KRUSKAL. 1954. Measures of association for cross classification. *Journal of the American Statistical Association,* 49 (December): 732–764.

MATZA, DAVID. 1964. *Delinquency and Drift.* New York: John Wiley.

MERTON, ROBERT K. 1957. *Social Theory and Social Structure.* Glencoe, Ill.: The Free Press.

MYERHOFF, HOWARD L., and BARBARA G. MYERHOFF. 1964. Field observations of middle-class "gangs." *Social Forces,* 42 (March): 328–336.

NYE, F. IVAN, JAMES F. SHORT, JR., and V. J. OLSEN. 1958. Socio-economic status and delinquent behavior. *American Journal of Sociology,* 63 (January): 318–329.

PILIAVIN, IRVING, and SCOTT BRIAR. 1964. Police encounters with juveniles. *American Journal of Sociology,* 70 (September): 206–214.

POLK, KENNETH. 1965. Those who fail. Eugene, Oregon: Lane County Youth Project.

1967. Urban social areas and delinquency. *Social Problems,* 14 (Winter): 320–325.

PORTERFIELD, AUSTIN L. 1946. *Youth in Trouble.* Fort Worth, Tex.: Leo Potishman Foundation.

REISS, ALBERT J., JR., and ALBERT L. RHODES. 1961. The distribution of juvenile delinquency in the social class structure. *American Sociological Review,* 26 (October): 730–732.

SHORT, JAMES F., JR., and FRED L. STRODTBECK. 1965. *Group Process and Gang Delinquency.* Chicago: University of Chicago Press.

SKOLNICK, JEROME H. 1966. *Justice Without Trial.* New York: John Wiley.

TAPPAN, PAUL W. 1946. Treatment without trial. *Social Forces,* 24 (March): 306–311.

CHAPTER FOURTEEN

Implications for Intervention

The first requirement for an efficient use of research in correctional program development is an organizational arrangement that calls for integration of the functions of administration, treatment and evaluation. Prior to the introduction of research, there was only one communication channel within the system: the channel between administration and treatment. With the advent of research, the channels of communication increase to three (President's Commission on Law Enforcement and Administration of Justice, 1967c: 14).

There are two major contributions that research can make to programs concerned with delinquency control: testing the empirical adequacy of the theoretical foundations upon which programs are based and assessing the operational adequacies of those programs. Since the first task for this experiment has already been addressed in the prior chapter, let us turn our attention to operational issues. Four major sets of implications merit our attention: (1) the relative success of efforts to enhance staff-offender collaboration through the use of group techniques; (2) the problems associated with establishing effective linkage for the program with the community; (3) the dynamic relationship between personal and social systems that was demonstrated by various bodies of research; and (4) the effectiveness of a community vs. an institutional program when assessed not only in terms of recidivism and danger to the community but in terms of financial cost as well.

Staff-Offender Collaboration

The evidence relative to the success of efforts to establish a collaborative social system in which delinquents play a key role was mixed. On one hand, findings from several different chapters indicated some positive results:

1. There was less evidence of a delinquent inmate system in the experimental than in the control program (Chapter Seven).
2. There was a greater tendency for experimental than control subjects to ratify organizational goals, norms, and expectations (Chapter Seven).
3. The experimental system seemed to develop efficient mechanisms for control. The number of critical incidents in the experimental program decreased over time and, as they did so, the number of group delinquencies declined also (Chapter Nine).
4. The degree of association between peer identification and post-program recidivism among experimentals—unsuccessful as well as successful graduates—was negligible, while among controls the association was stronger (Chapter Twelve).

On the other hand, in terms of negative findings, two things stand out:

1. There was evidence that the experimental system may have been overly concerned with control, overly constricted, and overly punitive (Chapters Seven, Ten, and Eleven).
2. The experimental system, no less than the control system, was far more inclined to punish boys for undesirable behavior than to reward them for desirable behavior (Chapter Seven). Despite the involvement of boys in the reformation process, there was little evidence that boys there found any greater intrinsic reward in the system.

By way of expanding upon these negative issues, several matters of importance might be considered. Since early runaways increased markedly in the experimental program, it appears that, as the program's capacity for control increased, both staff and boys became increasingly intolerant of deviance on the part of new boys. When this tendency was coupled with the personal dispositions of some boys to resist change anyway, a situation was set up that seems to have resulted in an unnecessarily high runaway and failure rate. Furthermore, because the system seems to have been effective as a control mechanism as measured by the small volume of in-program delinquency, it seems likely that the members of the experimental system were reacting as much or more to personal idiosyncrasies and to violations of in-program rules and demands as to violations of external legal demands. They may have been overly concerned with internal controls at the expense of losing some boys who might have been retained otherwise.

In fairness to both staff and boys, the possibility should not be overlooked that their apparent rigidities may reflect some of the realities that must be confronted in establishing a reformation culture. The problem is a complex one theoretically. Just as the members of a new religious sect are zealous in their conversion and intolerant of heretics, so also may the members of a new correctional system react. Those who are perceived as deviants because they will not accept the new demands are increasingly defined as nonbelievers and rejected. Furthermore, such a reaction is quite understandable in light of the extreme pressures to which delinquents and staff in a community program are subjected and in light of the insecurities experienced by boys in rejecting the delinquent value system for a non-delinquent one. Reform-oriented delinquents were faced with the necessity of not only changing themselves but also renouncing the accepted standards of their peers. This is a situation fraught with self-doubt and moral questioning, one difficult to handle psychologically and socially because it threatens old loyalties and points of view.

This problem speaks to some of the unanticipated difficulties inherent in trying to create a reform-oriented system among offenders. It is obvious that if the experimental program were to become more successful, it would have to cut down its runaway and failure rate. One simple expedient that has been introduced since the experiment ended is a three-day trial period for each new boy. If, after full participation for three days, he does not wish to become a part of the system or if boys and staff already in the program vote not to receive him, he will be placed elsewhere. This expedient seems to have lowered the runaway rate, probably by eliminating some of the boys who were most inclined to run earlier. This expedient has the virtue of increasing the self-determination of delinquents and perhaps enhancing their commitment to the program. However, it leaves unanswered the question as to how many rejectees might actually have succeeded in the program had they stayed. It should be noted that some of those who are the most resistant initially are those who do well later on. Second, such a sifting process inevitably sets up new kinds of problems for the courts and other correctional agencies. Someone has to deal with rejectees. Finally, since such a procedure would make difficult the use of a traditional experimental design in which offenders are randomly assigned to different programs, some other means would have to be used to determine why some people were not accepted, what their personal characteristics were, whether the program was improved thereby, and whether rejectees did any better elsewhere.

Another alternative would be to seek means by which the system could deal more effectively with newcomers. Even though it might be desirable to impose some demands and controls from the outset, those demands might be made more palatable if both staff and older boys in the program went out of their ways to be helpful and supportive of newcomers. The evidence was clear that more rewards and supports were needed. At the same time, one would also have to be concerned over the effects of increased flexibility. Conceivably, the cost to those boys who were willing to commit themselves to change could be sufficiently great as to counterbalance the beneficial effects of making the system more flexible. The magnitude of the problem is highlighted by the fact that the rejection of those perceived as deviant by the system is characteristic of most all groups, not just this one. It seems to be inherent in the nature of group life that in- and out-group structures develop, with the former rejecting the latter. To expect this particular group of adolescents, along with correctional staff, to overcome a tendency that other non-delinquent groups have been unable to overcome is asking a lot.

Another alternative for diminishing this problem might be to use group techniques in nonresidential rather than residential settings. Some of the problems that were noted were undoubtedly due to the nature of institutional life *per se* where people are forced to live together. Even in this small community-based operation those problems were present. But rather than expanding further on this issue here, let us turn to the problems of community linkage because they reflect on the question as well.

Problems of Community Linkage

Several themes regarding the relation of the experiment to external community systems merit attention. First, the experiment experienced its best relations with certain segments of the juvenile justice system, especially probation and the police. Relations with the juvenile court, however, were somewhat more problematic

The major difficulty had to do with the small number of problem offenders for whom legal processing and current procedures were so cumbersome that they made flexibility and program operation extremely difficult. For example, as pointed out in Chapter Seven, there were cases in the experiment where boys were probably lost to the program because they could not be detained temporarily. One source of difficulty was the presence of a few boys who continued to get into trouble unknown to legal authorities and for whom some controls were necessary. At other times, such individuals were detected and removed from the program by legal action and incarcerated when it was felt that such a removal was unnecessary.

Without some means for the temporary detention of the most difficult cases, reformers at the experiment were limited to a choice of two basic types of formal sanctions, neither of which proved to be very satisfactory. On the one hand, reformers could punish troublemakers by placing them on work details, by prohibiting them from visiting home on weekends, or by imposing some lesser sanction. However, because the residence was an "open" institution and had no physical or custodial constraints, boys who encountered severe restrictions could escape simply by running away. This situation undoubtedly contributed to the inordinately high incidence of runaways at the experiment.

On the other hand, the only other major sanction was expulsion, with a recommendation that troublemakers be returned to court, perhaps for incarceration. This type of sanction also yielded undesirable consequences because it contributed to the high rate of unsuccessful terminations and because, in the hands of overly punitive reformers, it may have resulted in the premature failure of delinquents who, with a wider range of alternatives, might have been changed. If relationships with the courts had been more functional, this situation might have been improved through the use of a third type of sanction: namely, temporary detention in local juvenile facilities. If temporary detention could have been integrated occasionally with regular program activities—group meetings, work, and even school— it might have worked more effectively than the use of restrictions or expulsion. The placement of persistent troublemakers in detention facilities would have had the additional advantage of freeing the groups at the experiment from a preoccupation with the problems of only a very few individuals. Greater attention could then have been devoted to the problems of boys who, while they were not continually in trouble, exhibited a desire to change.

This is an issue that, in this time of concern both for community protection and the civil rights of juveniles, merits serious attention. The juvenile court and correctional agencies should not find themselves in the position of either having to leave a serious case free in the community or having to incarcerate him permanently when some other alternative would be more desirable. It is suggested, therefore, that greater preparation be made than was made in this case for developing effective sanctioning procedures prior to, and as a part of, any community program for serious offenders. Furthermore, since this is only one case in point, it would be wise to consider other problems of a like nature with court and correctional people so that the most flexible procedures possible might be used.

NEIGHBORHOOD RELATIONSHIPS

Second, relationships with the local community were problematic on occasion but, in the main, were not characterized by irreconcilable conflict. Instead, a greater problem was the impersonality of experiment-community relations. Boys were detached, for the most part, from local adults and adolescents rather than intimately involved with them. As a consequence, the program failed seriously in its endeavor to establish community linkage.

This problem was due, in part, to the urban character of life in a big city and to the degree of social distance between conformists and offenders.

But there were other difficulties inherent in the nature of the program design itself. The average length of stay, for example, was only six months and boys lived in a common residence rather than their own homes. These factors made the establishment of neighborhood relationships extremely difficult.

The result was that, although the program was located in the community, it was only relatively more involved in community life than a total institution. The task of making it an integral part of the boys' community life was not fully realized. Furthermore, when offenders and staff found themselves engaged in an intense relationship, internal to the program and lasting 24 hours a day, there was a strong tendency toward introversion—a strong tendency to become preoccupied with internal problems and interpersonal relationships rather than with external ones. When this occurred, the necessity for community linkage was forgotten, as though the only problems to be solved were those that lay within the "therapeutic relationship."

Still worse, such a relationship tends to polarize delinquents (and staff) into opposing groups. For some, the longer the relationship exists and the more satisfying it becomes, the greater the likelihood that the only place such people will feel comfortable is in an institution. They become dependent upon, rather than independent of, such a relationship. For others, the relationship produces resistances which only inhibit the change process. The danger is that, in order to avoid dependency, resisters may end up with stronger, rather than weaker, ties to deviant peers and patterns. Consequently, since neither result is desirable, some more functional balancing of external and internal influences must be sought.

A possible alternative would be to make such programs as this nonresidential in character, with boys living in their own homes. The chances for achieving a better balance between internal and external demands might then be enhanced. Whatever problems were addressed, and whatever steps were taken toward school and institutional integration, would likely have more lasting impact. Efforts to make the offender independent both of program and delinquent ties and to help him achieve in legitimate activities could then be more objectively pursued. However, since a nonresidential program also has its difficulties, let us consider them in light of the problems that were encountered by the experiment in attempting to establish linkage with the school. The inability of the experiment to make this linkage effective constituted one of its greatest failures.

RELATIONSHIPS WITH SCHOOL

Briefly, school-experiment problems were attributable to four major difficulties: (1) school resistance, (2) offender disabilities, (3) a preoccupation of some experimental staff with in-program operations, and (4) the

fact that, even when boys adjusted successfully to the school, that adjustment was only temporary. That is, since average length of stay was only six
months, any boy wishing to remain in school had to seek readmittance and
a new adjustment in his neighborhood school upon release.

On one hand, it would seem that a nonresidential program could address
most of the problems of school resistance as well as, if not better than, a
residential one. School officials in any given school might have less reason
to be apprehensive if they were concerned with only one or two boys from a
single neighborhood rather than a large group of offenders, as was the case
in the Silverlake Experiment. They could then deal more easily with a
situation of this type. The chief difficulty, of course, might be the fact that
the particular boy or boys involved had already failed in that school. In
that case, a whole history of past failures would have to be overcome and
new relationships established before he could succeed. Even so, it is difficult
to see how those problems would be any worse than the resistances encountered at Silverlake.

Furthermore, the preoccupation of staff and boys with in-program
operation might be decreased if boys returned to their own homes each
evening. Greater attention might then be focused upon community and
school issues, upon the problems of offenders outside rather than in the
residence. There would be some surcease for everyone from the intensity
of a living experience in which group techniques and a strong reformation
culture are omnipresent. In such a setting, it is difficult for people to escape
from the constant pressures that arise from involuntary group living so
that they might consider the meaning of those pressures, learn to deal with
them, and to benefit from them.

Finally, there is no question but that, if a delinquent could achieve some
success in his own neighborhood school, he would be better off than if he
achieved the same success in an outside school, especially if his stay in the
latter was only temporary and required him to withdraw and start all over
again. Whatever new adjustments he made would be cumulative and would
involve those people, adult and juvenile, with whom he would ultimately
have to establish a non-delinquent identity anyway.

On the other hand, there are problems of a different variety that might
emerge in a nonresidential program. First, if that program had to relate
effectively to a number of different schools, rather than just one as at
Silverlake, its task might be made more complex. Instead of one set of
administrators, teachers, and students, it would have to relate to several.
Even if resistance was lessened, the sheer number of linkage problems would
require greater time and staff. Furthermore, if there is great need for
curriculum revision in the schools in order to deal more effectively with
delinquents, then it would be virtually impossible for any single program to

introduce those revisions into a number of different schools, while it might
be possible to do so in a single school. Thus, the problems of linkage are
great, no matter what community model is used. And while a greater
attention to the linkage problem at Silverlake might have diminished that
problem, it could not have solved it. Instead, its experience merely highlighted a few of the complex issues that, quite aside from offender disabilities and motivation, require further experimentation and research.

Dynamics of Personal and Social Systems

A third major theme was derived from rather impressive evidence that
offender behavior is very much a function of correctional as well as personal
systems. It is a product of the interaction between these two systems rather
than something entirely unique in the personal makeup of offenders or in
the organizational characteristics of correctional programs that must be
improved.

This finding was documented in several ways:

1. Runaway behavior at the experimental and control programs was shown
   to be associated with different personal and background variables
   (Chapter Ten). Furthermore, runaway behavior in the experimental
   program was primarily a problem for newcomers, while the same was not
   as true in the control program.
2. In-program runaways and failures in the experimental program tended
   to be disliked and unattached people—people who have difficulty both
   giving and receiving respect (Chapters Ten and Eleven).
3. When organizational characteristics in both experimental and control
   programs were altered, the impact on individual behavior was great.
   The personal factors most predictive of offender behavior before the
   changes were not always the same after the changes. Furthermore, each
   time a change occurred, the predictive efficiency of personality factors
   increased, suggesting the likelihood that those individuals with personality problems were most affected by that change (Chapter Ten).
4. The configuration of personal factors most predictive of recidivism for
   experimentals was not the same as for the controls (Chapter Twelve).
   While some offender types might do well in one program, they would
   fail in another.

These findings suggest, then, that there may be no uniform sets of personal
and background variables that will be consistently predictive of offender
behavior, no matter what the correctional setting. Offender behavior,
indeed correctional effectiveness, are instead a product of the match between
personal and social systems. Thus, if prediction is desirable, research will
have to look more closely at the dynamics of interaction between these two

systems rather than at personal or organizational characteristics by themselves.

The findings also guard against the tendency to draw one simple conclusion from the entire experiment; namely, that because post-program recidivism rates were approximately equal, experimental and control programs possessed essentially the same characteristics or had the same effect on delinquents. That conclusion is simply not true. While recidivism rates were about the same, the personal and organizational factors that interacted to produce those rates were not the same. Thus, by beginning to document more carefully what those factors are, we might ultimately reach a stage where a much more efficient matching of offender and program types could be made.

Finally, the study indicates that some strain, organizational as well as personal, will likely be the inevitable consequence of any attempt to change correctional practices not only in the community but in total institutions as well. Basic alterations, regardless of their nature, will produce conflict and dissension among both staff and offenders, since the disruption of existing relationships is always disconcerting. The basic objective, therefore, should not be to avoid strain at all costs but, through study, to become more conversant with the kinds of strain that will be produced under different sets of circumstances and what their long-run effects are likely to be.

Effectiveness of Community Programs

There are several ways that this experiment speaks to the issue of community program effectiveness: (1) whether it constituted a special danger to the community; (2) whether it was as effective as an institutional program; and (3) what its relative costs were.

With regard to a community danger, the data indicated: (1) that the program was of little danger to the community. In fact, as the program progressed, it seemed to increase its capacity to control offenders and became far more efficient than regular control agencies in detecting new violations (Chapter Nine); and (2) that the police were willing to testify publicly that there had been no increase in official delinquency as a result of the program (Chapter Eight).

As a reducer of recidivism and, concomitantly, as a help to delinquents, the effects of the experimental program were more questionable:

1. The runaway and in-program failure rates for experimentals were high, as high as those for controls.
2. The post-program recidivism rates for experimentals were about the same as those for controls, certainly not markedly superior as might have been hoped.

3. Yet, when before-and-after recidivism rates were considered, it appeared
   that both programs may have had significant impact in terms of delinquency control. Among experimentals, for example, the per cent
   reduction in number of delinquent acts for those who successfully
   completed the program was 85 per cent, and even for runaways and
   failures the figures were 63 and 64 per cent, respectively (Chapter Seven).

Such findings merit careful consideration, especially when it is recalled
that a very stringent measure—arrest rather than conviction—was used
as the criterion for recidivism. They suggest, first, that we must be careful
in using "either-or" measures of recidivism—*i.e.*, did or did not the offender
recidivate—to avoid imputing greater criminality to him than he actually
posseses. It may be that while he recidivated once, his overall rate of
violations may have declined significantly.

Second, we cannot answer this issue conclusively until better information
is available on the "regression effect." If the chances of arrest are small,
relative to the actual amounts of law-violating behavior in which an
individual engages, findings such as these could be due to chance. In seeking
to determine the effects of chance, we may have to use additional control
groups or gather recidivism data on undetected, as well as detected, violations. The goal would be to determine the extent to which official records
are inaccurate or to measure the degree of association between official and
unofficial lawbreaking.

Finally, we need better assessments of correctional effectiveness in terms
of cost—personal cost to the delinquent boy as well as financial cost to
society. From the perspective of the delinquent boy, the foregoing findings
might be seen in a much different light. It is difficult, for example, to say
whether the experimental (or control) program was helpful or harmful.
On one hand, both programs "lost" about half of their boys either through
runaway or failure. If this fact resulted in a further reduction in the self-
and social respect of these individuals, the programs may be seen as harmful,
even though only a small number of them were subsequently incarcerated.
Thus, for this particular group, one does not know whether community
intervention of this type (or commitment to an institution) was better than
doing nothing. It may have been worse.

On the other hand, the picture for experimental graduates was not so
bleak. It is significant that, while the community program was at least as
effective as the more complex institutional program, it completed its
intervention in less than half the time (six *vs.* thirteen months). From the
perspective of the delinquent in this group, therefore, a significant payoff
may have occurred. However, this payoff is associated with a choice
between only the experimental and control alternatives. We still do not

know whether the same results might have been achieved with even less, or no, intervention.

The answer to that question, however, is not likely to be provided because the delinquent wishes it. Instead, if it is obtained, it will be the result of other kinds of considerations, one of which is financial. What are the relative financial costs of different kinds of intervention? In this case, how did the costs of the experimental community program compare with those of the control program? Perhaps if there were significant differences, ways might be provided for considering yet even other alternatives, such as experimenting with no intervention.

In seeking answers to these questions, a detailed analysis of program costs was made that included all conceivable expenses: for personnel (salaries, health and retirement insurance, workmen's compensation, etc.), for physical plant (rent, depreciation, repairs and maintenance, etc.), for food, clothing, and utilities, for outside professional expenses (medical, dental, and legal), for administrative and office costs, and for miscellaneous expenses such as staff recruitment, staff training, and even public relations. The results of this analysis are summarized in Table 14.1.

It will be observed that the average monthly cost per boy was less in the experimental than in the control program, $303 *vs.* $363. However, since the average length of stay for experimentals was only about half of that for controls, this difference was magnified considerably. The result was that the average cost per experimental boy was only about 40 per cent of the cost per control boy, a significant difference indeed in light of the fact that recidivism rates for the two groups were approximately equal. It means that,

Table 14.1. Relative Costs for Experimental and Control Programs

Subjects	Average monthly cost per boy	Average length of stay in months	Average cost per boy	Ratio of experimental to control cost per boy
Program Graduates:				
Experimentals	$302.86	5.73	$1735.39	$\dfrac{1735.39}{4594.23} = 38\%$
Controls	363.18	12.65	4594.23	
Runaways and in-program failures:				
Experimentals	302.86	2.23	695.15	$\dfrac{695.15}{1576.20} = 44\%$
Controls	363.18	4.34	1576.20	

although both programs brought about a significant reduction in overall delinquency rates, the cost for this service in the noninstitutional community program was less than half as much.

One thing the figures do not totally reveal, however, are educational costs. Some exceptions must be noted. Except for a tutor, educational costs for the experimental program were borne by the Los Angeles City School District and, as a result, were not included. In the control program, by contrast, some educational costs were included. While that program does receive the same average daily expenditure per child from its local school district as other schools, it finances the cost of considerable educational enrichment. It is difficult to say exactly what this additional cost is, but it is significant since it maintains a teacher-student ratio of 1 to 15 and provides the physical plant as well. The point is that if the control program had to finance education entirely, its expenses would be even greater.

By way of implications, these figures, in conjunction with the foregoing rates on recidivism, imply three important conclusions:
1. that there is considerable potential inherent in community programs for reducing correctional costs;
2. that such programs may not pose much increased danger to the community; and,
3. that it may be possible to help many offenders in much shorter periods of time and without all of the debilitating effects of total incarceration.

The data imply, further, that by revising the ways in which correctional resources are used, it may be possible to realize a higher degree of success without significant increases in cost. For example, suppose that all 121 control subjects in this study had been placed in the community rather than the control program. Assuming the same costs as revealed in Table 14.1, and the same success and failure rates, a savings would have been realized of at least $2,859 per successful graduate and $881 per unsuccessful releasee. Taken collectively, this would have meant a savings of $171,540 for successful graduates and $53,741 for unsuccessful releasees, a total of $225,281. Even more striking, the same savings extended to larger numbers would mean a savings of almost $2 million for every 1,000 offenders.

Consider further what might be done with potential savings of this magnitude. The research costs for this project included approximately $95,000 for four years of data collection and the production of four progress reports and an additional $45,000 for data analysis and the writing of this book, a total of $140,000. The $225,281 savings realized from keeping control offenders in the community in this study would not only have financed a similar body of research but would have left an additional $85,281 for program enrichment and variation. In other words, by utilizing a community model similar to this one for more offenders, a great deal of research and program intervention could have been implemented without adding to operational costs or acquiring outside research funds. Furthermore, the above is but one of the methods of improving cost effectiveness implied by these findings. Two others, for example, might involve experimentation with shorter periods of confinement for offenders, having offenders in community programs live in their own homes, or choosing a control group that would remain untreated. The point is that by taking cognizance of alternative approaches and making experimentation a regular part of correctional operation, the chances for long-run improvement would not only be increased but would not always require vast new expenditures. Humanitarian, as well as financial, considerations argue for such an approach.

References

President's Commission on Law Enforcement and Administration of Justice. 1967c. *Task Force Report: Corrections.* Washington, D.C.: U.S. Government Printing Office.

CHAPTER FIFTEEN

Implications for Field Experimentation

An efficient steering of social action presupposes that fact-finding methods have to be developed which permit a sufficiently realistic determination of the nature and position of the social goal and of the direction and the amount of locomotion resulting from a given action. To be effective, this fact-finding has to be linked with the action organization itself: it has to be part of a feedback system which links a reconnaissance branch of the organization with the branches which do the action (Lewin, 1968: 442).

On the basis of what was learned in this study, there are several improvements that might be made in the use of the FEM in future research. Since a discussion of all of them would require the writing of another book, this chapter will focus on four areas that we felt were particularly important: the need for pilot studies, improvements in the study of program process, problems of experimental design, and the use of findings for the purpose of simulation.

The Need for Pilot Studies

It was pointed out in Chapter I that correctional personnel often make elaborate causation assumptions about offenders and what should be done to correct them. Yet rarely are those assumptions subjected to logical and empirical inquiry. The examination of assumptions in this study strongly supported the importance of doing so.

Several examples might be cited, but one good illustration was repeated evidence that the causation theory and intervention strategy failed to account adequately for the family problems of this particular group of delinquents:

312

1. Only about one-third of both experimental and control boys were still living with both of their natural parents and, similarly, only about one-third of them reported getting along well with parental figures (Appendix I).
2. Family disorganization was one of the single most consistent predictors of runaways and in-program failures (Chapter Ten).
3. Finally, family disruption also proved to be important in the analysis of post-program recidivism. Of all single predictors, it was the one most consistently associated with recidivism (Chapter Seven).

In drawing conclusions from these findings, it would be unwise to generalize from them to all delinquents and to assume that family disruption is the key to correctional problems. No such conclusion is warranted. However, the findings do suggest that the intervention strategy of the Silverlake Experiment might have been more effective had it identified these problems earlier in the study and attempted to address them. Thus, what is suggested is the importance of conducting more studies of offender characteristics *prior to assigning them to specific programs*. Such pilot studies might then provide a sounder basis upon which to construct field experimental models, whether in corrections or elsewhere.

Therefore, it is our suggestion that pilot studies be included as an integral component of future FEMs. A pilot study would precede all other aspects of research and would provide useful direction for organizing the field experiment. It would provide a validity check on any causal assumptions made about offenders and it would help to better pinpoint the areas that should be addressed.

The Improved Study of Program Process

A second area in which future FEMs might be improved has to do with the study of program process. Despite a great deal of process research in this study, we were disappointed over our inability to shed greater light on the evolution of the intervention program, its changing structure, and the problems that developed. This deficiency stemmed from at least two difficulties. First, the experiment constituted a very complex set of stimuli. Unlike laboratory experiments, where a single stimulus, or small number of stimuli are studied over short periods of time, the subjects of this experiment were exposed to many stimuli, internal and external, over prolonged periods of time. Because of this complexity, it was difficult to know in advance what should have been measured and how best to measure it.

Second, we were continually plagued by the possibility of over-burdening subjects with too many measuring instruments. For example, as was pointed out in Chapter Seven, attempts to monitor group processes were cancelled during the initial stages of the experiment because research began to interfere with program operation. The immense task of documenting this aspect of the program began to place too great a burden on boys and action staff. Thus, even though we had some relatively sophisticated research instruments by which to explore group development, we were forced to abandon them.

In view of these problems, we would like to suggest some ways in which the study of program process in future field experiments might be improved. First, one might want to revise or add to the two major data collection techniques we used: the research questionnaire and the unstructured interview. Although both techniques provided important information on certain aspects of program process, it is our feeling that neither provided sufficient description of the subjective views and interactional patterns of those who participated in the experiment. Our documentation of program process might have been vastly improved had such information been collected and utilized.

As a way of rectifying this deficiency, it was suggested earlier that data collection techniques might include the writing of personal diaries by selected subjects and a detailed daily log by staff members. In attempting to understand the changing nature of the program culture, or runaway and failure problems, it would have been of great value to have had more information on the day-to-day perspectives of both boys and staff. Since such information was not collected, crucial data were lost. Once boys ran away, for example, little could be gained from them regarding the factors that precipitated that behavior. Therefore, one possibility would be to select randomly a number of subjects and pay them to record their impressions of day-to-day events and routines. Perhaps through interaction with research staff, they might learn to observe routines and events around some loosely structured and agreed upon framework. The goal would be to obtain better information, subjective though it may be, on the factors preceding, associated with, and following both critical and more ordinary events.

Insofar as staff members are concerned, Klein and Snyder (1965) have demonstrated the utility of having them keep a detailed log of their activities. Their findings were revealing because they indicated a wide discrepancy between idealized prescriptions for staff and what staff actually did. For example, among street-gang workers, they found considerable variance in the time actually spent in contact of any kind with gang members, ranging from a low of one hour per day for one worker to over four hours for another. The average was $2\frac{1}{3}$ hours per day. Thus, if one had such a log, accompanied by additional personal information, he might gain a much different perspective of program operation than of the kind obtained here.

The collection of personal diaries and staff logs, however, would not necessarily rectify the problem of over-burdening subjects and staff and might even contribute to the burden of the small group of individuals who maintained them. Therefore, what is needed, in addition to the collection of such data, is the development of unobtrusive measurement techniques by which program process could be assessed without directly affecting respondents (see Webb *et al.*, 1966, for a discussion of such techniques). For example, in order to collect information on group development, a concealed video-tape camera, along with sound, might have been used to record daily group sessions. Staff and boys could have been informed that such data were being collected and the data could even have been used as a form of feedback to them, but the collection process *per se* need not have been disruptive. Researchers could then have analyzed tapes without ever having had to intrude directly on the group sessions. Likewise, the seating arrangements of boys in group meetings or at meal time might have been observed on a daily basis as an unobtrusive way of measuring the formation of friendship or power groupings (see Polsky, 1962, Chap. 6, for an example of the use of this technique). These groupings might then have been related to such issues as in-program delinquency, the runaway problem and the emergence of an anti-delinquent culture.

Another unobtrusive measure might have involved observations of the boys who accumulated around the living quarters of the experimental treatment director. His living room and bedroom were adjacent to the boys' living quarters and there was generally a small group of individuals who regularly congregated there. It would have been interesting to have listed the boys who comprised this group of "regulars" and to have studied their behavior in relation to such things as sociometric standing and the decision-making policies of staff. Since our recorded sociometric ratings by boys were almost identical to those of the staff (both groups tended to like and dislike the same persons), the regulars may have con-stituted an elite group of individuals who were favored by staff members and other boys. Conversely, they may have been comprised of "isolates" and "beggars" who were liked by no one but who were dependent on staff members for psychological support. However, since we didn't collect information on the groupings, we cannot make conclusions as to what really occurred. If we had measured this phenomenon over time and had done so unobtrusively, we might then have gained a valuable insight as to what went on during the life of the program.

Still another method might have involved the utilization of school personnel and records as a source of basic information. In fact, since the school constituted such an important external system, our failure to measure what went on there constitutes another very serious omission by this study.

We might, for example, have made a periodic check of school records to determine such things as which boys were tardy, who went to the dean's office and why, and the kinds of grades received on specific classroom assignments. These would have constituted a valuable body of information that could have been used as a validity check on the things that were discussed in group meetings, or which were identified as critical incidents.

The boys' teachers could also have been used as a valuable information source. While a great deal of resistance and suspicion was encountered from school administrators, teachers were generally favorable to the experiment and, in many instances, were highly amenable to helping boys and staff members solve school-related problems. They might also have been willing to provide important information to researchers on such things as the friendship patterns of the boys at school, their classroom demeanor, and their ability to understand and articulate classroom material.

There are an indefinite number of unobtrusive techniques that might have been developed and used by this study. The point to be made is that experimental subjects should be freed, as much as possible, from what must often appear to them as the incessant questioning and interviewing of researchers. At the same time, however, attempts should be made to provide as comprehensive a picture of program process as is possible.

Problems of Experimental Design

The initial experimental design of this study called for strict random assignment to experimental and control groups. Despite the elaborate steps taken to maintain this design, however, difficulties were encountered that might be instructive for those who wish to conduct experiments in other correctional and field settings. These difficulties reflected the problems inherent in attempting to maintain scientific goals and to meet the demands of two action programs at the same time; that is, to reconcile sound methodological research with sound programmatic functions.

The dispositions of the juvenile court do not always adequately take into account the bed space available in correctional programs. In anticipation of this problem—the possibility that the court might assign too many, or not enough, boys to fill the needs of the experiment—plans were made so that the control institution could be used as a temporary holding place on occasion, until space was available for assignment either to the experimental or control program. However, this plan proved to be unworkable. The primary reason for its failure was that the task of holding experimental boys, even for a short period, was disruptive to the overall program at the control institution. It could not be run effectively with some boys staying only a matter of days or weeks before being assigned to the experimental program. Furthermore, we were concerned that the interaction of experimental boys with boys at the control institution might contaminate the validity of our research design. Boys assigned to the experiment might be adversely affected by their short experience at the control institution. Therefore, this procedure was abandoned shortly after its adoption.

A second problem was inherent in the fact that, by design, boys stayed a much shorter period of time at the experimental community residence than at the control institution, an average of six *vs.* thirteen months. This differential turnover rate created an imbalance. On some occasions, the large number of boys required for the experimental group threatened to deplete the control population, while at other times the control program was overloaded and the experimental group was threatened by depletion. Both programs required a certain quota of boys to operate at optimum efficiency and imbalances were not always predictable and controllable.

In an effort to remedy the situation, a second design was set up. Regular intake procedures were maintained, except that instead of leaving the experimental group at the control institution for a short period of time, both groups were selected randomly from juvenile hall immediately after court disposition. Furthermore, in order to compensate for the differential rates of release, the intake for the experimental residence was increased to 60 per cent of the eligible population, while that for the control group was dropped to 40 per cent. Again, however, this design proved inadequate for many of the same reasons. There was still a shortage of bed space at the main campus for the control group, and the population at the experimental residence kept dwindling to small numbers.

There was no easy solution to this problem and it became clear that if the intervention strategy were to be tested adequately, some other method of selection would have to be devised. As a final resort, random selection procedures on rare occasions were relaxed, especially in the interest of the experimental program. When the number of subjects declined to such a low number as to affect seriously the quality of the group program, random selection was ignored and several boys were taken all at once. The problem was simply that of either altering selection procedures or destroying the program culture to which so much attention had been paid. It was felt that, if this culture were allowed to lapse, experimental conditions could not be maintained. Thus, a dilemma was created that threatened either the experimental or the theoretical design. A loss of either might destroy the quality of the experiment. There was no obvious way out and a resolution was worked out in favor of maintaining the population at the experimental residence at the cost of an occasional lapse in random selection.

It appears, however, that the occasional interruption of random selection was not seriously detrimental to this study (*a*) because such interruptions were not common, and (*b*) a careful comparison of the experimental and control groups indicated that comparability was not lost (Chapter Five). Nevertheless, it is our feeling that this problem could have seriously endangered the validity of the experimental design, even though, luckily, it did not.

Future field experiments that attempt to impose the rigid demands of random assignment on the ongoing activities and intake procedures of action programs should be wary of the dilemma that might be created (*e.g.*, whether program needs should have priority over research needs, or vice versa). Advanced planning should be undertaken between researchers and action people to anticipate the problems that might be encountered and to establish feedback mechanisms by which such problems might be resolved to the satisfaction of both parties.

An additional problem of experimental design had to do with maintaining program operation in a manner that was consistent with the intervention guidelines. Two major issues might be mentioned in this regard.

First, better mechanisms for quality control could have been developed to insure that operational guidelines were correctly implemented. As was pointed out in Chapter Seven, a serious problem developed relative to the feedback of research information to the action staff regarding their implementation of the intervention strategy. Because during the intitial stages of the experiment researchers were wary of presenting empirical findings that might be premature and unreliable, feedback sessions with practitioners were based, for the most part, on subjective observation. It is our feeling that a greater sharing of preliminary information, although risky, would have provided a sounder basis for decision-making than the subjective impressions that were used.

The need for such information was evidenced in Chapters Seven and Eight, where it was shown that the implementation of program design was less than ideal. The findings of these two chapters suggested very strongly that more efficient means of communication between researchers and practitioners are needed by which both parties can be assured that program implementation is commensurate with design. This would require the development of research instruments and feedback mechanisms that would take into account the dynamic nature of emergent social systems.

Second, feedback mechanisms are needed by which action and research people can effectively collaborate to deal with the unanticipated problems of experimentally induced social change. Any attempt to revise old social structures would seem inevitably to create new problems and dilemma for which ready-made solutions are not available. Consider, for example, the strain and high runaway rates that were experienced at both the experimental and control programs (Chapter Ten) as significant program changes were put into effect. As new problems are created, therefore, new means must also be sought to cope with them. This would seem to require considerable flexibility on the parts of both researchers and practitioners, a willingness to depart to a certain degree from pre-established design and to experiment with improving the components of a given social system.

There is always the danger, of course, of violating basic guidelines to such a degree that an experimental approach is never really tested. Short of that, however, it is possible to make changes that do not violate the guidelines. In this case, for example, the study of critical incidents, runaways, and failures all revealed that changes might have been made to make operations more, rather than less, consistent with design. Furthermore, experimentation designed to make improvements could have taken into account the counsel and collaboration of offenders, in addition to researchers and practitioners. Since a primary objective of this study was to increase that collaboration, there is no reason why an effort should not have been made to include them in the feedback process. Indeed, such an inclusion would not have been a denial of basic intervention principles but perhaps a better implementation of them, and it would have been conducive, rather than restrictive, to the knowledge-building function of the FEM.

Use of Findings for the Purpose of Simulation

A final area in which we feel future correctional experiments might be improved would be to use the findings from this and other studies as a means of selecting delinquents for participation in particular kinds of programs. Our findings (Chapters Ten, Eleven, and Twelve) have suggested that certain types of offenders may be predisposed to behave one way in one program and another way in a different program; that an individual's behavior is an interactive function of his personal characteristics and the nature of the social system in which he participates. This being the case, it might be possible to improve program effectiveness through the use of empirically derived preselection procedures.

For example, while certain types of delinquents might benefit from community intervention, their problems might be worsened by incarceration in a closed institution. Conversely, certain other types of delinquents may be incapable of handling the demands of a community program but might benefit from staying in a more structured institutional environment. If researchers and action people could work together to isolate these various types of individuals, then steps could be taken to make the *assignment* of delinquents more compatible with the theoretical assumptions of different programs.

Experimentation with purposive program assignment, however, would preclude the use of random assignment. Therefore, before it could be discarded, it would be necessary to accumulate information on the characteristics of different programs as well as on the characteristics of offenders. Since such information is generally unavailable, random assignment is used, as in this experiment, as a method learning something about the way people respond to different stimuli. However, once some clues are garnered regarding that issue, it may be possible to consider purposive assignment.

Using some of the input, process, and outcome findings of this study, the remainder of this chapter is concerned with providing an illustration of the way a computer simulation might be used to improve the purposive matching of offenders and programs. In other words, the data gained from an FEM such as this can be put to other uses than those already described. The following sections, therefore, will be concerned with two things: (1) with sketching, in ideal terms, the way in which the data from a study such as this might be used to simulate actual program outcome; and (2) with an exploratory attempt at constructing a partial simulation of the experimental and control programs as a means of illustrating the use of simulation.

Simulation Defined

Simulation may be defined simply as the operation of a model that is designed to replicate a specific phenomenon (Borko, 1962; Dawson, 1962). The term "simulation" is very generic in nature and could include any number of models, along with techniques for manipulating and operating them (*cf.* Guetzkow, 1962). For example, if one were interested in airplanes, he could build a physical model of an airplane, paying careful attention to such details as landing gear, wing span, movable rudders, and so forth. If the physical model were then placed in a wind tunnel, its various parts might be manipulated under various wind and weather conditions in order to assess its performance. This would be a physical analog simulation.

As another alternative, one could develop a mathematical model for use in a computer to simulate the effects of the same phenomena. Without using a wind tunnel and a physical model, the characteristics of an experimental aircraft, along with various weather conditions and wind velocities, could be punched on data cards and submitted as input to a computer. To do so, it would be necessary to program mathematically some general principles or relationships that are presumed to govern how the airplane would operate with variation in each of several conditions. Given proper programming, the plane's performance might then be manipulated and assessed under various conditions without ever having to build a physical representation of the plane.

Given mathematical knowledge of the principles that govern human conduct, simulations of the latter type seem to have a great deal of applicability to research in corrections. This is because the human systems are complex entities. They are comprised of individuals who react to, and are influenced by, a variety of stimuli: psychological, interactive, environmental, cultural, and situational. Sometimes behavior in any system may appear to be rational and purposive and thus amenable to systematic explanation. At other times, behavior may appear to be random or irrational. For these reasons, and because the social scientist must respond to many variables at once, his predictions must involve probabilistic, rather than deterministic, statements. As de Sola Pool (1964: 63) put it, "The thing that keeps the social researcher from enjoying the theoretical triumphs of his natural science colleagues is the complexity of systems he studies." Thus, the basic hope is that, through the use of simulation, the social sciences may be able to link up and use large numbers of single relationships which, although they do not yield a high degree of predictability by themselves, might increase predictability when taken collectively. They might enable social scientists to examine and explain complex social processes for which single propositions would be inadequate.

Model Construction

The initial step in constructing a simulation is that of selecting a model to represent the phenomena in question. Unfortunately, there are no standard or "cookbook" approaches to model building. There are, however, many ways in which models can be constructed, but such factors as the nature of the phenomena being investigated, the levels of measurement involved, and the nature of research design by which data are gathered greatly limit the choices that can be made. In the present study, given the nature of our measures and research design, we felt that linear regression models would provide the most simple and manipulable way of representing phenomena at the experimental and control programs. The following are the kinds of models we had in mind:

Model I, consisting of a regression equation for estimating from input data such process measures as sociometric standing, critical incidents, or school performance.

$$\check{P}_i = B_l + B_j I_j + E$$

Model II, consisting of a regression equation for estimating personal change and type of program release from input and process data.

$$\check{C}_i = B_l + B_j I_j + B_k P_k + E$$

Model III, consisting of an equation for estimating post-release outcome from the other groups of data.

$$\tilde{O}_i = B_l + B_j I_j + B_k P_k + B_e C_e + E$$

Where:

I_i = input variables (social background, personality, offense history, peer identification)

P_i = process variables (school grades, sociometric, critical incidents)

C_i = change and type of program release (changes on personality and peer identification scales, length of time in treatment, runaway, or failure)

O_i = post-release outcome indicators (measurements of recidivism and adjustment in the community)

B_i = empirically derived constants

E = error of prediction

Using this approach, separate models could be constructed for both experimental and control programs. Constants or "*beta* weights" for all three models could be computed using actual data collected from both programs. A flow chart indicating, in ideal terms, how these models might be used to replicate program operation can be found in Figure 15.1. The figure contains thirteen separate boxes, each representing a separate decision point in the simulation. Once the constants for all three models in each of the programs have been determined, it would be possible, hypothetically, to simulate any individual, or group of individuals, through either program.

The following kinds of things would be important relative to each of the decision points in Figure 15.1.

Box 1. Ideally, potential candidates would be simulated through both programs. Since it has already been shown that these programs differ widely, one basic objective would be to determine how different types of individuals do in each of them.

Box 2. Each candidate's input characteristics—social background, personality, offense history, and peer identification—would be determined.

Box 3. Based on input characteristics and the constants in Model I, process behavior would be estimated. This might include estimates of sociometric standing, critical incidents, and school behavior.

Box 4. This part of the simulate would use Model II. By using input data and process estimates, along with the predetermined constants of the model, it would be estimated whether or not the respondent would complete the program. If successful completion were estimated, the candidate would go to Box 6. If not, he would go to Boxes 5 and 7.

Box 5. If the candidate did not complete treatment, attempts would be made to estimate whether he ran away or was failed. Input data and process estimates in Model II would still apply at this particular point.

Box 6. Change data would be collected only from boys who successfully

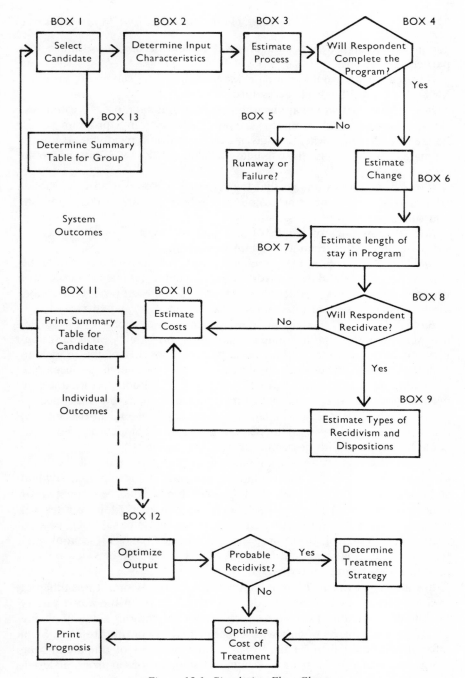

Figure 15.1. Simulation Flow Chart

completed either program, and Model II would be used to estimate this particular outcome.

Box 7. Model II would be used to estimate length of stay in the program for both successful and unsuccessful graduates.

Box 8. Model III would apply at this point. Input data, process estimates, change estimates, and estimates of type of release from a program would be used to determine whether a given candidate would recidivate. If it were estimated that he would, the candidate would go to Box 9. If not, he would go to Box 10.

Box 9. If it were estimated that the respondent would recidivate, Model III would be used to determine more precisely the nature of the recidivism and subsequent dispositions.

Box 10. Estimates of length of stay and recidivism would be used to calculate the cost of treatment in either program.

Box 11. Based upon the simulation, two summary tables would be printed for each candidate: one for the experimental and one for the control program. The summary tables would include estimates of process behavior, kinds of change, type of release, post-release behavior, and costs.

Box 12. This is another key point in the simulation process. For example, if it were estimated that a candidate had a high probability of recidivating, it might be possible to manipulate certain components of the models in order to determine whether the probability of recidivism might be decreased, to determine, for example, whether changes in school performance, in peer relations, or some other factors might increase the chances for success.

Conversely, if it were estimated that a candidate would not recidivate, the simulate could be used to determine whether comparable outcomes could be obtained with decreased time, effort, and cost.

Box 13. If estimates were being made for a group of candidates, systems outcomes (in the form of rates) could be calculated in addition to individual summary tables. For example, the following things could be estimated for either program on a group basis: (1) runaway rates, (2) failure rates, (3) recidivism rates, (4) fluctuation of these rates in time, (5) total cost of treatment, (6) extent of in-program delinquency, and (7) school performance. Information could be acquired that would be of value both in practical and theoretical terms.

In summary, by using a simulation to replicate behavior at these different decision points, it might be possible to learn much about the way a variety of different individuals or groups would perform without actually having to assign new subjects to either the experimental or control program. Such information could then be used in selecting the types of offenders to be assigned to either program or in deciding what alterations in program design might be made in order to improve their effectiveness.

Partial Test of Model

Neither time nor space permit a full implementation of the complex simulation just described. However, by way of conducting a partial test of both its accuracy and utility, a lesser endeavor was undertaken. Using input and process data, a series of 10-variable regression models, much like Models II and III, were developed by stepwise procedures to estimate two basic kinds of information for both experimental and control programs: (1) the length of time offenders could be expected to stay in either program, whether successful graduates or not, and (2) whether they would recidivate after release. On the basis of these regression models, two types of analysis were attempted.

First, attempts were made to see if the effectiveness of the experimental and control programs might be increased. This was done by simulating all subjects from the control program through the experimental program and vice versa. If effectiveness were increased, especially for recidivists, then some clues might be gained relative to a better matching of offender and program types. The second kind of simulation was concerned with the same matter. It involved the creation of a number of hypothetical delinquent types, whose characteristics were based on the theory of causation presented in the earlier chapters of this book. These hypothetical types were simulated through both programs in order to assess the capacity of each program to deal with them.

The analysis in each case is based upon 135 of the 140 experimental subjects and 102 of the 121 control subjects. Some individuals had to be dropped from the analysis because information on them was incomplete.

The accuracy of the simulation is indicated by the explained variances of the regression models. Variations in recidivism, it will be recalled, could be predicted with a 39 per cent accuracy for experimental graduates and a 32 per cent accuracy for runaways and failures. The figures at the control program were 43 per cent and 52 per cent, respectively. Length of stay in treatment was predicted with an accuracy of 25 per cent for experimental graduates and 44 per cent for experimental runaways and failures, while the figures for the controls were 32 per cent and 50 per cent, respectively. Thus, the simulation would be expected to contain considerable error and, thus, its outputs should be interpreted with caution. Even so, the results obtained are highly suggestive of the types of simulations that might be conducted in order to improve program effectiveness.

Optimization of System Outcomes

The first concern in our simulation was with indicating ways by which to optimize correctional outcome. How well would recidivists in the experimental program do in the control program and vice versa? Are there some offenders who would do well in both programs and others who would do well in neither? What should be done with both kinds of people? Better answers to these kinds of questions might make it possible to begin assigning offenders to various programs, not on some arbitrary basis but on the basis of which program would most likely alter their delinquency. Indeed, if simulation techniques could contribute to an optimum use of correctional alternatives, this would be one of the most dramatic contributions it could make.

By way of illustration, let us consider what might have occurred had all 135 experimental subjects in this study been assigned instead to the control program. In Table 15.1, it will be observed that 79 subjects (58 per cent of the total) were nonrecidivists, while 56 subjects (42 per cent) were actual recidivists. If they had been assigned to the control program, however, some striking differences might have occurred, differences that dramatically illustrate the value of seeking to optimize correctional placement.

Table 15.1. Comparison of actual Experimental Group Recidivism with simulated Recidivism in Control Program

Actual experimental program	Simulated control program		
	Nonrecidivism	Recidivism	Total
Nonrecidivists	33	46	79
	(24%)[a]	(34%)	(58%)
Recidivists	21	35	56
	(16%)	(26%)	(42%)
Total	54	81	135
	(40%)	(60%)	(100%)

[a] All percentages based on total N of 135.

First, there was a significant minority of 33 boys (24 per cent of the total) who would have succeeded in either program, raising the question as to whether intensive programming was needed for them. They may have done just as well, at much less cost, under lesser supervision.

Second, there was an even larger group of 46 boys (34 per cent) who, while they succeeded after the experimental program, might have recidivated had they been placed in the control program. Conversely, there was a smaller group of 21 boys (16 per cent) who, while they recidivated after the experimental program, might have succeeded after the control program. Such findings suggest, therefore, that greater harm than good may have been done in this case because there was no prior information by which to effect a better matching of offender and program types.

Finally, 35 boys, or fully one-fourth of the total, were double failures; that is, they were boys who would apparently do well in neither program. They represent types of offenders for whom both approaches would seem to be inappropriate and for whom the most careful study would be needed and new correctional alternatives developed.

Yet, even if one responded only in the crudest of ways to these problems, he might be able to make improvements. For example, suppose that one's program alternatives were limited to those which were used in this study. And suppose further that some general information was available on the types of boys most likely to fail in the experimental program. By the simple expedient of assigning all such failures to the control program, the information in Table 15.1 indicates that the success rate might be raised from 58 to 74 per cent (16 plus 58 per cent), the reason being that of the 56 boys who would ordinarily recidivate in the experimental program, 21 would succeed if assigned to the control program. This improvement alone would be significant and would be worth pursuing.

A much better approach, of course, would involve a concerted effort to be precise about all offender types and how their assignment to various programs could be optimized. Information on which to base such an approach might be derived in a variety of ways, depending upon available resources, offender populations, and correctional alternatives. By way of illustration, let us turn again to this study to consider what types of boys do best in either of the two correctional alternatives available. By using the theory upon which the experiment was based and the data that were gathered to test it, it is possible to create a number of hypothetical delinquent types whose characteristics would be based on the central concepts of the theory. Since the experimental program was designed to deal with a particular type of delinquent—*i.e.*, one whose origin was lower-class, who lacked achievement, who experienced strain, and who ultimately identified with delinquent peers—it would be important to learn how effective it really is with this type of individual, even if he only exists hypothetically. Furthermore, since other individuals rarely conform to a single theoretical type, it would be important to learn what happens to those who depart in varying degrees from that type. How would they do in the experimental as well as the control program?

Simulation of Theoretical Types

In order to derive the various theoretical types, the following scales described in Chapter Five were used: *social class* as measured by the occupational prestige of the father; *achievement* as measured by school interest, academic performance, and work behavior; *strain* as measured by family disorganization, self-concept, aspiration, and the nine scales of the Jesness Personality Inventory; *peer identification* as measured by the Ratfink, Ace-in-the-Hole, Sociability, and Deviance Scales; and *delinquency* as measured in terms of the Theft, Personal Disorganization, Street Corner, Automobile, Family Problems, and Habitualness Scales.

Table 15.2 displays the six different theoretical types that were constructed on the basis of these measures. As will be observed, Type 1 conforms most closely to the type of delinquent for whom the experimental program was created: the person who had the lowest possible scores on social class and all of the measures of achievement, and the highest possible scores on all of the measures of strain, peer identification, and actual delinquency. The other types, it will be observed, gradually depart from this ideal type until the opposite extreme is reached. It must be remembered in reviewing the analysis that all of these types do not necessarily conform to the traits of actual individuals, since they were theoretical rather than real people.

Table 15.2. Definition of Theoretical Types—Theoretical concept

| Type | Theoretical concept | | | | |
	Social class	Achievement	Strain	Peer identification	Delinquency
1	(Low)[a]	(Low)	(High)	(High)	(High)
2	(Low)	(Low)	(High)	(High)	Low
3	(Low)	(Low)	(High)	Low	Low
4	(Low)	(Low)	Low	Low	Low
5	(Low)	High	Low	Low	Low
6	High	High	Low	Low	Low

[a] If variable is in parentheses, its value is theorized as leading to delinquency. In constructing these types, age was held constant at 16 years.

Once the hypothetical characteristics of each type were created, they were punched on data cards as though they were real people and simulated through the regression models used to represent the experimental and control programs. Then, based upon the way different boys actually performed in the two programs, we extrapolated the possible ways in which the theoretical types might have performed had they been assigned to experimental and control programs. Thus, even though findings will reflect the possible performances of theoretical people, the models that were used to derive these findings were based empirically upon the performances of actual delinquents.

The results of the simulation reveal a very interesting and consistent trend. This trend is exemplified most clearly by contrasting Types 1 and 6. Type 1, which conforms most closely to the type of delinquent specified in the causation theory (lower-class, low achievement, high strain, high identification with peers, and high delinquency), performed relatively well in the experimental program but did very poorly in the control program. Type 6, the opposite theoretical type (higher-class, high achievement, low strain, low identification with peers, and low delinquency), did just the opposite. He performed poorly in the experimental program but quite well in the control program. Meanwhile, the other theoretical types tended to be located along the continuum between these two extremes. That is, the more they departed from the theoretical ideal, the worse they did in the experimental program, and the better they did in the control program.

Table 15.3. Simulation of Theoretical Types

Theoretical type	If run or fail, length of time in treatment		If graduate, length of time in treatment		If run or fail, frequency of recidivism		If graduate, frequency of recidivism	
	Exp.	Con.	Exp.	Con.	Exp.	Con.	Exp.	Con.
1	4 mo.	0 mo.	6 mo.	16 mo.	0	4	0	1
2	6 mo.	0 mo.	6 mo.	16 mo.	0	3	0	1
3	6 mo.	0 mo.	6 mo.	12 mo.	0	5	0	0
4	1 mo.	17 mo.	12 mo.	12 mo.	3	0	2	0
5	0 mo.	17 mo.	12 mo.	12 mo.	4	0	2	0
6	1 mo.	17 mo.	12 mo.	12 mo.	3	0	2	0

Since the experimental program was specifically designed to deal with the problems of the Type 1 individual, this result provides some support for the theoretical framework upon which the program was based. The simulation suggests a surprisingly strong match between theoretical Types 1–3 and the experimental program and between Types 4–6 and the control program.

For example, Table 15.3 indicates that if Types 1–3 were assigned to the experimental program, they would not only be tolerated longer, even if inclined to run away or fail, but would graduate in a relatively shorter period of time than Types 4–6, and, further, they would be less likely to recidivate. Meanwhile, the picture for the control program was just the reverse. Types 4–6 were the ones who did well there. These findings, then, if they legitimately reflect the relative impact of the two programs, seem to contain three major implications.

First, they suggest that experience in a "total" institution, as represented by the control program, may have very little impact on the problems of lower-class, under-achieving group delinquents, Types 1–3. Instead, the types who do well in the control program, 4–6, are those who according to this theory have the fewest problems, *i.e.*, they are not lower class, are doing well in school, are experiencing little strain, do not identify with other delinquents, and have relatively low delinquency rates.

Second, the findings suggest that the experimental program may be well suited to those types who conform most closely to the "ideal" hypothetical type suggested by the theory. If the simulation of Types 1–3 can be construed as one means of assessing the adequacy of the theoretical design, and its operational program, the findings are strongly supportive.

Third, the simulation of all six theoretical types suggest that when offender and program types are ill matched, the result may be harmful. This was demonstrated in two ways. First, as mentioned above, Types 1–3 did poorly in an institutional program. Second, when Types 4–6 were simulated through the experimental program, they were also affected adversely. They were inclined to run away early and to have longer stays in the program before completion, and, in either event, were more likely to recidivate after leaving. Thus, while it is the case that Types 1–3 might benefit from the group-oriented community program, a kind of "boomerang" effect seems to occur with Types 4 through 6. Exposure to the experiment, in their case, would seem to do a great deal of harm.

One can only speculate as to the causes of such findings. For example, they suggest that in the case of the experimental program, those individuals with the fewest problems (Types 4–6) may be socialized inadvertently in delinquent patterns of behavior. The truth of this possibility, and the discovery of the mechanisms by which it might occur, are beyond the scope of this study and would require further research. Whatever the explanation, these findings provide confirmation of a theme that has been struck repeatedly; namely, that a poor matching of offender and program types may do more harm than good.

In summary, this exploratory work with simulation techniques suggest that they may have important contributions to make in increasing correctional effectiveness. However, a great deal of work has yet to be done in terms of refining measures and increasing their predictability before attempts at simulation can attain a degree of accuracy necessary for their actual use. If decisions were based on simulations that contained a high degree of error, the situation could conceivably result in the decreased efficiency of correctional programs. If placements were inappropriately made, they could add to the already existing problems of offenders. Furthermore, if the day is ever reached when highly accurate correctional simulations are developed, a whole series of ethical issues may emerge. For example, in the hands of a malevolent government, simulations could be used for the control and dehumanization of man at the expense of his growth and well-being. Despite these problems, which we will not discuss at length here, we feel that future attempts at simulation, if properly executed, also have many beneficial functions to perform for scientists and practitioners.

On the scientific side, they could function to test hypotheses concerning the efficacy of using different types of intervention for different types of delinquents, to bypass certain ethical objections of experimenting with "real" people by simulating hypothetical types, to examine the inter-relationship of structural and individual characteristics as they relate to specific types of behavior, and to examine quickly and with ease complex sets of data and their interrelationships.

On the practical side, simulations could be an invaluable aid to decision-making. If properly developed, they could help to determine which types of characteristics should be the target of a change of strategy. Furthermore, they could help determine optimal treatment strategies in terms of minimum time and costs for both offenders and to society. This could hopefully result in a much more humane and efficient use of our present correctional alternatives by decreasing the costs and dangers of crime to society and by helping offenders to better cope with their own particular problems.

Conclusion

In conclusion, it appears to us that, despite its many limitations, the use of the FEM was more productive than unproductive in this study. By pursuing knowledge-building, as well as delinquency reduction objectives, it was possible to clarify basic theoretical inadequacies, to shed some light on the mysteries of program operation, and to highlight basic research problems. However, the conduct of the study was also expensive, especially in terms of time and human resources. The actual dollars spent and the problems encountered in obtaining them were also significant, but these monetary problems were merely symptomatic of a far different and more complex set of problems and practices. By way of example, let us consider just a few of them as they relate to the task of involving different organizations, research people, and practitioners in the conduct of a field experiment.

First, the ideology of the research person tends to be incongruent with that of the practitioner. The research ethic implies skepticism regarding any human service, correctional, educational, or otherwise, and places its faith, instead, in the efficacy of research findings regarding that service. In contrast, it is difficult for the practitioner to be skeptical regarding his work. Unless he reposes implicit faith in the validity of the assumptions underlying his practice techniques, it is difficult for him to maintain a high degree of commitment and enthusiasm. He must have confidence that what he is doing is constructive, that it will, in the last analysis, be helpful to his client and to society. Otherwise, the nature of the problems he faces may immobilize him. Furthermore, the status of the helping professions, in general, their position of eminence in the society, depends upon the extent to which both the professional and the ordinary citizen have confidence that current practices are constructive and helpful and that they will also control such problems as delinquency.

The result is that practice assumptions, if not specific practices themselves, tend to become doctrine; they are not treated as hypotheses regarding human behavior but as articles of faith upon which practice should be based. Thus, while the practitioner may be willing at times to question a specific approach or the particular way that approach is administered, he may find it extremely difficult to question the fundamental assumptions upon which it is based. It is obvious, therefore, that if experimentation is to be conducted successfully, some resolution of research and practitioner differences will be required. Unless practitioners can be found who will be willing both to state and to examine the validity of the basic assumptions they are called upon to administer, field experimentation cannot be conducted.

Second, there are personal career problems that must be confronted in establishing objectives. Experimentation in a correctional organization, for example, has different implications for the career patterns of research and professional persons. The conduct of experimentation for the research person may be a significant stepping stone in building a reputation and establishing a successful career. He gains from a study.

In contrast, the career potential for the practitioner who involves himself in experimentation is much less clear. The reason is that an appropriate career pattern for most practitioners entails the accumulation of training, experience, and credentials in the use of a particular set of practice techniques, not in skills concerned with testing the validity of those techniques. In fact, the successful acquisition of training and credentials often depends upon the capacity of the novice to perform according to the standards of those who have preceded him, those who are considered expert in the field. The more skilled he becomes, according to their standards, the more acceptable he becomes. It is certainly not his job to question those standards or to set about examining them. His capacity to perform well is what is of greatest importance.

It is also asking a great deal of the practitioner to spend years acquiring a particular set of skills, and the prestige and security that go with them, and then to have him participate in an experiment whose findings might seriously question the utility of many of his previous efforts. Moreover, it is somewhat of an affront to ask him to limit his efforts on behalf of the client in an experiment to the pattern of services called for by the theoretical design, especially if that pattern runs counter to the professional doctrines in which he has been trained. His basic beliefs are challenged and his professional sense of what is important is questioned.

In sum, the major problem confronting practitioners who may be interested in experimentation is the lack of institutionalized subspecialties in corrections, universities, and the professions that grant advancement for those who participate in experimental programs. Career lines for them are still blurred.

Third, there are organizational issues that have to be confronted in attempting any field experiment. As with the individual worker, some accommodation has to be effected between the practices and other demands of service organizations and the organizations that fund and conduct research.

As with the individual practitioner, more than abstract principles and personal selfishness are involved. Any change in the prevailing practices of a service organization would represent more than an alteration of abstractions. It could affect the very foundations upon which existing organizational arrangements were based, both within and outside the organization. Policy-makers have to be concerned not only with the impact of the innovation upon their employees, but with their relationships to other agencies such as the juvenile court, probation departments, the schools, and others. Innovations often lead to interorganizational difficulties. When this occurs, a significant portion of the energy that might be used to test some new approach is expended instead in organizational conflict. Different organizations often have greater investment in preserving the *status quo* than in seeking alternatives to it.

Thus, the problem with experimentation is that it not only threatens to introduce change, it is change. Research is intrusive; it adds new people, new methods, and a new ideological stance. Disciplined skepticism and a careful look at existing practices, for example, are not characteristic of ordinary relationships within and between organizations. Consequently, as the poor relations of the Silverlake program with the school and family illustrate, the failure to address interorganizational problems seriously reduced the effectiveness of the experimental innovation. Furthermore, given the political, bureaucratic, and social arena in which service organizations exist, it is virtually impossible for any field experiment to meet organizational expectations. Politicians, bureaucrats, indeed society at large, expect final solutions, not small increments of information or negative findings. The practical solutions it can provide are usually so small that administrators are inevitably disappointed and usually angry. It is their usual inclination, therefore, to quote the old saying: "The program was a flop, but the research was a success. I'll never do that again!"

Finally, existing funding and organizational arrangements for the research person are poorly articulated with the time and other demands of field experimentation. Usually, he has to engage in such endeavors on a part-time basis, attempting to maintain other commitments that are equally compelling. The result is that, if he fulfills his obligation to the experiment, he must do so at extreme cost to himself or others. Even worse, the demands of his profession are such that his career can be damaged if the findings of his research cannot be completed and reported in a relatively short period of time. Yet, field experimentation, in addition to the problems already mentioned, can require years of data collection and analysis before results can be reported. The consequences may not only discourage him from engaging in this form of research but can contribute to the disillusionment of those who work with him if he does. He is able to meet neither the expectations of his peers, nor the agencies with whom he collaborates.

What all of this means, of course, is that the systematic and successful conduct of field experiments in the future will depend heavily upon the extent to which there is growing support for new institutional arrangements, and sources of funding, that will facilitate this kind of research. Better funding for organizations and people willing to engage in long-term endeavors and changes in the career patterns of both practitioner and researcher will be required. The long-range view that now enables legislators and the public to expend large funds on the protracted study of problems in the natural and physical sciences will have to apply in the social realm if better understanding is to be acquired.

References

Borko, Harold, Ed. 1962. *Computer Applications in the Behavioral Sciences.* Englewood Cliffs, N.J.: Prentice–Hall.

Dawson, Richard E. 1962. Simulation in the social sciences. In Harold Guetzkow, Ed. *Simulation in Social Science: Readings.* Englewood Cliffs, N.J.: Prentice–Hall.

Guetzkow, Harold, Ed. 1962. *Simulation in Social Science.* Englewood, Cliffs, N.J.: Prentice–Hall.

Klein, Malcolm W., and Neal Snyder. 1965. The detached worker: uniformities and variances in work style. *Social Work* 10 (October): 60–68.

Lewin, Kurt. 1968. Feedback problems of social diagnosis and action. In Walter Buckley, Ed., *Modern Systems Research for the Behavioral Scientist.* Chicago: Aldine Publishing Company.

POLSKY, HOWARD W. 1962. *Cottage Six: The Social System of Delinquent Boys in Residential Treatment*. New York: John Wiley.

DE SOLA POOL, ITHIEL. 1964. Simulation of social systems. *International Science and Technology*, (March): 62–70.

WEBB, EUGENE J., DONALD T. CAMPBELL, RICHARD D. SCHWARTZ, and LEE SECHREST. 1966. *Unobtrusive Measures: Nonreactive Research in the Social Sciences*. Chicago: Rand McNally.

Appendices

Characteristics of Delinquent Population

The following brief description of the delinquent population is presented because of the interest other research people may have in replicating the study or comparing this with other populations. This description covers eleven major areas: family stability, mobility, social and ethnic status, school history, role model, delinquent history, work experience, self-concept, and personality characteristics.

It should be remembered that the following analysis includes boys both in the experimental and control groups, a total of 262 respondents.

1. *Family Stability*. There was evidence of considerable instability in the families of this delinquent population. At the time they were assigned to this study, one-half of the boys reported that their parents were either divorced or separated. Furthermore, relationships were so strained in some cases that boys had been sent elsewhere to live, even though their parents were still living together. Thus, only about one-third of the boys were still living with both of their natural parents. Of the remainder, one-fourth were living with their mothers only, one-fifth with stepparents, and one-fifth with other relatives. It is not surprising, then, that only one-third of the boys reported that they got along reasonably well with their parents while a remaining two-thirds rated their parental relationships as poor. It is significant, in addition, that 42 per cent indicated that one or more other family members had been arrested for law violations, the majority of whom were siblings.

2. *Mobility*. Despite the foregoing evidence of family instability, there was little evidence in this population of a high rate of transiency. The majority of the boys had spent the major portions of their lives in Los Angeles County. Only 9 per cent of them were immigrants from other

states. Thirty-six per cent had lived in the same community for longer than an eleven-year period and 40 per cent between seven and ten years. Only 5 per cent had lived less than three years in any one city. Thus, while instability within the family was high, instability in terms of geographical mobility was not.

3. *Social and Ethnic Status.* About three-fourths of the boys in the study were Caucasian, about 10 per cent were Negro, and another 10 per cent were Mexican–American. There were also four boys of Oriental ancestry. As mentioned earlier, this population distribution reflects the desire of Boys Republic to maintain an ethnic intake rate that approximates the population of the larger community and is not therefore necessarily representative of the ethnic breakdown of Los Angeles delinquents.

The socioeconomic status of the boys in the study was weighted toward the bottom of the status ladder. About one-half of them came from families in which the occupation of the father was as an unskilled, semiskilled, or service worker of some kind. Approximately a third came from the families of skilled workers (electricians, carpenters, machinists), small businessmen, and white-collar clerical jobs. Only about one-fifth come from the families of parents who were from the more prestigious business and professional occupations.

4. *School History.* The educational aspirations and actual school performance of these boys was a study in conflict. About seven out of ten boys said that they are interested in school and that an education was very important to them. Less than one-quarter of them felt that high school was sufficient, and over 56 per cent aspired to go to college. Yet seven out of ten reported having left school at one time or another, usually as a result of disciplinary problems. Most boys indicated that they had left school at age 15 and were out for a period of at least one semester. Furthermore, their grades were low. More than a third had received failing grades with only 12 per cent having received grade point averages above C. A little more than seven out of ten boys reported that they had participated in extracurricular activities at school. However, the bulk of this activity was involvement in athletics and only 10 per cent reported participation in leadership or social activities. In addition, 48 per cent of the boys reported they had won awards at school, but again the awards were for recognition of athletic activities. Only two boys of the 262 in this study claimed to have ever won an award for academic achievement. It was evident that unless the school performance of these boys could be altered, their academic aspirations would be extremely inconsistent with their actual performance and were, in fact, tinged with fantasy.

5. *Role Model.* In addition to reporting their backgrounds, boys in the experimental and control groups responded to a series of open-ended

questions in which they were asked to describe the person they "look up to most". Contrary to presupposition, the average ideal image they projected was not unlike one that would be expected from any non-delinquent population. Their ideal image was a person in his late teens or early twenties. He was depicted as a popular clever person who wanted to be a professional or businessman and aspired to membership in the upper-middle to upper classes. He liked to talk about general topics and hated to get into trouble. He was described as having a good personality, an average dresser, and as one who was well in charge of his emotional faculties. He had a positive attitude toward his parents and felt very strongly that school was beneficial.

As with academic aspirations, this projected ideal was highly inconsistent with the boys' actual behavior. Nevertheless, these findings confirm those of other investigators who report that delinquents are inclined to legitimate societal aspirations and prescriptions. The findings are supportive of the argument made in Chapter II that most major theories of delinquency may have failed to make sufficient allowance for the meaningfulness of middle-class values to delinquents.

6. *Delinquent History*. Seven out of ten boys in the study were repeat offenders. One-half of them had three or more recorded offenses; one-third, four or more; one-fifth, five or more. About one-fifth of the boys had already undergone prior institutionalization at county probation camps. Furthermore, one-third of the population had runaway histories, either from home or from places of incarceration. This tendency to run away posed a significant problem for both the experimental and control programs in this study.

The boys' official offense records revealed a variety of different offenses. As can be seen in Table AI.1, Runaway from Home, Incorrigibility, Automobile Theft, Breaking and Entering, and Petty Theft were the five most common violations. Only a very small percentage had ever been apprehended for narcotics and sexual offenses.

7. *Work*. About four out of five boys have held at least one job during their lifetime, while 60 per cent reported that they had held three or more jobs. This was a rather surprising finding in light of the general belief that delinquents do not ordinarily have access to job opportunities. But, as was indicated in Chapter Eleven, there is considerable evidence that these job histories were characterized by instability rather than opportunity, failure rather than success.

When work aspirations are considered, 57 per cent of the boys said they want to make more money than their fathers, although 41 per cent rated their fathers' jobs as satisfactory for themselves.

8. *Self-Concept*. There was little surface evidence of a lowered self-

Table AI.I. Number of officially recorded violations in each of 36 Offense Categories for the 262 boys in this study. Offenses are ranked in order of those most frequently committed

Offense	Number of violations			
	0	1	2	3 or more
	%	%	%	%
Incorrigible	65.6	26.0	7.3	1.2
Runaway from home	66.0	19.8	9.5	4.7
Automobile theft	67.6	22.5	7.6	2.3
Petty theft	69.1	21.4	6.9	2.7
Breaking and entering	70.2	22.1	5.7	2.0
Malicious mischief, damaging property	83.6	13.4	2.3	0.8
Fighting	85.5	9.9	3.1	1.2
Curfew violation	86.3	10.7	2.7	0.4
Truancy from school	88.9	9.2	0.8	1.2
Probation, violation, ineffective rehabilitation	88.9	9.9	0.8	0.4
Glue sniffing or other toxic sniffing	91.6	6.5	0.8	1.2
Drinking alcoholic beverages	92.7	6.9	0.4	0.0
Destitution, no proper guardian	92.7	5.7	0.8	0.8
Runaway from previous institution	93.5	4.6	0.8	1.2
Traffic offenses other than driving without a license	93.9	4.2	1.5	0.4
Loitering, gambling, improper companions	95.0	4.2	0.4	0.4
Welfare and institutions code—offense not specified	95.0	4.2	0.8	0.0
Aggravated assault	95.4	4.6	0.0	0.0
Robbery	96.2	3.8	0.0	0.0
Using narcotics	96.2	3.4	0.4	0.0
Possession of dangerous weapons	96.2	3.8	0.0	0.0
Grand theft—$50 or more	96.6	3.1	0.0	0.4
Arson	96.9	3.1	0.0	0.0
Buying, selling, or possessing narcotics	97.3	1.9	0.8	0.0
Nonforceable heterosexual behavior	97.7	2.3	0.0	0.0
Homosexual behavior	97.7	1.9	0.4	0.0
Forceable rape	97.7	2.3	0.0	0.0
Other sex behavior—voyeurism, exhibitionism, etc.	98.1	1.5	0.0	0.4
Buying, selling or possessing liquor	98.1	1.5	0.4	0.0
Driving without a license	98.5	1.1	0.4	0.0
Other theft—purse snatching, etc.	98.5	1.5	0.0	0.0
Forgery	98.9	1.1	0.0	0.0
Child molesting	98.9	1.1	0.0	0.0
Defiance of authority—teachers or police	99.2	0.4	0.4	0.0
Smoking	99.6	0.4	0.0	0.0
Drunk driving	100.0	0.0	0.0	0.0

concept among these boys. When asked to compare themselves with others in terms of their leadership, smartness, and maturity, the majority rated themselves as about average. Only a few said they were inferior, while one-fifth conceived of themselves as leaders and smarter than other boys. Three out of ten also said they were more mature.

9. *Religion.* Forty-three per cent of the boys reported their religious affiliation as Protestant. Thirty per cent were Catholic and 16 per cent belonged to other religious denominations. Only one out of ten boys reported no religious affiliation. One-fourth of the boys reported that they attended church regularly on a weekly basis while only 15 per cent said that they never attended at all. Whether this fairly high rate of reported attendance was accurate or not could not be ascertained. It could be a function of a significant minority among boys in trouble who wish to impress others with their respectability.

10. *Psychological Characteristics.* A series of nine indexes, developed by Carl Jesness of the California Youth Authority (Chapter Five), were used to measure the psychological attributes of the boys. The indexes measured a variety of psychological dimensions including autism, alienation, value orientation, repression, social maladjustment, affect, withdrawal, social anxiety, and asociality. Suffice it to say here that, with rare exception, no one exhibiting severe psychological disturbances was included in either the control or experimental group.

Summary

The average boy in this experiment was a 16- or 17-year-old who had a history of problems in many areas of his life. Although he was not a transient and lived most of his life in Los Angeles County, he came from a disorganized family, had considerable trouble in school, and was likely to be a repeat offender. There was even a good chance that he may have been incarcerated at some prior time.

There was also some evidence of strain and difficulty due to contradictions between extremely high fantasy-tinged aspirations and ideals and extremely poor performance. Even though the majority were lower- or lower-middle-class youth, they had high educational and occupational aspirations that were highly inconsistent with their past history and performances. There was considerable evidence, even in this limited description, of accumulated disabilities that probably contributed to the delinquent history of this group.

Scales for Measuring Offense History, Peer Identification and Social Background

A series of scales were developed in this study by which to measure the three general areas of offense history, peer identification, and social background. The rationale for the scales themselves and the uses to which they were put were discussed in the various chapters of the book. Consequently, this appendix will be limited to a brief discussion of the steps that went into their construction.

Each scale was developed through a two-stage process. First, techniques of factor analysis were used to help identify possible clusterings (or dimensions) among the separate items that comprised each content area. All factor analyses utilized a principal axis method of factor extraction with a varimax solution for othogonal rotation. In all instances, the squared multiple correlation coefficient of a given item with all other items was used as a basis for communality estimation. The content or meanings of the factors obtained will not be discussed in this appendix because of space limitations. Suffice it to say that some of the factors were considered meaningful enough to proceed to the next stage of scale development.

In the second stage, factor clusterings with two or more items were subjected to Guttman-type scaling techniques. Factor scores were not computed because our levels of measurement were ordinal or dichotomous and thus did not seem suited to this technique of scale construction. The development of the Guttman-type scales within each of the three areas is discussed below.

THE OFFENSE SCALES

From a long list of different kinds of offenses, five clusters of offenses were isolated by factor analysis and subjected to Guttman-type scaling.

Prior to scaling, all offense categories were dichotomized to a "0 *vs.* 1 or more" pattern. As can be seen in Table A2.1, for the most part, the Coefficients of Reproducibility are quite high. Whether or not these high coefficients are a function of the small number of items used and the dichotomous nature of the responses is difficult to ascertain. However, in light of the factor clusterings, it does not seem unreasonable to attribute unidimensionality to the scales.

Table A2.I. Guttman-type Scales based on Offense Data

Scale name	Item	Coefficients of reproducibility
Scale I Theft scale	[a]1. Petty theft, grand theft [a]2. Breaking and entering, burglary	.92
Scale II Personal disorganization scale	1. Runaway from institution [a]2. Destitution, bad companions, loitering	.96
Scale III Street corner scale	[a]1. Fighting; aggravated assault 2. Curfew 3. Alcohol	.91
Scale IV Automobile scale	[a]1. Auto theft, joy-riding 2. Traffic violations	.97
Scale V Family problems scale	1. Incorrigibility 2. Runaway from home	.89

[a]These items represent combinations of two or more similar offenses.

A major issue in connection with the use of any Guttman scale has to do with the *a priori* definition of the universe of qualitative data—in this case, information on delinquency—that a scale is supposed to represent. Guttman (1945) has said that in developing items for a scale, "items are constructed which contain the content implied by the name of the area. Whether or not a given item has the proper content defining the area remains a matter of intuitive judgment; perhaps the consensus of several people versed in the area could serve as a criterion."

In this case, "consensus" regarding delinquency is represented by legal statute and official practice. The major question, therefore, is whether there is any common characteristic either in the situation surrounding the commission of delinquent acts or in offenders themselves that would lead to classificatory scales that could divide respondents into different subtypes.

There is no intent to suggest that these delinquency scales represent the whole universe of delinquent behavior or whether each of them adequately represents a subscale of that universe. The proof of the pudding is in whether there seem to be any meaningful relationships between the offense scales and other indices of behavior.

PEER IDENTIFICATION SCALES

A series of sixteen items measuring identification with delinquent peers were factor analyzed. Four clusters of items were isolated and submitted to Guttman scaling. (All response categories were dichotomized.) As can be seen in Table A 2.2, the coefficients of reproducibility are, for the most part quite high. Consequently, because of what they seemed to be measuring, the four scales were arbitrarily designated as "Ratfink," "Ace-in-the-Hole," "Sociability," and "Deviance" dimensions of peer identification.

As with the offense scales, the high coefficients may be a function of the small number of items used in each scale. However, there were two things that might support assertions of unidimensionality. First, the original factor clusterings suggested that four distinct dimensions were present.

Table A2.2. Scaling attempts: Peer Identification measures

Scale name	Item	Coefficients of reproducibility
Scale I Ratfink scale	Would you "fink" to police? Would you "fink" to parents? Would you "fink" to teachers?	.95
Scale II Ace-in-the-hole	Would you hide friend who had run away from home? Would you hide friend in trouble with the law?	.97
Scale III Sociability	If you were watching TV, would you go mess around with friends instead? If you were going to church, would you go mess around with friends instead? If you were doing homework, would you go mess around with friends instead?	.95
Scale IV Deviance	Would you do something parents had told you never to do with friends? Would you do something you knew was wrong with friends? Would you skip school with friends? Would you go steal gas with friends? Would you break into a place and steal some stuff with friends?	.93

Second, the same two developmental steps resulted in an isolation of the same four dimensions of peer activity among an entirely different population of delinquents and non-delinquents in Utah, thus lending strong support to their possible generalizability (*cf.* Empey and Lubeck, 1968). A list of the scales and their coefficients of reproducibility may be found in Table A 2.2.

THE SOCIAL BACKGROUND SCALES

As was done with the offense scales and peer identification scales, a preliminary factor analysis was performed on a series of social background measures. Again, the results of the factor analysis were very suggestive of areas in which Guttman scaling might fruitfully be attempted and a total of six background scales were developed. The results of these scalogram analyses may be found in Table A 2.3. For the most part, the coefficients of reproducibility were greater than .90, the only two exceptions being Scale I and Scale IV.

All of these scales contained less than five items. This, combined with the fact that all of the items were dichotomized, again might raise questions

Table A2.3. Description of Background Measures

Scale	Item	Coefficients of reproducibility
I School interest scale	1. School interest 2. School interest compared with friends 3. Grades in school 4. Number of school activities 5. School aspirations	.89
II School frustration	1. Ever left school? 2. Grades in school	.92
III Family disorganization	1. Parents living? 2. Parents get along? 3. Boys get along with parents?	.91
IV Self-concept scale	1. Leadership self-concept 2. Smartness self-concept 3. Maturity self-concept	.88
V Aspirations	1. School aspirations 2. Decide on life's work 3. Money aspirations	.91
VI Work experience	1. Had job before? 2. Ever fired from job?	.98

regarding the actual unidimensionality of the scales. Nevertheless, it was again felt that the ultimate test of the validity and utility of a scale is a pragmatic one. The extent to which the social background scales contribute to the understanding and prediction of behavior is assessed in the analyses of this book.

References

EMPEY, LAMAR T., and STEVEN G. LUBECK. 1968. Conformity and deviance in the "situation of company." *American Sociological Review,* 33 (October): 760–774.
GUTTMAN, LOUIS. 1945. *Questions and Answers About Scale Analysis.* I and E Division Report No. D-2. Washington, D.C.: Headquarters Army Services Forces.

Name Index

349

Subject Index